DATE DUE

MY 2 8 '98			

DEMCO 38-296

BEGGARS AND THIEVES

R

BEGGARS AND THIEVES

Lives of
Urban Street Criminals

MARK S. FLEISHER

THE UNIVERSITY OF WISCONSIN PRESS

The University of Wisconsin Press
114 North Murray Street
Madison, Wisconsin 53715

3 Henrietta Street
London WC2E 8LU, England

Library of Congress Cataloging–in–Publication Data
Fleisher, Mark S.
    Beggars and thieves: lives of urban street criminals/
  Mark S. Fleisher.
    346 p.   cm.
    Includes bibliographical references (p. 293) and index.
    ISBN 0-299-14770-3 (hardcover: alk. paper). —ISBN 0-299-14774-6
  (paperback: alk. paper)
    1. Marginality, Social—United States—Case studies.
  2. Criminals—United States—Case studies. 3. Ethnology—United
  States—Case studies. 4. United States—Social conditions—1980–
  I. Title
  HN90.M26F54   1995
  364.3'0973–dc20   95-18431

Contents

Acknowledgments

The research for *Beggars and Thieves* was funded by the U.S. Bureau of the Census, Center for Survey Methods Research, and the Harry Frank Guggenheim Foundation. Leslie Brownrigg (U.S. Census Bureau) and Karen Colvard (Harry Frank Guggenheim Foundation) supported this research over many years. Thanks for your assistance and encouragement.

Numerous law enforcement agencies contributed to this research. The Federal Bureau of Prisons granted me permission to interview inmates at USP Lompoc. The King County Correctional Facility gave me access to its premises. All over California, city detectives and state parole and probation agents, as well as staffers in the California Department of Corrections and California Youth Authority, assisted me in many ways. The California Prison Gang Task Force listened to ideas at the earliest stages of analysis and offered streetwise opinions. I'm grateful for their advice.

In years of full-time employment in the Federal Bureau of Prisons I had experiences few scholars have had. During those years I had two mentors. Dr. Calvin R. Edwards tossed me onto the playing field of correctional administration and management and taught me how a professional administrator makes the right decisions in the sensitive, high-profile business of federal corrections. Dr. Richard H. "Dick" Rison supported me at the very beginning of this research, and years later he had confidence in my ability to work in federal corrections. Cal's and Dick's kindness, generosity, and thoughtfulness led to experiences I would have missed without them and to opportunities that dramatically altered the trajectory of my professional life.

Dale Welling and Lenny Lopez, Sacramento Intelligence Unit, Federal Bureau of Prisons, helped me bring this research and analysis to federal, state, and local law enforcement officials. Thanks for your friendship.

Street officers and administrators in the Seattle Police Department treated me wonderfully. These officers were helpful, honest, and encouraged my research from the first day I arrived in Seattle. Seattle's police officers do a tough job, often in dangerous neighborhoods, and they do it fairly with a high degree of personal and professional integrity. Every Seattle street cop I accompanied, watched, listened to, and interviewed had a genuine concern about lost kids on the street, and they showed it with kindness toward these kids. I wished many times that street kids' parents cared as much about their children's well-being as Seattle's street cops did. Were these children's parents as vigilant and as kind as these cops, they wouldn't have had to take the kids to prison.

Years of prison and street research touches numerous agencies and dozens of critics and colleagues in the academic world. Philippe Bourgois, Fox Butterfield, Scott Decker, Jeffrey Fagan, James B. Jacobs, Lynette Lee-Sammons, Bob Littlewood, Nancy McKee, Matt Salo, Carl Taylor, Tom Ulen, David Ward (Minnesota), Ralph Weisheit, Neil Weiner, Ed Wells, Tom White, Kevin Wright, as well as many others, listened to field tales, offered opinions about my perceptions and interpretations of ethnographic data, and read portions of the early versions of this book. Thanks for your assistance, support, and good ideas.

This book was reviewed for the University of Wisconsin Press by three world-class scholars: H. Russell Bernard (University of Florida), Robert F. Meier (Iowa State University), and James F. Short, Jr. (Washington State University). With their comments, criticisms, advice, and suggestions I was able to transform a manuscript into this book.

This research began while I served in Washington State University's Department of Anthropology. My colleagues there supported me by showing patience for the time spent off campus conducting fieldwork. Dr. Geoffrey Gamble, then chairman of the Department of Anthropology, now vice provost for Academic Affairs, has been a friend and strong supporter of my street and prison research since 1976. I am grateful, Geoff, for nearly 20 years of friendship.

After leaving the Federal Bureau of Prisons I joined the faculty at

Illinois State University, which is firmly committed to scholarly activity and demonstrates it with substantial support for its research faculty. Colleagues in the Department of Criminal Justice Sciences listened to my street stories and offered good criticisms while I wrote this manuscript. Dr. Betty Chapman, dean, College of Applied Science and Technology, encouraged the writing of this book, and has supported all my current research.

Dr. Ann McGuigan, my wife, has traipsed around the country with me for some 17 years while I pursued a quest to understand prisons and street crime. Ann even let me sell our home in 1984, to help fund my research at USP Lompoc. Can you imagine that! She stuck with me in emotionally tough times and helped me do things better than I could have done them on my own.

My literary daughter, Emily, is editor of her high school newspaper. Emily read portions of the early versions of this manuscript, checked references, and with a keen eye, she found grammatical glitches. I've never met a finer 15-year-old editor.

My creative son, Aaron, patiently listened to me talk about the organization of this book, and offered good comments while we drove hundreds of hours and thousands of miles between Normal and Champaign, Illinois, to the Illinois Gymnastics Center, where he is training for the 2004 Olympic games.

Dr. Rosalie Robertson, senior editor, University of Wisconsin Press, saw value in this ethnography of urban street criminals and its implications for anti-crime policy. Working with Rosalie was a valuable experience because she truly understands how well anthropology, sociology, and criminology mesh.

Dr. David Alexander made a special contribution to this book: his clear thinking and good counsel kept me going in the right direction.

State and federal law enforcement agencies, federal and private funding agencies, and officials of Washington State University and Illinois State University aren't responsible for my opinions, analyses, and policy recommendations. I am solely responsible for everything I have written here.

Foreword

Most people have opinions about crime and criminals—perhaps because they have at some time committed a crime themselves—but few people can fully identify with persistent criminals. Most people don't know how such criminals feel about themselves or others, how they see the world, or what it is like to keep daily company with other criminals. Most people have no personal experience of what it means when crime becomes a central life-interest around which other activities revolve. Most people do not know what it's like when other people are seen not as persons but merely as criminal opportunities. Most people do not realize that some criminals make many of their choices from a narrower repertoire of alternatives than what other people choose from. But Mark Fleisher knows these things. He has seen them, and lived with them, first-hand, over a long period of time. His insights didn't come easy, however; they were the result of a long series of field observations made possible by his anthropological training.

Knowledge of this kind is rare, because, although there has been much written about criminals, most accounts have been written by people who have not studied them up close. Perhaps most criminologists have not spent much time with criminals, instead opting to study crime from the safety of computer programs and secondary data. Even those criminologists who have obtained their information first-hand often have done so under controlled circumstances. For example, Donald Cressey (*Other People's Money*) interviewed 133 embezzlers already in confinement, and Shaw and McKay (*The Jack Roller*), and Sutherland (*The Professional Thief*), obtained first-hand information from single sources they happened to stumble across. Few criminological investigations have involved systematic information from participant observation, although many would agree that such a technique has obvious advantages. Some types of crime do not easily permit such a technique (e.g., organized criminal syndicates, violent juvenile gangs), and the opportunity to study some other crimes seldom presents itself (e.g., family violence, white-collar crime). As a result, where observation as a method is employed, ethical investigators have usually disclosed their identities, hoping that such information will not alter the behavior they wish to study.

Beggars and Thieves is real data collected in real situations from real people. Although Mark Fleisher was not dishonest about his identity, neither did he maintain his distance by hiding behind a cloak of professional degrees. Showing only normal human concern (and some grubby clothes), Fleisher was able to penetrate elements of the street culture in Seattle and bring forth a picture that is obviously and sometimes painfully honest.

The story is often brutal and almost always disheartening. Fleisher reports that the street people he studied have very high rates of criminality. They also engaged in a variety of other risky behaviors that may not be illegal, but have long-term negative social or medical consequences. Fleisher finds most characterized by low self-control, insecurity, anger, poor or negative self-concepts, and inadequate mental health; most have feelings of depression and a strong sense of emotional insecurity; most express feelings of sadness, regret, self-hate, and fear. They have been neglected at home, rejected by peers and school officials, and cast into deviant roles on the street with few verbal or intellectual skills. Most have no prospects for the future, no motivation to go straight, and no resources to facilitate conventionality even if they were to want it. Money is spent quickly, usually on a "high" or some other immediate pleasure, rather than food or shelter. Compared with their everyday lives, prison may actually look attractive to some. To others, imprisonment longer than a few days is to be avoided because of the pain of withdrawal from drugs and alcohol. It is a depressing portrait framed in hopelessness and despair.

Repeatedly, Fleisher's street criminals reported comparable backgrounds, including similar family experiences. The theoretical tone is set in the opening pages, where a behavior pattern is established in the actions of inadequate parents. The behavior will be perpetuated later in life as the children grow up and repeat the actions of their parents, thus creating a cycle of parental abuse and neglect that virtually guarantees the perpetuation of poverty, crime, and social disability. Angelo's anecdote about Ace depicts a key social process and illustrates Fleisher's central theoretical argument about the development of a particular outlook on life that is reinforced in the daily experiences of the street people. This *defensive worldview* comes to be the glasses through which the world and its events are defined and interpreted, and it is unchangeable once established. This immutable worldview is the manifestation of the street culture that stresses individualism and manipulation. Fleisher's argument may be controversial to some criminologists who identify the locus of crime in other dynamics or conditions, but critics will have to grapple with the strong evidence Fleisher provides.

Also likely to be controversial are the implications of Fleisher's observations on crime control. The criminals society fears most are those who commit violent crimes, but the most dangerous criminals may really be those for whom we have no effective response—those who commit crime repeatedly and for whom jail or prison is little more than a welcome respite from life on the streets. To be sure, these street criminals form only a part of the total crime problem, but they pose the most difficult problem because, as Fleisher argues, there is no remedy. Once the behavior pattern is established, it is too late.

Fleisher argues that the only solution to this type of crime is prevention. Prevention is a hard sell in the current political climate, where leaders of both major political parties attempt to capitalize on and reinforce public fears about crime and public disillusionment with criminal rehabilitation. Public opinion about crime reflects a strong sense of cynicism. People fear that crime is escalating and that we are becoming increasingly impotent to stem the rising ride. To many, the only alternative seems to lie in increasingly punitive measures. Americans treat the relationship between crime and punishment as an article of faith. To make this observation is not to deny that some offenders require imprisonment, nor is it to say that the sole purpose of the criminal law is to prevent crime rather than extract retribution. But, there is little doubt that punishment is the central tenet of current penal philosophy, and it plays out politically in more police and prisons, the use of determinate and mandatory sentences for an increasing number of crimes, and in longer prison sentences generally.

Fleisher's account shows the folly of the current strategy which focuses solely on the "back end"—the criminal justice system—

rather than the "front end"—prevention. All the street criminals Fleisher studied were products of dysfunctional families. Children raised in nonnurturing family environments, Fleisher argues, come to perceive the world as exploitative, a place where one is either aggressor or victim. Left on their own, unsupervised children have only each other from which to learn community values and individual responsibility. It is often one of the blind leading the blind. Community protection demands incarceration of current offenders, but it also requires more attention to those devices that might reduce future criminality. We need to invest more in those measures that have some promise of reducing the conditions of crime, rather than simply reacting to crime after it has occurred.

These are not new ideas. Thirty years ago, and at times prior to that, the national policy agenda was led by an investment, or proactive, strategy that emphasized parenting skills, child care, Head Start, Peace Corps, family reunification efforts, drug programs, deinstitutionalization, and community corrections. The current policy agenda is virtually entirely reactive and dominated by debates over restricting welfare, new jails, longer prison sentences, boot camps, the death penalty, and orphanages. It is hard even to keep the latter alternatives in mind while reading Fleisher's book; they are simply irrelevant. If the American Medical Association were to have the same opinion of prevention as is found in the present political climate, we would still be combatting plague by burning bed clothes and hunting rats. Fleisher's book brings vivid relief to the idea that some kinds of problems are best dealt with early, before they develop; indeed, there are some problems that can be dealt with *only* in this way. To be sure, there is no guarantee that we will be able to reduce street crime immediately with such a strategy, but virtually the only guarantee current punitive strategies provide is repression without hope and a continuing burden on the criminal justice system.

Mark Fleisher studied the toughest offenders. What makes them tough is not necessarily the crimes they committed, but their resistance to change. In many respects, the report of his fieldwork is pessimistic. As Fleisher suggests, though, we don't have to experience this kind of crime if we are willing to make social investments early in the life cycle. At least we have a choice to make, which is more than Fleisher's street criminals seem to have.

ROBERT F. MEIER

BEGGARS AND THIEVES

Introduction

Tattoos, faded from decades of wear, adorned Angelo's forearms. "Ink," he said, "tattoos from when I was a kid on the street." I'd seen hundreds of tattoos on the arms of active criminals hanging around street corners and prison inmates filling cellblocks, but these tattoos seemed out of place poking out from under the turned-up cuffs of Angelo's long-sleeve dress shirt. Angelo, now a veteran motorcycle cop in southern California, was reporting eyewitness accounts about youngsters he's known whose parents are criminals, fathers like Maniac.

"We busted Maniac, me and my partner did," said Angelo with anger in his voice. "This motherfucker was a slime ball. We went to his house, a fucking shack. They live in these awful, filthy places, but every one of 'em got a shrine, a fucking altar to the Hell's Angels. It's the only clean spot in the house. They put their plaques on the walls neatly, sweep the floor, set out their trophies.

"I got inside; my partner was outside watching for any more of 'em comin' up. I cuffed Maniac, told him to put his fat, ugly fucking ass down in the living room. His ol' lady was there. Sleazy bitch!

"They had a kid, a son, maybe about three years old. The kid was dirty and had a shitty diaper. Looked like it wasn't changed in days. Kid had shit dried on the back of his legs. Cute little guy, too. Ace, they called him.

"That asshole Maniac sat there and cursed and yelled at the kid, 'Come 'ere you little motherfucker. I'll kick your fuckin' ass if you don't get over here, *now*.' Ace stood there looking at that asshole. 'Get over here you little motherfuckin' asshole. I'll kick your fuckin' ass. Come here, you shit!'

"It was brutal. There was nothing we could do. The little guy walked over to that asshole, stood in front of him, looked up at him with his big eyes, and put his head on that motherfucker's leg, and stood there like that, didn't move.

"I knew the kid'd get the shit knocked out of 'im. There was nothing we could do. Nothing!"

Beggars and Thieves is an ethnography of the life trajectories of teenage and adult criminals ("hustlers").[1]* The hustlers, or informants, that you'll meet in this firsthand, participant-observation account are the drug dealers, the cocaine and heroin addicts, the street-corner alcoholics, the gang boys, the burglars, the violent men, the beggars and thieves, the flesh-and-blood street criminals who plague cities and crowd American prisons.

The lives of these hustlers are similar in many ways, but the most significant similarity is this one: The lives of all these hustlers, without exception, began in unloving families like Ace's, with often violent but always neglectful and unloving parents like Maniac.

The goal of this book is to describe the human dimensions of juvenile and adult criminals. It will be apparent that I am less interested in crime itself than in the familial factors contributing to the social, cognitive, and emotional traits typical among chronic street criminals. Consistent with this goal, I didn't write this book to test a criminological theory. Rather I chose to explore the social and cultural processes that shaped informants' character, setting them off on an inevitable trajectory toward a criminal lifestyle.

The nature of natal family life is the central issue that affects criminals' life trajectories. The quality of hustlers' social attachments to parents, teachers, and schoolyard companions, the quality of life within neighborhoods, and the styles of interaction between neighborhood companions are important too, as is the tension between social classes, the haves and have-nots, in American society. But this book isn't about poverty and crime, class structure and crime, and culture and crime. Its purpose is to trace the lives of teen-

---

*Data for this book were furnished in two studies. The first one, conducted in black, Hispanic, and American Indian communities from October 1988 through March 1990 for the U.S. Census Bureau, Center for Survey Methods Research, sought to understand the social and attitudinal dynamics of the undercount (the difference between the number of people residing in a community and the number reported to census enumerators; see Fleisher 1990). This research was pursued further in a second study (CY1990), funded by the Harry Frank Guggenheim Foundation.

age and adult street criminals who began life with brutal treatment from bad parents.

The analysis of each hustler's life history was integrated with daily participant-observation and interview data collected from dozens of active hustlers within numerous natural settings (street corners, bars, police stations, jails, prisons, missions, shelters, etc.). This daily process of data collection and analysis influenced the next day's participant observation as well as the collection and analysis of life histories and interview data. Slowly while the months and years passed, a narrative description emerged that captures the details of hustlers' daily lives as well as the lifecourse for the aggregate of hustlers in this study.

Beggars and Thieves is a narrative analysis based on core generalizations, or concepts (street culture, street lifecycle, defensive worldview) that I derived from life histories and participant-observation and interview data. These concepts may be valuable in understanding the lifecourses of other hustlers in even larger samples of chronic street criminals and may lead to testable hypotheses.

It will become clear, if it isn't already, that I consider socialization to be the key process shaping these informants' cognition and life trajectories. Angelo's account of Maniac and Ace will be referred to again and again as the central metaphor of what's wrong with anti-crime policies in America: Our crime control policies pour billions into police and correctional bureaucracies, drug and alcohol treatment, social service agencies, and education and vocational training for convicted juvenile and adult felons, yet we do little as a society to protect children from parental brutality, even though we know that brutalized children are very likely to exhibit deviant and criminal behavior. The policy recommendations offered in this book will tell us what to do about Ace and boys like him.

The approach in this book is holistic; I consider cultural, social, psychological, and environmental factors, significant influences on individuals' cognition and behavior.[2] Given this multiple-perspective approach to human behavior, I link these ethnographic data to criminological perspectives[3] as a *bricoleur* seeking numerous sources of interpretation.[4] Had I selected just one criminological perspective to complement these ethnographic data, the value of these firsthand accounts would be constrained and the usefulness of the interpretation itself as a basis for crime control policies would be strictly limited as well.

Ultimately my purpose is to construct a coherent interpretation of firsthand ethnographic observations and narrative interviews.[5] Readers will judge *Beggars and Thieves* as an interpretive portrayal of a subpopulation of American criminals, the chronic criminals. Their judgment should be made on this book's accuracy in describing how these informants think and act, which should serve in effect as a set of instructions for appropriately anticipating street scenes.[6]

An Ethnography of Street Criminals

The goal of ethnography is to grasp the point of view of the people (informants) being studied, realize their unique vision of the world, and describe their relationship to life.[7] Using a long-term ethnographic and linguistic approach to study street criminals is a radical departure from most studies about crime and criminals.

The actual speech of street hustlers as well as street and gang cops, parole and probation officers, and prison psychologists, among others, is presented as natural conversations unaffected by interview rooms and formal interview schedules that prescribe questions and responses, and is documented in numerous social contexts in Seattle, Washington, the principal ethnographic study site.

Natural speech is a powerful analytic tool.[8] Untouched by political rhetoric or researchers' ideological and theoretic bias, natural speech in social context is a metaphor for speakers' feelings, attitudes, drives, and emotions, a looking glass into the human character[9] that exposes hustlers' social world as they see, label, and act in it.

Prisons, jails, police-station holding cells, shelters and missions, street corners and parking lots, police stations and police cruisers, bars, "drug houses" (houses or apartments where cocaine is made into a smokable form, "rock cocaine," and heroin is packed),[10] and many other places were the venues for collecting ethnographic and speech data.[11]

After many years of studying inmates, street hustlers doing time in prisons and jails, I perceived order in social regularities of institution life, but the street scene seemed different at first. I began street research with Popcorn, a cocaine dealer, as my guide. We spent days and weeks together, and at first I didn't see social order and patterns among dozens of hustlers standing around street corners and wandering through parking lots. I didn't understand how hustlers' natal family life blends with adolescent years on the street, how adolescent social life is transformed into adulthood, how months served in jails and years in prisons affect hustlers' social street lives, and how aging street hustlers cope with pressures of the street and imprisonment. But eventually, after years on the street, I understood hustlers' words and wanderings around the city.

Ethnographers face a danger of adding too much structure, too much rationality, to ethnographic analysis.[12] A lifestyle model borrowed from lawful society, where years are structured by work weeks, weekends, holidays, vacations, and so on, doesn't apply to street life, which is missing these sociocultural frameworks. The other danger I faced with these ethnographic data was adding too much theory, overinterpreting data and distorting the scene depicting the actual lives street hustlers live. This ethnography doesn't do that.

These ethnographic data show that the lives of these hustlers are, for the most part, monotonous, colorless, flat. These are shallow people with little or no experience at anything but standing on street corners, committing crimes, and doing time. Their day-to-day natural conversations are mundane, covering topics such as: panhandling and buying wine; places where shoplifting is easy; who's in jail now, which street women were beaten up by their boyfriends, and which sleeping drunks were attacked and beaten in the alley the night before; hopping a freight train out of Seattle for warmer climates; recent arrests of drug sellers.

Research shows that criminals are versatile.[13] These ethnographic data support this fact, and show hustlers to be opportunists, moving between petty crimes as fluidly as children move among play structures on a schoolyard, taking advantage of what's available. Some do, however, prefer a certain type of crime (drug selling) to another (burglary, car theft). Popcorn said he wouldn't steal a car (he didn't know how to drive) or commit burglaries. He thought the risk of doing those things was too high, so he just sold cocaine. We all have preferences.

They don't talk about themselves as entrepreneurs or bureaucrats.[14] They don't ask "big" questions, think big thoughts, or seek big solutions. These hustlers are poorly educated, addicted, emotionally maladjusted men and women whose social interactions and criminal lives have become mundane rituals. Many of them even see their own lives as meaningless.

Documenting the criminal economy of the street life is straightforward; however, describing these hustlers' life trajectories and understanding their worldview are complex issues, and are the main points of *Beggars and Thieves*.

Concepts and Definitions

Ethnographic data, gathered in interviews and by an observing participant of street life, are the basis for three concepts. Below are the definitions and a brief discussion of each one.

Street Culture

Culture, as the term is used here, does not refer to a statistical description of behavior. Rather, culture

> consists of whatever it is one has to know or believe in order to operate in a manner acceptable to its members. Culture is not a material phenomenon; it does not consist of things, people, behavior, or emotions. It is rather an organization of these things, a set of unique rules that guide behavior and structure meaning, the form of things that people have in mind, their models for perceiving, relating, and otherwise interpreting them.[15]

The collective knowledge of the street, its content, structure, and meaning, is "street culture." Street culture is a logical, coherent system of adaptational rules that meet the conditions and perils of street life and is strongly influenced by how street criminals perceive and interpret the social world surrounding them. My informants are as firmly committed to street culture as lawful citizens are to their version of American culture.[16]

We can understand any culture from two perspectives. A description of the culture of any given set of informants can be based on opinions, observations, and beliefs imposed from outside the culture studied. Or it can be based on the "natives'" points of view obtained from natural (unprompted) conversations and long-term observations. The former is an "etic" perspective, the latter "emic."

This book is an emic ethnography. An emic study "helps one to appreciate not only the culture or language as an ordered whole, but it helps one understand the individual actors in such a life-drama—their attitudes, motives, interests, responses, conflicts, and personality development."[17] With an emic description in hand, an outsider would have sufficient detailed information about the form and content of cultural traditions as well as a knowledge of speech to pass as an insider.

I learned street culture from its "actors." There was Popcorn, a black cocaine dealer and cocaine addict in his early 30s. He was my principal guide to the social network of the street and the beggars, the thieves, the homeless, the addicted, the drug addicts, the drug dealers, the ill-fated optimists, and the former prisoners who dwell there.

Popcorn introduced me to T-Cool, a former California state prison inmate in his late 30s, an "original gangster" among the Compton Crips, a founding member of the Crips youth gang that originated about 25 years ago in Compton, Los Angeles.

There is T-Bone, who, in his mid-20s, is the reputed leader of Seattle's Compton Crips and organizer of its cocaine business. T-Bone gave me access to Crips, and through him, I met Twin, a Hoover Crip and cocaine dealer in his early 20s, as well as a collection of Crips on Hoover Street in south-central Los Angeles.

There is Shy, an alcoholic, homeless, former inmate in his late 30s. He is the central figure in a group of others who share the same history and characteristics and hang around Seattle's Capitol Hill, a neighborhood just east of downtown.

And when I strolled through Seattle's Pioneer Square on a warm afternoon, I found David, a homeless, alcoholic former inmate in his early 40s. He was leaning against a brick wall, eyes bloodshot, fingers trembling, left hand extended, asking for change. Many others will be introduced later.

Street Lifecycle

The street lifecycle is this book's core organizational theme. Street culture provides the rules for adjusting to street life and negotiating within it. Street lifecycle is hustlers' dominant socioeconomic adaptation, and the unique sociocultural path of life traversed by my informants while they move from birth to death.

Each culture organizes social life into discernible categories (infancy, adolescence, young adulthood, adulthood) and expects native participants to express appropriate behavior in each category when cultural expectations for social and chronological age merge.

Cultures impose social expectations on natives as they age.[18] Cultural expectations for performance are limited by biological maturation. I am a middle-aged man and can't perform feats of strength like those of my 12-year-old son, who's a competitive gymnast; nor can he compute the mathematics necessary to orbit the space shuttle around Earth.

Chronological age, the biological timetable measuring aging from birth to death, isn't necessarily synchronized with changes in social life, such as individual roles, identities, and opinions.[19] Street culture defines a unique link between social expectations and chronological age that's quite different from the chronological age–social age patterns typical in lawful society.

Lawful American society expects personal responsibilities to increase as we mature: At 20 years of age we're not supposed to speak as if we were 10; we are expected to finish high school, to attend college, to obtain employment; we are expected to get married and raise children. Eventually, at some culturally appropriate age, we are expected to relinquish responsibilities, to "slow down," to retire.[20]

Street lifecycle doesn't use these life events as indicators denoting social maturation. It allows hustlers at any age to speak and act like adolescents and never acquire responsibilities similar to those marking social maturation in lawful society. In the sociocultural world of hustlers, youth is marked by gang membership, "kids' crimes," the onset of drug and alcohol addictions, and juvenile detention; young adulthood is marked by going to prison; and aging is denoted by the number of times a hustler has been there, the number of decades of addiction, and the number of years on the street.

Years of participant observation and hundreds of interviews led to the identification of street lifecycle stages. Preteenage and teenage informants were close to childhood and offered excellent data about delinquency and gangs as well as natal family issues. Young adult informants (aged 19–29) were also close enough to teenage years to offer fresh opinions about gangs and delinquency and insights into survival in the jails and prisons and on the street. Adults (aged 30–39) were veterans of the street and institutions, and many were still surviving in familiar, old ways. Middle-aged informants (40 years and over) provided data about street survival as well as "aging out" of crime.

Street lifecycle is a life trajectory with transitions denoted by a series of life events: running away from home;[21] membership in delinquent groups and gangs; first commitment to prison; and residential living (apartment, shelter, mission, jail, prison) to homelessness.[22] A street lifecycle is disturbing to our view, but it keeps the natives of street culture alive.

This analysis of ethnographic data identifies four stages of the street lifecycle. The sequence begins with a childhood stage, progresses to a teenage stage, moves to a system stage, and ends with a postsystem stage. Each stage is distinguished by a distinctive style of social adaptation.

Street lifecycle is not a "crime career" with a different label. *Crime career* has been defined as the "longitudinal pattern of crime events for offenders and assessment of the factors that affect that pattern"[23] or a "longitudinal sequence of delinquent and criminal acts."[24] All these informants' lives also meet the criterion of a violent crime career, with "at least one violent infraction, indicated by either official records or self-report interviews."[25]

All informants self-reported either minor incidents of violence such as simple assault, often on girlfriends and legal or common law wives, or major incidents such as aggravated assault, with and without weapons, on the street and in prison. All informants, except Popcorn, who reported only several minor assaults on girlfriends, reported both minor and serious incidents.

Gottfredson and Hirschi suggest that an original notion embedded in the concept of crime career, the notion that criminals' offenses become more serious with time, is inappropriate.[26] Some scholars and policymakers think the career concept is useful in the formation of crime-control policy;[27] however, the reification of street deviance as a career shields outsiders from seeing the disorder, dysfunction, and irrationality of deviant behavior.

The concept of career projects a sense of order, planning, and design, which applies to physicians, businessmen, professors. But in the daily lives of hustlers, order and planning and design are absent. Hustlers' lives are created less by design than by default. After all, their first culturally defined social role is victim.

The term *crime career* is a metaphor for criminal activity through time,[28] but the use of the term *career* in regard to street culture is inappropriate, even oxymoronic. This use tries to understand behavior in one culture (unlawful society) with a concept appropriate in a distinctly different culture (lawful society). On the street, natural conversations among hustlers aren't about career planning. They bounce from one crime to another, one jail to another, one prison to another, one scam to another. This research shows that life as a criminal is more than a series of delinquent or criminal acts. There are no ethnographic data suggesting that a criminal lifestyle is a career.

Worldview

A worldview is a "reflection and mastery of a repertoire of forms and meanings . . . below the threshold of awareness."[29] How is a worldview acquired?

A genetic predisposition for culture and language acquisition allows all human infants and toddlers to acquire quickly and accurately the cultural perspectives and speaking abilities typical of their communities.[30] This universal process is enculturation.

An outcome of the enculturation process is a worldview, a unique design, a cognitive impression, for conceptualizing and perceiving the social world which reflects the conditions of the environment as well as a set of "operating instructions" (tacit rules) for adapting to and negotiating within it.[31]

Children's innate ability to acquire culture, language, and a worldview exists independent of cultural and social context.[32] The key issue in acquiring a culture's unique perspective, its worldview, is social context. Young children in American society are exposed to variations in social interactions,[33] that is, variations among the people with whom children interact, the nature of the interactions, the social situations themselves in which interaction occurs, and the goals of interaction within these social situations. Youngsters are also exposed to speech and speech variations in social contexts where speech varies, for instance, by dialect (determined by social class and/or geographic region) and by speech register (determined by social context).

A worldview can be metaphorically divided into two complementary components: a "sociocultural" grammar, a set of tacit rules that guide behaviors and interpretations of those behaviors; and a "sociolinguistic" grammar, a set of tacit rules that generate utterances in social contexts.[34] Sociocultural and sociolinguistic grammars interact to allow a youngster to behave, speak, perceive, and interpret the world around him in ways considered appropriate by others in the youngster's family, neighborhood, community, and culture.

Exposed to the sights and sounds of a Toraja-speaking community in central Sulawesi (Celebes), a youngster will likely formulate a worldview that conforms to these grammars of others in the community. Likewise, if a child grows up in a family culture like Ace's, where being battered, neglected, and harshly criticized are the typical sights and sounds in the immediate environment, he will formulate a worldview that reflects this environment and allows him to cope with and adjust to its conditions.

Enculturation's effects are permanent. Once a person acquires a sociocultural grammar and a sociolinguistic grammar these are never lost or replaced by other grammars. Learning a second language by living in a foreign country or in an ethnic subculture in America doesn't replace a person's original sociocultural and sociolinguistic grammars, nor does a new community's worldview supersede the original one.

How an informant thinks—that is, adjusts to the immediate environment, displays emotions, handles interpersonal situations, copes with anxiety, expresses fear, displays anger, among numerous other things—depends on the enculturation environment typical in his early years of life. Tumultuous emotional and linguistic displays, such as screaming and harsh criticism, for example, when commonly used as a child-rearing device leave permanent impressions on young children's worldview.

Ace will acquire an idiosyncratic worldview based on his family's enculturation environment. Maniac's unloving emotional displays and venomous speech are likely to have permanent effects on Ace's perceptions and interpretations of actors in his social world, as well as they are likely to guide his speech and behavior toward these actors. In the end, the test of this interpretation of enculturation and its relationship to thought, behavior, and speech will be whether Ace becomes a criminal like his father.

This study of the behavior of adolescent and adult street criminals shares its mission with archaeology. An archaeologist excavates material artifacts and re-creates physical environments with a goal of creating a model of sociocultural life at an earlier time. My job as an ethnographer is harder. Early-life enculturation conditions, such as parent-child interactions, are transient and leave no direct traces, no material artifacts. These early-life impressions can be inferred in later life, however, by focusing on actual behavior and speech as these occur in natural social contexts.

My informants' typical forms of behavior and speech in natural settings are maladapted to peaceful social life. Common expressions of physical violence and verbal assaults, irrational problem-solving, self-destructive behavior (substance abuse), social irresponsibility (adolescent truancy; the inability to hold a job or even seek employment), the inability to meet even simple requirements for peaceful social interactions (poor adjustment to school and work situations outside controlled institutional settings), and other things as well, are expressions of harsh early-life experiences that permanently affected their worldview and its constituent sociocultural and sociolinguistic grammars.

An analysis of all my informants' early-life recollections, as well as a firsthand view of their natural behavior and speech over several years, led me to posit the concept of a defensive worldview (see chapter 2, the section "Radical Effects on Enculturation") as the core feature of street culture, and as an adaptation which, in large part, determines hustlers' natural styles of social interactions and sustains a street lifecycle.

Street Ethnography and Social Policy

Criminological research and ethnography are dissimilar.[35] Irwin and Austin comment on the comparison between firsthand observation and participation and the analysis of records data:

> . . . are the popular images and the social scientists' ideas about contemporary criminals accurate? We think not, for the simple reason that most of these popular images of crime and criminals are shaped by the media, and media depiction consists mostly of selective attention on sensational crimes, politicians' rhetoric, and studies of career criminals. . . .
> In these studies, social scientists have formed most of their ideas in "armchairs" . . . using evidence that is unreliable and skimpy—police arrest records, prison files, and convicts' penciled-in answers to questionnaires. . . . Very few of these criminologists have spent any significant time observing or talking to their subjects, the prisoners, something absolutely necessary to develop an accurate understanding of offenders' motives and criminal practices.[36]

Criminology and ethnography can complement each other, and together these research paradigms can provide a more detailed picture of crime and criminals than either can do alone. *Beggars and Thieves* joins criminological perspectives with ethnographic details of the real life of dozens of actual street criminals.

Choosing one research paradigm over another is often a matter of personal experience, and, for the most part, both styles are exercises in academic scholarship; however, the seriousness of data collection and analysis significantly increases when government officials seek scholars' advice on crime control strategies. Until now survey methods and analyses of social science have dominated crime control policy. But this approach, with its focus on crime data obtained from police and court records and brief interviews, has failed to generate recommended strategies that effectively diminish street crime.[37]

America's response to street crime is based on aggregate analyses of crime data and on voters' and policymakers' beliefs about the causes of crimes, the efficacy of drug and alcohol rehabilitation to alter substance-addicted criminals' life trajectories, the deterrent effect of prison on juvenile delinquents' and adult criminals' behavior, and the effects of education and vocational training on altering delinquent and adult deviant behavior. We know these anti-crime efforts have had little effect on altering the thinking, feelings, attitudes, and behavior of street criminals.

Policymakers need to know what tools work best for each target population,[38] and qualitative research can give them this information. This ethnographic research provides detailed information about the actual behavior of street criminals in natural social circumstances and about their distinctive worldview. A close-up look at street criminals is essential information for policymakers.

Rist has said:

Qualitative work can provide to program managers and policy makers information on how confident they can or should be in the measures being used to determine program influence. Although the intent may be that of a highly reliable and replicable instrument that allows for sophisticated quantification, it is the qualitative work that can address the issue of validity.

. . . Suffice it to say that policy makers and program managers have been misled more than once by investing a great deal of time and effort on their instrumentation without equal emphasis on answering the question of whether their measures were the appropriate ones to the problem or condition at hand. Studies of school desegregation and busing or health care in nursing homes are but two areas where a heavy emphasis on quantifying outcomes and processes have left key aspects of the condition undocumented and thus unattended to by those who should have been paying attention.[39]

Beggars and Thieves shows that chronic street criminals don't choose a lawful, or "straight," lifestyle. They choose to be outlaws. Straight life has too many responsibilities, obligations, and pressures, say my informants. Many say that altering their established lifestyle is too difficult. Personal change is, for the most part, an anathema for these hustlers, who say that lawful citizens should meet their needs.

A criminal's life, including doing time, is easy, they say. Going to prison doesn't scare them. Education and vocational training as well as substance-abuse treatment are useless programs, as they see it, unless an immediate material benefit is an outcome of these programs. Street life is OK, in the opinion of hustlers; however, street criminals' lifestyles are not OK for lawful citizens.

Anti-crime programs are based on the education model of social change. This model suggests that behavior depends on knowledge.[40] Here's how it works: If criminals were to know about the destructiveness of overusing drugs and alcohol, they would stop overusing them; if criminals were literate and trained in a vocation, they'd get jobs and wouldn't have to rely on crime for money; if criminals were to know how much their offensive behavior hurts people, they would stop doing it; if criminals were to go to prison, they'd learn a lesson and refrain from criminal activities after release; if adolescents and adults on the margin of committing serious crime were to see companions go to prison, they'd learn that crime doesn't pay; if Maniac were taught to be a better father, he wouldn't abuse Ace.

Education-based anti-crime programs have failed to produce the desired outcome. But the education model is popular anyway, because it produces quickly implemented programs that fit middle-class policymakers' and voters' worldview (education brought them success and kept them crime-free and can do so for others as well). Also, education-based anti-crime programs have an obvious political benefit: This policy model has enabled state and federal policymakers to spend billions of taxpayers' dollars on tens of thousands of new government jobs filled by bureaucrats who design, implement, and oversee government programs. Unfortunately, however, these expensive government programs are ineffective; yet taxpayers and victims of crime must continue to pay a very high financial and social cost for them.

There are no simple, effective solutions to America's crime problem. This research shows that ending deviant and criminal behavior is a complicated issue that requires much more than remedial education for criminals, and that reducing street crime depends on creating and maintaining safe, healthy, early-life social environments for children. Ace and other boys like him must be protected from parents like Maniac. We must do more than ask parents like Maniac to stop beating their sons and daughters; we must permanently remove children from brutal parents.

Overview

Chapter 1, "Street Ethnography," presents a detailed look at an ethnographic methodology and problems of analyzing criminals' interview data. I discuss interviewing, issues that affect interviewing, and being a participating observer in jails and prisons and on urban streets. Also discussed are the ethical and legal dilemmas resulting from long-term participation among active street criminals.

In chapter 2, "Distorted Families," the socioemotional dynamics of early family life dominate the analysis of the childhood stage of the street lifecycle. This chapter is a series of informants' accounts detailing facts and events about early family life. These accounts show the socioemotional forces that lead to a defensive worldview and the forces driving boys away from home. These tales are often frightening, and you'll wonder how these children survived. Here in this stage you'll see why informants don't, under daily conditions on the street and in jails and prisons, establish close emotional ties with anyone. I show how the brutality and neglect of early lives effect a defensive worldview whose impact on the informants' social worldview is permanent.

In chapter 3, "Adolescent Survival," adolescent behavior, social networks, and survival strategies are the key points for a discussion of the teenage stage of the street lifecycle. This chapter explores social network ties as a system of social adaptation among homeless teenagers. I discuss the formation of youth gangs, analyze gangs as social networks, analyze the material conditions that perpetuate gangs, and discuss gangs' expressive, or symbolic, culture. The theoretical position is that a gang is a multigenerational social network that offers homeless youth material benefits; a youth gang isn't designed to be a criminal organization. The effects of a defensive worldview, low self-control, and weak natal-family social ties are indicated by irresponsibility (truancy, dropping out of school, hanging around street corners, joblessness), deviant behavior (criminal activity), self-destructive behavior (drug and alcohol use), and a lack of companions outside an immediate peer group. When these rejected boys remain among boys like themselves, their social world shrinks and social isolation intensifies.

Chapter 4, "Sanctuaries," analyzes how the system stage of the street lifecycle is initiated when street criminals learn to rely on jails and prisons as sanctuaries, safe havens from the chaos of street life. This analysis shows that jails and prisons offer hustlers a way of life that is otherwise beyond their grasp. These institutions offer the easiest, most direct ways to obtain a semipermanent residence, good food, planned recreation, and cost-free drug, medical, and dental treatment. The analysis shows that the institutions operated by America's law enforcement system to punish, deter, and rehabilitate offenders have become incorporated into the street criminals' survival mechanism. Jails and prisons are sites of comprehensive social welfare programs for the uneducated, the poor, and the indigent.

Chapter 5, "The Street," demonstrates that nearly all street hustlers, when released from terms of imprisonment, return to the street, where they must rebuild social and economic survival networks. These street hustlers don't use the vocational skills acquired in prison to obtain legitimate jobs. Rather they continue to rely on public institutions, such as missions, shelters, food programs, residential substance-abuse treatment centers, and criminal behavior, as means of support. This ethnography shows how the social lives of street hustlers are stabilized by the medium of bartering cocaine and heroin. Drugs are bartered for companionship, cash, and sex. If hustlers were without "drug buddies," they would have no companions at all. However, drug selling and other crime eventually lead these hustlers back to the jails and prisons, back to the sanctuaries they know well. Hustlers' dependency keeps them in the system stage of the street lifecycle while they go the round from the street to institutions, from institutions to the street. Sometimes this lasts a lifetime.

In chapter 6, "Aging," we see that some hustlers do escape the street-to-system cycle and move into the postsystem stage of the street lifecycle. These male and female hustlers, usually middle-aged and older, have become so addicted to alcohol and drugs that the threat of going to prison (or into alcohol or drug detoxification) then becomes a serious deterrent to their criminal behavior because they don't want to risk becoming deprived of easy access to alcohol and drugs. These ethnographic data take a close look at the street life for middle-aged former inmates whose lives are devoted to addiction. Substance-abuse treatment doesn't guarantee them a crime-free life, because many "dried out" hustlers return to the system stage of the street lifecycle.

Chapter 7, "Ethnography and Anti-Crime Policy," evaluates current anti-crime policies in light of the findings in this research, suggests that policymakers have chosen the wrong theoretical model as the basis for rehabilitation programs, and posits anti-crime policies and programs designed to protect children from brutal and neglectful parents and to transform prisons into work communities.

Policymakers have implemented anti-crime policies without a clear idea of how street hustlers actually live day to day and without understanding how hustlers exploit the criminal justice system. These ethnographic data show that the only long-term solution to street crime is to remove children from abusive, neglectful, irresponsible parents permanently, and for state and federal officials to fund and operate long-term residential child care facilities.

However, institutional care for youngsters won't protect lawful citizens from already-violent street predators. These offenders must be sentenced to long terms in prisons with well-developed industrial work programs whose products are sold on the open market, lowering prison operating costs and enabling more tax money to be spent on public institutions such as schools.

Nonviolent offenders, including drug sellers, shouldn't be sentenced to prison. Rather they should serve their terms doing full-time community service, such as painting public buildings, cleaning neighborhoods, shoveling snow, and serving the community they have injured. Full-time hard work may be our best crime deterrent.

1 ———————————

Street Ethnography

Many excellent field researchers have recognized the value of an ethnographic method in studying subjects whose lives are played out on urban streets.[1] Adler recognized the value of intensive ethnography:

> . . . investigative field research . . . , with emphasis on direct personal observation, interaction, and experience, is the *only* way to acquire accurate knowledge about deviant behavior. Investigative techniques are especially necessary for studying groups such as drug dealers . . . because the highly illegal nature of their occupation makes them secretive, deceitful, mistrustful, and paranoid.[2] (emphasis added)

Linguistic anthropologist and ethnographer James Spradley conducted ethnographic field research on First Avenue in Seattle, among "urban nomads," about 20 years before I conducted this study on the same street.[3] Spradley showed clearly how valuable detailed linguistic data are to establishing a coherent picture of life in street culture from the perspective of its participants. This ethnographic study of mine was inspired by his valuable insights.

Researchers face numerous problems trying to study street criminals with probability-sampling designs, and have found ethnographic research to be an optimal choice for data collection.[4] This ethnography includes more than interviews conducted in bars and offices and on street corners.[5] As a true participant-observer, I sampled behavior by direct observation, conducted informal, unstructured, and semistructured interviews,[6] and became enmeshed in my informants' social and emotional lives.

Ethnography relies on participant observation and improves data validity. Bernard writes that participant observation gives us "an intuitive understanding of [street hustlers] and allows [us] to speak with confidence about the meaning of data. It allow[s] [us] to make strong statements about cultural facts . . . [and] extends both the internal and the external validity of what [we've] learn[ed] from interviewing and watching people."[7]

Regularities in culture, social life, psychology, and language exist even in small samples. We don't have to survey 10,000 households to know children speak the language(s) and the learn the culture(s) of their socializers. Nor do we have to interview 5,000 English speakers to write a competent generative grammar. When an ethnographer has studied a population, however small the sample, he or she knows a lot about the lives of the people in it. The observations and interpretations of ethnographers can be combined with survey methodologists' aggregate analyses to effect a better understanding of spurious, directly causal, conditionally causal, and common cause relationships of criminal behavior.

Full participation provides a broad range of data and further minimizes problems of external validity. These hustlers, like major drug dealers, have a vested interest in protecting their identities, maintaining secrecy, and keeping outsiders outside. Adler found that her years of experience in the drug world were a useful research tool. My own years of experience with inmates, former inmates, and street hustlers were a reliable mechanism to verify informants' statements.[8]

I distrust data gathered in a few interviews with informants whom I don't know well and for whom I can't verify facts with reliable documents. Hustlers', inmates', and former inmates' self-reports are, until proved otherwise, just "folklore," simply informants' comments, opinions, and explanations often engineered to sound legitimate. After all, these informants have been shown to be untrustworthy, manipulative, and disingenuous. Why should they be otherwise with me?

Street ethnography is a valuable tool. However, it is difficult to set up, often dangerous, and I found it to be emotionally draining. In this chapter, I discuss how this research began, how informants were contacted and selected, and how I developed rapport and trust. I discuss techniques for interviewing and validating data, and some ethical and legal pitfalls that might befall anyone doing criminal ethnography, that is, the long-term ethnographic study of active street-level criminals in their own neighborhoods.

Getting into the Field

Ethnography requires knowing where to collect data as well as choosing good informants and asking them things they know something about.[9] There are dozens of good informants waiting on the streets and in jails and prisons.

The principal ethnographic data-collection site was Seattle, Washington, but interview data were also gathered in Arizona, California, Oregon, Washington, D.C., and several other places in Washington State. Table 1 summarizes my informant sample by age grade and place of first contact.

The demographic requirements of the Census Bureau research limited the informant sample by race/ethnicity and sex. However, the Harry Frank Guggenheim research expanded the size and demographic composition of the informant sample; I included two black women and six white men. Table 2 summarizes the racial composition of the informant sample by location of first contact (the female street informants aren't distinguished in Table 2).

Participation-observation data were gathered on Seattle's streets

Table 1. Informant sample, by age grade and location of interviews, October 1988 through 1990

Age	Jail	Prison	Street	n
9–18	9	0	18	27
19–29	10	40	10	60
30–39	12	24	24	60
40–49	5	12	24	41
≥50	0	0	6	6
Total	36	76	82	194

Table 2. Informants, by race/ethnicity and location

Race/ethnicity	Jail	Prison	Street	n
Black	26	48	53	127
Hispanic	4	19	3	26
American Indian	5	9	21	35
White	1	0	5	6
Total	36	76	82	194

from among hustlers ranging from boys in their preteens to men in their 60s and provided information about the day-to-day happenings. Sidewalks, street corners and sidewalk benches, empty parking lots, cars parked in parking lots and along sidewalks, bars and restaurants, police cars and police stations, informants' apartments and houses, drug houses, and alleys and parks are the places criminals hang out, where conversations occur, where drugs are bought and sold, where plans are made.

Two sampling strategies were used to select street informants. I conducted a focused sample[10] on a few hustlers to monitor behavior and speech (two to four days, every week or every other week, for the entire study). I also spot sampled[11] the behavior and speech of dozens of the same hustlers on selected days (Friday and Saturday night, for example), at particular times (early morning, late afternoon, and evening), for the duration of the study. These sampling procedures provided in-depth, long-term data about key informants that were complemented by detailed, long-term data about dozens of hustlers.

In addition to spot and focus sampling, I collected interview and observational data at particular locations (Pike Place Market, Pioneer Square, specific missions and shelters, and so on) from dozens of hustlers with whom I had just one or several contacts. These were more than convenience samples. While I chatted with hustlers I screened them, informally choosing those of particular age grades, racial/ethnic status, and state prison experiences, and with self-reported crime preferences and addictive substance (heroin, alcohol) preferences.

All informants were selected in purposive and "snowball" samples.[12] Fagan used snowball sampling in a three-city study of street gangs and found it useful: "The snowball strategy provided flexibility in targeting, locating, and recruiting [informants]. Moreover, because the snowball process involves respondents nominating other respondents and identifying other possible chains of respondents, the likelihood of excluding [street cohorts] is minimized."[13]

All informants had self-reported criminal histories, which were verified whenever possible. Local police assisted by recalling hustlers' recent arrest records and, if possible, more detailed criminal histories. The self-reports of all prison and nearly all jail informants were verified with official records.

Jail interview data were elicited from inmates who had been off the street in the King County Correctional Facility in Seattle ("Seattle jail") for a relatively short time (less than a year). To gain access to the Seattle jail, I met with a senior official there, explained the research project, the data to be collected, how it was to be collected, and how it would be used. Jail officials made calls verifying my identity and the legitimacy of this research. It helped that a senior official at the jail had been a senior administrator at USP Lompoc during my research in 1985–86. Within days, I received a photo badge that granted access to move freely on a dormitory floor where hundreds of inmates in their late teens and 20s milled about, and on another floor that housed work-release inmates, that is, inmates who ventured out to work daily and returned to the jail afterward.

Located among high-rise office buildings in downtown Seattle, the jail was not too far removed, either physically or socially, from the neighborhoods where many inmates hang out when not doing time. The following are examples of questions I wanted to have answered: What was an inmate doing the day he was arrested, the day before, a week before? What did he plan to do the day he was released? Where would he go and with whom? Ideally I wanted to meet informants inside the jail who would take me into their social maze outside.

Extensive life history interview data were collected at USP Lompoc from inmates who had been off the street for many years. These men, whose average age was 36, had been committed to jails and prisons numerous times. The institution confined black, Hispanic, and American Indian men who grew up in rural settings and in cities throughout the United States. I interviewed minority inmates from numerous major and midsized cities.

My interview goal was to collect detailed life histories, personal accounts of early family life, school relationships, friendships, work experiences, marriages and divorces, work and education histories of parents and siblings and cousins, plans for the future, and so on. Life history data were also collected at state prisons in Washington and California. Experiences at USP Lompoc and the Washington State Penitentiary at Walla Walla taught me that collecting life histories would take time, patience, and endurance.

To gain approval to conduct these inmate interviews at USP Lompoc I followed standard Bureau of Prisons policy requirements for research.[14] I submitted a research application, an interview schedule and an informed consent form, and a justification for the proposed interviews to the bureau's Office of Research and Evaluation in

Washington, D.C., and to the warden at USP Lompoc, where it was reviewed by the institution's research committee. I was granted permission to conduct inmate interviews by officials in the bureau's central office and by USP Lompoc's warden.

Gaining access to prisons and jails was easy, but I still had to gain access to the street. I needed several "guides," I thought, gatekeepers who would open the door to the street and bring me into their unlawful world.[15]

I found them while I was eating lunch in a Seattle restaurant on a Friday afternoon in October 1988. Sitting in a corner booth were three Seattle policemen, drinking coffee and chatting. I decided that I wanted them to be my first guides. I walked to their table, introduced myself as an anthropology professor, explained my research project and current dilemma: I needed someone who knew every street person, every drug house, every runaway teen, every youthful hustler, and every former inmate, and who was willing to introduce them to me.

The police officers welcomed this personal approach to studying street hustlers. The East Precinct, their precinct, had everything and everyone I needed, they said. They told me whom to speak to at the East Precinct and gave me the name and phone number of the Seattle chief of police, and suggested that I write him and explain the research project. Before long, I was riding in a police car.

Before the first time I rode with Seattle cops, I thought that hanging around with them might inhibit or damage potential relationships with street hustlers. My choices were limited though. Either I could wander around minority neighborhoods and parking lots where cocaine was being sold and hope to find someone to answer my questions, or I could let the police introduce me to hustlers they thought would cooperate.

Actually I did both things. But before I went to the street alone, I had to learn something about its people and its culture. Seattle police were good teachers. I wanted to see Seattle's "social areas," where gangs hang out, where drugs are bought and sold, where drug houses are located.

Connections

My street ethnography (data collection) depended on my ability to weave through T-Bone's, Shy's, and Popcorn's social networks, in much the same way as they did. My success in doing it depended entirely on my ability to maintain positive face-to-face relationships with each of them and members of their social networks.

Popcorn

Popcorn is a key informant who connected me to cocaine dealers, street hustlers, former prison inmates, and to the Bloods, a black youth gang originating in Los Angeles. We met in Seattle's Central District (called the CD by locals), where once-glorious Victorian houses stand empty and dilapidated. The first-floor windows of most two-story, single-family, woodframe houses have been barred, a sign that something bad has hit this once-elegant neighborhood. Small apartment complexes, new in the 1960s and 1970s, now show years of neglect. Up-down duplexes are squeezed side by side along narrow streets, protected by a canopy of tree limbs.

Neighborhood barbecue and catfish restaurants serve good food. Windowless taverns, a few private social clubs, and local white churches protect the neighborhood's multiple personality. On the weekends, gas stations in the heart of the CD hire security guards to keep patrons safe.

Lush green, sloping hills flank Garfield High School. West of and across the street from Garfield High is Ezzel's at Jefferson and Twenty-third, serving fried chicken, savory rolls, and sweet potato pie. Deep-fried gizzards sell quickly on weekend afternoons. It's the finest food in Seattle, but it's take-out only. Ezzel's removed their indoor picnic tables after Garfield students hung out, skipped school, caused trouble.

Traffic speeds along several busy east-west and north-south thoroughfares. Citizens of color and whites walk slowly, peacefully, on cracked sidewalks, stopping in neighborhood stores, meandering in small shopping plazas composed of five or six stores. Rows of houses and rolling hills deflect the echoes of kids playing.

In the daytime, the CD belongs to straight folks and to the officers of Seattle's East Precinct. At sunset, however, the street changes character like Dr. Jekyll to Mr. Hyde. Kids' sounds are replaced by cracks of gunfire.

One Friday afternoon in November 1988, when it was nearing dark in the CD, the cops I was with cruised slowly along a street a block or two from Blood territory, a neighborhood of ramshackle houses. The street and sidewalk were dotted with squashed beer cans and broken beer bottles, their jagged glass awaiting a child's bare foot. Along this street and others in this area many houses were boarded up, sheets of plywood tightly sealing windows and doors. These houses had been rock houses, places of business for gang members and private cocaine entrepreneurs. Now repossessed by Seattle, they displayed plywood GONE OUT OF BUSINESS signs.

Cruising slowly, scanning the neighborhood, the cops saw red. In the drizzle with darkness overtaking the CD, Popcorn's red sweat-pants and sweatshirt flashed brightly, sending an unmistakable message. Slowly and nonchalantly, as if he had been equipped with police sonar, Popcorn felt their eyes on him, spun on his left foot, turned an aboutface, and sauntered off in a direction opposite to the cruiser's. No matter. The cruiser turned too, finding Popcorn slithering up an alley.

The cruiser rolled next to him and stopped. He had stopped next to a dumpster overflowing with ripped grocery sacks full of garbage spilling onto the ground, mixing with garbage already there.

These cops didn't recognize Popcorn. The CD wasn't their regular territory. But it was his territory, though he didn't tell them so. A few years earlier, a handful of Bloods moved to Seattle from Elm and Piru streets in south-central Los Angeles. The Elm Street and Piru sets* found Seattle's CD a bright new spot to sell cocaine.

Popcorn is a demure fellow, about 5 feet 6 inches and 135 pounds, with a stutter that is accentuated when he is nervous. He asked, "Wha'cha stop *me* fo', anyways?"

"This is a high crime neighborhood, and we're just being careful, trying to protect everybody. There's gangs around here and drugs."

Popcorn's dumbfounded look seemed to say, "Crime and drugs in this neighborhood? Oh my, no!"

In this neighborhood cops are cautious. They are suspicious of everyone they don't know. New gang members come into town from Los Angeles or from other cities, bringing plague with them. The cops' questions started: "Got ID? . . . Where ya going? . . . Where'd ya come from? . . . Where'd ya live? . . . Got any relatives

---

* *Set* has three meanings: *Set* most generally refers to a person's neighborhood, independent of gang affiliation. It also refers to an entire gang (Hoover Crips), or to one of many local neighborhood gang groups (Santana Block Crips). Black and Hispanic gang members use the term *set*, preferring it to *gang*.

around here? . . . How long ya been in Seattle? . . . Carrying drug paraphernalia? . . . Mind if we check your pockets? . . . Why ya wearing red?"

Popcorn responded to the barrage of questions, stuttering and stumbling and waiting for the cops to get an armed robbery or a burglary call, or just get bored. But they didn't.

Popcorn feigned ignorance: he knew nothing about a Bloods gang, thought red was just a color, had never been in that particular neighborhood either. All lies.

Seattle police are lie detectors: an alias or a phony address can cost a liar six months in jail and a $500 fine. But that doesn't matter. Street folks lie anyway. Popcorn told the cops his name.

A cop called dispatch and asked for outstanding arrest warrants on Kenny Mitchell, alias Popcorn. While we waited, a cop shook down Popcorn and found in the pocket of his hooded sweatshirt a straight shooter, a glass pipe used to smoke "rock" cocaine.* And he found three playing cards—two black, one red. That's illegal too—gambling paraphernalia.

While the one cop shook down Popcorn, his partner stood back from the cruiser, scanning the neighborhood, looking up and down the streets and at the windows of the surrounding houses, watching for snipers.

I asked Popcorn, "Hey, what's the game you play with those cards? I've seen guys do that in Manhattan." Playing dumb gets information and explanations.

"Three-card molley."

"You any good at it?"

Popcorn stuttered, "Y-y-yeah, p-p-p-pretty good."

"Lemme see ya play."

---

*A cocaine rock is a mixture of powder (flake) cocaine, baking soda, and water that has been "cooked" in a glass dish, either in boiling water or in a microwave. When the mixture has cooked it "rocks up." In daily conversation, Seattle cocaine sellers don't use the term *crack*, so I have not used it either, although across the United States the terms *crack* and *rock* are often used as synonyms (see Inciardi 1986: 82).

There are many styles of rock pipes. Popcorn's was a three-inch glass cylinder, three-eighths of an inch in diameter. A small piece of metal mesh (plain steel wool) is stuck in one end, leaving three-quarters of an inch open for a rock. This style is known as a straight shooter, also called a glass dick. Street folks say rock smokers suck a glass dick.

Popcorn looked at the cops for approval.

The shakedown officer said, "OK, show 'im how you do it." Popcorn's hands caressed the cards as though they were old, reliable friends. The scam man started running his game.

"Here. I even bend a corna' on the red card. Make it easy for ya." He said it with a straight face.

The two cops and I gathered around Popcorn, who used the left front fender of the cruiser as a card table. We watched a master "shake the red card." I bet imaginary $100 bills; so did the cops. We lost every time. The cops laughed.

Dispatch called and it was bad news. Popcorn had told the cops his real name, and a computer search revealed an arrest warrant issued after Popcorn's failure to appear in court. Charge: possession of stolen property. The cops were surprised: they never expected Popcorn would give them his real name. On the street, truth is a rare commodity. Time for the card game to end and for Popcorn to go to jail.

Scamming, that's how Popcorn got his street name. A tag reflects a street specialty. In this case, "pops co'n" (to run confidence scams) has become Popcorn. He is an efficient shoplifter too, relying on dexterity to steal plastic Taiwanese watches from Pay 'n Save. He sells them for $5 or $10 to beggars (panhandlers).

Now cuffed, with his hands behind his back, Popcorn sat in the backseat of the cruiser, the cops whisking him away to the Seattle jail. As we rode, Popcorn stuttered, offering facts about his case, telling tales about shaking the red card, conveying little anxiety about going to jail. The cops reassured him that his charge was minor, that he would be out of jail soon—as if he didn't know.

The Crips, Fly Boy, and T-Bone

Years earlier, Pimping Slim, a Compton Crip, was one of my best informants at USP Lompoc.[16] I knew Seattle had youth gangs—Crips, Bloods, and Black Gangster Disciples (BGDs). Seattle media had been regularly reporting for many years alleged gang activity, such as drug dealing and drive-by shooting. But, when I did my research, Seattle didn't have an "official" gang problem. Seattle politicians called them opposing community factions. City leaders hide, or deny, the menace of gangs from lawful citizens.[17]

The day after I met Popcorn, Fly Boy, a Seattle gang cop, introduced me to T-Bone. An added benefit of having street cops as guides is an opportunity to do police ethnography.

Fly Boy boxed in college, and in the army he flew helicopters. On the street, his boxing reputation was well known. Over the years a few challengers emerged from the ranks of gang boys, but only a few. The street recalls a good jab. Gang bangers (gang members) said Fly has delivered many gang members to the Seattle jail. But, they said, Fly is a fair cop.

As long as a cop plays by street rules, local gang boys do not hold a grudge against him or other cops who arrest them. "We know we gonna get busted," commented Ice, a Blood. "But we don't wanna get the shit beat outta us in the station. You do us fair, we do you fair. Them's da rules, man. Fly, he fair wid us. Good dude. Tough, you know. There be some motherfuckers [street cops] better look out. Dem m'fuckers cuff ya, slap ya 'round. Fuck that shit, man. I'm waitin' fo' 'em. They stick they head through my window some night, I blow it off with a 0.357. Yeah! That right. You know what I'm sayin'?"[18]

Fly took gangs and gunfire seriously. Friday on a noon-to-8:00 shift, he rode alone, with me at his side. At about 4:00, a dispatch reported gunfire in Blood territory. He cruised the area, saw nothing unusual. Kids were still playing on the street.

Fly said, "If we're under fire and I go down, get on the radio 'n call for backup. Take the key off my belt, unlock the shotgun, and blast the motherfuckers. You know how to shoot, don't you?"

"Yeah. I was an honor graduate of the Federal Law Enforcement Training Center."

"Ever been under fire?"

"No," I answered. Fly said nothing; I understood his silence: polite rejection.

Later that evening, Fly Boy asked, "So you want to meet a Crip?"

"Yeah," I said.

"Let's see if Bone's home," he said.

We walked through a light drizzle along a newly poured concrete sidewalk up to the front door of T-Bone's duplex. Fly rapped on the door using the end of his nightstick; we waited for someone to answer. A young pregnant woman in her 20s opened the door slowly, sticking her face into the crack between the door's edge and jamb.

"Evening. T-Bone here?" asked Fly.

"Nah, he not here now," she replied, quietly.

"Would you tell him that I got somebody here I want him to

meet?" he asked politely. Fly didn't have to tell T-Bone's girlfriend who he was.

She nodded, pulling her head back to safety. She said nothing.

Next night we returned to T-Bone's. Again Fly knocked on the front door using his nightstick; again T-Bone's girlfriend answered the door.

"Bone here?" Fly inquired quietly, politely.

She nodded and walked away, leaving the door slightly ajar. We backed away from the door and stood on the sidewalk. The cop's eyes never left the front door.

Within seconds, T-Bone appeared, gliding out of the door like an actor making an entrance on center stage. He approached us. Fly just nodded at him and looked at me.

"He wanted to meet you," Fly said quietly to T-Bone. Fly then disappeared into the darkness of the neighborhood, leaving me alone with the T-Bone.

Finally, the infamous T-Bone, I thought to myself. I had read about him on a flier a few days earlier in the East Precinct house. Hanging on a small bulletin board along with pictures of confiscated guns taken from gang members, crime reports, and other artifacts of the street was a *Seattle Times* article about him. The article noted that someone had tried to kill T-Bone at a party, but T-Bone had shot first, killing the other guy. Self-defense, claimed T-Bone, but the prosecutor's office said it was a gang shooting.

T-Bone was a picturesque figure. Well over six feet tall, he had a thick chest and shoulder-length dreadlocks, shining from hair dressing in the dim light cast by nearby street lights. His dark waist-length leather jacket, its supple sheen reflecting the street lights, showed small beads of rain water.

• T-Bone was in his mid-20s, too old for a teenage youth gang. But his purpose in Seattle was not to hang out with gang boys; he was there to sell cocaine, an entrepreneurial activity. To do it, he took advantage of his teenage Crip affiliation and the young boys on Seattle's streets. •

"You da dude I heard about?" asked T-Bone.

I explained who I was, why I wanted to meet him.

"Wha's up?" he asked rhetorically.

In answering his question, I did three things: I tried to garner his support for a government effort to remedy the undercount in Seattle's black community; I told him I was interested in the social life of teenage boys in black street gangs; and, I linked myself to Pimp-

ing Slim, telling T-Bone that Slim and I had met in the Lompoc penitentiary. I described Slim's physical appearance, his mannerisms.

"Yeah, I know 'im," said T-Bone. It didn't matter if T-Bone knew
Pimping Slim; it only mattered that I did.

Standing in the drizzle on T-Bone's muddy front yard, we got
along well. Soon, from behind a large dumpster in the rear of T-
Bone's duplex, the shadows released Crips. Four, five, six of them
appeared. One wore a Crip jacket. Emblazoned across the back in
bold letters at the 12:00 position it read, Compton's Finest. At the
6:00 position there were three letters, SBC: Santana Block Crips. At
10:00, BK: Blood killer. At 2:00, PM: Piru murderer. Scrolled across
the front left side was his tag (nickname): Hollywood. That jacket
was street art.

I chatted with T-Bone, Hollywood, and the others, too, about
inner-city Los Angeles. Fly, who had been leaning on his cruiser
parked up the street not too far away, joined our group. The conversation was casual, friendly. The gangsters kidded Fly about chasing
them over lawns, between houses, and around the local high school,
trying for one reason or another to apprehend them.

Fly warned Hollywood about his gang jacket. Seattle police do
not allow teenagers, whether or not they are gang members, to wear
gang paraphernalia, such as red and blue bandannas, anywhere in
the city. Fly told Hollywood he would confiscate it. Fly looked at
me. "You can have it for your collection," he joked. His warning was
offered in an advisory, calm, fatherly tone. After that evening, I
didn't need a police escort in Crip territory.

Several months after we talked on his muddy front lawn, T-Bone
was jailed on a murder charge and was housed on a maximum-
security floor in the Seattle jail. T-Bone alleged it was self-defense,
but a jury disagreed. A judge sentenced him to prison.

Shy

Just a few blocks from the restaurant where I introduced myself to
the police officers who assisted in setting up the research, I met Shy.
The bridge of his nose had been flattened by a fist thrown in a thun-
der club, a bare-knuckle boxing club in Canada. Greasy shoulder-
length black hair lay straight and limp at the nape of his neck; his
facial scars were barely visible because they were covered by three,
four days' growth of beard stubble.

We met on a snowy afternoon. Shy and his companion, Mark, were huddled in sleeping bags, sharing a bottle of cheap wine. Shy was petting Wimpy, a tame husky. The three of them were sitting under the eaves of a church known among Seattle's street people for its generosity: it was a place to shower, to wash clothes, to get a free breakfast Monday, Wednesday, and Saturday, from 9:00 to 11:00, and dinner on Sunday afternoon. On Sunday, the church fed all comers a meal such as spaghetti and bread—filling, cheap, plentiful.

When I approached them, Wimpy stood up. I used my standard opening line: "Hi, my name is Mark Fleisher. I'm an anthropologist at Washington State University. I'm doing a research project."

Mark asked, "You're a what?"

"An anthropologist," I answered.

Shy blurted, "You a cop?"

"No! I'm an anthropologist," I exclaimed.

"I'd rather talk to the cops," noted Shy. "You guys stole my grandparents' bones. You're nothing but a fucking grave robber. You got any money, Mark?" he asked me. "I'm kinda dry."

Once connections were made and rapport established with Popcorn, T-Bone, and Shy, they led to other connections. I also learned how connections from earlier prison research could be useful years later.

Inside the Seattle Jail

Popcorn was inside the Seattle jail. Now it was time to begin jail ethnography, assuming, of course, he would introduce me to inmates. A few blocks from Seattle's Kingdome, next to Interstate 5, stands the Seattle jail, a lifeless, gray, high-rise building. We drove under the building and entered it through several steel doors.

The arresting officers delivered Popcorn to a booking clerk, a deputy sheriff, who didn't smile. Popcorn was now the property of the jail, and before he slipped into jail clothes, he would be stripped, searched, deloused. Some officers search incoming inmates too quickly, said jail inmates, and in their haste they forget to peek into inmates' ear channels, a hiding spot for small cocaine rocks. Cigarettes are also smuggled. In this smoke-free jail, they are prized possessions; inmates smoke huddled around exhaust vents in dorms or sneak a smoke in the toilet. Other things are smuggled in, too. A female officer in the booking area told me she had strip-searched a female inmate and found a loaded revolver in the inmate's vagina. The officer laughed and asked, "How da ya think da bitch was gonna shoot it?" Jail humor.

Popcorn was booked at about 5:00 in the afternoon. Holding tanks, large rectangular rooms made of steel and concrete that hold dozens of inmates, were already filling up. Street hustlers, dope dealers, street drunks, and gang members were among the dozens already there. They sat crouched in corners or leaned against the tank walls. It was a familiar place; they were veterans.

Opposite the main booking area was a padded tank with one occupant. Wearing a beard several days old and disheveled hair, he smashed his face nose-first into the tank's shatter-proof plexiglass door. The inmate was about 25. He glared at me the whole time his left fist pounded the door. He shrieked a wild message: "Seattle Police Department's the Green River killers. Green River killers. Seattle police is the Green River killers. Motha'fuckers. Faaaags," he exclaimed, spinning his shredded T-shirt over his head with his right hand. "You punk motherfuckers, I'll fuck ya up your asses. You punk bitches. Lemme out of here. I'll fuck you up, motherfuckers. Fuck you up the ass. Cocksuckers, lemme out a here, you bitches." (Green River refers to a serial murder case. A member of the Green River Task Force in Seattle said the estimated number of murder victims is about 40; the murderer dumps his victims, usually prostitutes, at or near the Green River, which runs past the SeaTac Airport.)

I spent five months inside, walking around, chatting with inmates and staff, eavesdropping, and interviewing sentenced misdemeanants and felons on an L-shaped dormitory floor. Large dormitory rooms at each end of the L were crowded sleeping areas. Inmates slept on bunk beds and single beds placed just a few feet apart. The jail's horizontal windows are too narrow for an inmate to squeeze through, but they do offer a view. Looking through the windows, inmates peered down at homeboys, visitors, hustlers, or former jail inmates out on bail. Now and then after visiting, girlfriends and wives stood on the sidewalk waving up at their men. Jail tales abound on the floor about female visitors who remove their conservative visiting room clothes once visiting hours end, and replace them with sexy short skirts; they stand on the sidewalk, lifting their skirts in view of their boyfriends and husbands, who yell to them through the windows.

At the short end of the L, there were several ping pong tables, and suspended from the ceiling was a color television. At the end of the long leg of the L was a reading area with a few armless plastic chairs and several small bookshelves half-filled with tattered paperback novels. Suspended nearby was another color television. The long leg of the L was filled with a dozen rectangular tables. Lined up at each table were red, blue, and gray armless plastic chairs.

This floor was an ethnic and racial potpourri. Black, American Indian, and Hispanic inmates mingled un-self-consciously among white and Asian inmates. I hung out with minority inmates, except for Jason.

Jason, a former Oregon State Penitentiary convict, had spent six weeks short of a year in the Seattle jail on an armed robbery charge. Jason felt good about his time. "It coulda cost me 10 years. I had a good lawyer. . . . How did I pay for it? When you're in my business, you got to prepare for the worst. I always keep 5, 10 grand aside for bail and lawyers. Good lawyers ain't cheap."

Jason and I met on my first day in jail. He stopped me while I wandered around and asked if I were a lawyer. I gave him my Census Bureau rap (the rap I had given the cops in the restaurant), and he asked if I knew anything about inmates. I told him about my 14 months at USP Lompoc, and we had a connection.

Animal, Jason's stepbrother, was a lifelong outlaw and a member of the Outlaws Motorcycle Club, a gangster-biker outfit that terrorizes California. Animal had done six years at USP Lompoc for bank robbery. Animal's time had overlapped with mine.

Jason said he had visited Animal. I asked Jason a few questions to verify his claim. Jason described the details of USP Lompoc's visiting room; he knew Animal's cellblock designation; and he remembered the prison nicknames of inmates whom Animal had "walked with on the compound"—nicknames that I remembered, too.

After this initial chitchat, we sat together for about an hour. Jason wanted to know more about the Census Bureau project and more about me. I assured him that I was not collecting "intelligence" about jail inmates on the floor. He offered to help me get informants, but he refused to become one.

"You want who? Blacks, Hispanics, American Indians?" he asked. He stood up and yelled at inmates of each color to come over to meet me. A group of about 10 inmates huddled around our table. "Tell 'em whatcha doin'." I did, and each one agreed to be interviewed. I handed each an informed consent statement (which I used to determine if an informant was literate), and assured them that law enforcement officials would not see my interview notes. I trusted them; they had to trust me.

I told each inmate that I wanted details about his social life prior to his present imprisonment and life history information, particularly his places of residence, with whom he had shared each one, and how he obtained the money to pay rent and buy food and other necessities. I also told each informant that I did not want to hear tales about his wrongful imprisonment or innocence, and that I would not do favors inside or on the street. I said I would not mail letters, make phone calls, give loans, smuggle cigarettes or drugs, and would not talk to a jail administrator about an early release. "Just talk. If ya can't handle it that way, split and I'll find someone else to talk to." My rules let each man know I had been in prisons before. Two inmates, American Indians who were members of the American Indian Movement, chose not to cooperate. I found other American Indians who did.

Weeks passed, inmates on the floor forgot about me and my interviewing, my nosey questions. I knew I blended in when heads did not turn as I walked by and when inmates did not stare while I conducted interviews.

Working with the Seattle cops was a highly successful strategy. It worked because Seattle cops had earned respect among their street people. Gang cops were respectful of young gang boys. They were stern, yet showed these boys warmth. They joked with the boys about chasing them around the neighborhood, asked if they were attending school, gave them second and third and fourth chances before arresting them for selling drugs. And they always cautioned them about the threat of street violence. These cops knew the boys' families and asked about their aunts, grandmothers, sisters, and brothers by name. From my vantage point, Seattle's cops cared about street kids, and the kids knew it.

Learning the Neighborhood

Popcorn stayed in jail 49 days, time enough for us to develop a good relationship and for him to introduce me to many informants. Among them, I met 'Dre (Andre), a former inmate at the Washington State Penitentiary and an active Seattle cocaine dealer who was doing a short sentence for a minor assault.

Just before Popcorn obtained his release, he gave me an address and a telephone number where I could reach him. One afternoon, I drove around looking for the address and called the phone number. The street address didn't exist and neither did the phone number.

On a Friday morning at about 8:30, I walked to First Avenue and Pike. Pike Street dissects midtown Seattle into north and south and joins First Avenue in front of the Pike Place Market, a busy tourist attraction. Its elaborate displays of fresh salmon and mysterious sea edibles, as well as its fresh fruits and vegetables, are bait for schools of tourists.

Street life flourishes at First and Pike. This downtown neighborhood belongs to drug dealers and runners, drug addicts, thieves, prostitutes, alcoholics, ex-cons, runaway teens—and to the Seattle Police Department's West Precinct.

There he was, standing on the northeast corner, poppin' co'n. That day a blue curling rag was pulled tightly over Popcorn's head, keeping his hair dry in the cool drizzle that often fills the air in winter, blowing eastward off Puget Sound.

We spent the morning drinking coffee in a crumpet shop, getting reacquainted, laughing about the cops playing the red card, learning more about each other. We still got along well.

I didn't beat around the bush: I told Popcorn I wanted his help with my research: I wanted him to guide me, to get me into the street drug scene, to introduce me to adult street criminals, to members of street gangs. He agreed. I don't know why.

The next day we entered his world. We met at the same corner for a walking tour of downtown Seattle. We sauntered slowly south, down the west side of First Avenue, Seattle's former skid road, to Pioneer Square, a renovated business area, tourist haven, and gathering spot for the homeless. Nearby, to the east and north, is the Seattle jail, and to the south is the Kingdome. Extra bleachers stored in its parking lot provide a slanted roof for homeless folks sleeping beneath them.

In the center of Pioneer Square is a picturesque plaza that is home to Wandering Raven, a Tlingit totem pole. Wandering Raven tells a story about how the world began, how men acquired culture and knowledge, how social life started, and how life is renewed in the Raven rituals of Tlingit, a Native American people of southeastern Alaska.

Alcoholic beggars, many of them American Indians, shuffle

around Wandering Raven or find shelter sitting or sleeping on the sidewalk benches under a nearby ornate cast-iron gazebo. Their roof is an umbrella of broadleaf trees. Life renewal for these American Indians begins with a handout and ends after swigging mind-numbing, high-alcohol wine.

By midmorning, we were walking slowly uphill, northward on the east side of First Avenue. Sunlight had just broken over the peaks of the downtown skyscrapers. We were heading toward the Pike Place Market.

While we walked, Popcorn stopped now and then to chat with a soup or dog food seller (in Seattle, cocaine is "soup," heroin is "dog food"). Some he had met in the Seattle jail over the years. Others he had met in a city mission. A few men were acquaintances from his most recent stay in jail.

We bumped into CJ, Popcorn's companion. CJ and Popcorn had been buddies for about a year; cocaine brought them together. As their story goes, CJ wanted a rock and asked Popcorn, who was hanging around a street corner, where he could buy one. They smoked a few rocks together and became "drug friends."

CJ's second addiction is "syrup." Nodding drugs, such as prescription cough syrup, make him dull and numb, leaving him in a painless state. "You can sit around and nod for days." Being a "syrup head," CJ is also a drugstore burglar.

Three blocks south of the market we walked past the First Avenue Service Center, a daytime hangout for street folks. Inside are men, women, and teenagers curled up in corners, on wooden benches, and on the floor, trying to sleep, covered by their torn dirty coats. Here street folks get a meal and a shower, play cards, and, until closing time, sit in a dry, warm place. Some folks sit alone, staring as if in a hypnotic trance, seeing nothing, hearing nothing.

It was there I introduced myself to Kelly, a 19-year-old, tall, skinny, black and Puerto Rican fellow from East Harlem in New York City. I asked him casual questions, which he didn't pay much attention to but answered with shotgun energy. He ate there, but he didn't nap at the Service Center. Kelly claimed that he didn't sleep at all, spending his nights on the streets, walking by himself non-stop, hour after hour. He spent his hours punching a heavy bag that hung in a recreation area downstairs; he had a coach, a man in his 60s who had boxed as a youngster (old newspaper clippings, with photographs, verified his tale). One morning Kelly and I sparred a few rounds; we got to know each other pretty well. He had a sharp left jab. I rationalized the swelling on the right side of my face as rapport building. I'm not sure what he thought.

It takes time to do ethnography in an urban neighborhood. An initial ethnographic objective was to understand how informants perceive their social world. To do that, I took Popcorn back to First and Pike early one morning, to watch the street wake up.

A cool drizzle fell at 6:30 in the morning, while I leaned against crumbling old brick in the side of a tavern known for selling heroin. The street awakens slowly, achingly, as an alcoholic beggar crawls out from under a cardboard blanket.

Looking east down Pike, I saw Benny, a legless fellow in his 40s. He had parked his wheelchair in a doorway out of the drizzle; a tattered, greasy, dirty raincoat pulled over his head was his blanket. Swollen capillaries filled his eyes, coloring them red; two, three days' growth of beard shadowed his face, outlining its scars; gray pants too dirty to touch bagged around him with their zipper half down; institution-style, thin, leather boots gapped untied, their soles worn thin, almost gone; cotton socks, threadbare, once white, drooped and curled into his boot tops.

Hawk is Benny's American-Indian "road dog" (street partner) from British Columbia. Standing next to Benny, Hawk bounced slightly, foot to foot, shadow boxing, throwing jab after jab, snorting through his nose. On the street, Hawk was everyone's light-middleweight punching bag. A black eye showed it.

Hawk and Benny were panhandling (a panhandler sticks out his hand, holds a cup, or puts a box or hat on the street; since passersby usually don't move close to or touch beggars, a box or hat works better for collecting money than sticking out a hand). A once-water-resistant cloth rainhat was tossed in the middle of the sidewalk as a collection plate. It couldn't be missed. Hawk scanned passersby in the same way that T-Cool and others read the street. Along came a woman. He stepped away from his partner, but not too far: according to him, "the cripple is sympathy bait." Hawk greeted the woman pedestrian with a bow at the waist, a smile, an arm extended, finger pointing at the hat. She and most others ignored him.

Hawk ignored tall, well-built businessmen and students who were built like middle linebackers, as well as other street people.

Slightly built men who looked nonaggressive were his targets. When he saw short thin men walking toward him, Hawk jumped half in front, half to the side of them, slowing his pace. He stuck his face out too close to the target's, pointed at the hat, shook his head side to side, jabbering. A coin or two fell into the hat occasionally. Most targets kept walking. For them, Hawk was invisible, inaudible, a nuisance too early in the day.

Frustration overtook Hawk in about 30 minutes. Like a country dog, Hawk chased cars when they slowed to a stop at a red light at Pike and Second. Running from his dry post next to Benny, Hawk accosted cars and yowled at drivers. Drivers saw Hawk in time and closed their side windows, pretending his face was not inches away. With his face mushed onto a car window, Hawk created distorted angry masks on the transparent canvas, leaving behind stains of greasy unwashed skin and tracks of saliva that had drooled from his mouth and slid down the glass. Hawk pounded on glass and screamed a grotesque opera, reminding me of an alcoholic's performance street art. When the light turned green, drivers were rescued.

At 7:30, I picked up Popcorn, and we drove downtown for breakfast at a cafe on the southeast corner of First and Pike. It's a bar, too; eight men and two women were drinking wine or schooners of cold beer.

"Tell me about the street, Popcorn. What do you see when you look at the folks walking by out there?" Popcorn heard my question, but he didn't know what I wanted him to say. He said nothing. I tried a paraphrase.

"Look out the window at the folks walking by. Tell me about them. Where did they sleep last night? Where are they going now? How do they get their money? Tell me a story about 'em."

"We got it all out here. Drugs and 'ho'es. What else do a man need?" Breakfast humor. Then he became serious.

"Men and women out this early come from missions. The women, they from ladies' missions. Most of them got a boyfriend. Women got it easier than men. Guys send women out to work. She can make money a lot faster, whorin'. Even the ugly ones get $5 or $10. Winos be ready to go [to have sex] for alcohol.

"No. All the women ain't sleepin' in missions. The real winos [women] are sleepin' outside.

"Who else? The real crazy ones. They be stayin' up in the shelters, waitin' on a welfare check. Some guy be lovey-dovey wit' 'em two

weeks before the first. She give 'im $100, $200, he be gone, motherfucker, gone.

"Addicts out there too. You see 'em later, after they be smokin',
smokin', then they be geekin',* runnin' around crazylike out there.

"Cluckers out there too, you know [clucking is a tweek]. They
lookin' on the ground for drugs. They look like chickens cluckin',
you know, lookin' down at the ground all the time.

"You got serious winos out there. They stay on the street, go into
detox, back to the street. Now, you see them people there with
packs. They stay in a shelter or the woods. The ones with sleepin'
mats sleep outside.

"There [are] some halfway dressed kinda nice. They be stayin' in
a shelter or just out of jail.

"Some of them stay with friends or relatives. Come here to hustle,
come to an area where they know people. They can run dope,
heroin, or rock. They be drug laborers, get a day's pay or day's hit.
Dealers say, 'You rush me five customers and I give you a $20 [a
rock].' Most of 'em you see out there at night, you know, when the
street's full, ain't dealers, man, they be runners.† They down but
they ain't out."

Popcorn and I visited gang territory. He provided a chronology
of drug houses, who ran them, and their opening and closing dates.
Popcorn ran one too, in the upper half of a duplex, not far from
Ezzel's.

Gangs carved up the Central District, without asking for permission from Seattle's city fathers. Bloods stay on Cherry. Crips hang
across from Garfield High. BGDs stay on Yesler in Bryant Manor. To
be sure, gang members can be found staying in other areas of the
city, too.

At night, packs of Crips and Bloods wander around the Pike

---

*Crack sellers and addicts use the terms *geek* and *tweek*. Inhaling crack has psychological effects on crack smokers. The effect crack has on a smoker is a tweek.
Crack smokers identify many types of tweeks. A crack addict who runs around the
street hustling money for another rock is geeking; geeking is the anxiety of a rock
addict who needs another rock.

†A "runner" sells ("runs") crack or other drugs on the street and is paid by a
"supervisor." Runners always face the risk of getting arrested, whereas a supervisor
"lays back" away from the street and is less likely to be arrested. A small drug operation includes, for instance, a dealer, who buys drugs from a supplier, and his
runners. A large drug operation has numerous hierarchic levels.

Place Market area, dominating the sidewalk. Blood packs include teenage girls who carry the drugs and guns of the "bangers." Young women and girls are less likely to be shaken down and less likely to go to jail than teenage boys are.

At night, Popcorn and I enjoyed cruising the CD, checking Blood and Crip hangouts. We often coasted by Hills Brothers Barbecue. There on the corner of James and Twenty-first, a few teenage girls and some in their 20s often join the Bloods. In clear weather, to the south of Hills at a bus stop, dudes are usually clocking. (Selling drugs in the social context of a gang is easier and safer for teenagers than doing it alone; also, gang members have regular connections to drug sources. In addition, "jackers," people who steal money and drugs, are less likely to jack gang members.)[19] Popcorn knew most clockers. Hanging his upper body out of the car window, he smiled and yelled, "You cool brother?" A drug laborer smiled back and nodded. "I cool. I be workin', man. Clockin' befo' one-time roll by."

Many clockers at that bus stop were Popcorn's relatives. Late one evening when a clocker's supply of rock cocaine dwindled, he asked for a ride to a rock house to pick up vials or plastic bags of $10 and $20 rocks. I ran a taxi for rock cocaine sellers. For my trouble, one of the clockers wanted "to take care of" me: he offered me a rock or two. A generous offer, but one I always refused (see the section "Fieldwork and Ethics," below).

Popcorn was comfortable among Bloods. Crips made him nervous. He did not know them and did not want to stay with me when I hung out with boys in blue. One night, Popcorn and I were cruising slowly around Cherry and Twenty-fourth, just north of Garfield High and the Medgar Evans public swimming pool. A three-story, brick apartment house in that neighborhood was a temporary home for the Rollin' 60s, T-Cool's set.

Rollin' 60s' graffiti adorned the building's exterior walls. Some of it had been sprayed over by authorities, leaving a neutral gray background that Crips used as a canvas. Once, twice, three times, we slowly cruised by. Crips stared. I stared back. They threw signs. Popcorn got nervous.

"They gonna start shootin', man. Go! Go!" I drove around the block and cruised by again. I was looking for Twin, an informant from Los Angeles.

Crips and their girls were jammed together on the stoop. A few guys huddled out front, under the umbrella of tree branches. Folks under the tree saw my car, turned and walked, climbed onto the stoop. I stopped near the tree. Signs were coming our way. Popcorn was nervous; he closed his side window. "That's glass, man. It ain't gonna stop a slug, homey," I teased him. He worried.

A dim light on the first floor shone through the glass of the entry-way, backlighting the stoop. I stared intently. Then I saw it: on the top step, a Crip had turned around, back toward my car, dropped his pants, and mooned us. They laughed. I laughed, and left them alone.

Popcorn has simple advice for dealing with Crips and Bloods: "Don't fuck wit' 'em. They'll hurt you bad." Popcorn proudly claims to have "started da Bloods in the cocaine business. I set 'em up."

After the tour and initial ethnographic interviews, I knew what I would face in doing street ethnography. Drug laborers, drug run-ners, drug dealers, cluckers, dealers clocking, tweeking addicts, and drug whores, among numerous other social categories and social processes, were out there on the street, waiting for me to understand them. Watching the street also taught me that, if I were going to blend in or at least look less conspicuous, I would have to develop a street identity.

Whenever an explanation to police, storekeepers, jail and prison inmates and staffers, prisoners and street informants was necessary, I used a brief outline of the undercount research and its purpose. I didn't distinguish the practical aspects of the Census Bureau re-search from the more theoretical issues in the Guggenheim project.

Street Identity

I wore street attire, armor protecting me from looking too middle-class, too much like an undercover cop or a social worker, or worst of all, a social scientist.

A two-day beard was a facial mask. The costume included faded and ripped blue jeans; torn heavy-weight socks (cement sidewalks are cold); beaten up ankle-high boots with worn-out soles and oddly angled heels (with padded inserts for warmth); a down vest covered with paint stains, looking as if it had come from a dumpster; dirty and unclipped fingernails; scratched metal-frame eyeglasses; and a 20-year-old, stained, hooded parka, which also looked as if it had come from a dumpster. Wearing rings, bracelets, necklaces, and a watch would have made me a target for robbery.

In warm weather, the down vest was removed, but the parka was useful for its pockets, where I stored a large notebook for sit-down interviews and a small one for quick thoughts and ideas, observations, and sidewalk chats. Used unobtrusively, a notebook can be nearly invisible. A large pocket concealed a microcassette tape recorder. When conversations were taped, I imagined myself in an informant's position: Would I allow a stranger to tape record the facts about yesterday's drug sales? Questions which informants wouldn't answer on tape, I asked later. Transcription of taped and natural conversations in the International Phonetic Alphabet was useful in capturing speech variations.

I used flash money. Dollars bills folded several inches thick and stuck in my jeans were a sharp hook for thirsty, penniless hustlers. A quarter will not buy anything on the street. A dollar buys enough patience to answer a half dozen questions. The trick is knowing six good questions. On a good day, I would spend $20 to $30 or more buying coffee, donuts, beer, and wine, and adding to various collections used to buy heroin. Experience is expensive.

Cash is scarce on the street and takes on added value. Hustlers, short of cash, barter with drugs, stolen property, and promises (debts). They needed the cash I had, and that brought me into informants' social networks. I knew when they bought alcohol or drugs, or both, how much they used, and how much it cost. Many informants sent me companions who needed money or a ride. Before long, I was a link in informants' social networks, standing between network members and serving as a transfer point for cash and information.

Weaving through Social Networks

Popcorn was a social link to Bloods, adult drug dealers, former inmates, and to a middle-aged Crip, T-Cool. Popcorn said he had met T-Cool years earlier. Popcorn's brother and his brother's girlfriend shared a house, in south Seattle, with T-Cool and his girlfriend. In those days, Popcorn and his brother were in business together selling heroin. One night, Popcorn visited his brother, knocked on the door, and T-Cool opened it.

Popcorn introduced me to T-Cool around noon one day, when he and I were strolling near the Pike Place Market. Crowds of locals and tourists were shopping and browsing; others were waiting for the free bus that runs along First. From the corner at First and Pike, I heard, "Hey, Popcorn, Popcor'."

"Hi," Popcorn replied, quietly.

T-Cool stood at the corner, looking up and down the street "reading" it, as if it were a prison yard, while talking in a continuous stream of jabber to anyone who would listen.

T-Cool is a good-looking man in his late 30s, but appears to be in his late 20s; the skin above his eyes is marred with thin scars. His knuckles and backs of hands show thick skin, rough scars.

That day, as always, he wore blue—blue pants, a blue nylon windbreaker, a blue hairnet to keep his curl dry. The blue caught my attention. So did his style of speaking. T-Cool's speech reminded me of convicts' speech I had heard over the years in many prisons. T-Cool acted and sounded like Pimping Slim.

T-Cool's eyes were bloodshot, his breath smelled of alcohol. That day his mood was jovial. A bright smile, nearly straight shining teeth, and a pleasing wit gave T-Cool public charm. Slim was charming too—and he was a killer. In two decades of listening to criminals tell tales, I ranked T-Cool's gift for storytelling among the best. A charming character I thought; I should have known better.

T-Cool was suspicious of me. "I'm Mark." My hand went out to shake his: a test. Convicts don't shake hands. Ex-convicts don't do it either, unless they must, and then they do it awkwardly. T-Cool looked at my hand, slowly his hand grasped mine. We shook, chatted, laughed. Nothing but rapport building was on my agenda at that moment. T-Cool kept reading the street.

An hour passed, I slid out a few questions in casual conversation. Where you from? How long you been in Seattle? Where do you stay? Where do you work? He answered them with vague responses, sounding like every prison inmate I ever heard, every cop's suspect on the street.

Seattle had been home for the last few years. But he had grown up in Compton, he said, and in California's Youth Authority (CYA, for juveniles and young adult offenders). He spent his teenage years, beginning around 1964 at about age 12, "cripping." Then he was a "BG," a baby gangster.

Twenty-five years later he is an "OG," an original gangster, a member of the first generation of Crips.* He had pride in the title. Slim was a Crip OG, too. I asked T-Cool if his blue (the Crip's color) outfit meant anything. He smiled.

"Nah. I just like blue, that's all." Sure.

"Come on, cuzz," I said, "You know I know better than that." He paused. *Cuzz* is a term Crips use among themselves.

I asked T-Cool if he knew Pimping Slim.

"Who?"

He should know Slim, I thought. Slim had turned 32 before his parole in November 1985 from the USP Lompoc. T-Cool and Slim were about the same age, both from Compton (there were fewer Crips then), and both had grown up in California's prisons for teens. If T-Cool were a legitimate Crip OG, I thought, he would know Slim.

"He goes by Slim. A 'CC' tattoo is on the back of his left hand." I added unnecessarily, "He was a pimp, too," which goes without saying in regard to men like Slim, who inevitably pimp at one time or another.

"Yeah, I know him. He's tall, thin." T-Cool described Slim, or someone like him, right down to his taste for extravagant, full-length leather coats. I guess there are many tall, thin men who like leather coats.

T-Cool's face changed expression; he became serious, curious. "Who are you, man? How do you know Slim?"

"We were in the penitentiary together." I waited for his reply.

"You did time?"

"Nah. No federal time for me. Feds don't fuck around, they say, huh? I was on the street for years in New York City when I was a kid. I did time on the street."

"Do jail time?" T-Cool asked.

"Got close a couple times. I was lucky—and white. I got busted a dozen times, threatened with reform school, state prison, but a

---

*This definition of an OG is consistent among all middle-aged criminals who claim to have been members of the original generation of gangs now known as Crips and Bloods. Young Crips and Bloods today say an OG is someone who's "deep into a gang," with many serious physical injuries and prison time being the criteria that distinguish OGs from others. An initiated male member of the West Side 6-Deuce set of Bloods in Kansas City, Missouri, said an OG "has been shot 'for real' like seven times, been down in the pen[itentiary], come out, and is still in it . . . not in the gang [as a regular member], but giving orders."

judge let me go to college instead. Scared me, so I stayed in college for 30 years." I laughed. He didn't.

I was evasive about my professional involvement at the Lompoc penitentiary. I didn't want to tell T-Cool or Popcorn that I had worked for the Federal Bureau of Prisons at USP Lompoc as a line correctional worker. That might have killed rapport in a hurry. So I bent the truth by omission. Everyone on the street does it.

"I'm a writer. I was in the Lompoc penitentiary working on a book. That's how I met Slim. He wanted me to make him famous. I did too. You want me to make you famous?" My hook.

"A what? A writer? You write books?"

"Yeah, yeah. He's cool, man. He all right. He's my friend. He a writer, man," Popcorn explained.

"A writer! Man, I figured you fo' a undercova'. You never know who you gonna run into out here," quipped T-Cool. "What do you write about?"

"About the street, drugs, gangs. I'm gonna make Popcorn a star. I write about street people, how people live on the street, how they got here. You know about gangs and the street, huh?" A poke.

He stared at me, nodded. "I should. Been on the street all my life. On the street—and in the joint."

"Do you know any of the Crips in the CD?"

T-Cool avoided my question. I dropped it too. We talked, we laughed, T-Cool read First Avenue.

Down First walked a very pretty, thin black woman pushing a baby in a stroller while carrying another infant in a baby carrier strapped to her chest. Popcorn stopped her. "Hi, Dorene." He didn't stutter this time.

"Hi. How ya doin'?"

"G-g-good."

T-Cool smiled, showing all his teeth. Quite interested in her, it seemed.

"Where you stayin' now?" Popcorn asked.

"Wid my sister in south Seattle. I moved outta dat ol' place up there." Her head motioned toward the CD. "I better be goin' now. I gotta catch da bus." Dorene smiled and strolled away.

"Hey, Popcorn. You never told me about her," I teased. "She's fuckin' pretty, man. Where you be knowing her from?"

Popcorn hesitated.

"Where you be knowin' her from, brother man?" T-Cool asked.

"She a strawberry, man. I had dat," Popcorn answered.

"No!" I questioned his honesty. "She's a strawberry. I don't fuckin' believe that."

"Hey, brother man," T-Cool exclaimed, looking at Popcorn. "Dude here wanna know where da strawberry patch at." They roared with laughter.

"Yeah, I tell you, man. She lived with her sister and a *bunch* of folks up near me [in the CD]," Popcorn went on.

"You had her?" I asked.

"Yep," Popcorn smiled. "Rocks, man, rocks. They be doin' anything for a hit." A strawberry, a rock whore. How depressing; I wondered, Where are her parents?

Working Street Connections

Standing at First and Pike, T-Cool yelled and waved to folks across the street and said hi to dozens of men and women, boys and girls, when they walked past. He knew them by name. His verbal skills made him the center of attention, at least for a moment, and he loved it. I wanted to meet the people T-Cool knew and to understand the nature of these social relationships.

Drizzle and wind coming off Puget Sound were starting to whip around. I suggested heading for a dry bar and cold beer. I don't drink, neither does Popcorn, but T-Cool does. After a pitcher or two of beer, I hoped T-Cool would talk all afternoon. We climbed aboard the First Avenue free bus and exited near Wandering Raven, strolling toward the Doubleheader, a tavern on the east side of Pioneer Square. While we walked, T-Cool teased the beggars lining the sidewalks like human parking meters reaching out for spare change. Sometimes, he reached into his blue pants pocket in a highly theatrical way and pretended to feel around for spare change. Or he paused to ask a beggar about his day's tally. Once he removed a few quarters from a beggar's collection plate, a small cardboard box that once held a tourist's coffee and donuts, and walked off, leaving the grayish-white puttylike facial skin of the beggar creased in shock. T-Cool laughed and tossed back the quarters.

Some panhandlers use signs to advertise desperation: JUST ARRIVED IN TOWN. NO RENT. NO FOOD. WIFE AND KIDS HUNGRY. T-Cool laughed about these signs and the gullibility of tourists who believe their message: "Motherfuckers are ex-cons and mission rats. Nothing but drunks and drug addicts. Shit!"

At first, I believed those signs, particularly when a woman in her 20s was proclaiming: NO RENT, NEED MONEY FOR HUNGRY KIDS. I tossed dollar bills into their collection plates and felt good, until I saw a lady beggar with the same sign on the same corner six months later. Some street folks said these women are single rock addicts with no kids. On the street, there is no truth in advertising.

Close to the Doubleheader are the Salvation Army and a large city shelter known as the Morrison. The Morrison is across the street from a small grocery store with aisles as narrow as a thin person. Behind the cash register and to the right of the cashier at eye level, and beyond anyone's reach, is cheap wine and hard liquor sold in pocket-sized bottles. A scan of the shelves shows that Wild Irish Rose is a top seller. Many shelves are reserved for its supply, though they're always half empty. But cases of pints and quarts are always stacked on the floor, waiting to be opened.

The hinges on the Doubleheader's swinging doors squeaked off-key when T-Cool, Popcorn, and I pranced into the tavern. A few men sat at the ornate wooden bar, nursing 75¢ schooners of draft beer. The jukebox hummed Kenny G's "I'm Missing You." A couple of pool tables were resting empty. I suggested sitting in a four-person booth near the door. There I could breathe fresh air that pushed its way in from the street, mingling with a fog of cigarette smoke that had accumulated since the joint opened in early morning. And in that booth, I could see each person when he or she pushed at the squeaky hinges. Some of them entered the tavern and stayed; others peered in and ran off.

I moved toward the booth, trying to slide in on the side facing the door. But T-Cool nudged me out of the way. He watched the door. I faced inward, viewing the bar, pool tables, and the dozens of wooden tables in the rear of the joint.

When we took our places in the booth, the bartender howled, *"Can't stay here if you ain't drinking!"* Those words prompted T-Cool's glance at me. I nodded at the bartender: "We got money. We got money." I bought the first of many pitchers of Rainier beer. Popcorn doesn't drink alcoholic beverages. Nor does he smoke anything a citizen can legally buy.

Popcorn didn't sit with us. He kept his distance from T-Cool, standing behind him, moving from foot to foot, looking very bored. I didn't want Popcorn to wander off or think I had abandoned him, preferring T-Cool's company. I needed him; he was my key informant. I knew I couldn't trust T-Cool.

"Play pool?" I asked Popcorn.

"Yeah."

I gave him four quarters, enough money for two games. He slid the quarters into their slots; striped and solid balls dropped. He took a cue, broke the pack. Squeak, the doors opened, and a tall black man walked in. Popcorn smiled a welcoming grin. It was CJ. I gave up my cue and sat down with T-Cool. Popcorn and CJ played pool, laughed and talked, and spent my money.

I took out my notebook, sipped Coca-Cola, asked T-Cool questions. At first, he gave me glib answers, clichés. His answers told me that he had been interrogated but never interviewed. However, I had my allies: patience, specific follow-up questions, and beer money. He relaxed, smoked, and gave away Lucky Strikes I bought pack by pack. They were over two dollars a pack. Informants' fees.

Folks ambled in, saw T-Cool, and headed for our booth. Hour by hour T-Cool introduced me to pimps and strawberries, heroin addicts, and mission rats dressed in three-piece suits. Most of them had a bottle of Wild Irish Rose tucked away in the waistband of their pants. I bought beer and cigarettes; T-Cool served them to his guests.

In walked a black woman with a grim look on her face. She saw T-Cool and recognized him, but walked past him, disappearing into the back of the tavern. She wore blue jeans with no label; brown, ankle-high, thin boots; thin white socks; an institution-issue, fiber-filled jacket zipped up to her neck; a blue stocking cap pulled over the tops of her ears.

A few minutes later, another woman walked in. She was short and round and had a softness about her face. Her eyelids drooped. She looked around, walked to our table. A drop of dried blood on the inside of the collar of her blue shirt revealed her addiction. Skin on top of her neck veins on both sides was scarred and puffy. She looked at T-Cool and in a quiet voice asked, "Is she here?" He nodded yes. She walked toward the back of the tavern toward the women's room.

By midafternoon the tavern was full. The bar had a beer sipper at each stool; the second pool table was busy; the back tables held patrons and their beer. No one was a tourist.

The bartender watched me all afternoon, and so did a few men at the bar. "I'm gonna hafta tell these motherfuckers who you are, buddy row," slurred T-Cool. He, too, saw folks watching us. "Motherfuckers gonna think you a undercover, man."

The black woman with the grim face, who was dressed as a convict, returned and sat on the outside of the booth across the table from me and next to T-Cool. But she had her back toward him, her right side toward me. When she talked to T-Cool, she leaned back and twisted her head to the right. T-Cool leaned forward with his elbows on the table top, sitting on his right knee with his head twisted to the left to talk to her. She didn't look at me. I felt invisible.

"Wha's your motherfucking ass doing in here?" she asked T-Cool.

"Taking da dude to school. He's a writer."

"What? You a what? A writer?"

"Yeah. I'm working on a book about street folks, gangs, that kinda stuff. I'm an anthropologist at Washington State University."

"Yeah! I hearda dat," she said, glancing at me before turning her head toward T-Cool.

"Listen, darlin', you telling him bullshit?" She laughed.

"You wanna know about gangs? I'll tell you about gangs. I knows every one of dem motherfucking punks. Fucking Crips. Shit! Ain't nothing but punks," she said sincerely. T-Cool said nothing.

"How do you know about Crips?" I asked.

"Shit, I lived up there in the CD wit' 'em. I did business wit' 'em."

"What's your name?"

"Ann. Miss Ann." A pack of Luckies sat in the middle of the table. I handed it to her and stood up, walked to the bar, bought her a beer. Miss Ann relaxed.

Miss Ann talked; T-Cool got bored. He felt left out and climbed over the back of the booth, walked away, and talked to some dude at the bar standing with his arm around the waist of a lean black woman dressed in a waist-length fur coat and a short skirt. She colored her face with red lipstick and heavy pastel eye makeup.

The woman with the drooping eyelids came to the table. Miss Ann invited her to sit down. She pulled up a chair, sat next to Miss Ann. I offered her a beer. She refused.

"My name's Mark," I said to her.

"Da dude, he a writer. Writing about us." Miss Ann grinned.

"Us?"

"Folks on da street," Miss Ann explained.

The other woman leaned forward, and with some effort she lifted her right arm high enough to shake my hand.

"Ruth's my name. They call me Cuzz." The words squeezed out between lips barely able to move.

Ruth said to Miss Ann, "We gotta go. You need help."

"Yeah I do. I'll make a call." Miss Ann looked at me and asked, "Got a quarter?"

Miss Ann got up, Cuzz remained motionless, nodding, eyelids drooping. Heroin's effects on its victims.

When Miss Ann walked away, T-Cool returned. He didn't disturb Cuzz, leaving her alone to nod. Without my prodding or even asking a question, T-Cool told me about the Crips in south-central Los Angeles in the early days of the organization, when he was a teenager on the street.

Soon Miss Ann returned. Cuzz looked in her direction. Miss Ann said, "Yeah. He gonna take us to see somebody. Pick us up out front in 10 minutes."

Miss Ann squeezed between Cuzz, who was sitting on a chair at the end of the booth, and the top of the table, pushing T-Cool to the end of the bench seat. This time she sat facing me. Miss Ann and I talked, laughed, enjoyed ourselves.

For hours a fellow at the bar had been watching the scene unfold at the booth. Suddenly he stood up, walked to the booth, stood behind me, looked over my shoulder, read my notes. That made me very uncomfortable. For all I knew, he was an undercover cop.

Miss Ann asked, "What do you want, motherfucker? Get on up out of here. Leave us alone man. We doin' bi'ness."

Unaffected by Miss Ann's aggression, the stranger calmly asked, "What's going on?"

"Dude a writer, *motherfucker*. Now get outta here."

The stranger said, "I'm a writer too. What are you writing about?"

"The street, street people," I answered.

"OK? Now get the fuck back to the bar, motherfucker," said Miss Ann, my protector.

The stranger said, "Lemme give you my phone number and name. I been out here on the street for 10 years. I can help you."

"Thanks," I said. He scribbled his name and phone number on the top of my notebook and then walked back to the bar.

"You got a wife?" asked Miss Ann.

"Two kids too," I said.

"I better call her, buddy row, that motherfucker wants *you*," announced Miss Ann. T-Cool roared. Cuzz didn't hear a thing.

Ten minutes passed. Miss Ann and Cuzz walked out, the swinging doors squeaked open, allowing street light in for a moment, announcing the reality of an outside world.

I looked at my watch. About four hours had passed since Popcorn, T-Cool, and I had walked in. I'd lost track of Popcorn hours ago. I looked around the room for him and asked a pool player if Popcorn was still there. "He left with CJ," he told me. I sat with T-Cool for another hour.

Miss Ann and Cuzz squeaked back inside about the time my note-writing hand got too tired. That was also about the time T-Cool ran out of tales of street life for that day.

"Listen. It's about dinner time. Let's go up to Ezzel's and I'll buy." Miss Ann and Cuzz were sedated, nodding on their feet.

"Why you wanna buy us dinner?" Miss Ann drooled.

"To thank you for talking to me." That was a lie. I wanted to get them into the CD, into their home territory.

"Yeah, all right," Miss Ann said quietly.

"I'll get my car. It's parked a few blocks away. I'll be right back. I'll pull up out front and come in to get you, OK?"

"Sounds good," said Miss Ann. "Hey, lemme aks you something. Sure you not a undercover? Why you wanna take me up to the CD 'n buy me chicken?"

"Guess I'm jus' a nice white motherfucker, huh?" They laughed.

New Social Connections

It was convenient to have had police officers introduce me to Popcorn and T-Bone. And it was handy to have these informants introduce me to others. But it was necessary to find informants who were, for whatever reasons, perhaps newly discharged from prison, hanging around the street alone. Should these informants remain alone over weeks and months, it would be important to understand why they chose to remain alone. However, if they were to become connected to other street men and women, it would be necessary to understand the nature of those new connections.

Years of studying prison inmates helped me identify former inmates. Institutional clothing, such as distinctive shoes, shirts, coats, and tattoos, are telltale. A teardrop tattooed on a cheek just below the outside corner of an eye or a tattoo on a neck just above the shirt collar is a common inmate marking. So is FTW (fuck the warden), often found on the outer surface of an upper arm.

Sometimes, the status "former prisoner" became part of a street hustle. On Capitol Hill in Washington, D.C., aggressive panhandlers, former inmates, approached me on numerous occasions, displaying a District of Columbia prison identification card with a photo.

However, most street folks do not have, or want to have, a photo identification card. So I asked a potential informant, "Have you done time?" Then I watched carefully. Men who had not done time averted their eyes, shuffled their feet, and tried to change the topic of conversation. Or, they made grandiose pronouncements about prison's cruelty and how society forced them into crime.

A former prisoner, on the other hand, stood his ground, looked me in the eye, nodded yes. Or he said, "So what?" or "What the fuck do you need to know that for?" I asked where he had done prison time. If I was familiar with that prison, I made comments about it and asked him questions about its location or unique construction features. Those questions weeded out a "wannabe" prisoner from former inmates. If I didn't know anything about a specific prison, I told the informant that and talked about similar prisons.

If an informant answered my questions coherently, a second interview was scheduled. However, before I did that, I asked if he would discuss social life on the street—crime, money, and drugs— and if he would talk about his natal and conjugal family life. If he appeared for a second interview (at least 50 percent were no-shows), we spent time hanging around the streets.

Soon I encouraged the informant to introduce me to his companions. When he did this, I bought wine and cigarettes and engaged in light conversation and in the scatology of the street. I always thanked the street group for allowing me to join them, and shook hands with each one. By doing that, I signaled that I wasn't fearful of getting close to them and, most probably, was not a street cop. For about a week afterward, I stayed away from the group. However, I tried to locate some of its members individually. If I found one, we talked. That was difficult though, since group members usually spend all their time with a companion or two, and those I found alone were uncomfortable talking away from group. When I revisited the group, I again bought wine and cigarettes.

Prison is a major component in the social lives of street criminals. It was fortunate that I knew as much as I did about dozens of state and federal prisons. Familiarity with the speech and behavior of prisoners gave me the confidence and the verbal skill to walk up to potential street informants and start a conversation.[20] That's how I met David.

Nearly six feet tall, thin, short light-colored hair, no facial scars, dressed as I was, and with a beard several days older, David posed casually against the brick exterior of a renovated building on First Avenue, smack in the heart of tourist country.

"Got a quarter for coffee, man?" he asked politely and quietly.

I pulled out my roll of ones. His bloodshot eyes stretched open wider, pulling at the yellowing gooey slime stuck in their inside corners.

"Sure do."

I peeled off a dollar and held it out, waiting for him to reach out for it. When he reached out, I looked carefully at his extended hand. Criminals tatoo their hands.

Faded but still visible on the first joints of the fingers on the back of his left hand was inscribed LOVE. One finger, one letter. In the V formed by his left thumb and index finger was a cross I had seen worn by Hispanic gang members. It was a *pachuco* cross. Oh, I thought to myself, an adventure lies ahead.

"How ya doin'?"

"Hungry."

"When was the last time you ate?"

"Couple days ago."

"How come? Do you know about the missions in Seattle?"

"I just got in town yesterday." That was the first lie.

"From where?"

"North Carolina." Probably another lie.

"How'd ya get here?"

"Rode the rails, man." I didn't want to listen to train stories so I changed the topic.

"You got a wife, kids?"

"Got a wife and kids. Nice kids too, man."

"How come you left 'em?"

"Ol' lady left me." He thought himself a victim. That's common.

"She came home from work and found me with a needle in my arm. She took the kids and went to Buffalo. That's where her mother is."

"What's your name? My name's Mark."

"David."

I extended my right hand; he stuck his out. There it was, another faded tattoo: HATE—LOVE's mate. Love is what street criminals never had. Hate is what they become. His handshake was too soft and hesitating, an unfamiliar style of greeting another man. He was an ex-con.

"Hungry, David? Come on, man, I'll buy you something to eat."

At first my invitation was refused. But I knew he would refuse. He needed a soft touch.

"Hey, you ain't eaten since yesterday. Come on, man, let me buy you a coffee and a sandwich."

"I can't."

"You can't? Why not?"

"I been kicked outta all of them places."

"Hey, when you come with me, they can't throw you out unless they throw me out, and they ain't gonna do that 'cause I got money. I'm respectable, huh?"

He smiled. Slowly we walked to a take-out restaurant near Wandering Raven. When we approached its door, David's walk slowed to a crawl. He absolutely refused to go inside.

"Look, man, I don't want no trouble. I got thrown out of there couple weeks ago."

"Drunk, huh? Raising hell?"

"Shit, Mark. I had money too. Guess I smelled too bad for them motherfuckers. Fuck 'em."

"I don't wanna hear none of that shit. You're a man. You're sober. And fuck 'em if they think you stink. My money don't stink!"

David joined me. It was like accompanying a five-year-old to kindergarten on the first day. When we walked in, I led him to the coffee pots and poured a large container full.

"Want anything in it?"

"Sugar. Lots of sugar." Alcoholics consume sweets, calories.

"You do it, David. I don't know how you like it."

He hesitated, looking around the place as if he were preparing to hold up the joint. He fixed his coffee. I asked him about food.

"How 'bout a sandwich? The menu's up on the wall there. What d'ya want?" That was my way of determining if he could read. He stared at it, doing nothing, saying nothing. I got my answer.

"How 'bout a hot dog?" He smiled yes and put everything on it—relish, mustard, onions, pickles. More calories. The clerk wrapped it to go and tossed it in a small brown bag. David walked out of the place before I did, still very uneasy. I put several sugary glazed donuts in the bag along with the hot dog; found O'Henry bars, and bought those too. More calories.

David was sitting on a varnished wooden bench long enough to seat four small people side by side between curled wrought-iron armrests. We sat together, our outer legs crossed inward. He didn't eat his hot dog or donuts, but he did drink his sweet coffee. I asked him why he didn't eat his food.

"I don't wanna eat in front of ya. I'll eat tonight in my bedroll."

"Your food'll get cold." On the street, food's food, hot or cold. How middle-class I am, I thought. David said he had to leave.

"Where ya goin'?" I asked him.

"I gotta meet some people. I need money." An informant interview often ended this way; a man just walked away. He always had somewhere to go, someone to meet right now. I thanked David for the time; he thanked me for the food. After that Saturday afternoon at the foot of Wandering Raven, I thought I would never see him. I thought he would hop a freight, or hitchhike out of town, or die in detoxification.

Before he wandered off I found that street hustling, staying drunk, and petty crime had occupied him since he had been released from the Arizona state pen in Florence, Arizona, about 12 years earlier. He said he had not returned to prison since then, but he has been in and out of jail too many times to count.

Interviewing

The details obtained in interviews depend, for the most part, on rapport with informants, informants' state of mind (drunk or high; mentally ill), and the location of the interview. Rapport is affected by the duration of our relationship (how long we have known each other before I ask intimate questions); the frequency of our contact over weeks and months; where we met (street, jail, prison, mission, shelter, police station); whether we like each other;

and whether an informant thinks I know something about the street, jail, prison, and crime. If an informant thinks I know about his world, our conversation is much richer. Always, to encourage rapport, I use the lexicon of the street, which is, after all, the native language of street people.

Interviews are affected by location (jail, prison, street corner, police car, bar, apartment, drug house), social scene, and time of day. Is an informant alone or with someone? Whom is he or she with? What is their relationship? Is an informant "clean" or high? What drug or drugs has an informant taken? When did he or she take drugs (informants don't respond to questions after shooting heroin)? What time of day does the interview occur (mornings are rocky for an alcoholic)?

In jail and prison settings, an important issue is informants' perceptions of each other. In these closed social contexts, it seems that every inmate has an opinion about every other inmate. In selecting informants, I try to choose "stand up dudes," inmates who are reputable in the eyes of other inmates. The following episode indicates how location, social setting, and one group of inmates' opinions about another affect interviewing.

Early in my research at USP Lompoc, I met Paris on a Wednesday evening at 7:30. I went into the lieutenants' office for black coffee, gossip, and 30 minutes of ambient cigarette smoke. I told them I was going to C-unit to find a convict who'd talk to me.

I always checked in with the lieutenants at night, just to be sure they knew where I was. Cellblocks at USP Lompoc are relatively safe, day or night. But in a maximum-security prison the only thing anyone can be certain about is the uncertainty of convict behavior.

I rapped on C-unit's steel door and waited for the officer to open it, ask me who I was, and what I wanted. This was Thanksgiving Eve 1988. I had left my job at the penitentiary two years earlier. Few correctional officers remembered me. The officer looked at my identification, locked the door behind me, and wandered off.

C-unit was one of my favorite cellblocks. I had done my on-the-job training there, among others, and it had housed some of the institution's most troublesome inmates. Pimping Slim and a few Crips. Pinto. White Nazis. Mexican Mafia. Hispanic street gang bangers. Bloods. All walking around, living together without violence.

About 8:00, three black inmates were shooting pool; other inmates were watching one of the two color televisions. Others were playing cards at a square folding table covered by a greenish army blanket. Some were hanging over the rails of the upper tiers, smoking, staring, talking.

I got down to business, and used my "look innocent but suspicious" approach to hook an informant. A Hispanic inmate would never approach me, I knew that. Most were associated with the Mexican Mafia. They'd stay away from this strange white man carrying a large vinyl-covered notebook, stuck in the waistband of my pants. Always keep your hands free in a penitentiary cellblock.

I stared intently at the black inmates shooting pool, waiting for a black addict from Los Angeles or Washington, D.C., to make eye contact. I slowly moved closer to the table, not wanting to disturb the natural order of things.

Getting closer forced them to recognize me, and they began to ask me questions. They wouldn't let me get too close without knowing something.

"You a new counselor?" asked one of them.

"Nope." I stood my ground, not saying another word, forcing their hand. I knew they wouldn't become aggressive. For all they knew, I was a new associate warden or the FBI.

Cues were chalked; inmate players talked among themselves and pretended I didn't bother them. They didn't know that I was aware of their tactic. It was my game, my rules.

"You a reporter?" asked another player.

"Nope."

Finally one of them laughed, blurting out, "FBI, CIA?"

That cleared the air and lightened the mood around the pool table. They laughed. That was my cue to hook an informant.

"Census Bureau," I stated calmly.

"What?" said a short stocky fellow.

"Census Bureau," I repeated.

"Feds?"

"Yeah, the feds, but I'm not a fed."

"Who the fuck are you?"

"An anthropologist." I gave them my Census Bureau rap on the minority undercount. If they wouldn't help me, I suggested, they'd be irresponsible minorities, hurting their own people. There was no response. Guilt and community responsibility never work to motivate criminals. But self-promotion does.

"I'm a writer, too."

"Whatcha write?"

"I wrote a book about this ol' joint."

"Wha's it called?"

I told them.

"I seen a copy of that. Yeah. I seen one in [a staff member's] office. Yeah."

"Ya make money on it, man?"

"Damn little m' man, damn little. Listen, I'm gonna use the stuff inmates tell me in my Census Bureau work to write a new book about the lives of criminals like you guys."

"Yeah?"

"Yeah. No shit."

"How much we gonna get?" asked a black inmate who was leaning against the wall near the hallway that led to the TV room and soda machine. The pool players looked at him, smiled odd looks at each other, and returned to eight-ball. About 5 feet 11 inches, broad shoulders with a narrow waist and big chest, handsome with no visible scars on his face, Paris came off the wall and began interviewing me. I had my man.

"Writer, huh? Come on man, I'll talk to ya. I got nothing better to do now. I got to be here another hour or two." He laughed.

Paris didn't let my interview questions stop him from telling me whatever was on his mind at the time. It didn't matter to him if his answer had anything to do with my question. Using shotgun speech, changing topics before I knew it, Paris didn't answer specific questions. But we got along well.

Paris was an entertaining storyteller and knew a lot about pimping, drug dealing, and bank robbery (I verified his involvement in these activities). But every inmate, every one, said Paris was "crazy," "whacko," "nuts," and "a psych case." And they said it freely: "Man, whatcha doin' talkin' to dat crazy motha'fucker fo'?"

Many black inmates refused requests for interviews, claiming that my relationship with Paris would affect their "rep." Some said if I were to sustain a relationship with Paris many black inmates would lose respect for me and wouldn't cooperate. I couldn't take a chance, so I spent less time with Paris and more time among other black inmates. That, of course, angered Paris. Social manipulation among inmates and between inmates and staff and outsiders is common in prison cellblocks. But I had interview data to collect, so I chose to gain 12 informants at the risk of losing 1.

Wolf Man opened the social network to Hispanic inmates at USP Lompoc. Prison folklore said that Hispanic inmates, particularly a former gang member like Wolf Man, would not talk to an outsider. Wolf Man was a long-term federal penitentiary inmate and former inmate in several California state prisons as well; he was well respected by Hispanic and non-Hispanic inmates. Wolf Man and I got along well from the moment we met. He introduced me to his companions, vouching for me. Even black, white, and Hispanic inmates whom I approached without an introduction from anyone said they had seen me talking to Wolf Man, so I must be OK.

Doing Interviews

Interviewing criminals is challenging. I created a list of topics, based on preliminary interviews with inmates and street people, and developed questions about each topic. These questions were asked of all informants, to develop a uniform database. But I never stopped an informant from telling me stories about anything he thought was important.

Tattoos were good starting points for interviews. Informants enjoyed telling stories about them, and at the same time, I uncovered details about their social lives and prison histories, which I used to formulate additional questions.

David had an interesting tattoo. It looked like a prison tattoo. Outlined in black, its negative space was filled by flesh color and by blue ink made from water mixed with the ash of a burned Bugler (cigarette tobacco) package. A straight needle stuck into the end of a wooden match had implanted the ink in his flesh.

A female image adorned the outer side of David's right biceps. It led to a good tale about a lover. He was 23, she was 17. Kneeling, back to the viewer, the female's head was lowered reverentially. Flowing hair caressed her neck, curving back across her left shoulder, dropping halfway down her naked slender back. A thin black line in the distance formed a high desert mountain. An American Indian woman praying, I thought, so I asked him.

"No! That's Ester. She's puking. Ester drank a lot, and one time we were out in the desert camping and she got drunk, kneeled down, puked in the sand. That's what this tattoo is. She's a lady. A woman. A woman who protects her man. Wherever you want to go, she'll be there with you. Not a bitch lady. Not a woman who won't stick with you. Ester, she was a woman."

"The Puking Ester tattoo, huh?" I asked, tongue in cheek. David smiled lovingly, longingly.

Interview sessions had a discrete purpose, so if I were never to interview a particular informant again, I would still have specific data about him. Interviews were a series of questions, offered in a smooth, flexible, and informal style, even though each session was carefully planned. Street hustlers who feel pushed, defensive, interrogated, prodded, and poked disappear.

Criminal informants aren't dependable. Asking a few questions about a topic today and planning to ask a few more questions about the same topic tomorrow is risky. There might not be a second, third, or fourth interview.

No hustlers on the street volunteered to be interviewed, but jail and prison inmates often did. I avoided them. In my experience, inmates who have become good informants don't ask to be interviewed. Inmates who volunteer details about themselves, as Paris did, or about other inmates and the prison itself are often viewed by other inmates as disreputable and "marginal," and they often are.[21] Marginal inmates usually have a specific reason for aligning themselves with an outsider. In their view, they try to trade answers to a researcher's questions for a favor.

In the early 1980s at the Washington State Penitentiary, an inmate whom I had met briefly became "my friend" within days. We talked and laughed, and he told stories about his life. Within weeks, he asked me to pick up a package ("wrapped in brown paper") mailed to a post office box at the Walla Walla Post Office and bring it to him. For each package he wanted me to deliver, "someone" on the street would have given me $150. Drugs.

Interviewing Strategies

Memory lapses and semantic circles are an interviewer's nightmare, but asking very specific questions helps resolve these problems. "Have you ever done prison time?" often elicited a long discussion about crime and society, people who were "really" responsible for an informant's crimes, terrible prison conditions, and abusive street cops. That question is too general. These questions are better: "Have you been in (name of specific prison or jail) in the last four weeks?" or "Have you done time in (Washington, Oregon, California)?"

"Are you married?" seems to be a simple question, but the responses were complicated. Informants had present and former marriages, both legal and common law. Many informants had both legal and common law wives simultaneously, and practiced a serial residence pattern, living with a legal wife for a few days, then moving in with a common law wife. To be sure, there were girlfriends, too, who were considered by some informants to be common law wives. And then there were strawberries. Imprecise questions elicited rich, but confusing, ethnographic data.

The first interview mistake was asking jail informants this question: "Where did you live before you were arrested this time?" Nearly all informants responded by talking about natal families and childhood residences in Mississippi or North Carolina or South Dakota. But I didn't get the answer I wanted. So I changed the question: "Where did you live just before you were arrested this time?" That did not work, either. Finally, I asked: "Where were you living the day you were arrested this time?" Success. Most informants responded by saying, "I was staying with ———." With that response, I discovered my informants' semantic distinction between *stay* and *live*, a significant cultural distinction made by all street and imprisoned informants.

I sorted informants' statements into categories, or domains, that are important in their culture; these are cultural domains, topics they talked about that were important to them. Some cultural domains are prison or jail; conditions in prisons and jails; street cops, how cops treat street people; drug distribution, the price of drugs, everything about selling drugs; people who had participated in drug distribution and the informants' relationships to those people; girlfriends, common law wives, legal wives, strawberries, skeezers;* parents, stepparents, other socializers, extended family members; crimes they had committed, how they had committed those crimes; and street companions.

Psycholinguistics and Interviewing

Illiterate informants posed unique interviewing difficulties with semistructured, open-ended interviews. Interviewer flexibility is a necessary skill. At first, I tried to collect interviews by using "cultural" stages that made sense to me, moving from early childhood and preschool to early adolescence and primary school, then to teenage years and middle school, and so on, proceeding through high school. But their memories didn't seem to be orga-

---

* A skeezer is a woman who trades sex and companionship for drugs.

nized by this cultural sequence. I switched, instead, to an event sequence of interviewing that focused on major turning points: alcohol use and first involvement in crime; parental divorce; gang membership, drug use, and delinquency; first arrest and first commitment; first crime partner.[22] This technique improved the retrieval of life history information, but the ensuing discussion was still circular.

I speculated about these responses and their link to education, reading ability, language acquisition, and the psychological reality of language and its effect on worldview. Informants' reading level was estimated by unobtrusively asking them to read something—an informed consent statement, a newspaper or menu, prison paperwork, and so on. Although an imprecise measurement, I did have a reading level estimate, as indexed by my children's level of reading ability in each grade. Educational achievement, as indicated by the last grade completed, is an inaccurate indicator: If a 25-year-old informant claimed to have completed ninth grade, how could I know how well he read then? The only effective fieldwork technique to gauge educational achievement is reading level as indicated by listening to informants read (a senior administrator in one of the largest state correctional agencies in the country told me that, on average, adult inmates read below fourth-grade level).

Only Popcorn, a native speaker of English, had a high school reading ability. He said he had remained in school through high school. All other informants, including English and Spanish speakers, reported excessive truancy in primary school, dropping out of middle school, and little or no literacy socialization in the natal home (their parents, or others in the natal home, had not read to them as preschoolers). American Indian informants in their 30s and older reported being monolingual in childhood, speaking a native language and learning to read English as teenagers or adults in prison.

Circular discussions might be tied to linguistic expression, either as a narrative style spoken in the natal homes of all my informants, except Popcorn, or as a cognitive effect based on a lack of early-life reading socialization, which would impair the order of syntactic processes generating speech.[23] My informants had limited linguistic resources, as indicated by relatively small, simple vocabularies, and few syntactic transformations, which constrained their expression of complex ideas and feelings. Lexical inventories and grammatical transformations are the building blocks of complex speech, and their absence is clearly discernable in natural speech. For instance, my informants never used passive constructions to add subtle nuances to sentence semantics, and question transformations were always performed with lexical additions ("wha's up?"), rather than with transformations that shift phrase order and sentence stress. Also noticeably absent in my informants' natural speech were the terms *think* and *feel*. This linguistic fact may provide insights into and support for a defensive worldview and may assist future researchers in creating an ethnopsychology of street culture.[24]

During the formative years of cognitive development, my informants' socializers did not stress literacy. This resulted in permanent linguistic impairment, which in its worst form left informants unable to verbalize complex emotions, and left them without the cognitive skills required to process complex thinking issues.

Linguistic impairment has significant implications.[25] Inadequate linguistic skills will surely have a negative influence on school performance, which may further reinforce truancy and increase school drop-out rates. Then too, a simple linguistic scheme may serve as a model for social organization ordering informants' elementary social networks. Finally, rehabilitation efforts may be hampered if informants can't retrieve recollections of early life and feelings accompanying those thoughts, as psychotherapy requires.*

If this is true, nonlinguistic therapies, such as music, art, and dance therapy, or even nonlinguistic modes of education, such as on-the-job training for physical tasks, may be more effective than language-based depth psychologies or educational techniques.

Informants seemed trapped by their own cognition and linguistic abilities. Should grammatical categories have psychological reality, these informants are doomed to live on the edge of the literate world.[26] In many ways, their involvement in street culture—with its simple social situations, limited demands for complex decision making, open expression of irresponsibility, and tolerance for bursts

---

*I talked to Dr. Paul Hofer, chief psychologist, USP Lompoc, about the difficulty of getting intimate informants to discuss their early years. At first, I thought I was asking the wrong questions or had inadequate rapport with informants. In explaining the situation I told Dr. Hofer that "it's as though their lives didn't start until they were 12 or 13 years old. They don't seem to remember anything about childhood." He agreed, and said "forgetfulness" can be attributed to childhood emotional trauma, and is a major impediment to psychotherapy.

of irrational anger, coupled with often playful, childish verbal and nonverbal expressions—may be an indicator of informants' limited natural, cognitive ability to reason.

These conjectures aren't meant to suggest linguistic determinism. There is always room for thought; rather, the issue is understanding how thought is guided. I am suggesting that an analysis of informants' speech may provide the basis for a cultural psychology of street culture that will give researchers a more comprehensive picture of criminals' lives and therapists a clearer diagnosis.

These linguistic issues affect field research. In narrative form, "semantic circles" are stream-of-consciousness speech, which, in the worst cases, approximate either "word salad," a linguistic aberration typical of schizophrenics, or unique linguistic expressions such as glossolalia, coprolalia, or echolalia.[27] Illiterate informants often spoke as if unable to focus and order their thoughts. Eventually, perhaps, they would be able to retrieve cognitive information locked away, but there were no guarantees.

Most informants had memory gaps. I thought at first that these lapses, most commonly associated with the childhood stage, were symbolic of emotional trauma. Then I considered another possibility: these memory gaps may be a result of very poor linguistic socialization so that portions of memory became unretrievable, as if a file name on a computer hard disk had been erased, leaving behind data that are inaccessible.

These speculations made me suspicious of all early-life recollections that I couldn't verify or that seemed anomalous among other data collected about an informant's early life. I considered the possibility that the things informants told me about early-life events were automatic, or unconsciously created, spontaneous stories used to fill memory gaps. However, finding common themes in the dataset made me more comfortable about data validity.

Verifying Data

Years of interviewing produce an abundance of data. I sorted available facts from beliefs and attitudes, from memories, and so on. Some facts were easy to verify; for instance, how much did a gram of flake cocaine cost in March 1990? To verify that, I asked five or six cocaine sellers how much they had paid for a gram of flake cocaine, at a particular level of purity, on a certain date.

The only things I knew for sure about informants' lives were those things I watched. Most things informants said about their past lives were impossible to verify. To follow up on things they said they would do, such as "go straight" the next time they were released from prison, I had to be on the street, watching them.

David said that at age 19, after serving a tour as an infantryman in Vietnam, he did two years and four months at the Louisiana State Penitentiary in Angola for safe cracking in Shreveport. For years, I had heard many tales about Angola from inmates in numerous state and federal prisons. It was a harsh place, they said.

David said he had spent months in a concrete cellblock, a monument to Angola-style inmate discipline, for supporting a strike of inmate fieldhands who refused to work without water along the Mississippi in the steaming, humid cotton fields. The punishment cellblock, David said, did not have heat in cold weather or air conditioning in the blisteringly hot summer months. Dozens of inmates in each tiny cell slept on the concrete floor and urinated and defecated into a hole in a corner of the cell's floor. The daily diet was bread and water.

I visited Angola in 1989 and verified, with a senior prison official, the details of David's story about the disciplinary cellblock. A federal court order had closed that cellblock in the late 1970s, proclaiming the living conditions to be cruel and unusual punishment.

Data verification is a concern of field researchers.[28] I verified interview data whenever I could by checking records. Law enforcement and correctional agencies are bound by agency policies that define public information about detainees and inmates. In jail and prison, with an interviewee's permission, I could read his file. On the street, however, verification is tough. Long-term participant observation, on the street and in prison and jail, does compensate for a lack of objective means to verify informants' claims. Although participant observation can't take a researcher back into an informant's history, ethnographic research is the only accurate way to verify informants' claims about their current and future behavior.

Time among criminals, on the street and in jails and prisons, has helped me assess the veracity of interview data and the meaning of participant-observation data. It's easy to be misled by informants' claims, particularly if a researcher has established a close rapport with informants. Tales of early-life abuse, mistreatment by prison officials, difficulties with street police and the courts, society's responsibility for criminal behavior, and so on, are common, often believable elements in informants' stories. My exchange with Donut illustrates this.

Donut and I met in Portland. He was a part-time donut cook at a neighborhood donut shop and a part-time pimp and heroin dealer. In his mid-30s, he had fond memories of his mother. "She was always there. It was tough when I was a kid, but she loved me, man."

Donut bragged about protecting his "girls" and told many tales about tracking down johns who hurt his girls and, with the help of several street companions, "thumping 'em real good." I asked him if he had ever hit a girlfriend or prostitute. He was emphatic: "No." Had he ever beaten a child? He was emphatic: "No." He had ever done prison time? He was emphatic: "No."

A short time later, Donut was arrested and imprisoned for conspiracy to distribute heroin. There, I read his prison dossier. Donut was born in Chicago, Illinois, and had been beaten and neglected by his mother and abandoned by age two. With help from a social service agency, his mother's relatives had sent Donut to Portland, to live with his mother's mother.

Donut had a long adult criminal history. He was a convicted killer and an armed bank robber, and had served two prison terms prior to the current commitment to prison. Many times he had been arrested for beating several of his common law wives and, on several occasions, for beating the preschool child of one of them. His juvenile record was lengthy too.

Many informants evade answering questions. They use a sincere, calm tone and extreme politeness as verbal camouflage, and they construct an answer that, to them, sounds like a direct response. It's also common for them to suggest associations with famous people and important events. The following is an excerpt from an interview with William, a maximum-security prisoner in his late 20s:

"How long you been in here?" I asked.

"Six years and change. Murder, sir," he answered in low tone.

"You programing good?"

"Yes, sir. I'm taking some classes, correspondence courses, you know. I wanna go da college when I get up out of dis ol' place, sir." Sincerity.

"Where did you grow up?"

"Maryland, man. Nice back dere, you know, man. Outside o' D.C. Grew up in the same town Sugar did, man."

"Sugar?" I knew he was going to link himself to the former Olympic and world champion Sugar Ray Leonard.

"Sugar. Sugar. Sugar Ray Leonard. There's a street, man, named after him. I boxed too, man. I coulda been like Sugar Ray too, you know, man. Me and Ray, man, we alike, man. Ray's wife, Juanita, went to my school."

"Did you know Juanita?"

"We went to the same school."

"So you knew Ray's sister?"

"Told you man, we went to the same school." A bit defensive.

"Did you know Ray?"

"Man, we grew up in the same town and ran on the same streets, man, doing roadwork. Me and Ray be out there runnin', yeah. We worked out at the same gym."

I verified that William was a murderer who grew up in Washington, D.C.; in fact, he had killed several more people than he admitted to killing.

Fieldwork and Ethics

Illegal behavior, to some degree, is required of researchers studying criminals.[29] I think street ethnographers seek the excitement of crime without the responsibility for it and have empathy for the folks on the street. Adler writes that she was "well suited to study drug dealing. . . . [She] had a generally open view toward soft drug use, considering moderate consumption of marijuana and cocaine to be generally nondeviant." Did she use cocaine and marijuana, too? She admits to knowledge of international drug dealing.[30]

Was my knowledge of cocaine distribution excusable as part of a research project funded by the U.S. Census Bureau? Or was it simply misprision of a felon? Could I be forced to testify against informants?[31] Or was my knowledge of the street protected by the same confidentiality that is ensured with all Census Bureau data? Would a professional relationship with local police protect me from arrest? Or would I become an inmate at the Seattle jail?

In fact, a senior Seattle police official told me that police officers would be compelled to arrest me if I were standing in a rock house during a police raid, within an arm's length from cocaine. At the time of my research, Seattle practiced "zero tolerance": anyone possessing illegal drugs at the time of a traffic stop by police would have his or her car impounded and sold at auction by the city of Seattle. I reported that conversation to my department chairman, and asked if Washington State University or my colleagues in the anthropology department would pay my legal bills if I were arrested and charged with cocaine possession or conspiracy to distribute cocaine? After all, I was conducting university-related business, which the university sanctioned by accepting overhead costs from the U.S. Census Bureau. He just laughed nervously, and told me to be careful.

I watched and listened to "straights" buy cocaine. And I saw their license plates. I bought wine and beer for alcoholics, and gave addicts cash to buy heroin and cocaine. Should I have refused to give informants cash, preferring, instead, to give alcoholics and drug addicts food and clothing? Was my involvement in their addiction a violation of research ethics, or was it an indispensable element in the study of criminals?

Adler was personally involved with her informants, and I was too. Cash, rides, food, alcohol, and drugs were exchanged for information, and that was an indispensable feature of our research relationship.[32] A few months into my research, I had the following encounter with Miss Ann.

Sunday, at 9:00 in the morning, I walked to Wandering Raven. The sidewalks around Wandering Raven were sprinkled with men who had walked out of missions a few hours earlier. Some of them were panhandling for breakfast wine. No one asked me for money.

I walked near the city shelter. There they were, Miss Ann and Cuzz, panhandling near the convenience store.

"Where you go?" Miss Ann asked me. I had planned to meet them the night before; we were going to Ezzel's.

"Me! You guys disappeared. I drove all over this town looking for you."

Miss Ann laughed. "You think I was goin' up in the CD with some white man driving a Maxima. Shit!" Then for a moment she got serious. "Can't go up there with you yet, buddy row. Don't know enough about you to take you to where my people can see me with you. My people be thinkin' that I rolled over and be sleepin' with a white man."

Miss Ann and Cuzz laughed. But they were in pain. Cuzz hurt more than Miss Ann. She had fixed hours before Miss Ann had last night. Now they had no money.

Miss Ann asked, "Got 20 bucks, buddy row?"

"Twenty bucks. For what?" As if I didn't know.

Cuzz said, "We're trying to get well."

Miss Ann added, "Can't get high on 20 bucks. They selling bunk* out here ever since the Cubans came in."

"I got $12 and a Visa card."

Miss Ann said, "I take the cash. The Cuban [Miss Ann's heroin dealer] don't take Visa." We laughed. Miss Ann and Cuzz combined my cash with some money they already had and walked to the Pike Place Market to "score some shit."

I questioned myself during this entire study about the limits of my obligations to informants. Did it end with payment of informants' fees? Or did our relationship mean I owed them more?

In jails and prisons a research relationship is established by policy. Federal inmates can't be given informants' fees no matter how these fees are conceived: no money, no cigarettes, no coffee, no candy, no favors. After my experiences at USP Lompoc, I knew relationships with inmates had to be that way.[33]

However, the street is a different ethnographic scene. I decided to allow the rules of social street life to influence my relationship with informants. Reciprocity and frequent contact were vital to sustain open relationships, but the degree of intimacy and personal involvement I expressed toward informants was entirely up to me.

Intimacy is optional in street relations. On the street, relationships live in the moment, and "players," including a street researcher, are responsible only for themselves. It was easy for me to feel this way, perhaps too easy.

I gave money to Miss Ann and Cuzz, and many others as well, in payment for spending hours with me day after day. How they spent this money was their business. If they chose to use the money for heroin, it was their choice. I didn't suffer pains of guilt or existential angst because of a life choice they made.

All my informants were cantankerous. A request for an interview

*Bunk is heroin too weak to cause a high but strong enough to ease the withdrawal pain that comes with a craving for a fix.

might be met with a shoulder shrug, a distant stare, or "too busy" or "fuck you, asshole!" Too often they blamed me for their failures, too often they were irritable and angry,[34] as is illustrated by the following event.

I was in the first few months of this research, and I wanted another guided tour of the Central District and introductions to my informants' companions. T-Cool, Miss Ann, and Cuzz agreed. We arranged to meet late on a Saturday afternoon at the Doubleheader. I arrived, they didn't. Late the next morning, I went looking for T-Cool.

T-Cool was walking down the sidewalk near the Doubleheader, his left arm hanging lazily from around the shoulders of a chubby woman in her early 20s. T-Cool had his blue fishnet hairnet on, and yesterday's blue clothes. His eyes were bloodshot; his breath smelled of wine or beer.

He saw me walking toward him. When we met he gave me a big hug. The top of my head fit under his chin. He issued an abrupt goodbye to his woman friend. "Da bitch took care o' me las' night, buddy row. Where the fuck did you go las' night?" he asked.

"Me? I came here just like I said I would. You were gone. So was Miss Ann and Cuzz. I drove all over this fuckin' city looking for your ass."

"Now that pisses me off, man."

"What pisses you off?"

"I talked to you all fuckin' day. Tol' you 'bout my personal life, my people, Crips, gang banging, all kinda shit right in front of my people, and you leave me out there on a corner waitin' for you. I stood right there [he pointed to the nearby corner] for a fuckin' hour. Shit!" He turned and walked away, heading toward the Doubleheader.

I was flabbergasted. I thought to myself, What is going on here? Then I realized the problem and its implications. In prison or jail, I could walk away from outrageous behavior like T-Cool's and find another informant. But on the street I couldn't do that. I couldn't develop a reputation as someone easily pushed around by aggressive talk. And that's all it was, street talk. At least that's what I hoped. I followed T-Cool into the tavern.

"Hey, T-Cool. I'm sorry if I made you look bad in front of your people. I didn't mean to." I didn't like groveling, even as a fieldwork technique.

"Fuck you."

"Lemme buy you a beer." He didn't answer or look at me. He walked to the bar.

"Give me a schooner," I said to the bartender.

"Make it a pitcher," ordered T-Cool. The bartender looked at me. I nodded yes.

"Shoot pool?" I asked T-Cool.

"I beat your fuckin' ass, man." I put two quarters in the coin slot, pushed in the plunger; the balls dropped. I racked them and looked up at T-Cool.

"Break?"

"You break, motherfucker. Once I shoot won't be nothin' left." He stood in front of me, the heavy end of his cue resting on the unpolished wooden floor. His right hand held it near the chalked tip.

"You made me look bad, motherfucker. I should kick your ass. Why'd you leave me out there on the corner? It was fuckin' rainin', man. Shit!"

"By the time I got my car and came back, I guess I took longer than I thought I would. You know I wouldn't want to embarrass you in front of your people." I hung my head and looked down at his feet, feigning contrition. I hated it.

T-Cool asked, "Did you break 'em?"

"Yeah. Shoot."

He shot, made one ball, missed the next. My turn. I missed. I missed every shot.

"You one dumb motherfucker. White men can't shoot. Shit! I'm pissed man. Leavin' me out in the fuckin' rain. I told you everything you wanted to know. You write a book about me, you get rich, and what the fuck do I get?" He glared.

"I ain't gonna get rich. It's just a hobby."

"Fuck you!" T-Cool sank the eight-ball. The pool game ended, but his verbal game continued. It was a bore, I was annoyed with it, I needed a legitimate escape. It walked through the squeaky doors.

An American Indian fellow, maybe 21, stood in the doorway. He was about 5 feet 5 inches, 125 pounds at most. He said he was a kick boxer and an amateur fighter. The kid was scared of the street's people. Pretending was his defense.

He looked lost, somewhat dazed. Standing there, he assaulted invisible enemies with leg kicks and waved his hands around in a chopping motion. Grunts and squeals added zest to his game. With his enemies defeated, he stopped.

T-Cool watched him, holding a schooner of beer. He looked at me, forgetting to wear an angry mask.

"What the fuck is dis?"

"Just a kid," I answered.

"A motherfuckin' fool is what dis asshole is."

The kid walked up to T-Cool. His nose came to T-Cool's chest, about midsternum high.

"Got a quarter? I need to get a bus to a powwow."

"Fuck you," growled T-Cool. The kid stood motionless.

"You hear me, boy? *Fuck you, asshole.*" T-Cool waited. The kid remained motionless. T-Cool was not an imaginary foe. I felt badly for the youngster. I interrupted T-Cool's verbal assault.

"I remember you," I said to the kid. T-Cool looked at me. "I met this kid at the Service Center yesterday."

The kid said, "I remember you. You boxed that black dude."

"Yeah, that's me."

"Know what? I whipped three guys last night," the kid offered.

T-Cool asked, "Think you can whip me, *motherfucker?*"

I interrupted again. "Where'd ya sleep last night?"

"I didn't sleep nowhere. I walked around all night."

"Where you going now?"

The kid answered, "A powwow, but I need some money for the bus." I gave it to him, escorted him outside, and pointed to the bus stop. T-Cool stayed inside.

The kid said, "I don't know how to get there."

"Ask the driver," I said. The kid walked off. So did I.

All my informants are racists and aren't afraid to show it: black informants hate whites, whites hate blacks, American Indians hate whites and blacks, blacks and whites hate American Indians and Hispanics. In their mixed company, my patience wore thin, and their tempers flared. Witness the following encounter between David and Dog, a Yakima Indian.

David and I were sitting in Pioneer Square on a bench in front of Wandering Raven. The day was overcast; the wind was getting colder; drizzle filled the air. I got up to buy a container of hot coffee at a nearby store. When I exited the coffee joint, I saw David in front of the bench, pacing and looking agitated. A heavy-set American Indian man had taken my seat on the bench. I walked over to the bench, and sat next to him.

In speech slurred by wine, he said, "Dog, Dog, that's who I am." Swollen lips marred his speech, too. Blood had caked into the corners of Dog's mouth and had oozed out of lip wounds and trickled onto the front of his shirt, drying into a brownish-red patina. Blood, smeared onto the upper right side of Dog's paperweight nylon windbreaker, had dried into a thin crust. Dog's face carried old wounds too. Several thin knife scars visible on his left cheek testified to the right-handed skill of an opponent. His brows and forehead were marked with rough scars, jagged from punches and scratches.

The Yakima Indian Reservation south of Yakima, Washington, is his home. Dog said his misery is my fault: I am a white man. It bored me, but patiently I listened. Dog wanted me to study him too. Apparently David was not as naive as I thought. He knew my research game.

I showed little interest in Dog, nodding my head while he talked, drifting back in my mind to USP Lompoc, remembering the interviews with American Indians that eventually turned into outbursts against all white men. I had grown weary of paying for the sins of whites, particularly when my judge was a street thug. But when I became less attentive, Dog got angrier. And Dog's anger stirred my protector, David, into action.

David paced faster, scarred white knuckles clenched into fists. Trouble was afoot. Politely, as a sign of respect to me, David told Dog to hit the road. Dog didn't hear it that way and persisted in telling me things about his life that I didn't want to hear, that I couldn't understand spoken in a drunken slur. Having too many informants can be more annoying than having too few.

David reached his peak of frustration. "Hey, Dog, leave us the fuck alone."

Dog stood up, wobbling into a fighting stance, ready to bleed again.

"This guy's my parole officer, man. We need some time," David said.

Dog's face was flattened by surprise. "You his parole officer?"

"Yep."

"Why didn't you tell me that?" Dog asked.

Glibly, I said. "You didn't ask. Get the fuck out of here! I need to see David now." Proud of my aggressiveness, David smiled his consent. He was a street mentor, my road dog.

"I'm goin'. You got some change for the bus?"

"The bus is free, Dog. Beat it." I had power. David smiled. Every time I needed an escape from a tight spot, the magic words *parole officer* worked well. Why hadn't I thought of it?

After several months on the street, I created a short list of field-work "dos, don't, and maybes," and tried to stick to this list. Informants could earn money with interviews, but I wouldn't lend it. I wouldn't write letters to judges or testify at parole hearings. I wouldn't provide excessive transportation around Seattle. I wouldn't participate directly in drug distribution by handing packets of drugs to customers. I wouldn't knowingly commit a crime by participating in robbery, burglary, or car theft (I was asked on numerous occasions to assist in car thefts). And I promised my wife I wouldn't bring my informants home. She was pleased.

Finally, I don't drink alcohol, smoke marijuana, smoke cigarettes, or use cocaine, heroin, or any other illegal drugs. I also refused offers of "strawberries." In numerous situations I felt as if not drinking or sharing a joint might damage rapport. But public drinking among street folks is ritualistic, and my abstention gave them more to drink and didn't negatively affect rapport or the ritual. It wasn't too long before no one offered me a joint or a bottle of wine or beer.

I found Itch, School Yard, and 'Dre drinking a bottle of Wild Irish Rose, the first one of the day around 10:00 in the morning. They stood in circle, a huddle I joined. The bottle passed clockwise, passing by me.

"Gimme a kick* off that motherfucker," Itch said to School Yard, who held the fifth between his hands.

School Yard said, "Ge'cha own bottle, asshole."

Itch replied, "Dis here is *my* bottle, ugly motherfucker. Give it over here o' I kick you ugly motherfuckin' ass, bitch." Onlookers chuckled.

"*You* bought it. Well let dat be da reason," said School Yard, passing the bottle to Itch.

In a tender gesture, Itch reached for it as a parent lured by the cry of an infant. The fingers of Itch's right hand carefully grasped the bottle, lifted it to his mouth, his dry lips extended to meet it. With each long thirst-quenching gulp, Itch's Adam's apple raised and lowered, plunging down the debilitating liquid. The bottle drained, Itch discarded it to the sidewalk; it shattered, its usefulness sapped.

Wobbling, Itch, an intravenous drug user, an ex-convict in his late 30s, pivoted on his right foot, stuck his hand in his pocket, pulled out a few crumpled food stamps.

---

*A portion of something is a "kick." Someone who needs a loan might ask someone for a kick or a "kick out."

He looked at me and slurred, "Dolla' fo' five dolla's worth of dese food stam's?"

"I don't need food stamps," I said.

He stuck his face inches from mine. "Well den gimme da motherfuckin' money anyway. You a rich motherfucker."

A fine mist of saliva droplets projected from his mouth, landing on my cheeks and lips. I handed him a few bucks and walked away, wishing I could disinfect my face. Thoughts of AIDS overcame me.

Years of fieldwork among street hustlers left me feeling like a surrogate father. I was straight and encouraged them to stay straight too. What's more, I worked hard to resist an urge to stop them from doing what they do. They are alcoholics, drug addicts, and criminals; the decision to remain on the street is theirs.

I also realized that if the HIV virus and continued intravenous drug use, homosexual and heterosexual promiscuity, prison sentences in penitentiaries, months of boring hours spent in jail, and the potential of being beaten or killed on the street haven't altered my informants' lifestyles, then badgering them surely wouldn't do it. Over and over again I told myself, I am a street ethnographer, an observer and a participant, not a cop, social worker, or surrogate father.

2

Distorted Families

The famous anthropologist Edmund Leach shocked his audience during the 1967 Reith Lectures with these words:

> Today the domestic household is isolated. The family looks inward upon itself, there is an intensification of emotional stress between husband and wife, and parents and children. The strain is greater than most of us can bear. Far from being the basis of the good society, the family with its narrow privacy and tawdry secrets is the source of all our discontents.[1]

In this chapter, informants report memories of early-life family, school, and peer relationships. Life history data were self-conceived stories, and they provided important information that I would use to understand the social and emotional dimensions of street culture. I conceived of these life histories as personal stories.[2] Bruner writes that

> stories define the range of canonical characters, the setting in which they operate, the actions that are permissible and comprehensible. . . . they provide, so to speak, a map of possible roles and possible worlds in which action, thought, and self-definition are permissible (or desirable). As we enter more actively into the life of a culture around us . . . we come increasingly to play parts defined by the "dramas" of that culture. Indeed, in time the young entrant into the culture comes to define his own intentions and even his own history in terms of the characteristic cultural dramas in which he plays a part—at first family dramas, but later the ones that shape the expanding circle of his activities outside the family.[3]

These life history stories illustrate family culture and parenting style as well as informants' initial expression of antisocial feelings and delinquent behavior. Despite spotty memories, forgetfulness, and distortions, life history data show that children like Ace who are brutalized by parents like Maniac are likely to grow up and live a street lifecycle.

The Family

Teenage and adult anti-social behaviors, those acts that violate the individual rights of others as well as societal norms, begin in early childhood and endure for decades.[4] Family disintegration, as assessed by interviews and statistical studies alike, leads to juvenile delinquency, juvenile homicide, drug and alcohol abuse, suicide, and depression. Widom, for instance, notes that "being abused or neglected as a child increased the likelihood of arrest as a juvenile by 53 percent, as an adult by 38 percent, and for a violent crime by 38 percent." Predictors of anti-social behavior can be seen in children as young as 6 and are obvious by age 10.[5]*

In this chapter, I report informants' accounts of early life as if they were facts; obviously, I didn't watch my informants grow up. Whenever possible I verified their claims by checking official records, which I did with inmates. However, even law enforcement records are too often inadequate for social scientific research. Presentence investigations (PSIs) frequently present a spotty picture of offenders' early family life. Interview data are collected by probation officers, who have too little training in interviewing techniques and analysis of qualitative data, and have too little time to spend on individual PSIs when their case loads and paperwork grow.

PSI interviews with an offender's mother, father, uncles, aunts, siblings, grandparents, and neighbors, among others, often yield generic information, and claims that the offender is "really a good

---

*Nearly all black informants whose accounts are presented here are children of Wilson's urban black underclass; Wilson (1987) discusses an emergence of a black underclass and its relationship to joblessness and crime (also see Bernard 1990; Coleman and Hoffer 1987). Hispanic informants were reared in families and in neighborhoods characterized by social and economic marginalization (Vigil 1990). American Indian informants, whose families were removed from mainstream society decades go, were reared in desperate squalor on Indian reservations in the United States and British Columbia.

boy." I recall frequent conversations with the mother of an inmate in the federal correctional system. She claimed that her son was led astray by former navy friends, that her son was really an honest fellow, and that his crime was her fault: her husband died when the offender was a boy, and she didn't have enough time to spend with him. The offender, age 41 at the time of commitment, controlled marijuana farming in a western state and was responsible for its distribution in numerous West Coast states; he had a history of numerous arrests and convictions for possession of firearms, beating women, and sexual assault on minor females, including his stepdaughter.

Patterson found that many parents do not recognize their children's criminal behavior and often argue that their children are innocent of alleged misbehavior, such as stealing or rule violations at school. These parents usually blame a child's offense on prejudicial treatment by teachers or others.[6]

Informants' self-reports, as well as reports of family members, are always susceptible to memory lapses, exaggerations, intention distortions, self-serving rationalizations, lies, forgetfulness induced by drugs and alcohol, and distortions from altered psychological states, among other things.[7] Despite distortions of all sorts, despite growing up in different cities or in the same city in different decades, despite affiliations with different ethnic and racial groups, all my informants' often sketchy early-life accounts reported similar social circumstances.[8]

These informants' reports of early family life might be part real and part imaginary. Perhaps reports of physical and emotional abuse, neglect, and other trauma are adult informants' self-serving excuses for their own lifelong irresponsibility. But these tales should be carefully considered anyway. After all, these informants became adult and teenage drug addicts, alcoholics, and street criminals.

Family Memories

Popcorn

Popcorn was reared by an aunt and uncle in a town not too far from the Market Cafe, a popular breakfast spot near the Pike Place Market.

On weekends, when I took Popcorn to the cafe, it was jammed with folks sitting at six padded seats at a short counter, in five old wooden booths, and at four small, roundtop tables stuck between the front windows and the counter. The *Seattle Times* had usually been pulled apart by patrons, and sections of it were spread out on a narrow shelf attached to the back of the booth closest to the entrance. Omelettes, fried potatoes, bacon, and wheat toast at the Market Cafe are better than similar fare in other local cafes, and this cafe serves Starbuck's coffee. Street people do not eat at the Market Cafe, but I enjoyed taking Popcorn there.

Market Cafe patrons sitting at the roundtop tables up front have a clear view of First Avenue and a bus stop across the street, which serves as a part-time rain and wind shelter for career women in white Reeboks as well as for street minstrels hustling coins by playing 20-year-old folk tunes off-key, homeless winos. A pay-n-park lot is across the street too. Vacant now, it had been packed shoulder-to-shoulder from late last evening until nearly sunup with beggars and thieves and peddlers of heroin and rock.

The smell of bacon grease filled the air, mixing with patrons' conversations. Folks around us talked about shoe sales at Nordstrom's, the perennial losing season of the Seattle Mariners, local politics, and home remodeling. Why aren't these folks interested in poverty and drugs? I asked myself. It's all around them, but they don't see farther than their eggs and toast. I wanted to know about street food—soup, dog food, and strawberries, staples in Popcorn's diet.

I asked myself, Why has Popcorn done what he has done? How did he get here? I wanted him to take me back to his early life, believing my questions might be answered there.

We sat far to the rear at a small table stuck away to accommodate weekend crowds. Back there, Popcorn and I were out of the way. We usually didn't eat, even though I wanted to. Popcorn always refused breakfast. Even prodding and guilt didn't work. "I'm hungry. If you don't eat, I won't eat, either!" Guilt doesn't motivate a rock addict.

"I don't wan' nothin'."

"Have something, man. The stuff looks good."

"It's against my religion. I got to cut down. That's the way Muslims are. Know what I mean? Uh-uh, no thanks."

"Sure?"

"Yeah, yeah."

I know Popcorn likes to eat. Whenever I took him to a nice restaurant, he ate and ate and ate. He liked my choice of restaurants, too. Chinese. Thai. Fried chicken at Ezzel's in the CD. Ezzel's opened a second store on University Avenue (called the Ave), near the University of Washington. At Ezzel's on the Ave, you won't see cocaine-dealing gang bangers waiting in line to pick up chicken and biscuits. We never ate there.

Before Popcorn accompanied me to middle-class eateries, he had not eaten in one, he said. We made a deal: I would take him to places where he had never been; he'd take me to places I could not go without him. We began by going into his childhood.

Popcorn was one of his mother's nine children fathered by three men; he spent his first four years in Tyler, Texas. Up to age four, the only father he knew was a man nicknamed Bozo; Popcorn had no memory of him, and he had just a few recollections from those years.

"My earliest memory is roasting weenies over a gas stove. She'd [Popcorn's mother] give us beer with dinner. She ran a cafe, the Chicken Shack. It was a gambling and bootleg house."

At age four, Popcorn was moved to Bremerton, Washington, America's most livable city, according to a 1990 issue of *Money* magazine. There Popcorn lived with his mother's sister, a housewife, and her husband, a handyman, carpenter, and cement worker. "My aunt wanted me 'cause they didn't have no kids. My brother before me died in a fire and my twin died; there was a lot of anguish on them."

Life was satisfactory until junior high school,* when he learned to shake the red card. "I started going out more and more. That's when I smoked my first joint. My cousin [the son of another of his mother's sisters] from Seattle used to come over, and we started chasing women. I was raised up in the church, and I was deep into it. I was a junior deacon and in the choir. I played the trumpet for four years. But I lost interest in it."

Life began to sour at age 12, 13, he said, when he encountered

---

*Several theories suggest that the institution most responsible for delinquency is school. Labeling theory (societal reaction theory) first identified school as a contributor to delinquency by giving negative labels to students who fail and who are troublemakers (see Tannenbaum 1938; Kelly 1982; Rosenthal and Jacobsen 1968). Strain theory suggests that school might frustrate students' aspirations and goals (Cloward and Ohlin 1960; Cohen 1955); disorganized schools lead to cultural deviance; schools give inferior education to poor and minority children (conflict theory; see MacLeod 1987); and, poor school environments do not allow students to form positive attachments and commitments to school (control theory).

racial prejudice. "I ran into a lot of prejudice against me," he said, reflectively. "Kids teased me about being black. I started drinking a lot at my aunt's house in Seattle. I was always going over there on holidays."

In fifth grade, Popcorn made two friends, boys who joined him in committing his earliest teenage crimes. They remained crime partners through high school.

"The adults [his aunts and uncles] let kids over eight or nine drink alcohol. Anything they wanted. Beer. Mixed drinks. We drank three, four times a week. My aunt and uncle [his surrogate parents], they didn't say nothing about alcohol."

Popcorn said his "parents" didn't say much about anything he was doing, but the local police did.

"They first noticed me, I was 15 years old. At school. Something happened with a girl, and I hit her one time. Just one time. We were going together after that."

"Didn't it bother you to hit a girl, Popcorn?"

"Ahh. That girl, she said something to my girlfriend that made her angry. Then she got angry at me. Pissed me off."

"Did you hurt her?"

"Man, no. It was a one short left to the face. I knocked her back some, but she all right."

"Is she the only girl you ever hit?"

"I hit another too, one time, but that one really pissed me off bad, man. I was 22 years old and I was selling heroin and Valium at three different schools in [south Seattle]. I got three high school girls to sell Valium and had another girl, she was my main lady. I had sent her to Wheeler [Washington] to turn some tricks and some bullshit happened.

"My sister's boyfriend had cheated her out of money. I told him to pay me. My sister came down to protect him. I picked up a frying pan and knocked in the window of their Cadillac and just went crazy man. I popped her good for losing my money, man. Shit, she pissed me off.

"I got through high school, but the principal didn't like me for some reason. I got kicked out in my senior year. I went to an alternative school. I was 15, 16.

"Them motherfuckers kicked me out, too. They said I had too many missed classes and too much tardiness. Shit, they didn't know what they was talking about."

He stayed part-time with his parents, part-time with his cousin in the CD, and part-time with his crime partner in Bremerton. Popcorn was selling weed and joints, and was arrested for his first burglary at 16.

"Did you date anybody special in high school?" I asked. Popcorn went silent. I repeated the question. "Did you have a steady girlfriend?"

Finally, he responded. "Not really."

"Not really? A handsome guy like you musta had a special girlfriend. Come on, man, you must have been getting laid." I goaded him.

"I dated a white girl, Karen. She was 14. I dated her sister, too."

"How old were you?"

"Eighteen," he said, calmly.

"How'd it go with her?"

"I used to sneak around to her house after school, before her parents came home. It was all right for a while, but then she got pregnant. I'd go to her house to see her. One time, you know, her sister's boyfriend came to the door and said, 'He's [Karen's father] going to kick your ass.' I went in anyway and sat down. [Her father] came in and sat down and said he wasn't prejudiced. He said he had black friends, too." Popcorn sneered.

"Eva' hear da sayin', 'Don' nothin' die faster than a dog chasin' cars and a black man chasin' white women'?

"Karen, she put the baby up for adoption. I didn't want that. Her father *was* prejudiced. [Karen's parents] wouldn't let me into the hospital after the baby came.

"Karen had a boy, my son. She named him Isaac. Right out the Bible, man."

"Did you get to see your son?"

"Couple o' times. I sneaked in the hospital."

"I bet it hurt you to lose Isaac when Karen gave him up."

"Yeah, yeah. It be the best way though, man. I wasn't ready to be a father, you know. I going to find him one day, you know. I find him."

David

David grew up in a rural setting, reared by foster parents. We met one afternoon and had a chance to talk about his childhood.

I was hanging around near the Morrison at Chinaman's Corner early one afternoon, watching street folks standing at the entrance to the Salvation Army mission a couple blocks away, and listening to Popcorn complain about how long it takes to get free food there. "You could waste your whole motherfucking day in this town just waiting for meals!"

Coming at me from across the street was David, clean shaven, a bounce in his step, scabs on his wrists, bubbling to see me.

"Motherfucker! Where'd you come from?" David greeted me.

We shook hands. David put his arm around my shoulder, pulling me into him. Two companions were with him, both ex-cons—they had the look. While David and I talked, his companions huddled together, staring at me.

"David, meet Popcorn. Popcorn, meet David." They looked at each other. Neither extended a hand. Popcorn nodded. David turned his back to Popcorn. Introductions are irrelevant on the street or in prison. No one cares who you are.

David disliked Popcorn. It was mutual. Popcorn suddenly had to meet CJ uptown, right now. He walked away.

"David. I was out looking for you. Where you been? You looking pretty good. Shaved. A change of clothes. What's going on? Chasing women?"

"Just got out of jail yesterday morning. Met up with Dale and Bobbie last night in a tavern." He pulled me farther away from them, away from their hearing range.

"How'd ya get busted?" I asked.

"I was drunk, real fucking drunk. Friday night in the park. Me and this dude was sharing some 'I' [Wild Irish Rose wine], and these niggers they come over and was fucking with us. So we got down with 'em. Beat their asses good. Motherfucking niggers. I hate niggers. Cops came, took us to jail."

"Did you go peacefully?" I laughed.

"Fuck no, man. They said I *re*sisted arrest. *Re*sisted. Look at my wrists, man, where they put the cuffs on me. Them motherfuckers almost broke my arms off. Look here, man." Testimony to resisting arrest. Go peacefully.

"Look, David, you know better than I do, man. They say you don't fuck with the SPD."

"I don't want no more of them. Next time I don't fight."

"How long were you in?"

"Five days," he noted. "Nothing. No time at all."

Five days were long enough for David to dry out a bit. Symptoms of serious alcohol withdrawal plagued him in jail, but he kept quiet, not asking for help. A few days of pain in jail were better than a few weeks in the detoxification hospital, he said. Dale and Bobbie got bored, wandered away.

Forty-two years old, an alcoholic, an ex-convict. That's what I knew about David, so far. I suggested getting some lunch, which I'd buy. We always went to one of two places in Pioneer Square, the only two places that still let David in the front door. Drinking and fighting had gotten him barred forever from the other joints.

Budweiser, bottle after bottle, was David's lunch. His alcohol level lowered in jail. I ate pancakes. Cheap food left more money to buy David beer. Some favor.

One of 11 brothers and sisters, David had grown up on a small farm that his mother worked alone after his father was executed.

"I was three years old [in 1951]. My mamma took me to see my father, my real father, die in the gas chamber in North Carolina. I 'member standing next to her and jumping as high as I could, trying to see him through the glass where they had him strapped down. I 'member the big leather belts. She picked me up and showed him to me." That, he said, was his earliest memory.

David's mother did not remarry and, said David, she could not control her children or handle the financial burden of raising them alone. "I started drinking when I was seven, eight years old. I got popped the first time for busting into a church and taking the wine. At age nine, she gave up David and his six-year-old brother; they were taken by foster parents, a farm family in Tyler, Texas.

"I knew they [the foster parents] did it for the money. [My foster father] beat my brother almost to death, and I hit that motherfucker with a hot iron and almost killed him. He was in the air force. Trained special forces troops in survival. I hated the motherfucker. [My foster mother] was a good lady. When you're a kid, you're expecting the best, and you don't know you didn't get it 'til it's too fucking late."

Pimping Slim

Pimping Slim grew up in inner-city Los Angeles. He stole U.S. Treasury checks and did a five-year sentence at USP Lompoc in 1985.

Slim had a dark career as a contract killer, pimp, gang banger, and heroin addict (all verified in his dossier). He was proud of his violence inside California state prisons and on the street. I verified most self-reported violent accounts, and had a chance to see one. Slim and two Crips brutally assaulted a Blood in the weight-lifting area of the gymnasium at USP Lompoc in August 1985. They beat his head and face with a barbell bar and weights.

"[The Blood] was talking shit, man. He came in there flying his colors and pushing his way around up in there. Look, Mark, we told him to be cool, but that Slob [Crip slang for a Blood] motherfucker, he wouldn't listen. We rode down on him, man. You can't run that bullshit up in here. This is a penitentiary, right, Mark!" He laughed.

One afternoon when we were sitting around in his cell, Slim told me about his earliest memories of family life. It took months before he talked about his early life. He preferred telling stories about prostitutes he said he had tortured with hot iron hangers as punishment for keeping more than their share of heroin money. Long before he talked about his mother, he described in detail how he had beaten a prostitute to death with a tire iron and tossed her corpse into a garbage dumpster. Killing was easy for him to talk about; talking about his mother was difficult.

Taking a long deep drag off a Lucky Strike, he told me about her. "The first time the cops brought me home [about age seven], my mother beat me with a belt she had around the house. The next time, the cops called her from the police station and told her to come get me. She came down. Man, she had that belt and started beating me with it. The cops had to stop her from hitting me. She told the police they could keep me.

"Yeah, Mark, she said she didn't want me around no more, that I was too much trouble, and that she couldn't handle me no more. So the cops, man, they kept me. That was my first time in juvenile hall."

Slim recounted his earliest family memory. "I was pretty young, probably five or six, but I don't know for sure. I remember being in a motel room with two of my uncles. I was lying on the bed. It was a big bed. There was a couple of whores in the room. One of them came over and started playing with me. I remember that! Yeah, that was all right. My uncles came in from an armed robbery and put their guns in the closet. I asked for one of the guns. He let me hold it. I knew then, *that* life was for me."

He lit a Lucky, tipped back on his metal folding chair, cocked his head back and smiled, peering through his mirrored sunglasses. "I really liked that gun. Pussy, guns, money, power. Yeah, Mark, that's for me."

After talking about his mother, Slim usually wanted to laugh, tell crime stories, and joke with me about the "girls in his boutique," a "stable of 'ho'es" in Las Vegas. Color photos of each girl were placed carefully on his footlocker and pinned to the bulletin board in his cell. Slim said he'd fix me up with Brenda, a very pretty 23-year-old "model."

T-Cool

Like Slim, T-Cool refused to discuss his mother. The only thing he told me is this: she had her first child by age 18 and had him at age 21 in McGee, Mississippi. He was one of four brothers. "Daddy," he said, "was a rolling stone. Daddy was a marine for 30 some years. He had nine kids by different women. He was hittin' and runnin'!" He laughed.

Week after week, I tried to get T-Cool to talk about his parents and home life. He wouldn't do it, except to say, "Respect and discipline, that's what they instilled in us. We got whuppin's 'n shit. But there ain't no scars."

Twin

It was a hot summer day in the C D. Twin was hanging on a corner in Crip territory, accompanied as usual by Vamp and Body Count. Each had scars on the back of their hands and on their faces. Some were long and thin, like healed knife wounds. Twin had a bullet scar on his chest. Baggy khaki pants were slung low on their hips, low enough to expose their boxer-style underwear had it not been hidden by billowing shirts hanging loosely outside their pants. Their shirts were buttoned from midchest to the collar, showing white T-shirts at waist level. Twin and Body Count had cornrows cinched at the ends by blue rubberbands. Body Count had blue laces in his high-top white sneakers and was wearing a blue nylon-and-wool stocking cap, pulled down over his head, covering the tops of his ears. A gang banger's uniform.

"Body Count." I got his attention. "It's hot as hell out here. Why are you wearing that hat, man? Why's your shirt buttoned up to your neck?" He looked at me like I was crazy.

" 'Cause that's what we do." Simple.

I talked to Twin about his family. At first, Twin was insecure about his ability to answer my questions, but that's common. He didn't mind talking in front of his companions; they were always together.

"My mother was a clerk, a cashier at a store, and my father worked at a house cleaning business."

"Your father—is that your biological father?"

"Nah. That's my stepfather, Freddy."

"When was the last time you saw your biological father?"

"I don't know, a long time, I guess. I haven't seen him since I was three or four. Willie."

"Is Freddy legally married to your mother?"

"Common law. They been together for 10, 11 years. There was five of us kids, three girls—28, 26, 15—and two boys, me and my brother. He's 11 months younger than me and we look alike. That's why I got called Twin."

"Freddy, he had the girls who's 28 and 15. Willie had the rest of us. Freddy took care of the girls."

"Was Willie around when you were comin' up?"

"No. Freddy was there."

"Did he drink?"

Twin stared. "Yeah, he drank."

"Listen. I want to ask you a few really personal questions about sensitive things, and you don't have to answer me if you don't want to. OK?"

"Yeah."

"Did Freddy beat your mother?"

"Yeah."

"Did he beat you or your brothers or sisters?"

"Not my sisters. Just me and my brother gettin' hit. It was a lotta stupid shit. It was like a quick three-, four-minute ass whuppin'."

"Did you get whupped a lot?"

"Enough."

"Tell me about the beatings?"

"They weren't beatings, man. I don't remember 'em." My cue to stop there.

"Did your mother beat you, too?"

"There was no mistreatment, man. She didn't beat us."

"But you said Freddy and your mother gave you ass whuppin's."

"Yeah, but they didn't beat us, man. I deserved the whuppin's I got. They didn't do it for nothin'."

"What's the earliest whuppin' you remember?"

"Last whuppin'—I was about seven years old."

"Who hit you, Freddy or your mother?"

"My mother always did it with a belt."

"Did she hit you real hard?"

"I deserved it. She whup' me for, maybe, five minutes with an ol' belt. She did it other times too. I used to get into a lotta shit. I deserved it.

"I look like my mother. We was real close. We had a good relationship."

Paris

Paris and I talked about his early life one evening, sitting in his cell. Before I got what I had come for, he gave me what he thought I should hear.

"I'm a pimp. P-I-M-P." Smile.

"You know what that stands for? 'Power in manipulating people.' A guy that's pimping, that's the most prestigious job in the world. I was slick, too, man. I had 21 birthdates and 19 social security numbers.

"The jungle creed says a man must feed on anything he can. Pimping isn't beating a woman and stomping her ass. This is my woman and I love her dirty drawers. I have a job. I got to be a bail bondsman. I have to manage the money. I got to fuck the bitch. I got to do everything. It's a job, a helluva job. Pimps need love, too.

"Diamonds, cars, physical things don't make a pimp. It's a lifestyle that you live. Pimping is like a religion, something you live, something you think and learn through experience.

"White bitches, I wanted white bitches. Don't give me none of them ol' mud hens [black women]. I noticed that the chemistry was there in white women who run away from home or been battered or abused, then they get with a black man to get with the psychology. Myth, you know, do black men have big dicks?"

He paused, fumbling in some old letters held together with a rubberband and some legal documents inside tattered envelopes in a shoe box, also holding photographs. There, he found it.

Proudly, he handed me a three-by-five color glossy photo of Alice, a middle-aged, bleached-blonde, wrinkle-faced white woman with an overcurled perm frizzed into a football helmet hairdo. Skintight jeans and a tight V-neck sweater completed her visiting-room costume.

The photo depicted a king surveying his empire, his queen at his side. Kneeling on her right knee, left knee cocked at a right angle and left foot planted squarely on the ground, Alice had both arms wrapped firmly around Paris' left leg. Paris stood erect with his back straight, right leg slightly forward of his left one, looking into the cameraman's lens. Hair done Super Fly, wearing jeans so tight that his queen's trousers looked like sweatpants, he pointed out that his groin bulged. It looked like a codpiece.

"Check it out, man. Look there."

"Where?"

"My 'works,' man. My works. Look there at my right hand [which framed the bulge in his groin], dude. Buff, too, huh? Bad motherfucker, man. *Bad motherfucker.* Bitches can't stay away." He roared with laughter.

" 'Works'? What the fuck are you talking about? What's 'works'?"

"Dumb white motherfucker," he laughed and looked to see if I'd bitch about his joke. It wasn't a joke.

"My works, man. That's what niggers call a *penis*," pronouncing *penis* in an African-American man's version of a white man's speech. He roared louder and harder. A proud man.

"Once a white woman she gets with a black man, she becomes an outcast. White men become tricks. She wants to be dominated by black men.

"Niggers are slick; she wants to be dominated by 'em. So she wants her [pimp] to have a nice car, so she can turn up her nose to them white men who fucked her up.

"Any bitch that's crazy enough to go out and suck 10 dicks a day, 3,000 dicks a year, that's a crazy bitch.

"Drugs don't mix with [the life of a pimp]. If you can't direct your own life, how you gonna direct someone else's?" Dark irony. Paris was a freaked-out rock addict when he got to the federal prison.

"White bitches, they the only ones I wanna be with. With black bitches, the chemistry just ain't there. If I fuck with anything black, I don't want nothing except a black Cadillac, and I'm gonna trade that in on a white Mercedes Benz. Once a white bitch go black, they never go back. Yeah!

"Some white 'ho'es come from suburban families. They don't have the love and support and attention of their mommies and daddies; that's why they run away from home. They meet some dirty ol' pimp. But pimps need love too. Read the Bible where King David meets the queen of Sheba.

"Women are whores by nature. A woman will give away $1 million worth of pussy before she gets one thin dime. When men give in to women, when we love them with an emotional faction, we lose our masculinity."

Paris showed me a copy of a letter written allegedly by a psychologist at the California Men's Colony. The letter noted that he had been diagnosed as paranoid schizophrenic. And he was proud of it. He didn't hear voices though, except for his own. Control over his emotions was brittle however, and he often exploded into verbal fury. I was a safe target. I could not attack or punish him.

Continuous chatter packed every tape-recorded minute with Paris. My tape recorder let him feel as though his words were important enough for me to keep. I asked him a question and sat back while Paris took control, answering any way he saw fit, changing voices from black to white, male to female. He created a space that he controlled. I tried to take some control, too. My only advantage was suggesting that I'd turn off the tape recorder and leave if I couldn't get the information I needed.

"I want to ask some specific questions about your childhood. I'll ask a specific question. You give me a specific answer, OK? Otherwise, I'll have to split. All right, Paris? We can talk shit later, now I need some straight talk. No bullshit."

"Yeah. Shoot, motherfucker.

"I was born in St. Louis, 1960. Grew up there 'til I was nine. My father used to beat the dogshit out of my mother. Mamma left him. He was a real violent motherfucker, man. A black man have two genes in his sperm, a light and a dark. He got a dark one. I wanted him to run away from home when I was seven. He did, but the motherfucker, he came back. Motherfucker.

"Yeah. My father said I wasn't his child, just to hurt my mother. I got a complex against real black men. He used to be mean to me, treat me, man, like shit.

"She protected me from that motherfucker, man. She say, 'I'm going to send you to Detroit to live with cousin Helen [his maternal grandaunt's daughter].

"Helen like to beat ass, too. I was too bad; she couldn't handle me.

"School? Everything I was learning in the fourth grade, I learned.

"I got along all right. I played with the little girls, showed 'em my dick and reach' under their dresses and grab their little pussies. I remember one, I said, 'I'm gonna bust your pussy after school.'"

"What? Paris, come on, man. You were nine, she must have been eight, nine. Don't bullshit me, man!"

He smiled, laughed. "That be good pussy, that young pussy. She went yelling and crying to the motherfucking teacher. That bitch come up, grab me, and I say, 'Fuck you, bitch. Get the motherfuck out of my way, you ol' bitch."

No surprise Paris was transferred to another school. On the first day, he waited for a special bus to pick him up. "The bus pulled up and it was filled up with crippled motherfuckers. Handicapped, man, motherfucking handicapped motherfuckers. The school had a floor for each of 'em. The top floor, that was Miss Bone and Miss Bart. That bitch, she had a black belt in karate. That top floor, it was for emotional kids, hyperactive kids.

"Motherfuckers, man. Miss Bart, she be wrestling me down to the floor, and she put her pussy right in my face. Yeah, she sat on my chest and put that big ol' pussy right in front o' my face. She be wearing panties, man." He roared.

"I be telling her, 'Get off a me, bitch, get off a me.' And she be sitting on my face like that every day. It went on for a month, and then she did it and she didn't have on no pants. She had a wet pussy like in the heat of passion. I had that shit all over my face and it stunk. She said she won't let me up 'til I told her I loved her. We went through this shit twice a week.

"Finally, my mom called [the school]. I ain't been hearing from her in two years."

Paris repeated her first words to him during the call. He changed the tone and quality of his voice when he switched roles, mother to son. He said softly, imitating his mother, "Hi, baby."

"Mamma, where you at?"

"California, baby. I miss you. I love you."

He laughed quietly and told me, "My mamma was a good provider." Then, he added, harshly, "Yeah. The bitch used to make me mow the motherfucking lawn. She made me study. She was a dirty bitch, but I loved her.

"My mamma sent for me 'cause she needed help. She sent for me 'cause she needed a slave. I'm 10 years old, and I got to clean up this shit [garbage left in the house from parties his mother and stepfather had]."

Paris left the special school and journeyed to California by bus, he said. He traveled alone.

"I got there and Donald left. Motherfucker." Donald was his mother's live-in boyfriend.

"Two days later she come home with a white man, Jerry. She come home with this white dude, but I ain't tripping." Soon Paris started to terrorize the neighborhood.

"I threw loaded soda bottles at a woman's front door and she ran out firing [a gun], and I ran 'n threw one into a plate glass window. Mamma said, 'It's time to move.'

"Her and Jerry put me in juvenile hall. He loved my mamma. She still uses his name, and he's been dead going on 20 years."

Paris was sent to Selmar, a juvenile hall in the San Fernando Valley outside Los Angeles. "I told the judge I don't want to be with them. The black kids teased me 'cause I had a white stepfather. I'm about 12 years old; they sent me to junior boys. I told them I wanted to be in with senior boys, where I can smoke and get pussy. I been jackin' off and I knew the feeling and I wanted pussy.

"I had trouble with da Crips, Bloods. I got into a few fights.

"The psychologist, Miss Crummie, didn't like me. An earthquake ruined the [juvenile] home [after he had been there for five months], and they moved me to an Episcopal home for children. I had to deal with them motherfuckers. They kept eight badass motherfucking kids, so they could keep the money for whatever they wanted. I started to love Mamma. I started to love Pappa.

"I used to go on home visits on weekends. Jerry grew his hair long like a biker. Mamma was in a car accident one day and stayed in the hospital a few days. She tol' Jerry not to fuck up [to stay off drugs] and take care o' me and da house. She came home and Jerry was fucked up, man, real good. She kicked his ass out. The next day Jerry came back and mamma jumped on him. She stuck a gun in his face, and *bam bam*, [fired it] next to his head. He tripped out. He said, 'Black ass bitch, give me that gun. I'm gonna break your motherfucking neck.' Mamma killed Jerry 'cause he had went crazy shooting dope, drinking, shooting heroin.

"He used her, man. She downed him. She emptied that gun in his ass, right on the front yard. The German shepherd was running around licking up the blood. My mamma took the diamond rings off his fingers and took his diamond watch. The police come. Cuffed her up. Took her off."

Paris lived with his "grandmother," Mamma Carrie, he called her. She was a neighborhood grandma. In his teens, when Paris wasn't in juvenile detention, which wasn't often, he stayed with Mamma Carrie. He made it to the 12th grade.

Paris described his life when he was 15 years old. "We'd go snatch 15, 20 leather coats. I had a low rider [a car whose suspension system allows it to ride low to the road]. I was high sidin' [publicly displaying goods "to show what you have"]. Nice clothes. Hair done right. Car. The world knows a man by the car he drives. We stole cars. I'm getting away with shit. I' beating cases, GTA [grand theft auto], all sorts of shit. Then they busted me for marijuana!

"I'm selling PCP [by the 12th grade]. I'm making money, carrying 3,000, 4,000 dollars. Gambling, throwing three-card molley."

Paris thought back. "I've done everything but child molestation, and I never killed somebody. I shot a motherfucker who fucked with one of my whores, but I never killed nobody."

Paris spoke in an imitation of a white man's voice, saying: "I done everything. I never wanted to be a fireman like Jimmy."

Porkie

Nicknamed by inmates as USP Lompoc for his favorite food, barbecued pork ribs, Porkie cleans tables in the dining hall. Iron Man, a Compton Crip and self-proclaimed founder of the Crips in Oakland, Fresno, and several other California cities, introduced us.

In his mid-20s, Porkie has a 50-year sentence. He's been a burglar, an armed robber, a heroin dealer, a thief, and he's done some pimping "when times got tough." Porkie isn't as violent as Pimping Slim, at least his rap sheet doesn't show any arrests for assault or killing. He said he never killed anybody, on or off the record. Who knows?

After he finished cleaning off tables and mopping the dining room floor, Porkie and I chatted, sitting together at a table bolted to the tile floor next to the ice machine, not far from where convict Shu knocked convict Garrett cold while he drunkenly slumped over a table early on a Saturday morning in 1985, after celebrating his birthday with cellblock-homebrewed wine.

"My father. Treat me good? He left my mother when I was seven. He was in and out of the pen. He's running the street with other women. He ain't had time for us children. He didn't want to spend much time with us doing what a father's got to do. If you grow up fatherless, you pick someone as your role model, like my cousin [his father's brother's son]. He was into the fast life—drugs, women."

Porkie didn't remember much more about his childhood. He did remember, however, that his mother often left him and his siblings alone.

"Some ol' bitches down the hall would come in looking in on us every now and then. She'd be gone for a long time. When I was six or seven, I started hanging out on the street. I lived in reform schools. I lived 10 out of 24 years on the street. Fourteen years in prison."

"I lived with my grandma [his father's mother] when my mother was incarcerated. I had a place in her basement," Porkie said rather passively. By age 11, Porkie was selling drugs and staying with his grandmother full time. Porkie's father's brother, his father's sister's three kids, and his father's brother's son lived with his grandmother, too.

Porkie sat quietly for a moment. "My mother is bailing out of jail right now, today, in Kentucky. Yeah, she wrote me. She's a professional thief—stealing drugs, jewelry. Some of her attributes came to me. She done took me out, and we stole together." He laughed.

Pinto

Pinto grew up in the barrio in Los Angeles, the youngest of 11 siblings.

"The ol' man [his father] was an alcoholic and beat my mother through the years. He had a few auto body shops. He was in the army in World War II. I think that's how he got his citizenship; he's from Mexico. Mom worked two jobs and was a nervous wreck. When I was three or four, my father wasn't paying his taxes. Feds took our house, and we all were in foster homes for a while. We all went to different foster homes.

"Feds put us on the street, and the church came in and put us in foster homes. It had a big effect on the family. My father was never there. He'd come home drunk, beat everybody up, and leave. He had girlfriends. One of them, he's still with today.

"My mother and father have been split up since '57 or '58. My father was never there and he never really helped financially with anything. Me and Gary [Pinto's brother] would live with him. He didn't want his kids to speak Spanish; he had a hard time with his accent from Mexico. He had a hard time and he'd meet these women and want to start his life over again. He'd tell his girlfriends I was his only kid. He'd show up, slap my sisters around, beat up my brothers, and never really did nothing for nobody."

"Did he beat you, Pinto?"

"Yeah, but only when I deserved it. He'd whip me real good. He was strict and that's good. I raised hell and I guess I wasn't that easy to raise up, so he hit me. I'm kinda like my dad. I had everything I wanted 'cause I worked for it. I didn't hate him. I lived with him from when I was 7 or 8 to 12. I left him when I was 12, and he waited for me to come back. If I would have lived with him [instead of leaving], my whole life would have been different.

"He brought my wife up here [to visit him at USP Lompoc] twice in five years. That's more than I can say for anybody else.

"I always liked Anthony [ninth in the birth order; Anthony and Pinto had different fathers]. He's an attorney now. He went to a [Catholic college]. He was an exchange student in Spain and taught in Bowling Green, Ohio, and in Seattle. He went to Argentina and met a woman there and married her. I helped him out his first two years of law school [with drug money], but I got busted. He struggled like the rest of us. He was in a foster home. He escaped to school and that kind of shit. I escaped to the street.

"My mother put a lot of hate in Lupe for my father [Lupe is a short form of Guadalupe, the youngest daughter and 10th in the birth order]. I guess Lupe knew all along that he wasn't her father. Lupe had a daughter; she never married the father. They [now] live in HUD housing. She worked different jobs and struggles along from job to job. She's into a heavy Christian trip now.

"She had an older boyfriend when she was in ninth grade; he had been in prison. He was 27 and an ex-con."

Wolf Man

Wolf Man was hanging around the pool table in the dayroom of D-unit, clutching some books and file folders under his left arm. Wolf Man's hair was coifed, every hair in its place. His khaki federal prison shirt was buttoned to his neck and his khaki pants were meticulously ironed, a sharp crease dividing each pant leg in half. A five-o'clock shadow, darkened by the dim light of the poolroom, gave Wolf Man an unmistakable image, a *cholo*, gang banger.

A 34-year-old bank robber and heroin addict, Wolf Man is about 5 feet 7 inches, with a thin waist, large chest, and pronounced cheekbones. The ends of his downward-curved dark moustache reach nearly to the line of his lower jaw, and remind me of fangs. A large heroin dragon on the inner side of his right foreman signals his addiction.

At 26, he did his first of 13 bank robberies and one attempted bank robbery. He robs alone. "I like to work by myself." An arm tattoo reads "Lone Wolf." Now he's doing 25 years, alone, at USP Lompoc.

Wolf Man's been legally married to Rosa since January 29, 1983. His entire back is devoted to her inked image, a tattooed portrait of a beautiful Hispanic lady whose hair flows down from her head around her neck. The tattoo depicts a gorgeous woman. Wolf Man explained that it was modeled on a Polaroid taken of Rosa at a prison visiting session. However, the Rosa I saw in the visiting room looks nothing like the fantasy on Wolf Man's back.

Wolf Man said he was sharing Rosa's bed, spending the night at her house without her parents knowing it, when he was 12. "I came in her window at night and left before they found me in the morning. We would have gotten married when we were 14, but her mother tried to kill me a coupla times. She shot at me one time and tried to drive over me once. We got engaged at 17."

Wolf Man is now the father of a 16-year-old son and two daughters, 12 and 9. Junior, Wolf Man's son, wants to grow up to be like his dad, said Wolf Man.

At 13 Wolf Man robbed three supermarkets. In the fifth grade, he started gang banging with the V-13s, a Hispanic gang in Venice, California. In the eighth grade, he first experienced heroin. "When I started [using heroin], man, I was trying to look bad, being tough. It was a form of getting respect." At 14, he entered his first drug rehabilitation program.

He enjoyed telling me about his teenage supermarket robberies. "I told people with grocery baskets and five, six kids to split. A detective in Los Angeles said people in the store and in the neighborhood said I was a Robin Hood robber." He smiled proudly.

"Incorrigible," he said, was the authorities assessment of him in eighth grade. At 14, Central juvenile hall in Los Angeles and the Los Angeles county jail were his homes. He's been in custody ever since, in juvenile detention, jail, prison, or parole.

Hour after hour, Wolf Man's lower lip curled upward, dragging at the long untrimmed hairs of his dark moustache draped unstylishly over his upper lip and into his mouth. "I got picked up for GTA and a burglary too, but my main thing was running away. They [his parents] were too strict." Wolf Man doesn't know his "real" father, he said. His stepfather, Victor, was a construction worker.

"Did Victor drink?"

"Friday nights, he only had one six pack. Saturday, his nephews would come over and they'd go out drinking."

"Did Victor hit your mother?"

"Yeah, not a lot. But she had it coming sometimes. I don't view the dude as being abusive. They're good parents. He backhanded her when she pushed the issue. I never wanted for nothing. Food. Roof. That was cool."

"Did Victor hit you, Wolf Man?"

"Yeah. I hated him. Finally, one day, I thought, no more belts from this day on. The belt can't hurt no more. He'd hit my little sister; that was his daughter. Sometimes I'd jump in and get him to focus on me. That was the wrong way to do kids. Once I wasn't scared of the belt no more, I realized that he couldn't stop me. I was gone.

"In junior high school, I stopped coming home sometimes, and when I was 15 or 16, I'd go to my mother's house on and off. [I was] sleeping with homeboys in garages or rooms when their mother doesn't know I was there. It was about eighth grade when everything started jumping off and I got into heroin.

"At a young age, I clicked in with authority. In high school, man, I assaulted a teacher the first week I was there. He insulted me. He grabbed me around the neck with a cane and I went off. That's it. I never went back. I went to camp [juvenile detention] when I was 16. When I went to camp, my ol' lady was pregnant, and I didn't know it. Then when this probation thing started [as a teenager], I felt like I was never free."

Leo

When we met in 1981 at the Washington State Penitentiary, Leo had served several years in a state prison on a long sentence. Leo's a veteran of state and federal prison. Now he was doing "two dimes running wild, boxcars," two 10-year sentences, one for armed robbery, one for the statutory rape of a 12-year-old girl, the daughter of his live-in girlfriend. "The kid wanted me. She sat on my lap, rubbed my neck, smelled good. What's the problem?"

Leo is about 5 feet 6 inches, 140 pounds, with straight blond hair, blue eyes, and a bright energetic smile. His skin is not marred by tattooes but is by a few scars, mostly around his eyes—mementos of street and cellblock fistfights.

He walks with a limp slightly to the right. A serious motorcycle accident caused massive injuries to his lower leg; he crashed at high speed, trying to elude the police after he had stolen the motorcycle. He was a teenager, then. His upper body is now assymmetrical, shoulders curving at different angles. A police bullet shattered his left shoulder during a gunfight after an armed robbery. He was in his early 20s then. Now, at age 32, he has nearly 20 years of crime behind him. After nearly three years of acquaintance, Leo told me about his early life.

"My mother was an alcoholic and my father tried to keep his farm running; her drinking was real hard on him. I hated the bitch.

"When I was a kid, she'd throw empty whiskey bottles at me, from across the living room. She brought her boyfriends home with her and used to fuck 'em on the couch; she didn't care if we were around or not. She was always drunk anyway. I remember when I was real young, she'd take me to bed and play with me.

"When I got older, she used to tie me to the clothesline pole out back—we had one of those free-standing deals, you know—in the summer. You know how hot it gets in Minnesota in the summer. She'd tie me up with clothesline. She'd wrap it around me, leave me out there all afternoon, and put a bowl of water down on the ground in front of me, but I couldn't get it. My father knew some of the shit that was going on, but he tried his best to keep the family together. It was nice when she died."

Donnie

One midweek night I was sitting with Donnie, a 23-year-old Plains Indian, serving a sentence of more than 50 years at USP Lompoc. Donnie has three brothers, and he's second in the birth order. His eldest brother, Warren (a former state prison inmate), still lives on the reservation and is always in trouble, according to Donnie. His second youngest brother, Davie, has "always [had] something wrong with him. If you give him an idea, he wouldn't think, he'd just do it." Sammie, the youngest brother, shot himself in the head at age 17. When Donnie was 13, he plunged a knife into the head of teenager.

"I was high on acid [LSD]," Donnie said. "I don't remember too much about it. I was sitting on the floor; there was music playing. I saw somebody lean over me, like they was going to hurt me. I picked up something I had [in my hand] and stabbed in the front of me. When I woke up, I saw what happened. I don't remember it."

Donnie and I had already spent several hours together a few days earlier, but I could not get him to talk about his preteenage years. This time I wanted to hear about his early family life on the reservation. Donnie has a hard time talking about it, and claims he does not have any memories about his life before the LSD killing.

Donnie said he ran away from his mother's house three times. At age four, he walked out and went to live with his mother's mother, who lived two miles away. "Grandma tried to treat me good," he said. But relatives brought him home. At age five, Donnie said, he ran away again, back to his grandmother's house. Again, he was returned.

"I had to leave my mother's house [at the age of six]. I don't know why. Life in my house to me was very boring. They [his grandparents] were too old, and we had to go out and do all the work. My grandmother didn't drink. My father drank, but he didn't beat me. My mother beat me. That's why I took off."

The third time Donnie ran away from his mother's house, he fled with a friend. Together they ran as far away from his mother's house as they could go. They had horses, he said, so they could ride to the distant areas of the reservation to avoid capture by the tribal police, and for good reason. "They'd pick you up, and beat the shit out of you!"

Donnie and his companion broke into reservation houses for food. Most were white people's houses, he said. After he was caught, the tribal council (some of whose members were his relatives) decided to send him to his aunt's house in Colorado.

Telling me about those events did not disturb him. When I asked how he felt about his childhood—if he had been treated well by his parents, if he had enjoyed being a kid—he said, "Yeah, I guess so."

Donnie and I were sitting together at a round cardtable covered with an old prickly army blanket, on the "flats" (ground level) of the cellblock. Bill, a chubby white inmate in his 30s, was sitting at the table too, left over from the card game I had interrupted and broken up when I arrived.

Donnie introduced Bill and said Bill could stay there during our interview. That was unusual. An inmate usually does not want other inmates to hear details of his personal life unless he can "construct" an interesting, exciting, and crowd-pleasing tale. An honest tale requires honest emotions.

Even stranger, Donnie wanted to sit out in the open area of his cellblock. That had not happened before, in many years of prison ethnography. American Indians, at other times, had always wanted to get out of the view of inmates and staffers alike. Donnie simply said, "I got nothing to hide." So there we sat.

Rastafarians leaned over the second- and third-tier railings, with their long braids packed into colorful knitted hats. Others just leaned against the railing, arms folded, staring downward, expressionless from their perches 20, 30 feet above us. I could read their faces: "What are these assholes doing?"

"What's your earliest childhood memory?"

Donnie paused, staring into the air. "I told you. The time I killed that kid."

"But you were 12 then, right?"

"Yeah," he nodded.

"Let's go back before that. How about when you were really young, three, four, five?"

He kept staring at the gray cellblock wall, but he was remembering back, as if there were something back there worth remembering. He said nothing. I primed the pump.

"Tell me about Christmas when you were really young. Do you have any memories of Christmas?"

"Nope."

Bill said he was an expert in matters of psychology and jumped into the conversation, thinking that he could extract information. "You mean you don't remember Christmas when you were a kid? Didn't you have a tree? You got to remember Christmas!"

Donnie kept staring into cellblock doors. Finally he said, "[My] only Christmas memory, I was living in Denver [with an aunt on his father's side]; we only stayed there a year. It was Christmas and I came down and found my uncle stabbed. He was pretty fucked up. They [his aunt and uncle] must have been drunk.

"We got sent there; we were just getting out of control [on the reservation]. We wouldn't listen to nobody or anything like that." Donnie, Warren, and Davie were sent away from the reservation to his aunt's house; Sammy, who later committed suicide, lived with his father.

"When I went to school, I didn't get along with anybody. I didn't get along with teachers. I thought they were all out to get me. I had problems all the time with the teachers. I didn't have problems with kids, always with the teachers. I couldn't face looking up to the teachers. My grandmother was always called to the school. I used to get in fights with teachers. If they wanted me to do something and I didn't want to, we'd get into a fight.

"Until I was eight or nine, I was all right. I decided I could take this for a while, as long as they don't get into my face. When I was 10, I didn't want to go back to school. I told my grandmother that nobody was going to make me go back. Me and Davie [his second youngest brother] took off at 10. That's when we started breaking into houses [again]. That's when the real serious trouble started."

Donnie's teenage years were spent in jails on American Indian reservations and in training schools. At age 19, Donnie went to federal prison to serve a federal sentence, which will be finished in the second or third decade of the next century. Then he will face kidnaping, rape, and armed robbery charges in Iowa and Nebraska.

Radical Effects on Enculturation

Recall that enculturation shapes a worldview, and that the nature of a child's early-life environment strongly influences a sociocultural grammar and a sociolinguistic grammar, which permanently guide an individual's behavior and speech. These recollections of early life clearly suggest that, as youngsters, my informants were reared in family cultures characterized by neglect, conflict, criticism, and rejection.[9]*

Many caretakers were criminals;[10] most had violent tempers;

---

*Research suggests a strong connection between parental substance abuse and neuropsychological impairment (central nervous system damage) in the children of alcoholic or drug-addicted mothers. Some of these impaired children later commit violent criminal acts (Spellacy 1977, 1978; Yeudall and Fromm-Auch 1979; Yeudall et al. 1982).

most physically abused their children; most had addictions to drugs and alcohol; most had little affection for each other or their children. There was no family intimacy; the parents had no commitment to each other or to their children's emotional, physical, or educational well-being. Most addicted parents were more attentive to drug and alcohol addictions than to their children. Children cared for themselves as if they were orphans.[11]

A defensive worldview is a cognitive outcome of early-life adult rejection and neglect, and is a way of perceiving, interpreting, and explaining social processes and events predicated on fear.[12] A defensive worldview is un-self-conscious; it projects meaning onto social forms and events in street culture, provides its connotations and denotations, and binds hustlers together into a recognizable yet diffusely dispersed subgroup. Hustlers with a defensive worldview are predisposed to see the world in similar ways.[13]

A defensive worldview has six traits: a feeling of vulnerability and need to protect oneself; a belief that no one can be trusted; a need to maintain social distance; a willingness to use violence and intimidation to repel others; an attraction to similarly defensive people; and an expectation that no one will provide aid. What sort of protection other than a defensive cognitive, psychological, and emotional strategy might a youngster develop in a household like Ace's, Donnie's, Wolf Man's, and Porkie's?

A defensive worldview is recognized by its emphasis on self-protection, suspicion, impulsiveness, insensitivity, reliance on physical force, propensity for risk-taking behavior, and a reluctance to become socially intimate. Gottfredson and Hirschi identify similar traits as indicators of "low self-control," and suggest that these traits are an outcome of poor socialization: an absence of parental nurturance, positive discipline, and positive behavioral training.[14]*

Defensive worldview traits have been noted by Sanchez Jankowski and Hagedorn as typical of gang subjects. Vigil says gang

---

*In the absence of psychometric measurements, long-term observation strongly indicates that my informants were insecure and angry, and seemed to have developed a poor self-concept (Erickson 1968). Kelly (1993a) refers to these traits collectively as low mental health (see Chesney-Lind and Shelden 1992:177; Ellis 1987; Douglas and Johnson 1977).

Research on self-concept has focused almost exclusively on white middle-class youngsters. Racial and ethnic identity is virtually absent in the literature (Banks and Grambs 1972; see also Helms 1992).

members are youngsters reared in economically marginalized, trau-
matized families with little adult supervision.[15]*

A defensive worldview enables youngsters threatened by forces
outside their control to protect themselves; they withdraw, become
aggressive, act moment to moment, and distrust adults (potential
abusers). These are, in an evolutionary sense, survival skills.

Although these traits are adaptive in early family life, they become socially maladaptive when these once-abused children age
and enter a broader social arena. Years of neglect by parents are followed by rejection outside the family too, when primary and secondary school teachers and peers can't cope with these children.[16]
My informants, even before their teenage years, were driven away
from homes and schools.

Over the years, my informants' fear of social interaction, except
with people whom they perceived as similar to themselves, further
isolated and shielded them from positive social interactions with
youngsters and adults outside their immediate social sphere. Once
they began to commit delinquent acts and were arrested and imprisoned in juvenile detention facilities, social isolation heightened,
and opportunities to acquire the social skills and daily experiences
that lead "normal" children into adulthood were gone. A defensive
worldview retarded their social maturation and left them in a pro-
longed state of adolescent dependency, because these youngsters
were kept from developing cognitive and social skills necessary for
adult independence in American society.[17]

Poor parenting often doesn't end in one family; it's transmitted
from one generation to the next. In a discussion about the psycho-
dynamic processes of child abuse, Dwivedi describes how parents
with a defensive worldview, or with the low self-control described
by Gottfredson and Hirschi, inadequately rear children, who in turn
also become emotionally damaged:

> Child abuse is a manifestation of the disintegration of genera-
> tional boundaries. Abusive parents are described as adults
> who are rather immature and cannot emphasize with their

---

*The relationship between economic conditions and crime has influenced nu-
merous theoretical paradigms, including conflict theories (Taylor et al. 1973), subcultural theories (Cloward and Ohlin 1960; Wolfgang and Ferracuti 1967), strain
theory (Merton 1949), opportunity theories (Cantor and Land 1985; Cohen et al.
1980), and social disorganization theory (Kornhauser 1978; Shaw and McKay 1942).

children. They may also have very unrealistic expectations about their children's abilities. They may be treated as if he or she was a parent figure. Thus, the child may be expected to satisfy the needs of the parents for love and nurturance of which they were deprived in their own childhood. Such an unconscious role reversal is bound to lead to frustration and aggression because a child is bound to fail in this enormous task *and the parents would perceive this as a wilful rejection.* Thus the child's lack of mastery of a skill is misperceived as wilful hostility, requiring punishment.[18]

These parents were probably reared by caretakers who had a defensive worldview and expressed semantic miscues similar to those noted here. Parents who perceive rejection by their children will automatically react with hostility, often leading to rage and violent behavior when they beat their youngsters.[19]

Distorted social semantics enabled by a defensive worldview generate interpretations, explanations, and perceptions that are faulty in a parenting situation; however, this faulty worldview was adaptive in childhood. In the way we are unaware of the linguistic rules guiding our speech (we can't list them on a page unless we've been trained to do it), a defensive worldview with its constituent sociocultural and sociolinguistic grammars is outside its carrier's awareness. People who carry a defensive worldview may misinterpret social situations and, from our perspective, say the wrong things and behave badly in those situations; they are likely to be unaware of these miscues and feel as if they are behaving and speaking the "right way."

Unbuffered, a defensive worldview will pass from adults to children within generations of family culture in the process of enculturation. If this is a plausible assumption, we should find propensities for inappropriate or illegal acts passing through families.[20]

Perhaps these statistics reflect, in part, this situation: 52 percent of juvenile offenders in state institutions, 37 percent of adults in state prisons, and 35 percent of adults in local or county correctional facilities have relatives who are or have been incarcerated.[21] Hammet and colleagues report that 52 percent of homicide victims are killed by a family member or acquaintance, and 35 percent of homicides stem from a conflict not associated with a felony.[22]

Social control theory and the theory of low self-control suggest that inadequate, or "defective," socialization processes lead to deviant behavior.[23] Enculturation is a natural and neutral process; even in these cases of my informants with abusive, neglectful parents, enculturation created for them a sociobiologically adaptive system of knowledge that enabled them as young human animals to survive in the immediate environment. The problem ensued when these young humans, adapted for one set of external environmental conditions, moved to other environments where their reactions weren't culturally adaptive.

A defensive worldview isn't abnormal; it isn't a mental illness; it isn't psychopathy; and it can't be easily "fixed" or replaced with grammatical rules that lead to behavior and speech that are more acceptable in lawful society.

The only effective strategy to prevent the acquisition of a defensive worldview (low self-control) is to remove children like Ace from households like Maniac's before the enculturation process yields a worldview that's unalterable. In a few years, perhaps just 36–48 months, Ace will have acquired a worldview that generates behavior and speech mirroring Maniac's.

3 _____

Adolescent Survival

This research among delinquents and gang members focused on life histories, social life and street survival, and social adjustment between these people and their families and peers. Unfortunately I didn't systematically collect data on aggregate rates of street offenses. However, street ethnography among delinquents, both gang members and non–gang members, brought me close familiarity with offense types, such as drug dealing, car theft, possession and sale of stolen property, and shoplifting.

In this chapter, I define and discuss the relationship between childhood rejection and the formation of delinquent groups and gangs, discuss gangs' social networks and expressive culture, offer a definition of the term *gang*, and speculate on a gang's politicolegal functions in chaotic neighborhoods. I make generalizations about gangs that are based on interview data from Hispanic, black, and American Indian inmates in jails and state and federal institutions, as well as on observational data collected on Seattle streets.

Ethnography of Rejection

Life history data for adult hustlers, as well as participant-observation data for teenagers, show disturbing trends. Here are a few examples. Popcorn gambled, used drugs and alcohol, had found two crime partners by age 12, and assaulted his girlfriend at age 15. David drank alcohol, committed burglary, and displayed violent behavior before he became a teenager. Slim was beaten by his mother and was arrested the first time at age seven. Paris was in training school by age 12, and by then he had been a target for peers' teasing and rejection and had begun to fight with them. Porkie was hanging around the street, abandoned by his mother and father by age seven. Wolf Man was staying with his girlfriend full time by age 12, and was a veteran armed robber by age 13. Donnie didn't get along with anybody. He fought with teachers and peers, refused to attend school, and had run away many times by age 10.*

Episodically homeless youngsters are an indicator of family neglect and rejection. All adult informants had "run away" or "stayed on the street" as children. Initial periods of homelessness were so short, a day or two at most, that at first I overlooked them as significant teenage events. These episodes were not "sleep aways" and slumber parties. Always these short episodes, which sometimes began at age seven or eight, extended into episodes of homelessness lasting weeks and then months. Informants who had consanguineal and affinal social ties to grandparents, cousins, or other extended family members temporarily stayed with them. A place of residence, even with a family member, did not heal the damage inflicted at home.

Some older teenage boys, like Wolf Man, stayed with girlfriends who still resided with their parents. Or as these boys aged they employed girlfriends who lived apart from parents. Some, like Kelly, the Puerto Rican teenager with whom I boxed, just wandered city streets, claiming to stay awake all night, because it would be too dangerous to fall sleep on the bench or in an alley near a garbage dumpster.

T-Dog, a Seattle Crip, said: "About 10, 11 I started staying on the street. Slept where I could. Usually with some other dude at his place." When I asked why, T-Dog was startled. "'Cause that's the way it *was*." This happens in other cities too. I found the ethnographic counterparts of T-Dog's remarks in the Central District.

I began ethnography in the CD without expecting to see preteenage boys and girls standing on street corners, or under limbs of 50-year-old trees, trying to stay dry in the Seattle drizzle, or leaning against boarded-up store fronts, between midnight and 3:00 in the

---

*Inciardi, Horowitz, and Pottieger (1993:119; emphasis added) write: "All of the 12–15-year-old boys interviewed, and 96% of the 14–15-year-old girls, were still living with *a* family. Among 16–17-year-olds, however, 18% of the 206 males and a surprising 76% of the 50 females had moved away from home. There were no differences by race/ethnicity for either gender." In general these authors find that teenagers who live on their own are "disconnected from conventional life" and have higher rates of drug use and crime.

morning. I thought children of this age should be at home in the middle of the night, or at least I expected to see frantic adults scouring the streets looking for them. Perhaps at first I was a bit naive.

There are usually more school-age kids on the street at 2:00 in the morning than at 2:00 in the afternoon. During school hours, police scan the streets picking out truants, so kids stay out of sight.* Cold weather also keeps boys and girls out of sight, but during warm seasons dozens of youngsters flock to the streets in the evening hours, when boys and girls can hang out together and drugs can be sold to passersby under a shield of darkness.†

Some of these kids are members of the local gangs, Rollin' 60s Crips, Piru Bloods, and Black Gangster Disciples (BGDs).[1] Other boys hanging out with gang boys are "wannabes," waiting for an opportunity to join. But now these kids, like other street kids, are used by gang drug sellers as pawns in the cocaine game to peddle drugs on street corners, visible to police.[2] These groups include girls too, walking with gang boys, laughing, talking, holding the gang boys' handguns, packets of drugs, but not the cash. Should young wannabes and girls get arrested, gang boys know the penalties will be minor.

In the wee hours of the morning they wander aimlessly and with impunity because local patrol cars are busy elsewhere, chasing down burglars, armed robbers, and street shooters.

Neighborhood blocks in the CD are not highly differentiated as gang territories, as neighborhoods are in cities like Los Angeles. But even so, the Rollin' 60s, the Piru Bloods, and the BGDs stay off each other's blocks. It takes little effort to drive or walk around the "enemy" in a place as small as the CD. It shows respect. No point in "dissin'" (being disrespectful toward) someone and getting shot.

Gang boys hang out and sell drugs in the CD. Sometimes on Fri-

---

*Johnson (1993:1, 8), in a story about violence among children in Chicago, Illinois, notes, ". . . among the 25 homicide victims this year between 10 and 14, at least seven besides [the current victim] had chronic attendance problems, a rate almost eight times Chicago's overall student population rate of about 4 percent. . . . Chronic truancy, experts say, is a red flag fluttering madly, a signal of family or other trauma, a clear indicator of children in trouble. . . . Experts think that if they could intervene at the point where students are frequently absent but still in touch with schools— before they can legally drop out at age 16—they could save some of them."

†Inciardi, Lockwood, and Pottieger (1993:59) provide an excellent "cocaine lexicon," including numerous terms for women who trade sex for cocaine. Drug terms collected in this research are presented in chapter 5, "The Street."

day and Saturday nights, when tourists cover the streets, they wander downtown near the Pike Place Market putting on a show, being loud, yelling, covering the sidewalk from side to side as they walk, pushing timid citizens off into the street or forcing them to stand aside lined up along building fronts, like a police line-up. It's just a show, however.

Gang boys don't sell drugs downtown. These corners, sidewalks, and parking lots are occupied by adult hustlers, hard criminals who carry handguns and knives and who know how to use them. These former black, white, and Hispanic convicts own these streets and aren't frightened by boisterous children. The men feared most downtown are the Mexican heroin dealers, who, as Popcorn says, "will cutcha bad." The men let the youngsters play the street game. Live and let live.

There are lone youngsters, too, in the CD. These are girls in their early teens who station themselves on sidewalks and street corners on busy streets. Motionless they stand, arms limply hanging by their sides, faces gaunt, cheeks drawn—lifeless children waiting to earn a $5 or $10 bill or a cocaine rock with the one thing young girls can sell in any city, sex.[3]*

Delinquency and Groups

The causes and conditions of juvenile delinquency are complex. Neighborhood and community characteristics, influences of peers on the street and in schools, individual personality and temperament variations, and family conditions are primary causes of juvenile delinquency.[4] Among the myriad of factors associated with delinquency, impulsiveness, a trait of low self-control, has been strongly related to social maladjustment among children.

Wilson and Herrnstein find that "the interaction between constitutional and familial factors has a powerful effect on later misconduct, especially physical aggression," and that "impulsiveness is strongly associated with other kinds of behavior—aggressiveness, hyperactivity, and having problems in school—that are, in turn, often precursors to criminality." Finally, they note that "chronic recidivists begin their misdeeds at a very young age. This means that

---

*Six years ago there were about 300,000 unsupervised adolescents on the street (National Coalition for the Homeless 1989; see Rossi 1989).

constitutional and familial factors are most important in explaining the behavior of the most serious offenders."[5]

Scholars have shown that group behavior has an effect on street offending. Delinquents almost never commit street crimes alone.[6] Decades of research have consistently shown that the likelihood of a child engaging in delinquent behavior increases as a child's number of delinquent associates increases.[7]

Hirschi points out that delinquents will seek out others who share their own values. Reiss shows that most adolescents commit offenses with other youngsters.[8] Other scholars suggest that delinquent groups are sources of delinquent values that children can easily learn.[9] In either case it is the group nature of delinquency which attracts the attention of criminologists.[10]

Delinquency and group association are inexorable components of juvenile offenses.[11] Esbensen and Huizinga studied the relationship of rates of street crime in delinquent groups as compared with gangs; I define the term *gang* below, but until then I will use Esbensen and Huizinga's definition of a gang as a "group involved in illegal activity."[12] They find that there are higher rates of street offenses for teenage gang members than for non–gang members,[13] and that "delinquent involvement precedes gang membership."[14] This finding supports Hirschi's contention, as well as Fagan's observation that "gang participation may not be a cause of delinquency, but a facilitator of it. In turn, the factors that explain the higher rates of delinquency among gang youths may lie in the social organization of gangs and their development in specific social and historic [*sic*] contexts."[15]

● Research literature in delinquency, social psychology, and child developmental psychology leaves little doubt about the causes of maladjustment and delinquency in preschool children through high school teenagers. Determinants for childhood disorders that lead to academic failure and to rejection by peers and teachers, as well as to the formation of delinquent groups and street gangs, are ineffective parenting and disturbed family social interactions. These determinants increase the risk for childhood depression, which then heightens the risk for involvement with a delinquent group. ◗

Life history and ethnographic data collected in this study show informants' gradual movement from abusive and neglectful natal families, to rejection by school peers and by teachers, to banding together with other rejected children on the street.[16] Left uninterrupted by outside forces, this process seems automatic and inevitable.

Liska and Reed (1985) suggest that poor relationships in school increase the likelihood of attachment to a delinquent group, which decreases attachment to school and encourages even more delinquent behavior.[17] Once delinquent children drop out of school their involvement in crime increases and so does their use of drugs.[18]

Also well known is that abused children have higher levels of aggression, fight more with siblings, show more aggression in school, and have a higher level of aggression toward parents and other children.[19] Olweus has shown that abused children have weak control over aggressive tendencies, possess strong self-assertion needs, and display dominance needs.[20]

Coie and colleagues in a sociometric study of 300 school children, aged 8–14, show that children identified as "least liked" by their peers are seen as committing many offenses, disrupting group activities, starting fights, and acting snobbish. Those children with the highest risk of peer rejection are seen by peers as lacking social skills, having limited social perception (unskilled at joining and behaving in groups), and committing peer identified offenses.[21]

Children rejected by peers and by teachers recognize themselves as unpopular and disliked.[22] Peretti and McNair interviewed rejected children. These authors felt the children's ability to interact socially was superficial; they were self-deprecating, and portrayed themselves as emotionally bland, depressed, and suspicious; also, they feared social rejection, and many had already withdrawn socially.[23]

Studies in social psychology show that children are keenly aware of their own intragroup variations, and that they readily identify with other children who resemble them in the slightest way. They use these self-identified criteria of similarity and difference to form groups, and may enter into bitter rivalries with groups that show a slight difference from their own characteristics.[24]

Delinquent groups are composed of self-identified rejected boys. Gang formation is just a short step away. Tajfel found that adolescents sort themselves into in-groups and out-groups, facing off as "us" versus "them," and being a member of the wrong group is likely to lead to social isolation and rejection. To gain acceptance to the right group, to gain recognition, children often make desperate attempts for membership. Their alternative is frustration and loneliness, which may lead to withdrawal and even more disruptive behavior.[25]

Interview and participant-observation data as well as findings from other research show a strong association between delinquent groups and peer rejection. Frude identifies characteristics among school children associated with high peer rejection: low sociability, lack of social skills, high aggression, low maturity, offensive behavior (as judged by peers), and identification with other rejected children.[26]

Hazen and colleagues show that rejected children display a lack of attention to other children, and are cited by peers as being socially inept, lacking in social skills, and displaying high levels of aggression. Rubin and colleagues and Milich and colleagues find that, in peer studies of school children, rejection by peers was consistently related to aggression. Cairns and colleagues emphasize that aggressive children 9 and 10 years old, while rejected by most peers, are popular with other aggressive children.[27]

Coie and Dodge conducted a four-year longitudinal study of children 8–11 years old.* They find the sociometric status of groups remains at a high level of stability, and that the status stability of rejected children was particularly high. Even among very young children, they find that sociometric status tends to be stable.[28]

This suggests that children rejected by school-yard peers will remain rejected, and that rejected children, without the possibility of acceptance by peers, will likely form a group among themselves.[29] Once formed, this group will function to accept other rejected children. Frude notes that rejected and aggressive children in gaining acceptance from an in-group may be highly aggressive toward an out-group, and the cognitive and affective expressions of their aggression are prejudice and hatred.[30] Intergang rivalries and drive-by shootings are likely an extension of these natural, albeit violent, social processes.

Rejected children look to groups composed of children like themselves for help and for validation of attitudes and opinions. These

---

*Esbensen and Huizinga (1993:573) found that nearly 43 percent of youngsters in their study were gang members by age 14. These researchers didn't report data about gang members' association with school teachers and peers, gang members' intrafamily processes, the nature of social ties within gangs for members and outside gangs for former gang members, the link between kinship and gang membership, and neighborhood influences on gang membership and street crime.

groups of school-yard and family rejects will be internally stratified by the rejected youngsters' own scheme for peer classification. Some will be popular, others neglected, still others rejected.[31] Esbensen and Huizinga find that 91 percent of youngsters in their sample remained gang members for less than two years.[32] Perhaps these youngsters were gang scapegoats or the neglected and rejected boys among other marginal teenagers. If so, did this group rejection lead them into social isolation and force them into further crime and violent behavior? Or did they find another group of rejected children and join it? Are teenage "lone wolf" boys similar to Pinto and Wolf Man, who were serious delinquents by age 14, victims of continual peer neglect and rejection, as Hirschi predicted?[33]

In the interaction between the disturbed processes of family neglect and abuse, peer rejection at school, and the effects of these on an individual's self-concept lie the socioemotional dynamics of delinquent street behavior and gang formation. To explore the expression of juvenile delinquency and social maladjustment further, it is necessary to understand the interaction between children with a poor self-concept and the dominant society's racial biases.

Clark writes that "children who are consistently rejected understandably begin to question and doubt whether they, their family and their group really deserve no more respect from the larger society than they received."[34] The following is an excerpt from an interview with Cliff, a black inmate at USP Lompoc, which illustrates the link between minority self-concept and delinquency:

"Darkness. I lived in a world of darkness. The ghetto, the slum," Cliff chanted, quietly. Born in Louisiana, Cliff and his family moved to Los Angeles when he was a boy. He spent 22 years in juvenile and adult prisons. While he talked about his youth, he became increasingly animated, spraying the air with tiny droplets of saliva. Then I remembered that Cliff had AIDS, a result of shooting drugs all his life. Cliff took out a scrapbook he had tucked away in his footlocker and showed me tattered and yellowed clippings from several Los Angeles newspapers about the "Pillowcase Bandit." Cliff was also a kidnaper, burglar, and convicted child molester. The Los Angeles district attorney once sought the death penalty for a crime Cliff had committed.

"I threw colored pillowcases at [bank] tellers and told them 'Fill 'em up!'" Cliff threw many pillowcases. He robbed 16 banks. He was convicted on just three counts of armed bank robbery, even though he had committed seven armed bank jobs, he said. Cliff was one of the eight children his mother had with five different men.

"I went to school and never learned how to read or write, and went through 10th grade. In those days, they passed you on age, no matter how dumb you were. I felt inferior, I felt ugly. Before 1965, blacks were considered ugly, so I imposed myself on people. I couldn't read so I didn't know what existed in the world, except the slum. I started stealing cars and joined a gang so I could be recognized. If you were a pimp, a dealer, or a drug addict you were somebody. You were recognized. I did all the things that couldn't be done and never learned to do things right.

"I robbed, raped, shot, stabbed, kicked, and bit. I did every indecent thing that was conceivable to the mind of man. Robbery, deceit—little mindless darkness. So I fiddled and fumbled through life.

"I wanted to be a real professional criminal. I told the judge, 'I been trying to beat you for 25 years.' John Dillinger was my ideal. The pimps and the dealers were my ideals. These were the people I loved. They gave me a feeling of being somebody. The judge said, 'It's a shame that a man of your caliber became a criminal.' It is a shame. But I took an oath that I was going to be a criminal.

"Caesar White was my best friend. He came from a Catholic house. He had a mother and father in the house. They were trying to teach him discipline. My mother didn't do nothing; she was used to it.

"We made a bet when we were children, who would outlive who. We bet a dollar. I met Caesar in fifth grade. We were together every day until he died. He got killed. A guy shot him at a party. Shot him in the heart. He was real beautiful, real beautiful. In 1968, Caesar got killed. My son's mother came up to visit [when Cliff was in state prison, just after it happened]. 'Caesar White is dead,' she said.

"I went to prison, I couldn't read or write. I couldn't spell *what, when,* or *why.* I went to prison [the first time] for kidnaping, rape, oral copulation, robbery, burglary, and for violating a 13-year-old girl. She was a week from being 14. She looked every bit of 18 or 19. Two weeks later, I got arrested, and I found out. For 22 years, I've had to live with being a pervert. She was white, so it was all fun 'n games [in court]. Ya know what I mean, Mark?

"I went to Folsom prison for five years, four months, on a five-year–to–life sentence [for that crime], and my partner was sentenced to CYA." Then he served seven years at Soledad—another soul on ice. "I learned to read and write in prison. I became a Black Muslim, and in those days, it signified cleanliness, uprightness, and that the white people was the devil. A guy would get up on the podium: 'The white man's the devil. The white man made you a slave, he made you a pimp.' I wanted something to believe in, so I joined the Muslims.

"I talked to my sister today for the first time in five years. I talked to my mother for the first time since 1983. I moved my safe to my mother's house, and I came up missing things. I told my mother that if I get out, I'm going to kill my stepfather and my brother. My grandmother was fair. If I gave her something to hold, I could go back 10 years later, 3 years later, or 10 minutes later, and it would still be there.

"If they parole me, I'd live with my son. I want to die with my family around me. The [parole] board can't give me freedom. I gave me freedom. The board can fix it so it can be more convenient to my family, but I gave myself freedom. I got seven brothers I don't know.

"I want to live with my family and die peacefully, not like I used to want to go out in a blaze of gun fire! I'm retired from my crime. Let the record show that I've officially retired from crime. From that day to this day, I tried to do things to change myself. It was hard in the beginning.

"In the dirty glass [his metaphor for life], I had all these hangups, all the dirt, garbage, dope. You got to empty it out. I got rid of the lies, the snorting, the masturbation, the homosexuals. I got rid of all those things that made me Cliff, that dirtied the glass for 37 years. I scrubbed out hate, madness, deceit, frustration. I scrubbed out all those things that made it a dirty glass."

Delinquent Groups to Street Gangs

These ethnographic observations and interview data show that all my informants were motivated to band together with other rejected and neglected children to form groups of similar boys.[35] Some boys hung around with just one or two others, while many found themselves among dozens of preteenage and early teenage boys on the street.

These groups shared behavioral, social, and cognitive characteristics. The quality of social interactions, patterns of behavior and

styles of decision making, and perceptions and interpretations typi-
fying these groups rested squarely on boys' low self-control and low
mental health. Depression and gnawing feelings of low mental
health were assuaged by the temporary excitement of the ritual process of deviant behavior (planning, acting, fleeing, and talking about
it)[36] and the numbing high of drugs and alcohol.[37]

Social relations were a series of instrumental (practical) or symbolic (nonpractical) negotiations, with little personal closeness
shown in forming long-lasting "friendships"[38] or in topics of natural
conversation. Boys' street talk is dominated by group jargon and
molded by speech proscriptions, and consists of mundane argu-
ments over money and discussions about crime and money and
purchasing goods (cars, stereos), but its distinctive features are verbal dueling, ritualized insults, verbal displays of daring, courage,
and male prowess.[39]

Verbal insults are involved in numerous teenage interactions:
jeers about former school peers and teachers and other street boys'
lack of fighting ability and sexual preferences; stories about "the
neighborhood" and its defense from outsiders; tales about "con-
quering" and propositioning young women and personal sexual
prowess; adventures about getting drunk and high on drugs; tales
about family members' (fathers, brothers, cousins) skill at theft,
fighting, "gang banging" (gang fighting), drug selling, and doing
time; predictions about making big money; and, of course, lore
about the thrill induced by committing petty crimes and eluding
capture by police.

What these boys don't talk about is revealing. Absent are conversations about the actual social and material conditions of their lives,
the circumstances that ethnography can uncover: parents' substance
abuse; natal household hunger, violence, and poverty; parents' illiteracy and joblessness; boys' substance addiction; boys' lack of education; boys' absence of medical and dental care and their suffering
and embarrassment from a mouthful of rotten teeth; boys' fear of
dying in a cellblock knife fight or in a shooting on the street. Ritual
street speech disguises the vulnerability of fearful boys by transforming them into courageous, fearless, brave street warriors. Adult
street hustlers express this verbal tradition as well.

These boys' socioemotional life is often out of control, and the
street offers numerous opportunities to commit deviant acts.[40] They
have little control over their own feelings, emotions, and behavior,

and there's no one on the street restraining them. They become truants and shoplifters and vandals; they fight with peers and teachers; and soon they become teenage drug addicts and alcoholics.[41]

Over months and years these boys' feelings of aggression and depression, displays of deviant behavior and substance abuse, and the inability to conform to social rules increase the social distance between them and conventional institutions—church, school, athletic teams, and the lawful socioeconomic world[42]—and their willingness to behave in deviant ways persists,[43] maintained by this social distance. Deviance becomes a group norm for these boys,[44] and a life trajectory acted out on the margins of society is set in motion.

I have argued that delinquent groups are a predictable extension of distorted socioemotional processes that characterize gang members' family cultures. Neglected and rejected at home, youngsters find little solace among school peers, who also neglect, reject, and isolate them. These rejected elementary school boys are too aggressive and socially and verbally inept to blend well with peer playgroups and to accommodate the academic demands of teachers. These boys know they are disliked, which further heightens their fear of rejection. To compensate they walk away from school peers and schoolroom activities, withdrawing to the neighborhood streets among children like themselves. These children stay within familiar neighborhoods, near places, people, and things they have seen since they were toddlers on the sidewalks.

The group behavior of rejected children follows the internal social processes that typify children's school playgroups. Boys and girls tacitly classify themselves into those who are rejected, neglected, accepted, aggressive, unpopular, disliked and liked, and so on. Like the groups they left behind at school, rejected boys and girls adopt the equivalent of distinctive school clothing and colors, the insignia of membership.[45] Members learn group cheers, rhymes, and folklore, wear group clothing, engage in rites of passage and intensification, uphold communal values (like school children's loyalty to their school), and they give themselves a name.[46] Now the delinquent group has become a gang.

The labeling process is the distinctive feature that separates delinquent groups from street gangs. All my informants had committed juvenile offenses with one or several crime companions; however, in instances like these, the informants did not have a name for their group. Those informants who were gang members belonged to named groups. A name brings pride, identity, and focus to the group, as it does to school athletic teams, and is the sine qua non of collective identity and action.

The expressive culture, that is, the style and feeling of social inter-actions within gangs or groups of rejected boys, is different from that of former schoolmates. The affective tone, order, coherence, and stability depend on the personal qualities of the members of these groups.[47] Gangs and delinquent groups are composed of aggressive, fearful, angry children who don't return home at night to the comfort of their parents.

These juvenile groups aren't based on positive values;[48] they exist for the sake of survival. Youngsters face real dangers. Major urban centers have predators, wild-eyed men and women and boys and girls, with semiautomatic and automatic weapons, who kill people without giving it a second thought. There are male sexual predators who entice teenage boys into sex for money, reward them with drugs, and then force them to work as prostitutes. Starvation and illness face these boys every day. In the winter, frigid weather can be life-threatening. Where on an urban street might a rejected and neglected, lonely young boy find safety except in a gang?

Expressive Culture

Gang life has two distinct components. Its instrumental culture is devoted to the purely practical activities of crime and gives rise to "tips" and "cliques" (see page 124) and neighborhood sub-rosa economies.[49] Unlike boys in Cub Scouts, gang boys have to worry about where they'll sleep, get food, and find protection from other gangs.

Expressive culture is ordered by symbolic dualism: Strength versus Weakness, In versus Out, Honor versus Dishonor, Life (Play) versus Death, with the last one being its overarching theme. It is this symbolic dualism that distinguishes the expressive culture of delinquent groups from gangs.

Gang social life has a playful side, where just the utterance of words and acts of boys feigning toughness bring them pleasure. Gang boys' banter, outlandish clothing styles, folkloric traditions and storytelling, verbal dueling, boasting, and youthful irrespon-sibility and overindulgence are boys' play. These things should be expected. After all, gang boys are just teenagers, and adolescent forms of expression like these happen in every high school in America.

However, there is also a dark side preoccupied with "loyalty or death," violence, and warfare. Gang boys share a mythology of death, tales of fallen warriors who are exalted and extolled, a symbolic land where killing brings dishonor for the enemy and honor for the dead, and where the reality of daily life involves ever-present blood, pain, and sorrow.

Mediating between play and death are gang boys' instrumental common crimes. Stealing, fistfighting, driving while intoxicated or without a license, burglary, car thefts, disorderly conduct, drug selling, among others, are just teenagers' crimes, acts of delinquent boys or boys just temporarily breaking the rules. If they can avoid arrest (the dark side) these boys are pronounced the winner in the game of "hide-and-seek" on the street.

Social Networks and Symbolism

The social network structure of a gang affects its expressive culture. Social networks exhibit strength called density.[50] In a high density network, members share mutual connections. If ego (a given person) is connected to alter (a person with whom ego interacts), then ego will automatically be connected to alter's companions. In the absence of alter, ego can connect to alter's companions. This network is balanced, or symmetrical, and is composed of numerous strong ties, with members sharing interests, an outlook on the world, and vocations, among other similar things. On the other hand, in a low-density network composed of weak network ties ego is unable to contact alter's companions. Eventually ego's ties become focused in the network among only a few alters who don't have access to each other's alters. That is, ego and his alters will, even in their own network, become isolated.

Klein notes that gang members come together out of necessity, know little about each other, including the others' surnames, and share a history of poverty and disturbed families.[51] This was surely the case in my study. These gang youngsters knew little about each other; no one knew his companions' surnames or even the slightest information about family history.

The significant finding of my social network perspective on gangs in Seattle is that gang members have relatively few daily companions and share few aspects of personal life. Boys use street tags as prison inmates do, and like prisoners, boys don't know their companions' surnames.

In natural conversations they don't use the term *friend,* preferring the symbolic classifiers *homeboy, partner,* and *road dog.* Gang boys do, however, borrow the term *friend* as it's used by non–gang members and substitute it for a specific street classification. In street talk the term *friend* is a generic label denoting anyone with whom one has social relations. It doesn't have the same connotation that the term *friend* has in middle-class vocabularies. Even in a gang, boys are alone.*

Gang networks are low density and involve weak social ties.[52] These two factors have three effects: (1) A gang network isn't an even matrix that allows for information flow and will not be an effective entity for collective action.[53] Although gangs do respond to external pressure and threats of violence,[54] these collective social responses are temporary. (2) Unbalanced social ties allow a gang's social fabric to become a patchwork of subnetworks (tips, cliques).

---

*Numerous scholars have explored delinquents' and adult criminals' social ties, but scholars rarely approach this research with an emic methodology (Spradley 1970 is an exception; see also Hill and Mannheim 1992). Rather, researchers have just assumed that a street criminal's social world is labeled, perceived, and conceptualized in the same ways their own social world is. This conceptual error leads to faulty conclusions about the nature of social life among adolescent gang members and adult street criminals.

Kandel and Davies (1991) use the denotative terms *friend* and *family* for social affiliation, and the connotative term *friendship* for the social concept, but don't define these terms as etic or emic concepts. Adler (1993:173) uses *friendship,* but doesn't offer emic or etic definitions. Fagan (1989:658; see also Keiser 1969) uses *good friend* and *family* to investigate social processes of gang membership, but doesn't give emic or etic definitions. Winfree and colleagues (1994:237) asked gang members to identify their "best friends," but don't offer an emic or etic definition.

Inciardi, Horowitz, and Pottieger (1993:158) asked subjects to discuss their "three best friends," but don't give emic or etic definitions for *friend* or *best friend.* These last authors do suggest (pp. 159–160), however, that the criterion used to distinguish the terms *friend* and *best friend* is the duration of social contact (that is, subjects distinguish friends from best friends by how long they've known these people). But on the street, duration of social contact has little to do with the presence or absence of emotional attachment or the degree of emotional attachment if one exists.

Lexical items have a culture-specific character. My informants on the street and in prison and jail never use in natural conversations the conventional lexical items *friend, best friend,* or *family;* nor do they borrow similar terms from straight culture for use in their street speech.

Weak social ties also allow for members to exit the gang as well as to recompose tip and clique alliances frequently.[55] (3) Marginal members or members who wish to exit the group can walk away.[56]

Assessing the strength of social networks and subnetworks using just ethnographic data (interviews and observations), without support from social network instruments, can be difficult. However, watching and listening to network members can provide a fairly accurate qualitative measure. I kept track of who talked to whom, counted the number of times people saw each other, and tracked conversation topics. These things also gave me clues about interpersonal intimacy.

An excellent indicator of network strength and substructure is how people find out about events and hear information about drugs, cops, undercover detectives, and welfare women, among other topics. Information is a matter of survival, and is called protection by some informants. By tracking information flow and the flow of exchanged goods (drugs, stolen property), an ethnographer can ascertain the membership in subnetworks. Money is rarely exchanged however, and has symbolic value in that it is believed to be in limited supply. I could not determine the total amount of cash in the possession of a gang's members. I never saw a gang member or adult hustler make a cash loan.

Gang vocabulary classifies its members into social categories using terms, or symbolic classifiers, that denote strength of the social tie to the gang. These terms are, in effect, a gang's emic sociometric map of subnetworks and cultural geography. All terms used by gang members are shared by all adult street hustlers, but the emotional significance of symbolic dualisms (In/Out, Honor/Dishonor, Strength/Weakness, Life/Death) is far less for adults than for adolescents. All speech has idiosyncratic, geographic, social, and subcultural dialect variations, and vocabulary is subject to diffusion across social class. Street speech is no different. The terms and definitions I use here are gang specific. I didn't investigate their historical or folk etymologies.

My informants who were gang members didn't recognize "the gang" as a social entity.[57] In day-to-day conversations, gang boys don't talk about the gang or refer to themselves as gang members.

"Were you in a gang when you were a kid, Wolf Man?" I asked. Wolf Man just stared at me. His face was blank. I repeated the question. Wolf Man shook his head side to side, as if to show his disbelief. I changed the question. "Were you real close to anybody in the gang?"

"Man, it wasn't no gang," he exclaimed. "A gang, man, we didn't have no gang."

"What do you call it?"

He didn't answer right away. Then he said, "It's the neighborhood, man, the neighborhood, you know, the set."

A gang's physical boundary is its "'hood" (neighborhood), and its social boundary is the "set." A personal network is sorted from nongang neighbors and everyone outside the 'hood by the term *homeboy* (diminutives: *homey, homes*). A set has no daily function and is the unit of collective action.

Sets compose gangs. In Seattle, the Rollin' 60s Crip gang occupies just one block; in this case, the set and the gang are coterminous. But in Los Angeles, there are hundreds of Crip sets, with gang membership in the tens of thousands.

Twin is a Hoover Crip. He explained, "Hoover Crips, yeah. De nine sets. Hoover and 43rd, 52nd, 59th, 74th, 83rd, 93rd, 104th, 107th, 112th. There's about 200 motherfuckers at each corner, plus dudes in the joint. Na' how da fuck am I suppose' to know dem dudes?"

Set recruiting ensures that potential members are similar to current members. As a member of the 59th Hoover Crip set, Twin hung around older members in his neighborhood set while he was growing up, before he was courted in.

A set has a vital connecting function. Set membership in one city offers access to a 'hood controlled by the same set in another city. But there is no guarantee, since Crip sets are often feuding; it is said that Blood sets don't feud. Twin gained access to the Crip set in the CD, just a few months before I did in 1988, through T-Bone, by asserting a common set affiliation in south-central Los Angeles. It is interesting, however, that T-Bone is a Rollin' 60s Crip whose set is often at war with Hoover Crips. But since they shared a desire to sell drugs and make money, the interset animosity ended.[58]

Sets provide opportunities for boys to develop personal relationships. Some homeys become partners and road dogs, and partners and road dogs merge into tips and cliques. Tips consist of a few men with a specific economic purpose. Tips don't have a social hierarchy, and if there is leadership, it's consensual. A clique is a group with a long-range plan for a specific purpose. A clique is larger than a tip, has a socioeconomic and political hierarchy, and forms to sell drugs.[59] Most significant among all social ties for gang members is the subnetwork road dog, which is the strongest social tie on the street.[60] Every boy I knew on the street, and most adult hustlers too, had at least one road dog.

My informants distinguished homeboys from road dogs. Twin explained, "About five dudes in the set that I really trust. I be hanging around with 'em ever since I was growing up. Ten or 11, and older. I had five road dogs; they're tighter than homeboys. I was in camp [CYA juvenile work camps] with some of 'em. State prison with 'em too. It's more funner to do prison time with road dogs. You know homeys inside from the street. But you still have enemies on the yard from the street. Got to be careful."

Body Count and Vamp were Twin's road dogs.* Popcorn had two road dogs in junior high school with whom he continued to hang out through high school. CJ is now his road dog. Miss Ann and Cuzz are road dogs, sharing a syringe of heroin at least once a day. Junior, Wolf Man's son, has two road dogs, Smiley and Wino. Wolf Man distinguishes homeys from *homeys* (with the emphasized form signifying road dogs). He had two road dogs on the street, Gilberto and Carlos, who were his fighting and crime companions. T-Bone is about 10 years older than all teenage Crips, and doesn't have a neighborhood road dog, but then again he didn't need one; he controlled cocaine trafficking and everyone worked for him. His road dogs were still residing in Los Angeles. T-Cool had no road dogs.

Next to road dogs, partners are the most significant social tie. Benny and Hawk hustle together and are partners.† Itch and School Yard are partners. David forms a partnership, on occasion, with two former penitentiary inmates. T-Cool has a partner now and then. He doesn't trust anyone.

---

*Fagan (1989:642) writes that "gang members were solicited in groups" for interviews as a variation of standard snowball sampling. Twin, Vamp, and Body Count were a cohort that acted together even during interviews. It took weeks before Twin felt comfortable enough to be interviewed alone.

†Two years after I finished this research, I gave a presentation on street gangs at the National Academy of Corrections in Longmont, Colorado. I talked about social networks and used Benny and Hawk as an example of partners. Afterward, an employee of the Washington State Department of Corrections told me that when he had visited his father, who resides in downtown Seattle, he looked out a window in his father's apartment and saw Benny and Hawk running their scam.

Pinto is the only informant who said he hung out with guys outside the set: "A couple older guys who'd been in prison. They was around 27. Ex-cons. I used to run with those guys. I was 12, maybe 13. Yeah, we was partners, man." These men were courting his sister Lupe, who was in her midteens.

Pinto developed a heroin addiction in his early teens and, with his two gang partners, he sold heroin. He said he stayed in an apartment near the beach, and had two houses and one trailer outside his neighborhood where he hid drugs, money, and weapons.

Homeboys, partners, and road dogs are functional ties. The day-to-day solidarity of a gang network is threatened by its own weak internal structure. Symbolic and economic exchange networks, rites of passage, founding mythology, warfare, folklore, group jargon, and death are expressive themes that help bind it together.

Symbolic Exchange

Loyalty and trust are symbolically exchanged and add group cohesion. An individual and a companion exchange trust; an individual and a gang exchange loyalty. Gang peers at least symbolically offer each other safety on the street and in jails and prisons, as well as opportunities to make money.* In return however, the gang expects members' loyalty. To ensure loyalty, symbolic threats are issued to members who wish to leave the gang, fail to comply with gang rules, or dishonor the gang.

Despite loyalty and trust, ethnographic and interview data show that gang networks do lose members when they go to jail and prison, are killed, die of drug overdoses, or move away from the neighborhood. Maintaining the value of membership is a vital issue to the perpetuation of the gang.[61] Gangs, like other groups, screen members, purporting to take just the bravest and most courageous boys who have the nerve and endurance to pass the rite of initiation. Once members, they are now responsible for maintaining the gang's size lest it fall prey to larger, stronger gangs. Exit rituals and folklore symbolically block the exit door.

Reciprocity operates with stunning accuracy. An addict or a former inmate might borrow cocaine or heroin for a personal habit or to resume drug selling. He may promise to repay his debt with

---

*Short (1990:3) notes, ". . . boys who join for 'protection' are often exposed to dangers that nongang boys are in a better position to avoid."

drugs or money. If he doesn't repay his debt, his exchange network quickly withers.

Reciprocity also has a symbolic dimension. Gifts are given in public contexts in full view of other gang members, community members, and outsiders in an overt attempt to boost prestige. Twin bragged about distributing drug money to relatives. "I took care o' everybody," he said. "[I] gave drug money to my mother. She was gettin' tookin' care of good. Everything was cool. She knew what was goin' on. I had my own place. She knew that I knew the consequences of the shit. She said, 'Be careful.'"

Economy Exchange

Loyalty, trust, and reciprocity combine with emic social classifications (road dogs, partners, and homeys) to yield the social and symbolic fabric underlying gangs' drug economy.

When gang boys weren't on the street in the Central District, groups of them, sometimes six to eight, shared a rundown, filthy, smelly apartment. I knew several young wannabes, 11- or 12-year-old boys, whose mothers were alcoholics and drug addicts, so they stayed with their (maternal) grandmother or aunts instead.

Black Gangster Disciples, ranging in age from about 13 to 17, rented a furnished, one-bedroom apartment, as other similar groups did elsewhere. The television always blared; the place was always filthy; there was never food in the refrigerator, but it was packed with quarts of beer. They smoked joints, drank, watched television, and listened to music. This is called partying. On occasion the partying became very loud and spilled onto the street in the front of the apartment house. Screaming, pushing-and-shoving matches between roommates, smashed beer bottles in the street, loud music playing at 2:00 in the morning always brought the local police. With order restored, police drove away.

Rollin' 60s stayed in an apartment building, using several apartments as drug houses where they prepared rocks of cocaine from flake cocaine and sold it through the front door. There was no furniture, just several battered, filthy mattresses tossed on the floor and the stench of urine so penetrating it nearly made my eyes water. When they heard from connections on the street that local police were going to bust them, they moved. If they could, gang members who sold drugs would rent all the apartments in a small apartment complex, live in two or three units, and set up rock houses in the others. Or they would rent a house and stay there for a few weeks and move on when they heard the police were going to raid them.

The rumors circulating in this network have two sources: paranoia, and the police. The Central District is a small community, and everyone knows when a drug house opens. Traffic flow increases down particular streets. The number of cars that stop for a moment as someone runs up to a door, looks up and down the street, knocks, hands something to a man at the front door, and runs away also increases. Drug sellers know that police know where they do business, because police tell street-corner drug sellers and gang members where new drug houses have opened. That, of course, increases drug sellers' paranoia. Drug house "half-life" is about a month, particularly when police are anxious to close down drug houses, as they were when I did this study.

Cops and drug sellers chase each other, block to block, house to house, until someone goes to jail. After this happens, drug houses open more slowly, and sites are selected off the beaten paths, but the pursuit continues.

When the police close a drug house, two or three gang members, a tip, invade public housing projects. In these projects, there are dozens of families and men the age of gang members, a lot of foot traffic, and no roads for police to cruise. A cocaine tip takes up temporary residence with children and their cocaine-addicted mothers. Gang members prey on drug-addicted welfare mothers, who spend an entire welfare check on rock cocaine sold by gang members sharing their apartment. As a courtesy these drug peddlers offer discounts for the rock cocaine or a few free rocks in return for the use of the woman's apartment.

This is high-risk behavior. A woman on public assistance in a public housing project would be evicted if authorities were to discover either drugs being sold from her apartment or gang members residing there. To avoid this, the gang boys just move.

Bepop, a teenage Crip, was "helping out da bitch" by giving her rock cocaine and buying food, diapers, and medicine for the children. But Bepop's claims about caring for children are "bullshit," declared T-Cool. "They all liars, man, you know what I'm saying? Dey move in, fuck her, eat her food, sell the drugs, party, roll out. Das all. They don' give a fuck if she get run outta dat ol' place. Shit." T-Cool had also done this when he was younger.

Gang boys in groups of 8 or 10 don't act together in any social event except partying. Tips pool their energy for low-skill crime, shoplifting, car theft, and rock selling.* Cash buys food, a temporary place to sleep, beer and tapes for the tape player, and perhaps an old car. Driving increases the risk of getting busted, since most gang members and hustlers have outstanding warrants and no one has a driver's license. A traffic stop will put everyone in the car in jail.† None of my informants, ranging from teenagers to middle-aged men, had official identification.

Wolf Man talked about a tip he belonged to in the 1960s and explained the link between tips and gangs.

I asked, "How about crimes? Would all gang members participate in a single crime?" It was a silly question as he saw it, but a good place for me to begin.

Wolf Man looked at me with a blank face, trying to understand my ridiculous question. "No, man, we didn't trip on that. Tips got into stuff. Tips were into run-of-the-mill stuff. Robberies. Drugs. Members of tips go about their own business."

There were many American Indian teenagers on the street who had run away from alcohol and violence on reservations and moved to urban areas. Many of these youngsters, as well as older American Indians, said they couldn't return to their reservations, where they had committed offenses so violent that if they were to return they would be subject to blood revenge. Their only choice, they said, was to stay on urban streets.

Some members firmly embedded in a gang structure form cliques.[62] Before Twin came to Seattle, he was busted several times for tip activities, car theft and burglaries, and did short bits in several California youth institutions. "Just camps, nothing serious." After he turned 18, Twin did prison time at Avenal prison (near

---

* In jails and prisons, inmates who share an interest in an athletic activity (handball, jogging, weight lifting) or who share a heroin habit may form a tip. In the latter case, a drug tip guarantees a supply of heroin (smuggled into the prison by the wife or girlfriend of a tip mate) and access to a syringe (a scarce commodity in a cellblock). The term *tip* is used by state prisoners in California to denote membership in a prison gang or street gang. Inmates say gang members are "tipped."

† Police know this, of course. They will follow a car conveying known gang members, and wait for the driver to violate a traffic regulation. Eventually the driver will run a stop sign, fail to use a turn signal or have a broken one, or block traffic when he stops the car for the boys to talk to girls walking down a street. From then on, its the cops' game, and gang boys often go to jail.

Fresno) and Donovan prison (near San Diego), as a member of a cocaine distribution clique. He explained that teenage gang boys follow the lead of the original gangsters, experienced adult men like T-Bone and T-Cool. "Dudes listen to OGs. Most of 'em's around 30, been in that shit [gang banging] for years, fuckin' with it since they was 10, 15 years old. Long-ass time. That the ol' days."

Twin had been a dealer in a cocaine clique in Los Angeles that had four levels.[63] The Colombians, whom Twin called the movers (importers), were at the top. Several Hoover Crip OGs, 25–30 years old, supplied the clique (suppliers) and negotiated the price, delivery details, and pick-up with the movers. Twin, Vamp, Body Count, and about a dozen other Hoover Crips were the dealers. They prepared it for sale and packaged it. At the bottom, a "pick-up" man delivered the rocks to 20–25 "workers" (teenage drug sellers) and picked up the workers' sales revenue, delivering cash to the dealers (networks for the distribution of rock cocaine are flexible and plentiful, and access to them is available on request).[64] Each worker was paid $2,000–$2,500 a week, said Twin; dealers and suppliers got the rest of the money.[65]

Twin's cliques lasted from 1985 to 1988. "In 1987, 1988, business slacked up. Police was really out then. Sales dropped to $20,000 a day for six workers." That's when Twin came to Seattle.

Founding Myths

Many Crips and Bloods in their late 20s and 30s say that these two gangs arose out of the Black Panthers. A law enforcement official in California said the Black Panthers were started by a white man.

Oni, a 14-year-old Seattle Blood, told me this origin tale. Before Crips and Bloods were different groups, boys hung around together on street corners and "free-lanced"; that is, they sold drugs on their own. Oni said the boys then began to fight among themselves over the right to sell drugs on particular corners. "So they all ran off the street in different directions and came back. Some of 'em had blue rags [bandannas] and some red. That's how it started."

Law enforcement officials tell tales about the Crips' origin, traditional rivalries, and gang colors. A California gang cop told me this tale, which I have paraphrased: Gregory Washington founded the

Crips in about 1969 after he had gathered teenagers together on the football field at Washington High School in south-central Los Angeles. The Crips' blue gang color was one of Washington High's school colors (blue and gold) (red was the color for the neighboring Centennial High School, which is where the Bloods started). Gregory Washington enjoyed Vincent Price's movie *Tales from the Crypt*, so he used the term *crypt* for the Crips. The traditional rivalry between Hoover Crips and Rollin' 60s Crips began after Hoover Crips killed Gregory Washington, a member of the Rollin' 60s.

Other law enforcement officials say that Tookie Williams, now on death row in California's San Quentin state prison, is the Crips' founder. Pimping Slim said Crips were organized and took their name from a crippled man ("a crip") from Chicago who went to Los Angeles in the 1960s and organized teenagers on the streets into gangs. Unrelated to Pimping Slim's origin tale, some California police say Washington was crippled, and when he was assaulted one day by teens who were later to become Bloods, he retaliated and beat his assailants. Washington purportedly said, "Not bad for a crip."

Yet another tale declares that Crips evolved from a neighborhood group, the Slausens.[66] Between the Slausens and the Crips was an intermediate stage, the Cribs (the terms *crib* and *home* are near synonyms in colloquial speech). It is unclear whether Cribs became Crips, or if Cribs were an off-shoot that disappeared.*

Original gangsters (OGs) are gang founders. They have folklore too, including tales about the days they were "coming up." TJ, an inmate at USP Lompoc, hung out with a high school group that became a Crip gang more than 20 years ago. His group was located not far from the campus of the University of Southern California. We met on July 4, 1989, standing in a line in Lompoc, each of us waiting to pick up a barbecued T-bone steak.

TJ is a handsome, strongly built black man who at that time looked to be in his late 30s, but was actually in his mid-40s. We talked, got along well; eventually I asked him if I could interview him. He agreed and later told me a little about his original gang

---

*Prison officials distinguish prison gangs from street gangs by the gang's point of origin. Prison gangs such as the Aryan Brotherhood, Mexican Mafia, and Texas Syndicate originated in prisons and now have members on the street. Conversely, most street gangs now have members in prison (see Daniels 1987; Fleisher 1989; and Jacobs 1977).

affiliation. He announced one day that it was the 20th anniversary of the Crips.

"Were you a Crip when you were comin' up?" I asked.

"Nah, we didn't have Crips back then. I was in the Van Ness Boys, out there on Exposition Ave and Martin Luther King Boulevard. I was in eighth grade, about 12 or 13 when I joined."

OG tales often stress how violent gangs are now. Red Dog told me about his teenage years in Los Angeles. "I was the leader of a gang. We stole sodas, stole donuts, hopped on trucks, and rode out of town. To go to juvenile hall was a big thing. You could lift weights and get big. You walked around with your back tilted, like you're tough. All those guys are dead. There's only a few still alive. We didn't kill each other. We went to school together. And after the dance, we fought each other. Fistfights, that's all."

Storytelling with Words and Signs

Street culture operates face-to-face. Storytelling (accounts of idiosyncratic incidents), folklore (street lore with common themes), and verbal dueling keep networks open, active, and vibrating with tales about money, drugs, women, and warfare.*

Gang speech involves ritual rhymes and sound proscriptions. Blood speech has sound rules. Bloods avoid uttering *k* sounds, as in words like *Crip*, or writing the letter *c*. In Blood graffiti, the term *block* is written with a diagonal slash through the *c* or without the *c*. Crip graffiti similarly distorts *block* as *blocc*.

In Blood speech, *Compton* become "Bompton," and *cigarette* is pronounced "bigarette." In Crip speech, *blue* is "flue." Piru Bloods, from Compton, also avoid *p* sounds in what might be called symbolically dangerous sound combinations, as in the name of the convenience store AM/PM. Bloods say PM stands for "Piru murderer." They call the store AM/CM: CM stands for "Crip murderer."

A Blood will say the name Crip means "cowards run in packs" or

---

*Storytelling is a significant cultural activity on the street and in jails and prisons. In this book, I have included several "action" tales told by 'Dre, David, and Paris, and "fantasy" tales with sexual and crime themes told by David. Storytellers often become emotionally involved in these tales, particularly when they've been drinking alcohol. In listening to and watching them, it seemed as if these men were reliving and once again experiencing the "thrills" of those incidents. As speculation only, it seems the pleasure hustlers and inmates obtain in recounting an exciting tale has an addictive quality and lets them (re)create and experience a thrilling chase, even if the actual incident didn't happen or happened with little excitement (see Katz 1988).

"crabs rest in peace." Ask a Crip about being called a CRAB, and he will say that CRAB means "Crips rushing all Bloods." Crips insult Bloods with the terms *SLOB* or *SNOOP*. Bloods say it means "super lopped out Bloods." Bloods also insult Crips by calling them E-rickets.

Gang exploits are published. *Teen Angel*, a magazine of limited distribution, published in Rialto, California, is dedicated to the public announcement of the activities of Hispanic gangs. The magazine publishes pictures of gang bangers' cars, group portraits of gang members, and individual photos of children "on their way up," some as young as three or four, dressed in gang clothes with their tags noted below their pictures. A common tag for the very young is Pee Wee.

There is nonverbal communication too. Seattle Crips and Bloods stand on opposite corners at Second and Pike. They "throw signs" (finger configurations conveying gang affiliation) back and forth. Downtown in tourist areas, Crips and Bloods don't shoot at each other as they do on rare occasions in the CD.

Gang clothing is distinctive too. Bloods and Crips wear baggy khaki pants slung low on their hips (this is called sagging) and a baggy shirt, sometimes wool, buttoned at the collar—an oppressive style in the Los Angeles summer. Their shoes are also revealing. Few Bloods ever wear British Knights sneakers; they say BK stands for "Blood killer." However, a Blood who does wear BKs says the initials stand for "bitch kickers." Bloods don't eat at Burger King either. But Crips do.

Sagging is functional. Handguns can be hidden in a boy's sagging pants. Prison inmates put knives in their underwear and conceal this with the baggy crotch of their trousers.

Warfare

Gang researchers have found that gang behavior is often violent, but that violence is infrequent and has literal and symbolic functions.[67] Violence, both in folktales and in fact, is gangs' most significant symbol. Violence heightens emotions, signaling a call to action, and serves as the occasion when gangs' symbolic dualisms (In versus Out, Strong versus Weak, Honor versus Dishonor, Life versus Death) coalesce.

Violence defines gangs' physical and social boundaries (In versus Out); it transforms boys into heroes or cowards (Strong versus

Weak; heroes become courageous warriors protecting the group and its honor, cowards become less-than-men); it brings Honor to victors and their gangs and Dishonor to cowards and weaklings; and, in an instant, it transmutes boys into dead heroes (Life versus Death) and neighbors into villains.

Significant in gang culture are physical, social, and emotional boundaries. A threat to gang viability comes with a loss of members, loss of internal social order,[68] and threats by outsiders.

Because gangs have a network of weak social ties, keeping members inside and nonmembers outside is an important issue. Should gang members develop social ties outside the neighborhood, they might move into those networks, leaving the gang with fewer members, weak defenses, and a poor reputation. It would then be moribund and an ineffective adaptive social unit.

Gang cultures are subject to forces of natural selection (differential death rates, differential membership rates) and use violence as a symbolic mechanism for internal cohesion, protection from outside threats, and social and physical boundary maintenance.

As previously noted, gangs denote a social boundary with the term *set* and a physical boundary with the term *neighborhood*. Often, these overlap, and the neighborhood corresponds to the set.* Graffiti marks the physical and social boundary, denoting it clearly and unambiguously for outsiders. Short points out that cars have disrupted the territorial dimensions of gang life, enabling members to reside in many places.[69] This would, of course, disrupt the correspondence between the neighborhood and the set.

The issue of boundary maintenance has a dominant place in gang folklore.[70] To ward off threats, gangs need warriors. Warfare mobilizes a gang, reinforces and stabilizes social status, and encourages group cohesion.[71] Violence makes (archetypal) heroes.

TJ explained, "Back then [gang life] wasn't like it is today. The Van Ness Boys were 16 strong. It was very rare to use knives or guns. Shit, today they use automatic weapons, Uzis, assault stuff, man. In the ol' days, we'd get it with chains, boards. Stomping was the thing then. We was fighting rival schools. It was a 'this-is-our-show [movie theater], no-outsiders-allowed' tip. I was in the diamond lane. That's the fast life."

---

* *Neighborhood* and *set* are culture-specific terms. Should non–gang members in a neighborhood be asked to define the neighborhood's boundaries, its demarcation may be different from what gang members would define as the boundaries.

T-Cool told me, "Teachers, mothers, or the DI [Marine Corps drill instructor] told me what to do, and I listened or they kicked my ass. Today, shit, today these kids, they don't do that. They don't give a fuck. They say, 'Fuck you!'

"When I was comin' up, gangs wouldn't allow you to kill another gang member. We'd fight, but not kill each other. Not today, man. They kill each other.

"Man, I don't believe how violent some of them motherfuckers are now. Them Hispanic gangs, man, they the wors'. The F-13s took a girl, I saw her body, man. They gang fucked her and put her body in lye. When the cops showed, there was nothing left of her but a ribbon. A fucking ribbon that was in her hair. That's cold, man. Real fucking cold."

Wolf Man added, "The guys who fought best were the leaders. Back then everything was on the respect for our neighborhood. We fought for our neighborhood. Wars, man. We got together with all the homeys when we went to war. You know which ones fight best, so you put your best fighters against best fighters in rival gangs." In gang jargon, the propensity of members to commit violent acts is clearly labeled. Gang talk has elaborated warrior ranks, stratifying them for special recognition.

"The real-deal Crips," says T-Cool, "their family was Crips. Original Crips started from their parents."

"What's a real-deal Crip?" I asked.

"They goes by their heart. Your craziness. All the real-deal ones are locked up. 'Blink your eye, you'll die.' That's a real-deal Crip. Main thing is your heart. If your heart pumps Kool Aid, you're a punk."

Real-deal Crips are also described with another term: "'N-sane [insane]. They are the craziest, most violent motherfuckers. They 'n-sane Crips," exclaims T-Cool. "Those dudes who do anything, killing, anything, they 'n-sane motherfuckers. 'N-sane. You know what I mean?"

Long Beach, California, has a Crip set called Nsane Crips. Several members have the letter *N* tattooed in mirror image on the outside of their left biceps. I asked one if all Nsane Crips are "'n-sane." He answered, "Nah, they just act that way to keep the real crazy 'n-sane motherfuckers away from 'em!"

Wolf Man said some gang members "half-step," others go "full-fledged."[72]

"You got homeys and you got *homeys*. Some of them will do

something; some won't. Sometimes I wish I didn't do anything. It's like you're damned if you do, damned if you don't. You can't be half-stepping, man. If you gonna be for real, you gotta get down, you gotta go. One time, man, I got a call from a dude to use my car for a robbery. He'd give me some money. I do it. I went full-fledged. I'm not going full-fledged like that anymore, homes. There was a time when I go full-fledged and go to the pen behind it. No more, man."

Real-deal and full-fledged boys protect a gang's outer boundary with violent acts or with talk about violent acts. It is significant to note that, within a gang's political structure, its leaders (sometimes called shotcallers by black gangs, *veteranos* by Hispanics) and warriors are distinctly marked and hold prestigious positions. In a gang's low-density network, with weak social ties, the mobilization for war of tens or hundreds of members is impossible, so warriors are protectors of the culture.

Warriors are few, but they are the carriers of gangs' radical values (endorsements for behavior). These values depend, in large part, on boys' predisposition, their temperament, personality, and mental state. Gangs facilitate the expression of radical values.[73] Gang folklore doesn't reward nonviolent behavior. Radical behavior finds its way into headlines, where it's amplified and mistaken for group norms.[74] Teenagers with a propensity for violence and aggression might easily become leaders in these weak social assemblages,[75] particularly if they display good verbal skills and charisma.

Boyish qualities of street play disappear when teenage boasting and victimless crimes become violent. Fistfighting, an honorable activity, revered in national and international competition, may become life threatening when fists are filled with knives, revolvers, and automatic weapons. Flying fists are abandoned in favor of flying bullets. Death signals victory.

Twin talked about gang violence: "Majority of time violence ain't about drugs. Most of the time it's about the set. Different sets don't get along with each other. Dudes ya hang wid get into it, you know. A argument lead to fighting or shooting. Sometimes the shooting comes right from the top. I lost 10 homeboys in '86, in '86, alone. Three of them was brothers. I didn't react to violence when I first seen it [as a child]. I didn't fear it, man. That's how this shit started, I guess, man.

"I was watching TV. The Geraldo [Rivera] show about drugs, gangs, violence. That be straight put-together shit! You got to be in there.

"A lot of killing going on behind broads. A dude going with this broad, and she get caught leaving a motel with some other dude. Some dude in my set seen 'em leaving the motel; he tell me, I go home get my thing [gun], and take care of it. I'd have to kill 'em."

Aggression as collective expressive behavior with charismatic leadership will solidify a gang.[76] Given the fearful and aggressive nature of gang members, violent and aggressive acts, or a threat of these acts, are a powerful emotional symbol that heightens social cohesion, at least temporarily.[77]

Rites of Passage

The family and gangs are threads woven into a social fabric of neighborhood life. "It's the way we live," said Ramon, a 65-year-old Hispanic grandfather and former gang member. "Our children have to face it, too."

Today's Hispanic gangs have a *pachuco* ancestry. Ramon did his teenage gang banging in Santa Barbara 50 years ago. He recalled his version of how Hispanic gangs originated in southern California in the early 1900s.[78] Ramon was a Zoot Suiter and so was his father, and a *pachuco* insignia, a tattooed cross placed on the middle finger of his left hand, denotes this affiliation. *Pachucos* arrived in southern California from Texas, 40–50 years ago, said Ramon.[79] The Maravilla, White Fence, and Keystone gangs have been in Hispanic communities in east Los Angeles for decades.

Rites of passage into gang culture in Hispanic communities are a family tradition when sons pass through the rituals of their fathers. In black communities too, gangs are traditional. Rites of passage reinforce gangs' principal symbolic dualisms. Like warfare, the initiation ritual calls attention to bravery, violence, group membership, and honor.

Cultural heritage and family dysfunction acting together are a powerful force.[80] Wolf Man said he had an alcoholic, overly strict stepfather whom he hated. He joined the V-13s, a Hispanic gang, in his early teens and now encourages his son, Junior, to join too. If Junior were to join, he wouldn't be a V-13 by virtue of Wolf Man's membership; he would have to cultivate his own gang network. Junior grew up in his father's neighborhood, which put him in close contact with the sons of his father's generation of V-13s.

Wolf Man was an absentee father whose criminal activity kept him in prison and on the run. He always refused to discuss his child-rearing philosophy. Junior wandered the same streets that his father had, at about the same age.[81]

Wolf Man brought me a copy of the September 22, 1988, issue of *Rolling Stone* magazine to show me a pictorial essay of the V-13s. We reviewed each photo, and he discussed each neighborhood scene and the relationships among the men, women, boys, and girls in each photo. Frankly, his matter-of-fact approach stunned me. I was taken aback by the photos of preteenage boys dressed in gang clothing. I showed my surprise.

"Why," I exclaimed in a judgmental way, "do parents let their sons join gangs?"

He reached into his left shirt pocket and took out a few photos of Junior posing alone, and of Junior and himself dressed in matching gang clothing. I felt foolish.

"When you going through those trips [gang involvement], you want your sons to be like you. Junior comes up here [to the penitentiary] and says to me, 'Smiley and Wino [two of Junior's homeboys] want me to get into their set.'"

I interrupted him. "You're not going to let Junior join a gang, are you, Wolf Man?" I insulted him.

Aggressively, but patiently, Wolf Man explained how he felt about Junior's involvement in gang life. "I'm his father, and I don't want to see him get hurt. When my kids were babies, man, and I was riding with them in the car, we'd cover them with a blanket so they wouldn't get hurt 'case anything jumped off.

"Man, the gang's the neighborhood. I counseled him about both sides, you know."

"But he can get hurt gang banging or even killed," I said.

"You can get killed anywhere, man. We talked about it and I said, 'The choice is yours. You got to decide yourself.'

"I said, 'Junior, remember the time I got down with those dudes?' [Wolf Man had beaten up three opposing gang members while his son watched.] Junior said, 'You were real bad, Dad.' I told him, 'Yeah, but you don't know what I went through [to learn how to fight that well].' I been able to keep up a good rep for being able to use my hands *real* good."

"Well, what did Junior decide to do?"

Wolf Man reached into his right shirt pocket and pulled out a recent photo of Junior. There stood Junior, his chest puffed out as far as the skinny chest of a teenager can be, dressed in a baggy khaki uniform, displaying his head band. Junior is a proud member of Smiley and Wino's set.[82]

Wilson and Herrnstein note, ". . . a parent with a criminal record rarely wishes his child to be a criminal also."[83] Wolf Man and Rosa had little buffering effect on Junior's desire to join the V-13s. Rosa ran with gangs too, married a gang member, and was in the heroin business. Once, when she and her son and two daughters visited Wolf Man, authorities apprehended Rosa trying to pass heroin to Wolf Man in the visiting room.

Recruiting occurs through recognized social ties. Hispanic gang culture has refined this notion with cultural rules for transforming a homophilous network into a system of age grades (subnetworks). Younger members are expected to become older members.[84] Intergenerational ties facilitate recruiting and provide social cohesion.

Wolf Man described age grades in the V-13s. "The young kids, man, they're the pee wees. They're not in school yet, still staying at home. In elementary school we had Juanitos, junior high Chicos, and high school Chucos. Girls, man, they had tips, too—Juanitas, Chicas, Chucas. Man, when they get old and they're on the street, then they are winos."

Gangs lose members, so recruiting is a vital issue. Gangs scrutinize nonmembers and at the same time encourage them to become affiliated as either members or closely linked nonmembers known as affiliates and wannabes.

Fear of aggression will force youngsters to join a gang.[85] But this decision is not rational; it is one made by a frightened child.[86] Twin said he was in the fifth grade, 9 or 10 years old, when he started hanging with the Hoover Crips.* "Yeah, I joined dem. Why? Shit! It was join 'em or be killed by 'em motherfuckers. You got nowhere to go. You got to stay on the set. Whatcha gonna do? You're in or you die." Folklore.

Blue, a Compton Crip, talked about being recruited: "Young boys jus' be hanging on the street with older guys, you know. Dis is wha' dey do every day. Guys they know. Cousins, sisters' boyfriends, shit like dat. You just can't walk in to them these days and hang around. They gotta know ya."

Then I asked Blue about the rite of passage. He explained: "You

---

*Hoover Crips have recently disassociated themselves from other Crip sets, and now refer to themselves as Hoover Criminals.

just tell 'em you want to get in. They seen ya, watch ya. If it's OK, they pick out somebody to fight. I fought three, four of 'em at once. In some I seen, they be tryin' to seriously hurt de motherfucker. Yeah."

"Is fighting the only thing you have to do to get in? Do dudes have to kill somebody?" I asked.

His reaction was predictable. He smiled a slight smile, leaned back a bit in his chair. "There's other ways in, too."

"You mean killing?" I responded.

"You know what I mean!"

"Does the fight that gets guys into a set have a name?"

"A name?"

"Yeah. What do you call that kind of fight?"

"When a dude do that, we say he courted in.

"When you were courted in, did you hurt the dudes you were fighting?"

"Yeah. I did all right, ya know. Yeah!" He smiled a winner's smile.

In Champaign, Illinois, according to gang folklore in November 1993, potential gang members must kill someone and from the victim cut off a bodypart and bring it to the group. Similar tales were popular in 1992 in the Kansas City metropolitan area. In the fall of 1992 folklore about a new gang initiation ritual spread throughout the United States among non–gang members in a matter of days. According to the rumor gang members were to drive at night with their car lights turned off, and when a passing car flashed its lights warning them, the gang boys would turn the car around, follow home the good samaritans, and kill them. One version of the tale had gang members killing just the elderly. Los Angeles County police received hundreds of phone calls about this initiation ritual. Apparently there were no "flashing light" killings, according to police there.

Once courted in, T-Cool said, it's hard to get out. "Rollin' 60s, motherfucker. Listen up here, man. If you not associated with a gang, you can't leave your house. They jump on you, man, take your lunch money. Those crazy motherfuckers beat your ass, man! I joined when I was 13. Back then the only thing I believed in was my colors. If he [another kid on the street] had the wrong color on, I'd say, 'Give me a gun, he got to die.'

"I was going to Manual Arts High School. It was a serious war zone. I hung with 'em there. I was getting into a lot of trouble with teachers, fighting, shit like that, ya know. The Watts riot was the first thing that scared me. That's when I started gang banging. Tough. Yeah! There was maybe 25 homeboys back then; now there's 10 or 12 still alive, and most of them are in prison. I was in a couple YA joints and state prisons. There ain't no way to get out, except to die, or if your family moves."

Gangs have members who drift in and out, depending on their needs.[87] Boys in Seattle sometimes "get tired," they said, of hanging out, so they stay away from the blocks where gangs usually hang out. T-Bone, a member of the Harvard Park 6-Deuce Brims, a Blood set in Kansas City, Missouri, was shot three times at age 16, and then decided to pull away from the set.

I asked T-Bone how he had done it, if there were "exit" rituals, or if he had faced the possibility of gang retaliation for leaving. T-Bone said he had just stopped "hanging out wid 'em" and didn't "go around 'em." He hadn't undergone an exit ritual, but many sets beat up exiting members, he said. Retaliation after leaving may occur, noted T-Bone, if "ya all went around dissing 'em. I see 'em, they tease me and shit like dat, but I can handle it." *

Decker notes that about 10 percent of his sample of St. Louis gang members said the only way to end gangs is to "smoke us all." An interviewer asked a Rollin' 60s member, "We couldn't give you guys jobs?" The gang member responded, "No, just smoke us."[88] Death, the ultimate exit ritual.

Drug use and its effects have become folklore too. Moore has found that young Hispanic gang members play peripheral roles in

---

*Boys who want to exit from some Los Angeles gangs, according to police, receive a beating from members and are chased whenever they are seen, and will be beaten again if caught. This ritual is called being beaten out. Peripheral members of Seattle gangs walk away without endangering their safety. Esbensen and Huizinga (1993) note that gang boys leave gangs after a year or two. Prison gangs (Mexican Mafia, La Nuestra Familia, Texas Syndicate, Mexicanemi, for example) have a "blood in, blood out" rule. Often members of these crime associations do kill former members, but not just because they want to exit. Always these marginal members have committed an act punishable by death, even if they were to remain in their own gang. Death penalty offenses include, but are not limited to: stealing drugs or drug money for personal use, testifying in open court against another member, failing to kill someone after being directed to do it, or betraying gang loyalty. For instance, a man could be an initiated member of the Mexican Mafia but sympathize with the Texas Syndicate and give its members free drugs and drug profits taken from the Mexican Mafia. In prison, the death penalty is meted out quickly.

drug distribution, with central roles going to older gang members, a structure similar to Twin's cocaine clique. Vigil's Hispanic gang members use alcohol and marijuana, but say heroin use betrays the gang and the neighborhood: an addict can't devote attention to the set and an addiction too.[89]

Every Hispanic informant I had in prison and jail, both gang members and nongang members, was a heroin addict. Most Hispanic prison gang informants had been, and still wanted to be, in the prison heroin business. The Mexican Mafia, La Nuestra Familia, Mexicanemi, and Texas Syndicate traffic in heroin, and most members are, in my experience, heroin addicts.

Nearly all Hispanic prison informants displayed arm tattoos of a gang insignia, an ideal lover (wife or girlfriend), and a heroin dragon, the three elements that structure a man's life.

This theme, the conflict between drug addiction and selling drugs, is heard in other ways. Seattle drug sellers said it's problematic to sell cocaine successfully and use it too. These activities are at odds with each other. Popcorn and other black cocaine and Hispanic heroin sellers in Seattle said a cocaine or heroin seller could "run his thing" with a heroin addiction, but "cocaine would bring 'em down." They also said cocaine is not addictive,[90] a contradiction to folklore (see chapter 5, "The Street").

Death

Gang territories in south-central Los Angeles have a "dead wall," a graffiti-covered wall honoring dead gang members. Names spray painted on the wall are assigned a label: RIP (rest in peace), BIP (blooding in peace), CIP (cripping in peace), or PIP (Piru in peace).* On walls in gang territories, graffiti denotes gangs at war, contracts issued for a killing, markings for gang neighborhoods; and names of gang members who've been murdered."[91]

Hispanic criminal organizations, such as the Mexican Mafia, La Nuestra Familia, and Texas Syndicate, as well as Crip and Blood groups, use *Teen Angel* to display the names of gang bangers who were killed and to announce murder contracts.

---

*A color photograph on the front page of the November 19, 1993, issue of the *Chicago Tribune* shows the gang jacket iconography of the Insane Cottage 75, a gang from Seventy-fifth Street and Cottage Grove Avenue, on the south side of Chicago. The set is sitting in a church, attending a funeral. Visible on the jackets is the inscription RIP.

There are gang death rhymes too. "Chitty Chitty Bang Bang" is a Piru Blood rhyme recited, they say, after killing a Crip. The tale is that Bloods, driving through a Crip neighborhood, stop when they see a Crip. Leaning out the window one says, "Hey cuzz, yo cuzz, come on, cuzz, come here." The Crip, without thinking about the danger, walks over to the car and is shot to death. The Bloods then sing,

> Chitty Chitty Bang Bang,
> It's all about that Crip thang.
> Hah, hah, fooled you.
> Undercover Piru!

Gang members' tags often connote death. I asked Body Count how he got his name. "When da shootin's ova', das what I do, coun' da bodies."

Funerals are the only events, according to Twin, Wolf Man, and others, at which all members of a gang gather together. Teenage gang members in the Kansas City metropolitan area purchase their own coffins, decorate them with gang graffiti, and pose inside the coffin for "death photographs."

Ethnography of "Staying on the Street"

A core theme in the life trajectories of all gang and non-gang boys on the street is mobility, as indicated by transitory residential patterns. Mobility begins in adolescence, sometimes before age 8 but always before age 14, when boys become episodically homeless: "homeless for a brief period because of circumstances such as the loss of a job, a house burned down, and abuse in the home."[92] Episodic homelessness keeps them out of abusive parents' reach.

Sometimes by their midteens but always by their early 20s, hustlers are literally homeless: they lack "a fixed, regular, and adequate nighttime residence [and rely on] a shelter for the homeless, [an] institution providing temporary residence, or a public or private place not ordinarily used for regular sleeping accommodations for humans."[93] This freedom of movement is an instrumental survival strategy in a deviant world.

Street survival requires two things. These boys must learn street culture and become embedded in the street's social networks. This has a paradoxical effect: It keeps them alive, but isolates them from the lawful world while they become increasingly dependent on street companions[94] and, eventually, on the criminal justice system for survival. They slide on a path from adolescent episodes of homelessness to juvenile institutions, adult jails and prisons, and in midlife to literal homelessness.

Knowledge of street culture is essential but not singularly sufficient to survive on the street. Men who stay on the street rely on each other with distinctive patterns of social organization.[95] I conducted a census among hustlers to determine with whom they had interacted and why, and found that hustlers in each age grade (teens, 20s, 30s, 40s, and so on) interact with other hustlers who share sociodemographic traits,[96] and form a homophilous network on the basis of criteria such as age, race and ethnicity, personal interests, addictions, and crime preferences.[97] Homophilous patterns of social ties among drug dealers and gang members have been noted by Adler for "Southwest County," by Decker for St. Louis, Missouri, and by Vigil for Los Angeles, California.[98]

Social ties in these teenage, as well as adult, hustler street networks are "weak." Granovetter (1973:1361) argues that social ties can vary significantly in strength: "Most intuitive notions of the 'strength' of an interpersonal tie should be satisfied by the following definition: the strength of a tie is a . . . combination of the amount of time, the emotional intensity, the intimacy (mutual confiding), and the reciprocal services which characterize the tie."[99] *

McPherson and colleagues note that the frequency of contact between ego (any given person) and alter (those with whom that person interacts) "is probably the most obvious measure of tie strength. The more often ego has contact with alter, the greater the amount of shared information . . . the greater the emotional bond. . . ."[100]

Laub and Sampson "emphasize the quality or strength of social

---

*In this study these criteria—contact, reciprocity, and intimacy—will be used to assess the strength of social ties. Contact refers to both frequency of face-to-face contact and duration of contact (people may see each other every day for a month, or every week for years, and so on); reciprocity denotes what people do for each other (middle-class neighbors may watch each other's house while on vacation; however, this example of reciprocity doesn't fit street culture, where people may take turns watching each other while they sleep in an alley); intimacy refers to how people feel about each other and the extent that they share personally intimate feelings, emotions, and thoughts (this never happened among my informants). The last criterion is used to distinguish weak social ties from all others.

ties. . . . marriage per se may not increase social control, but close emotional ties and mutual investment increase the social bond between individuals and, all else equal, should lead to a reduction in criminal behavior."[101] Their contention that social-tie strength affects the crime rate depends on culture-specific (ethnographic) definitions for these etic concepts. Insofar as personal predispositions and street culture's norms affect behavior, how do hustlers define (etic) concepts such as strength of social ties, marriage, closeness, emotional ties, mutual investment, and social bond? What social forms do these concepts have on the street?

School Yard, a youthful member of a teenage street gang, has an emic view of social closeness; he proclaimed: "People close to you are the ones who hurt you. I always keep my defense up. It's called cover your motha'fuckin' ass." All hustlers in this study share School Yard's opinion that closeness is dangerous.[102] This extreme defensiveness, an affective and cognitive effect of socialization, is the quintessential trait of a defensive worldview; it prevents the formation of strong social ties and further embeds street hustlers in a deviant world.

Hustlers see cognitive, social, and emotional protection in street cultures' weak social networks. Inside these networks they know many people, have frequent interactions involving drinking, hanging out, acting out impulsive crimes, and finding protection. Despite frequent interactions in the sharing of alcohol, drugs, and crime and its profits, hustlers don't express intimacy or confide fears or inner feelings to anyone. The street is a closed social world that allows hustlers to hide, shrouded by a culture that devalues intimacy and labels those who express feelings as weaklings (a well-reported tenet of prison inmate culture is not showing weakness).[103]

Weak social ties are an expression of boys' low mental health and low self-control. These boys on their own don't create social ties to non–gang members or nondelinquents,[104] nor do they build social capital,[105] except to bring themselves immediate practical gain. They don't have realistic future orientations,[106] nor do they care about others' feelings, except in regard to how these feelings might hurt them.

Embeddedness[107] in a homophilous network enables socially and economically expedient relationships, but it has a negative feedback on crime and poverty: it limits lawful economic choices;[108] separates adolescents, as well as adult hustlers, from lawful opportunities, which they don't want anyway;[109] and maintains weak social ties.[110] Under these conditions, a commitment to street culture and deviant behavior persists.[111]

Gangs: Definitions and Public Policy

Thrasher's definition of gangs includes these elements: a gang meets outside the home; has rules and definitions for membership; has a territorial base for group activity; has self-defined rights to occupy and use a territory; performs many activities; and has internal status and role differentiation.[112]

Klein proposes similar features. A gang recognizes itself as a group and is identified as one by others, usually denoted by a name, and draws a "negative response" from neighbors and law enforcement agencies because of the frequency of illegal activities.[113]

Cohen (1990:10) writes that when "criminologists speak of gangs, they usually are thinking of collectivities. Although the definitions they offer may emphasize size, organizational complexity, urban location, hierarchy, leadership, territory, and so on, I think the criterion they are operating with intuitively is collectivity, plus some propensity to disruptive, 'antisocial,' or criminal behavior."[114] Esbensen and Huizinga, following from Miller and Klein and Maxson, write that, "in order to be considered a gang, the group must be involved in illegal activity."[115]

By contrast, Short defines gangs as "groups whose members meet together with some regularity, over time, on the basis of group-defined criteria of membership and group-defined organization." Short also notes that his

> definition of gangs does not include delinquent behavior, since that typically is what we wish to explain. Nor does it include characteristics of dress, names, or types of organization, or any reference to most types of conventional behavior. . . . It is important to study all of these phenomena, how they vary between and within groups. We need to understand gang identity and behavior, and the reactions of others to gangs . . . and the *significance* of names, for gangs, and for others.[116]

My ethnographic experiences and interviews with teenage delinquents and gang members as well as adult former gang members and nongang delinquents have shaped my definition of *gang*, which captures a gang's core features and, following from Short,[117] doesn't include illegal activity as a distinguishing feature. A gang is a social group composed of adolescents who form a weak social network with intergenerational longevity: ego has natal or extended family relatives, or both, who were, or still are, gang members. A gang has a coherent expressive culture, which denotes the network's outer social boundary through various symbolic markers such as a distinctive name, origin tales, specialized vocabulary, and secular rituals and traditions. The unique distinguishing feature of a gang's expressive culture, as opposed to other types of adolescent symbolism, is its fatalistic ritualism predicated on a mythology of death.*

Crips, Bloods, and Black Gangster Disciples in Seattle each had about 50–75 members, membership numbers similar to Decker's St. Louis gangs. Just a few gang members, such as T-Bone, weren't native Seattle teenagers. These gangs show traits of Taylor's scavenger and territorial gangs, Fagan's Type I (social) gang and Type 2 (party) gang, Cloward and Ohlin's fighting and retreatist gangs, and Huff's informal, hedonistic, instrumental, and predatory gangs.[118]

My ethnographic data don't distinguish between gangs on the basis of criminal or predispositional criteria. Each gang had boys with similar predispositions for substance use, crime, and aggressive tendencies. Many teenagers had very poor verbal and social skills. Many were depressed. Many got high on alcohol, rock cocaine, and marijuana (hedonism); most committed petty offenses (shoplifting); some fought occasionally and hit their girlfriends (aggressiveness); some formed tips for car theft, rock selling, and burglary (instrumental economic networks); a few were noted by peers as highly assaultive and violent.

Fagan notes that, in addition to group rules, leadership structure, internal sanctions, initiation and exit rituals, among other traits, a gang is intergenerational; that is, it lasts more than one generation.[119] This point is distinctive, separating delinquent groups from neighborhood gangs.

Gangs do survive beyond their membership. Many generations of V-13s preceded Wolf Man, and now Junior will continue the tra-

---

*Scholars have noted the fleeting nature of criminals' interpersonal relations. Hirschi (1969:141) writes that deviants' social relations are "cold and brittle." Irwin (1970, 1985a:50) notes that criminals' networks disintegrate quickly and lack strong obligatory ties and emotional bonding (cf. Moore 1978).

dition. TJ was in an early generation of Crips, Pimping Slim was an original gangster, and Twin survives both of them.

These ethnographic and interview data show that gangs aren't perpetuated by an internal descent mechanism, a social rule of consanguineal membership, similar to a rule that forms lineages in non-Western, nonliterate societies.[120] Sons of gang members aren't members of their father's gangs by virtue of birth.

To explain the intergenerational character of gangs, I return to a predispositional argument. If rejected and neglected, children form ego's generation of gang members; then with similar socioemotional conditions in the conjugal families of ego's generation, a second generation emerges. Distorted families create children who are gangs' raw material. A son is molded by forces similar to those that molded his father.

Intervention might occur in a family if it weren't for exposure to distorted socioemotional forces in each generation. Neglectful parents, along with peers and teachers who reject disruptive children, don't provide a buffer from the ongoing effects of low mental health, low self-control, a defensive worldview, and neighborhood deterioration. These boys will inevitably find a place among others like themselves. Gangs' intergenerational character, despite long-standing cultural rationalizations, is the distinctive indicator of distorted family culture. Some cultural traditions signal a culture's destruction.

Gangs in Social Context

In this section, I offer some speculative remarks about gang formation and perpetuation that will lead to remarks about social policy and gangs.

Gangs are "minisocieties." As cultural entities they have a life of their own and soon become more than groups of children on street corners committing delinquent acts. They are complex metaphors. On the one hand, gangs symbolize members' predispositions and the cognitive and behavioral artifacts of poor socialization. On the other hand, they encapsulate a community's and neighborhood's history and become a mirror of the socioeconomic and politicolegal forces that have borne down on neighborhood families for decades from society's sociopolitical strata.[121]

Thrasher noted that gangs are connected by social disorganization and social instability, and things haven't improved in nearly 60 years. Shaw and McKay's research has recently been revisited, and numerous scholars have sought to understand the complex relationship between formal and informal social control, poverty, sociocultural heterogeneity, residential instability, and crime.[122]

These ethnographic and interview data suggest that economic conditions and the social degeneration of neighborhood cultures are conditional causes for delinquent groups and gangs. Most informants in this study are black Americans. It is clear from research in Afrocentrism[123] that heroin and cocaine use, illiteracy, violent behavior, gang membership, drive-by shootings, and personal irresponsibility aren't African-centered values and aren't socially accepted in the worldview of black communities.

Interview data show that alcoholism, drug dependence, crime, violence, and child neglect and abuse have dramatically deteriorated the nature of informal social control within families. Informants in this study displayed deviant behavior as youngsters, in some cases by age six, and were members of delinquent groups and gangs before community socioeconomic and political factors had a direct influence on them.[124] These ethnographic data suggest that substance abuse, street offending, motivation to join and participate in gangs, and violent behavior are direct results of disintegrated family socialization processes that have lasting effects in children's poor mental health and low self-control. Youngsters affected this way learn street life, and when they do, street culture offers self-serving rationalizations, justifications, and excuses for deviance. To some degree intrafamily disruption has weakened neighborhoods' informal social control.[125]

Gangs are a kinship-based community-level social phenomenon and are, after all, composed of neighborhood children with a small percentage filling "core" roles.[126] But street gangs seem to have a tacit relationship with communities and neighborhoods that have been disenfranchised by dominant society. From an etic perspective, gangs are a reification of intracommunity poverty and society's political and economic neglect.[127] From an emic point of view a latent function of gangs may be to provide communities and neighborhoods with a culturally specific way to act out feelings of extreme marginalization,[128] without condemning the community itself and blaming the victims.

In the way distorted family cultures endorse their own dysfunction either by not being conscious of it or by being conscious of it and ignoring it, cities and minority communities have ignored neighborhood gangs.[129] Now communities have begun to use street gangs as a primary local-level political pulpit and street violence as a bullhorn calling attention to neighborhood chaos.

The *New York Times* reports that the

> Los Angeles County Board of Supervisors has approved $2.9 million for a church-run program intended to deter youths from joining street gangs.
> . . . In addition to the county money, the city has pledged $2.5 million and the state $2 million for the program.
> The program was created last year by a coalition of community and religious leaders. . . . Cardinal Roger M. Mahony of the Roman Catholic Church is chairman. . . .
> The program will send teams of social workers, gang experts and teachers into some of the country's most troubled neighborhoods to help students and parents overcome family and social problems. . . .
> Critics of the program question spending public money on an untested program headed by religious leaders with little expertise in the field.
> Leaders of Hope in Youth say they will begin hiring and training workers with the aim of having them on the street by January.[130]

Neighborhoods in which informal social control mechanisms have deteriorated are left with a gaping hole in their social fabric.[131] This tear is filled by gangs acting as self-help groups.[132] Gangs' social relations take direct action to enforce and protect their members' own rights and have a self-proclaimed right to reprisal, blood revenge, and feuding.[133] Despite formal social control mechanisms,[134] gang members' low self-control determines the expressions of violent behavior.

A gang is a sociopolitical entity with informal legal duties and self-perceived rights and obligations. The political nature of gangs as self-help groups is apparent when feuding gangs symbolically unite for economic[135] or political purposes. An illustration of the political self-help dimension was the 1993 "Gang Summit" in Kansas City, Missouri, and Chicago, Illinois. This meeting of gang "leaders" drew the nation's attention to intergang violence and inner-city poverty, but most of all it drew attention to the summit leaders themselves.

In this public arena a symbolic transformation occurred: A few charismatic street-level gangsters assumed leadership roles[136] for several days, transforming them from warriors into street-level statesmen, administrators, and bureaucrats.[137] But when the television cameras were turned off, street-level statesmen once again became hoodlums. "Kansas City police found that some of the local summit participants soon returned to their gangbanging ways and police lock-ups."[138]

Perhaps Fagan's social and party gangs and Taylor's scavengers may progress into a complex economic and criminal organization, the next generation of the notorious Young Boys, Inc.,[139] with enduring charismatic leadership. Given the predispositions of gang boys themselves, the weak nature of the social ties among gang members and others, and the low density of the gang network, it seems highly unlikely that low-level gangs could evolve into complex groups even with charismatic leadership. Gangs, by their social and emotional nature, can never be armies.

Gangs emerge in neighborhoods characterized by socioeconomic and political conflict with dominant society.[140] All informants in my Census Bureau study said unequivocally that they and everyone they knew distrusted local, state, and federal government officials and disbelieved any government officials who discussed rebuilding inner-city ghettos and helping minorities find education, vocational training, and employment.[141] This distrust of government officials extended, of course, to all law enforcement officials (police, courts, attorneys, probation/parole officers).

Distrust and anger may provide a pro-active opportunity for developing a quasi-formal system of internal social control within high-crime neighborhoods. Effective community policing in these neighborhoods will be problematic unless targeted communities fully support outside intervention.[142] To do this, however, requires full awareness of how difficult it is to blend cultural styles of social control: anglocentric formal social control processes must be blended with Hispanic and black American neighborhoods' cultural norms and informal social control processes.

In coalition with outside law enforcement mechanisms, neighborhoods might develop "community courts," that is, a cultural blend of dispute mechanisms that use principles of anglocentric formal social control and familiar culture-specific social processes and styles of interpersonal interaction. A community court might be able to define guidelines for investigating neighborhood infractions, strategies to cope with young delinquent children, programs to assist families in need, and procedures to enforce community-based restrictions with emic sanctions.

Community policing should support and blend with, but not supplant, local-level social control initiatives. An outcome of a community court may be a reduction in conflict between anglocentric formal social control practices and informal culture-specific traditions in minority neighborhoods, mitigation of the destructive effects gangs have on neighborhood families and economies and the public's image of these neighborhoods and their people, and a sense of community restoration as the community regains informal social control in its neighborhoods.

Gang Definition to Gang Policy

The term *gang* is generic and has been used to label social groups ranging from a few delinquent boys hanging around street corners wearing the same athletic team jersey, to adult criminal organizations such as the Mafia, the Medellín and Cali drug cartels, white supremacist groups, and prison gangs (the Mexican Mafia, La Nuestra Familia). To develop effective anti-gang strategies, we must first be able to define target populations: 10–13-year-old gang boys can be diverted more easily from illegal street activity than adult criminals in their early 20s can be.

A street gang, as I've defined it, is altered in social composition and criminal activity by a social process that I call the gang cycle. Other researchers have classified gangs into different types rather than seeing *all* gangs as affected by the social dynamic of age-grade blending in a gang cycle.[143] Older teenage gang members return to home neighborhoods from juvenile detention; adult criminals who were once youthful gang bangers return to home neighborhoods too, from serving state and federal prison terms. These older gang boys and young adult criminals align with neighborhood teenage gang members who are on the street, and form a larger, potentially more dangerous street gang. Older gang boys and young adult criminals, now OGs, exploit teenage and preteenage gang boys as a way of expanding criminal activities; Twin's cocaine clique is an example. Young gang boys and gang girls caught in this network of adult criminal activity sell cocaine rocks on street corners and eventually are dragged into the criminal justice system as drug dealers and co-conspirators.

Age-grade blending may create very dangerous criminal street organizations too, if young-adult gang bangers doing prison sentences align with violent prison gangs. When these current prison gang members are released, they may return to home neighborhoods, where they were formerly teenage gang boys, with the purpose of escalating criminal activity. Prison gang members, such as those in the Mexican Mafia, are very violent. Wolf Man, once a teenage V-13, claimed a social-criminal connection to the Mexican Mafia. In June 1994, a confidential source in Kansas City, Missouri, said the Mexican Mafia is now trying to "organize" Hispanic street gang members in Kansas City, Kansas.[144]

The generic use of the term *gang* has confounded anti-gang policies and programs. To say that Chicago, New York, Los Angeles, Miami, Houston, Dallas, and Denver have gangs is the equivalent of saying these cities have baseball teams. But what does that tell us? Even the use of gang typologies has, to some degree, confused the gang policy efforts: a dozen early teenage delinquents who drink, use drugs, and occasionally fight are very different from a group of 25-year-old former inmates who have joined together to distribute cocaine.[145]

Policies should focus on the social process leading young boys and girls to the street (parental brutality and criminal activity) and on neighborhood age-grade blending, which escalates criminal involvement for youngsters.

Blended gangs are complex and likely to require different forms of intervention. Imagine, for instance, the complex intervention strategy necessary to hand the Eastside Freemont Hustlers, who control Freemont Avenue and Thirteenth Street in Kansas City, Missouri. According to G-Love and Sweet Pea, two female members, the set consists of about 100–150 members; I believe there are about two dozen. Some 5 percent are black, 35 percent Mexican, and 60 percent white; ages range from 12 to 22; there are five female members. G-Love and Sweet Pea said many males over 17 are either in jail awaiting felony trials or are "on the run" from Kansas City police. A few face murder and multiple murder charges. Most members of this set aren't killers, however. Rather they are chronic truants and school dropouts who drink high-alcohol-content malt liquors, smoke marijuana and "water" (Formalin cut with brake fluid or alcohol), and "cruise" other gangs' neighborhoods picking fights.

My definition of a gang suggests that family cultures must be altered. This will require more than just parenting classes. Family cultures are similar to any other culture and are composed of numerous complex interactions and functional components. Family social health depends in large part on economic health, and to recover neighborhood health will require reindustrializing and rebuilding inner-city neighborhoods. Realistically, this is not likely to happen. Billions of state and federal dollars are allocated to deterrence and incapacitation, rather than to inner-city development and early-life treatment for effects of abuse and neglect and for addiction to alcohol and other drugs, prevention of early-life involvement with crime and addiction, and diversion of children from gangs and illegal activity.

To explain the emergence of delinquent groups, I have made a predispositional argument: Boys attracted to delinquent groups share a predisposition for selected traits, such as social rejection, fear, low self-control, anger, and low levels of verbal and social skills. These traits typify delinquent groups and serve as the motivation for similar boys to join.

These social and emotional processes that alienate children from distorted families and push them away from schools and other conventional social systems are powerful. In 1993 in Los Angeles, about 1,200 gangs and between 100,000 and 150,000 gang members inhabited Los Angeles County.[146] In the California Youth Authority, there were 8,000 people, ranging in age from 13 to 25.[147] Kovnator said it's common to find boys in the Youth Authority whose fathers and grandfathers are or were in California adult institutions.

In its simplest social form, a gang is a group of children who have been abandoned by their families as well as society's adults in general, and who fend for themselves. They adopt the trappings of school-yard culture as a symbol of collective action as well as a personal and group identity. Most inner-city children don't join gangs, and gangs are a peripheral social phenomenon even in marginal neighborhoods.[148] However, insofar as gangs are likely to be composed of very angry youngsters prone to violent behavior,[149] gang expressive culture has become a target for political condemnation.*

The solution to problems posed by gangs requires two things. We must first know what a gang is and how it's formed.[150] Then we must decide how best to intervene. The former is complex but manageable, and numerous scholars have offered definitions and social theories that point policymakers in the right direction. But formulating social policy that adequately intervenes seems to be a serious problem.

If the predispositional argument is even partly correct, then these crime control policies must first address family abuse. While we do that, community programs must provide teenagers with a place to sleep, food to eat, an education, and support from the lawful community. We must be able to relocate gang boys. Leaving them in impoverished neighborhoods among distorted families and violent companions is a mistake. And we must find substitutes for the symbolic pleasures that gang association brings to delinquent boys.[151]

This ethnography reveals a fact about the implementation of crime control programs. To receive the benefits of remedial education and vocational training programs, drug counseling and psychological therapy, medical and dental care, among other services and programs, disenfranchised citizens—the impoverished men, women, and children of America—must go to jail or prison. To be effective for crime control, public programs must be implemented in places where the neediest people can access them, before they become delinquents, gang bangers, and prison inmates.

Gangs are a visual symbol of depraved families, of the painful family drama played out generation after generation, shrouded by tradition or ignored by society. Resolving the causes of delinquency will take the joint effort of schools, juvenile justice, and social services. Social service agencies and juvenile justice must act quickly, however, and be given the budget to do it.

---

*The 1993 anti-crime legislation before Congress included a provision to prosecute 13-year-olds as adults (Povich 1993). It seems that society has replaced the term *neglected child* with *violent gang member,* and as a consequence has begun to attack its children. This symbolic process is reminiscent of the 1943 Zoot Suit riots in Los Angeles, when the symbolic zoot suit "evoked only the picture of a breed of persons outside of the normative order, devoid of morals themselves and consequently not entitled to fair play and due process" (Turner and Surace 1965:220).

Recall that Wolf Man was incorrigible and a veteran of armed robbery by age 13. T., a teenage Blood in Kansas City, Missouri, became an alcoholic and marijuana addict at age 12, and by age 14 he resided in a drug house owned by his cousin and was a participant in many drive-by shootings. He said boys like himself were "wolves, urban wolves, you know, makin' it any way ya can." These wolves hunt in every city in America.

There are two courses of action. We can arrest all delinquents before they are 10 years old and imprison them forever. Or, by permanently removing children from brutal parents like Maniac, we can do something about the family abuse which eventually leads youngsters to gangs. Protecting children isn't just *a* solution to the problem of gangs and crime, it is the *most crucial* solution.

4

Sanctuaries

"'It's nice here,' [Red Hog] said by telephone from the Federal Correctional Institution at Terminal Island in Los Angeles. 'It's right on the ocean and the scenery's beautiful. You can look out and see the big ships go by.'"[1]

Red Hog is Dannie Martin's prison nickname. Red Hog was one of my informants at USP Lompoc,[2] and has recently become a published author.[3] He was paroled in the spring of 1993, soon got drunk and drove a car into a freeway abutment, and was returned to federal custody for violating the conditions of release.

Red Hog says prison isn't too bad: "'I rejected the work ethic. If you're lower-class and reject work, there's not much else except crime and prison.'"[4] Even Red Hog's editor at the *San Francisco Chronicle*, Peter Sussman, says Red Hog, an alcoholic and heroin addict, is "better off in the big house."

In this chapter, I discuss jail and prison life and its advantages over staying on the street. Data come from interviews with jail and federal and state prison inmates; many years of participant-observation research* as both a participating observer and an observing participant;[5] and full-time employment as a correctional programs specialist and executive administrator in two regions of the Federal Bureau of Prisons.

Street to Jail

From the sidewalks of Seattle, hustlers glide easily into the Seattle jail on weak social ties maintained on the street and sus-

*Some of the fieldwork data used in this chapter were gathered on and off between 1980 and 1987.

tained in jail.[6] These social ties are stepping stones for young adult gang members and adult hustlers who move from the outside to the inside, from the street to jail, jail to prison, prison to prison.

When hustlers go to jail, other hustlers are there too. Fact is, the social ties of the street are strengthened in jail because inmates' duration and frequency of contact increases.[7] There in a relatively stress-free environment even competing gang members forget their mutual street animosities. Bloods, Crips, and BGDs sit at tables 10 feet away from each other, talking and playing cards among themselves every day. Crips never sit on red chairs. Bloods never sit on blue chairs. BGDs sit on red or blue chairs, depending on their affiliation that day. There are no fights, and on occasion members of competing gangs talk to each other, although not often.

The day I met Popcorn he was detained and transported to the Seattle jail. The arresting police officers used the authority of an arrest warrant issued by the municipal court, for failure to appear. Popcorn had been arrested months earlier, a court date had been set for his minor offense, possession of stolen property, and he had been released on his own recognizance.

Jail is a revolving correctional door that slides open and closed in about the same way in every city. Offenders are arrested one minute, out on bail the next. In the United States among people arrested for felonies, only about 50 percent are prosecuted, and among these, 80 percent are convicted.[8]

Crime has a "bond" value, or price tag (the 1984 Comprehensive Crime Control Act allows a federal magistrate to deny bail for drug distributors, citing their threat to society). Rock selling on a street corner might have a bail bond value of $1,000, but selling rocks near a school will cost more, perhaps, as much as $3,000 (these are actual bail bond values used in a city in eastern Washington). Once a bond has been obtained, an offender can walk out of jail. But many don't.

Hustlers get arrested and choose to remain in jail, refusing to bail out. Some offenders get arrested for minor offenses, such as public drunkenness, spend a night in jail, and are then released by a magistrate who believes that the brief time the hustler has served satisfies the interest of the state in maintaining order. However, if an offender has been arrested for a serious crime and, in the opinion of a magistrate, poses a threat to the community, the offender will not be released unless he posts a bail bond, which will secure his appearance in court, or so it's hoped.

Popcorn could have bailed out for $160. Had he chosen to post a bond or pay cash he would have been issued another court date, and the process would have begun again. But he stayed in jail. "I wouldn't burden nobody like that," he commented. I pried. "I ain't got nobody, man. I'm out on my own, man. I been here alone all my life." Popcorn had no one to call, no one to help him. This is, for street hustlers, a common illustration of a weak social network.

To test the "weakness" of informants' social networks, I chose a crisis situation, an arrest, and I asked informants the same question, "Whom do you call when you get arrested?" Their responses weren't a surprise: no informant had anyone who would put up his or her own money or personal property to secure a bail bond for a companion or relative.

Irwin reports a bail account as an illustration of how jail stresses social ties:

> A young man who had been in jail for about a week told me that a group of friends had raised the money to pay a bail bondsman and that all he needed was a property owner to sign the bond. He gave me the name of an uncle who owned property, the name of a "close friend," and the phone number of a bar where the friend could be reached. . . . After several calls to the bar over a two-day period, I finally reached him, and he informed me that the group no longer had the money.[9]

Eventually, Irwin writes, the inmate's uncle bailed out his nephew, but the inmate's "friends" had lost interest. Irwin blames the friends' disinterest on a deterioration in inmates' social ties during imprisonment.

Informants don't have bail money, but they do have a rich collection of folklore about bail, stories always told as if they were true. Some jailed inmates said they keep bail money in a joint account with a trusted person—a lawyer, for instance, as Jason claimed. 'Dre said his grandmother held his bail money.

"Yeah, I figure it was a OK system, you know. Keep a few grand in an account downtown, call gramma when one-time come for me." 'Dre smiled, nodded, shook his head up and down.

"The motherfuckin' day come, man, and I was on the run. *Again!* Motherfuckers was chasin' me and my partner all *over* this motherfuckin' town. Burglary, man. They be gettin' tense 'bout that shit, you know.

"They be trackin' us like we Ted Bundy, man. I be thinkin' about this, man: they be gettin' me dis time and it back to Walla Walla [Washington State Penitentiary; 'Dre was then on parole].

"My partner drop me off up, see, up in Lynnwood [a community about 15 miles north of Seattle]. I be hidin' in one of them lots full o' vacation campers, you know, under a big motherfucker, man. You know, man, the kin' that block the road when you wanna get somewhere in a hurry. With some ol' white motherfucker drivin' wit' his ol' toothless bitch there next to him.

"I'm hidin', hidin' under there, pushin' up against a tire, wishin' I was home at my gramma's house. It was cold and rainy, be gettin' dark too, you know. That when I figure I get the fuck out from under this camper. In the dark, man, one-time never be seein' my black ass in the dark.

"I hear one-time cruisin' by, radio on. I know them motherfuckers is lookin' for my black ass. I could see them motherfuckin' bars down there at Walla Walla. Oh, shit! I don' give a motherfuckin' shit about goin' to that penitentiary; I was king of that motherfuckin' place before, I be king again. I don't want them fuckin' cops beatin' me, man. You know what I' sayin'?

"I pulled out my telephone, you know. I always carry a cellular phone when I'm out robbin' and shit, you know. You never know where you end up. Sometimes you don't have a quarter. The' don't be havin' 911 for criminals, man! Shit." 'Dre laughed, and he knew I liked his story. He was always a crowd pleaser.

"Call my gramma, figure she drive up here [she lived in the CD] and pick me up, and get me the fuck away from this mess.

"She say, 'I be right there, baby. Now don't you worry. Stay right there.' Shit! Where's I goin', man? Shit, a man of my stature shouldn't be doin' shit like this. Layin' under campers in the fuckin' rain. Cops be drivin' all around lookin' for me. I'm under there for fuckin' hours, man. Be gettin' colder, darker, colder, darker. All fuckin' afternoon I be under there. One-time driving around.

"Gramma never showed up, man.

"Why? Shit, I tell you why. She took all my fuckin' money, that why. I had a couple grand downtown, and she took it all.

"Nah, man, I don't say nothin' to her about it. It just the way it is here on the street. Easy come, easy go. You be killin' everybody who rip you off, you be killin' everybody and they be trackin' you' ass down like the motherfuckin' Green River killer or some mother-fuckin' bullshit like that. It ain't worth it. You lose money, you lose. You don't trust 'em next time. You don't trust nobody out here."

Hustlers say a reliable way to store bail money is to leave cash with a favorite bail bondsman. I heard street tales about "big time" criminals—burglars, fences of stolen property, large-scale drug distributors—who do this. I didn't see it happen. Tales like 'Dre's are the fantasies, the high-risk adventures, of street hustlers whose lives are usually dull.

Popcorn and other informants don't fight jail. It's good for "laying up" when hustling gets to be a hassle. "Giz ya chance to relax, you know," said Popcorn. 'Dre claimed that "jail's good for the rep." He assessed his reputation by counting the number of women who visit him in jail. "I get more pussy in here than on the street."

Jail, a Connection to Social Services

Irwin writes that the "jail is a location where the rabble life is not only controlled but compacted. . . . [It] socializes persons into deviant or outsider cultures. . . . jail disengage[s] people from the dominant society and embitter[s] them toward it."[10] My observations show that jails in urban areas and on American Indian reservations provide street people with vital resources, life-saving resources.[11]

Donnie, Paris, Slim, Popcorn, David, T-Cool, T-Bone, Twin, Vamp, Body Count, Itch, School Yard, 'Dre, and the others were marginal, disengaged people in society, and within their families, by age 12. As adults they are illiterate or semiliterate, unemployed, frequently homeless addicts whose economic alternatives have been reduced to a choice between committing property crime or selling drugs. Where else can these people get help as easily as they can in jail?

On American Indian reservations all over America, there are approximately 65 American Indian jails, so-called Indian Country jails. These are a vital, primary source of social, medical, and mental health services. I served on a curriculum workgroup at the American Indian Police Academy, Marana, Arizona; our mission was to develop a curriculum for training new American Indian detention officers for Indian Country jails (some detention officers are employed by a tribe's council, others are employees of the Bureau of Indian Affairs).

Nearly 100 percent of American Indians arrested on reservations have committed alcohol-related offenses.[12] In Indian Country the primary objective of jailing offenders is not detention. Some Indian Country jails don't even have operative locking devices. "If one of them leaves, I can be at his house before he gets home," said the police chief on a major Indian reservation in the West. Indian inmates are detained in reservation jails and screened for health needs. Some are released after regaining sobriety; others, however, desperately need medical attention and are referred to Indian Health Service hospitals.

Indian Country and urban jails have two sets of clients, the community and the inmates. The community is protected from street criminals, who are incapacitated before and after trial. And inmates receive access to cost-free medical and social services. True, the services offered in jail are also available outside; however, from offenders' perspectives, going to jail is the most direct way to get help.

In a study of 17 cities, 53 percent of males arrested in San Antonio and 82 percent arrested in San Diego tested positive for drugs; drug use rates were especially high for females arrested.[13] Jail rescued many of my informants.

Paris explained his situation: "I was smoking, smoking, smoking. My life was worthless. I wanted to die. The dope has did me like this. I wanted to die. I know my only hope was prison. 'I'm going to rob so many banks, these whities are going to stick so much dick in me, I'll never get out,' I says. The feds ain't to be fucked with."

Jamie, a kid about 23 years old, found help in jail. "I checked myself in. I walked in and said, 'You gotta help me. Get me off the street.' I was outta control out there. I was finding myself in bad places in the middle of the night, man. I knew I was gonna get killed if I didn't get help. Been here a few months, I feel good now. My ol' man freaked on coke, too."

In Broward County Jail in Fort Lauderdale, on a recent New Year's Eve, there was action on the "runway" (booking area). I was watching and talking to the runway officer, Deputy Dog, as his fellow officers called him. Dangling on a short chain hung around his thick muscular neck was a gold barbell pendant. Deputy Dog fingerprints, photographs, calms, cajoles, placates, and, on occasion, wrestles with folks fresh off the sheriff's wagon. These men and women are drunk and vomiting and barely able to stand; dazed on heroin and vomiting; tweeking or geeking; or angry and ready to fight. Deputy Dog looked as though he were having fun; he was the master of the runway.

Just a few minutes before midnight, a sheriff's van rolled up and deposited a horde of men and two boys, one 12, the other 14. They had been arrested for assault and for armed robbery with a sawed-off shotgun. Each one had a full rap sheet of serious offenses.

The orderly in the booking area was Pete, a Mariel Cuban brought to America in the Mariel boatlift. Booked seven months earlier, Pete had become a trustee, and was permitted to sweep and mop the runway. Pete shuffled around, holding a broom, but mostly he talked to Deputy Dog.

Pete slumped on a stool next to a bucket of dirty mop water. The mop handle leaned on the tile wall he rested against. He had just finished his dinner: chicken, Spanish rice, mixed vegetables, a roll, vanilla cake. Smoking a store-bought cigarette, and using his plastic foam dinner plate balanced on his right thigh as an ashtray, Pete confided in Deputy Dog: "I feel good now, you know. When I came in here, I was in bad shape. Strung out on coke, heroin. I was gonna die. Skinny, man, real skinny. I come here, been eating good. Sleeping, talking to a counselor. Think I can make it this time. Man, if they didn't bust me, I'd be dead."

Prison Life through Hustlers' Eyes

Primetime, a Hoover Crip in his early 20s, said, "Going to prison don't change nothin'. That be time for kickin' back, baby, layin' up in there. Chillin'. Know what I mean? Prison don't change *nothin'*, motha'fucker."

All my informants named someone on the street who had been to prison, as well as someone still doing time in a state or federal prison. A counselor at the Washington State Penitentiary and I walked together in the yard one morning. A young red-headed inmate in his early 20s approached us, bubbling with enthusiasm, a big smile creasing his face. He asked the counselor, " 'Member I was kin'a scared when I drove up?" The counselor nodded, and the inmate continued. "Man, this is great. I met my cousin. I didn't know he was here doin' time. And a couple of guys from home too. I'm gonna be all right. This is great!" He ran off.

Street hustlers said criminals would rather do a longer prison term than a short jail sentence.[14] 'Dre told a joke about doing time: "Dis Black motha'fucka', say 'bout 23, 24, stood befo' da judge, dat ol' motha'fucka'. Judge say, *'Boy,* the good folk o' dis here city don' want yow' ass on the streets no mo'. Hear dat, you little motherfucker?'"

'Dre had been speaking black street talk until now, but now he switched his style of speaking to his version of English as spoken by a white judge. Each word was slowly and precisely articulated: " 'I sentence you to two life sentences in the state penitentiary at Walla Walla, Washington.' "

'Dre switched back, and spoke as the man being sentenced: "Dat boy look up 'n say, 'Oh, yes, sir, judge, sir. Two life sentences. Oh, yes, sir, judge, sir. I do my bes', sir. I do my bes'. T'ank ya, sir. I likes it up in dere, sir."

'Dre continued in his own voice: "Shit. I be doin' three, four years at Walla Walla 'fore I do a year in that motherfucking joint [he pointed in the direction of the Seattle jail]. It be bad up in there, you know, man. Nothing to fuckin' do 'cept get into this tip or that tip and be getting in trouble all the fuckin' time, scamming for drugs 'n shit like that. It be too hard to have a good time up in that ol' jail. Now, in prison, that different.

"Yeah. You do more time, but you be gettin' a lot more action. Homeboys be in there wich'a. It all right.

"Nay, man. Ain't gonna be missin' me out here on the street. Anyway, man, sometime it good to go to prison for a few years, you know. Cops get to know guys like me who be gettin' into shit all the time. And they be hasslin' me every motherfuckin' day wantin' to bust me for every motherfuckin' thing. Dis way, I go 'way, chill wit' da brothers, you know, and they be forgettin' about me on the set. When I get out, I start fresh." He smiled.

A veteran prison psychologist with nearly 10 years experience, Dr. Joseph Kerman had an opinion: "While they're in prison, they say: 'Now I can relax, read books, lose weight, and let someone else do all the thinking.' When they're in prison, they take pride in it. They don't think they've done anything wrong, just gone too far. The risk is worth it, they say."

Prison isn't a risk that worries street hustlers. Things such as limited freedom, loss of privacy, violence, and variant sexual activity, which might frighten lawful citizens, don't frighten them. Popcorn talked about a loss of freedom. "If you ain't got no money, man, you may as well be in prison. You got all the worries out here. Food. Rent."

Sex

Sexual life for male street hustlers is concealed and difficult to investigate. A presentence investigation will rarely report an offender's sexual behavior as one of his characteristics unless he was previously arrested for a sex offense or is currently indicted for a sex crime. It would surely be awkward for a probation officer to question an offender's mother or grandmother about her son's or grandson's sexual preferences.

Numerous of my penitentiary informants had been arrested and convicted in their midteens for sexual offenses, such as forced anal or oral intercourse committed against preteenage and teenage girls and boys. Some penitentiary informants admitted teenage homosexual behavior (noncriminal offenses) on the street, and most informants who had had homosexual encounters on the street practiced homosexuality in prison, but some didn't. As adults these informants reported situational bisexuality: if they could have sex with a woman, they did; otherwise they would have sex with a man.

Street culture, as well as prison culture,[15] doesn't label these men homosexuals. Male street informants had sex with other male hustlers but weren't referred to by any hustlers as homosexuals, nor did they think of themselves that way. In street culture, homosexuals are male prostitutes ("raspberries"), men and adolescents who sell sexual favors to anonymous male nonhustlers on the street for cash or drugs, and men who hang out in gay bars. In bars patronized only by male hustlers, I saw men engaging in oral sex and mutual masturbation in full view of other patrons, who pretended not to see it.

Here is male hustlers' conceptualization of heterosexual sex. Strawberries and skeezers, who exchange sex with male hustlers for money or drugs or both, aren't labeled prostitutes. If a male hustler doesn't have money and won't relinquish drugs, his choice of heterosexual partners is limited to female winos, or bitches, as Popcorn calls them, who stay in missions and shelters or sleep on the street. T-Cool said, "There's too many good-lookin' strawberries around here ta fuck wid a dude or touch one of dem ol' ugly toothless bitches."

Male hustlers in this study had sexual liaisons with other male hustlers, but no one formed sexual unions that lasted even a few hours. Sex acts were quick, impersonal, and just as dispassionate as their other social relations. Male hustlers never say they have sex with men because they are unable to "get with a bitch." In prison, male-to-male sex and "dates" are consensual.

Violence

Informants perceive prison violence as less hazardous and less risky than street life. School Yard told me, "Man, ya get yo' ass killed out here on dis corna' a fuck of a lot fasta' dan ya can inside." Despite occasional violence, most informants said they find prison peaceful.

At age 16 Leo went to prison, and his life improved. "When I started getting into trouble, my father was real disappointed in me. He tried to help. But he didn't have much money for lawyers. My ol' man sold off part of the farm to get money to keep me out of the joint. My brother just went to state prison. He didn't even get a good lawyer.

"It's OK though, you know. Peace. I didn't get any peace until I went to prison. It was nice. I was 16 when I did my first [maximum security] time. It was real nice. I was in Stillwater [Minnesota]. I had to fight a couple o' times over the first six months, but that was it."

Just before 10:00 P.M., I was sitting in Paris' cell. The cellblock officer had just yelled, "Count, count!" It was time for all inmates in the penitentiary to be counted, one by one, cell by cell. Inmates who were wandering about the cellblock heard the announcement and moved slowly but deliberately toward their cells. If an inmate were outside his cell when the cell doors slammed shut, he would be given an incident report for "interfering with the count." An inmate in his late 20s stopped in front of Paris' cell, looked up at a companion standing on the cellblock's third tier and said, "Yeah, g'night man. See you in the morning." Peaceful words never heard on the street.

Social Connections inside Prison

Unlike street life, imprisonment enables a stable set of social ties to develop and be sustained for years. Durable and frequent social ties in prison focus inmates' social life in a small place, similar to neighborhood gang relations. But now these men are not youngsters; they are mature, often-violent prisoners who can organize the ranks well enough to enable collective action, namely, riots.

Over a number of years in an institution, inmates align themselves and form partnerships, cliques, and tips. They find road dogs and "row dogs."* Inmates redefine their social networks. Homeboys now include inmates whose residence is in ego's city, state, or coast area, namely, the West Coast and East Coast. Many informants at USP Lompoc said anyone who resides west of St. Louis is a West Coast homeboy.

Racial and ethnic animosities, once causes for street killing, are redefined too. It was common at USP Lompoc to see black, white, and Hispanic inmates walking together in the big yard, talking among themselves in the dining hall, or chatting while they walked the 110-yard main corridor of this maximum-security penitentiary. Inmates are required to live peacefully in a multiracial-multiethnic environment. Racial and ethnic segregation, self-imposed on the street, and street-gang animosities, once a cause to kill, are anathema in a well-managed prison.

Prison allows inmates to participate in activities missed on the street, such as vocational training and basic or higher education. Daily prison life exposes inmates to men and women staffers whose jobs are to educate, train, and counsel them. Inmate jobs put them in close contact with work supervisors, five days a week, eight hours a day.

Staff-inmate relationships develop too. It is common for work crew supervisors at USP Lompoc to volunteer support for a work crew inmate who has found himself in administrative detention for violating prison rules. I have known supervisors who have asked an associate warden to remove a member of an inmate work crew from disciplinary segregation or administrative detention, because the supervisor needed the inmate's electrical, plumbing, or carpentry skills on the job.

Time passes and inmates form heterophilous social ties among staffers and inmates. This network reaches well beyond the distance of sociodemographic separations[16] that either inmates or staffers have encountered and becomes a key mechanism in informal social

---

*A row dog is an inmate, alter, whose cell is on the same tier or row of cells that ego is on; a row dog relationship is slightly weaker than that of a road dog.

control. Inmates and staff see each other every day, month after month, and depend on each other's consensual behavior. Staffers provide all inmates' material and professional needs; inmates provide work for staff supervisors. Staffers and inmates offer each other companionship year by year. Strange bedfellows, but the system works peacefully if administered well.[17]

In this social context the stress of street life has been lifted. Inmates reassess social ties on the street, and soon once-valuable ties to homeboys, partners, road dogs, and legal and common law wives fade away. Wolf Man said his interest in neighborhood happenings had disappeared. He was content inside.

"No matter what happens, man, I lose. Never's nothing good out there for me, anyway, man. In prison, I can relax, man, you know. It seems like out there I get choked up. I've never been off probation or parole since I was a kid. It's not like I'm free, anyway. One thing leads to another, and I go off.

"I leave the 'hood to the younger generation. Anyway, I gotta learn how to choose between being a family man or not care if I'm in the pen all the time. It's got to be one or the other. If you're half-stepping, man, you're straddling the fence, man, you're not comfortable. I'm in the pen, man."

Wolf Man paused, raised both arms, pointed his palms toward the ceiling: "You know, man, I got a home [USP Lompoc]. It's my wife who's got it tough. I got everything I need right here. I got a house. I got all I want. My family—they're the ones who got it hard."

Inmates now disinterested in the outside world expand their working knowledge of the inside. When they do, their linguistic repertoire expands. Inmates participate in education programs, vocational training, drug counseling, and many other activities whose purpose is rehabilitation. In correctional jargon, these programs are called programing. Inmates are said to program, and a staff member may ask an inmate, "How ya programing?" The inmate responds, "Programing good."

Years of programing in education, vocational training, and on-the-job training in food service, factories, and business offices expose inmates to complexities in speech they hadn't encountered on the street. They learn new speech topics and acquire new vocabulary and styles of expression in their exposure to a wide variety of sociolinguistic situations, which they eventually master.

Many inmates new to prison soon learn they shouldn't speak to a warden or parole commissioners as they do to each other over a cellblock's pool table. Before long, many inmates sound like students or workers in offices, factories, and restaurants in the world outside, and they acquire the ability to switch quickly and smoothly between speech topics, speech styles, and vocabulary, depending on the audience. This multipurpose verbal repertoire is a valuable linguistic resource.[18] Now for the first time in their lives these inmates don't have to speak like poorly educated street hustlers. Sounding sincere and honest in front of a new girlfriend, researcher, judge, or the media is easier than ever before.

However comfortable stable social ties have made life inside prison, breaking those social ties makes leaving and staying out of prison very difficult. Over the years inmates' weak ties to the street have been lost. To ease the slide back to the street, inmates seek a set of weak social connections outside.

From the Joint to the Street

Women are an inmate's street connections. A wife or girlfriend can provide a place to stay and money.[19] Even though prisons usually have rules intended to prevent "instant" relationships, they begin anyway. High-security prisons often have policies stipulating that an inmate and a potential visitor must have known each other in a street relationship for at least a year before the inmate began the prison term. Potential visitors lie, and prison authorities don't have the personnel or time to check the veracity of every potential visitor's claim of social affiliation.

Prisons have visiting rooms, where inmates "date" street women. Inmates meet women in many ways. I've known inmates who made "blind" phone calls to numbers chosen at random in a local phone book; they called phone numbers one by one, until they reached a single or divorced woman. Others advertise in personal listings in newspapers. These techniques are effective, but slow.

An inmate's most reliable and fastest technique is to exploit his prison social network. To do that, he finds a prison homeboy, row dog, road dog, partner, or tip member whose wife or girlfriend is willing to bring to the prison a girlfriend, sister, cousin, or daughter.

"Most women are easy to get," said Leo. He met Donna, a Jehovah's Witness, at a Sunday afternoon Bible study group. "It was love at, what do you call it, first sight," said Donna. Church elders protested her marriage to Leo. She insisted he was a "good man who made bad decisions, but they weren't his fault."

Phone calls are essential to sustain a new relationship with a street woman. Many prisons monitor and record inmates' phone calls. A staff member talked about inmates' conversations:

"They use kids as pawns. They talk to their ol' ladies and tell them, 'Yeah, I'll take care o' you when I get out, but now I need money.' Then they'd call another girlfriend. A lot of 'em use their girlfriends or wives as mules [to smuggle drugs].

"Horny, man you should hear some of these guys. 'I want to feel your twat.' You can hear 'em panting in the telephone room, jerking off.

"They cuss at them and treat them like dirt. At the end, they tell 'em they brought it on themselves. What kind of mentality do these women have to stick with these guys?"

In state prison visiting rooms, during five years of research among women who marry prisoners, I saw "first" dates turn into marriage ceremonies and wedding receptions, watched inmates "cheat" on their wives by visiting wives one weekend, girlfriends the next, and observed inmates and their wives/girlfriends fondle each other's genitals and engage in oral sex and sexual intercourse in full view of children and adult visitors, who pretended not to see it.

Today, even maximum-security prisons employ female staffers as correctional officers, teachers, case managers, psychologists, counselors, physicians, lawyers, paralegals, food service workers, business office personnel, and senior administrators. More frequently than correctional administrators would admit freely, female prison employees, as well as outside female contract employees, develop emotional attachments to male inmates. Many relationships culminate with intimacies behind locked office doors and in examination rooms, closets, and inmates' cells.

Male prison employees too, correctional officers, factory staff, and even senior administrators, have become intimate with male inmates. No topic in prison management is more sensitive and closely guarded among staffers at each organizational level than that of male staffers who have had intimate relationships with male inmates.

Inmates perceive women (as well as male) visitors and staffers as vulnerable prey who can be easily manipulated into doing things. Women give inmates money, smuggle drugs to them, and wait for them on the outside. Despite tight security precautions, inmates conduct drug business inside as they did outside. For an inmate drug hustler to stay in business, he needs a woman (or several women, a wife and a girlfriend) who will "carry," or smuggle, heroin, cocaine, PCP, LSD, and marijuana into the visiting room.

Smuggling is easy. The following is a common technique, but, to be sure, there are many ways to do it: A female visitor might conceal drugs, which have been wrapped in a balloon or condom (the package is called a balloon) with the top tied tightly, in a baby's diaper, or under her tongue, in her vagina, or in her bra. The balloon is removed in the visitor's lavatory and passed to the inmate when she kisses him goodbye. The inmate swallows the balloon, and when he arrives back in his cell, he either vomits or defecates it. Sometimes, even a balloon filled with a laxative is passed with a drug-filled balloon. Frequently, many balloons are passed during a visit; I have known inmates who have swallowed dozens of balloons. On occasion, a balloon breaks and the inmate becomes extremely ill and needs emergency medical care.

If a woman is reluctant to smuggle, an inmate is likely to coerce her. He might threaten to leave her. If that fails, he might threaten to have her or her children beaten or killed. Or he might tell her that, if she doesn't smuggle drugs, he will be killed or beaten. This is a likely possibility for an inmate who has drug debts or has promised to deliver drugs to a prison gang, such as the Aryan Brotherhood (AB).

Drug smuggling is easiest in prisons that permit conjugal visiting. To afford a couple privacy, trailer houses are used for these visits. In an unsupervised trailer, smuggled drugs are passed with ease. In the recent past at Folsom Prison, the infamous maximum-security prison in Folsom, California, the Aryan Brotherhood, a violent neo-Nazi prison gang, controlled all drug smuggling and drug distribution inside the prison. Aryan Brotherhood members and AB wannabes had their wives smuggle heroin and cocaine into conjugal visiting trailers. The drugs were hidden behind a wall in a plumbing compartment. The inmate "trustees" who cleaned the trailers after visits were paid to smuggle the drugs inside cellblocks. Guards who were assigned to "shake down" (search) trustees were bribed by the Aryan Brotherhood, and drugs entered the prison freely.

The drug-smuggling scam continued even after Aryan Brotherhood members were paroled. After release, an Aryan Brotherhood member divorced his wife, a paid employee of the Aryan Brotherhood, who then married another Aryan Brotherhood member still in prison, and the drug smuggling continued through conjugal visits in the trailers.

Connections to the Street

Leaving prison can be an emotional trauma and can present a social dilemma. A rich body of prison folklore tells about inmates who had to be carried out of a prison, screaming and yelling, because they didn't want to leave. I have seen inmates who were near parole commit offenses, hoping to have their parole dates rescinded. Some inmates have resorted to offenses such as assault on another inmate; a few have committed a serious assault on a staff member and have then served additional multiyear prison terms. Some inmates leave prison grounds and immediately rob a bank or throw a brick through a store window. I have verified cases like these, where a newly paroled inmate broke a window and sat down on the sidewalk, waiting for the police.

An inmate informant at the Washington State Penitentiary was committed for a six-and-a-half year term for homicide. On three occasions, he escaped from the minimum-security building within 30 days of parole. For each of these escapes, he had to serve the term of the original sentence. We met in 1970. In 1990, he was still there.

Most inmates have nowhere to go, but have decided they aren't going to stop street hustling. The Black Hammer and Stan revealed this in a conversation after we had enjoyed a Mexican dinner, carefully prepared by Mexican American inmates at USP Lompoc, in celebration of Cinco de Mayo.

The Black Hammer prefers life in prison over the hassle of the street. Stan said he was going straight.[20] Stan, age 34, was first imprisoned in the California Youth Authority when he was 15. He has been inside ever since. The Black Hammer, age 36, went to the California Youth Authority at 14, and since 1972, he has served three separate sentences for bank robbery, and is a veteran in federal penitentiaries (USP Atlanta, Terre Haute, Leavenworth, McNeil Island, and Lompoc).

Stan has two brothers. "One of 'em is 22. He's in the navy. He's got a good future ahead of him. The other's straight too. He's married with kids. They nice, but they don't want no part of me." I asked Stan who else he could rely on out there. "Me, that's who. There ain't nobody else I'd trust."

The Black Hammer said after he had left prison he had no one to call. "I had a wife, a nice white Jewish girl, when I was up in McNeil in the mid-1970s. That's who gave me this [a mezuzah dangling from his neck]."

I asked, "So what are you guys going to do when you get out of here?"

Stan stood up from the table and grumbled, "I ain't coming back here, that's for fucking sure. I'm tired of this shit and the petty bullshit you got to deal with up in this ol' fucking prison, man. I ain't giving up, man. So many of these pathetic motherfuckers in here just give up when they're on the street. Not me."

"You ain't gonna get a job, Stan. Who's gonna hire a nigger bank robber?" asked the Black Hammer, with a smirk creasing his face.

Stan responded, "Fuck them. I'll live like them other homeless motherfuckers out there, selling drugs and sleeping on the street, before I come back in here to this motherfucking bullshit."

Black Hammer smiled. "Not me. When I get out there this time, I know that I'll get back into [bank robbery]. The next time, I'll get 28 years and I'll do 25 of 'em. That's all right. I don't mind this. I get everything I want in here. It's tough out there, man."

"You giving up like them other motherfuckers. That's bullshit, man," argued Stan.

"I'll watch, man. You'll come back." The Black Hammer laughed.

Angered, Stan exclaimed, "Fuck that bullshit, man." He stormed away.

After dinner Stan and the Black Hammer exercised. Stan enjoyed basketball, the Black Hammer lifted weights. Then it was back to the cellblocks to play a game of pool and watch color television, then on to a quiet night's sleep on clean sheets. At 6:00 they were greeted with a hot breakfast.

Lori Granger, an experienced case manager at a coed state prison, said, "The toughest thing to do is to find somewhere for them to go. Most of them don't have anywhere to go. The women stayed with their boyfriends before they were arrested, and the guys were on the street selling drugs. If I don't get a satisfactory release-plan residence for them, they could stay a lot longer. It's our job to find a place for them to go. But that's tough."

Ramon, a Hispanic inmate in an Arizona prison, was finishing his third prison sentence; he had numerous juvenile sentences. He asked my advice about getting a place to stay after his upcoming release.

He said, "I don't have nowhere to go."

"Where you from?"

"Yakima."

"Go back there."

"I'm tired of that, man. I said I was going to stay with my ex-girlfriend's mother. She's the grandmother of my kid. The [parole] board said, 'Huh-uh.'"

"Stay with your ex-girlfriend."

"Can't, man. We ain't talked for years. You know what I'm saying?"

"So what are you going to do, bud?"

"I don't know, man. Can I stay with you?"

Connections for Parole

Many inmates successfully exploited visiting networks. On Christmas in 1989, I saw Paris after he had visited with a "white bitch, daughter of a cop motherfucker!" He had a photograph of her standing next to a Ford pick-up truck: she was about 22 years old, a bit overweight, bleached and teased hair, wearing painted-on jeans.

Another "white bitch," said Paris, was planning to visit him for the first time. A cellblock partner's wife arranged the "first date." Paris was hoping to meet another woman like Alice.

"I met that fine white bitch [Alice] at a California state prison. Alice was a psychologist there. She was fucking these guys in there, you know, so the motherfuckers made her resign. Shit! Now *that* was a good program fo' inmates.

"I seen the bitch visiting Toad. She's a fine white bitch, a fine bitch. I had this big ol' fat broad then, a Jew, I met through Pam [a visitor].

"I seen Alice in the visiting room with Toad. Toad didn't need her, man. He was doing 10 years and I was getting out soon. I knew I was going to get that bitch, 'cause she was supposed to be with me.

"I needed a place to stay when I got out. I saw a letter she sent in to Toad, and I memorized her return address and sent her a letter. I knew she wanted me. I could tell. I'm small in the waist, cute in the face, and got muscles every place!

"I wrote her. 'What was a woman of status, stature and character doing up in there? I'm just writing you on a friendship tip. I don't want to put a burden on you, honey, but I need some money. How much? A couple hundred, baby.'

"Now I tell her I need a package. Tin cans of oysters, cosmetics. She sent the stuff and got me the money. Now I tell her, 'I want a double-breasted midgray suit, lizard skin shoes, and lizard skin belt.' She got that, too.

"The day came and she met me at visiting, and I was high siding it.* We walked out of there, the bitch hanging off my arm. We turned some heads!

"She had a new car. I took the keys. She lived in Santa Maria. We got to her place and I showed her my new works [he had recently been circumcised, he said], and I sexed her down real good. I fucked her in the pussy, up her ass, and she sucked my cock. I said, 'Oh baby, oh baby, I'm gonna cum,' and she tried to pull away. I grabbed her by the ears and say, 'Baby, take every drop, swallow it all.' I dominated her!"

Many informants told me about their passion for anal sex with a female or male partner. Paris was one who told me about it.

"'Cause it hurts 'em, man. When you fuck 'em up the ass and it hurts, you control the bitch, man. You control 'em. You dominate 'em! You got 'em.

"I sexed her down real good, man, and she gave me $500. She dropped me off with a friend in L.A., and I used the money to buy cocaine.

"We were into the money, the material things. I was back in business. Now all I needed was a 'ho'e. I prayed to the pimp-god, 'Oh, pimp-god, send me a 'ho'e, send me a good 'ho'e, send me a white 'ho'e."

Paris got back into smoking rock. "I was at this party and this bitch stuck a pipe in my mouth. One hit and I lost everything. Man, there's nothing like it. It feels like you're cumming when you blow the smoke out. I got so crazy, I started shooting heroin to come down.

"The drugs is what fucked me up, man. It can turn you to jelly-fish. I was shooting heroin and freebasing cocaine. Pretty soon, the girls [his prostitutes] left. I got violent with them, too, a couple of times. My bottom girl [his favorite], Debbie, she was the bitch that

---

* High siding is wearing flashy clothes, strutting.

sent me to prison one time. I assaulted her with a lamp, table, chair, and towel rack." Paris paused a moment, thinking. "I lost it all. I had everything. Fuck it, man."

Paris expects to be released from prison in the mid-1990s. In the meantime, finding a woman keeps him busy.

Getting It All Together

In 1981 I taught a college-level class, "Language, Culture and Society," to maximum-security inmates at the Washington State Penitentiary (WSP). Blue, in his early 30s, was a student in this class. His new wife, Anne, was in her late 30s and had been a music teacher at a high school in Spokane, Washington. She divorced her husband, a local businessman, ending 19 years of marriage, after she met and began "dating" Blue.*

It seemed that Blue's future would be bright. He was accepted as a student in a special education program, funded by Washington State, for qualified inmates at any adult Washington State correctional institution. A few qualified inmate-students, considered by authorities to be high-potential students and low-risk offenders, received full scholarships to the University of Washington. Tuition and fees, books and supplies, and room and board were paid by state taxpayers.

Anne was instrumental in gaining Blue's admission to the University of Washington program. He wasn't an extraordinary college student, just an average student among maximum-security inmates whose preparation for college took place in state prison education programs. His criminal history, as self-reported and as told by Anne and by prison staffers, suggested (to me) that he was a poor risk. Blue had nearly beaten to death a prison guard at the penitentiary, and as a result he had spent years in disciplinary segregation, according to a correctional supervisor. Blue was a drug addict and an alcoholic, and as a juvenile offender he had escaped from a Texas work camp. The offense that brought him to the WSP was breaking into and entering a pharmacy, to steal "nodding" drugs, for personal use and for sale on the street.

---

*Anne had a friend who was preparing a documentary film about inmate life at WSP. Blue played a guitar and was asked by the filmmaker to record the documentary's background music. The filmmaker played Blue's music for Anne, who was impressed and wanted to meet him. She accompanied the filmmaker to WSP and met Blue. Their love affair began soon afterward.

Anne believed education would offer Blue an avenue for rehabilitation. After all, she knew the benefits of education. Her father was a professor of mathematics at a regional university. Anne's network of personal friends contained college-educated men and women, including engineers at the Boeing Corporation.

It took Anne more than a year to spring Blue. She wrote letter after letter, made phone call after phone call to the WSP's superintendent and Department of Corrections officials in Tacoma, Washington. "I wore 'em down," she said. After graduation, Anne said Blue would attend the University of Washington's law school and then earn a Washington State political office, fighting for prison reform and prisoner rights.

Anne, Blue, and I visited in Seattle each weekend in Anne's sparsely furnished apartment, a few blocks off campus. Blue gave me a tour of his dorm. He stayed on a floor with college students in a high-rise dormitory overlooking Lake Washington. Blue had a wonderful view of the Cascade Mountain range, the lake, and Husky Stadium. Blue wasn't permitted to leave campus without permission, but he did it anyway.

Fall classes began. Blue didn't attend classes and failed to appear for his part-time job, which also had been arranged by Blue's on-campus advisor. Blue disappeared; Anne didn't know where he was either. Days passed, Blue remained lost to the street. Two weeks passed into the semester. One day when Anne returned home from work, Blue met her in the underground parking lot of her apartment house. Drunk and angry, Blue slapped and punched Anne and threw her into her car's windshield. I saw her multiple bruises and black eye.

Anne forgave Blue. Anne said she understood the stress Blue must be feeling. Several more weeks passed, Blue still hadn't attended classes, and Anne saw him just a few times a week. One night Blue, drunk and angry, knocked on Anne's door. She answered it, and he punched, slapped, and kicked her. Before he left, Blue threw Anne into a hollow closet door, shattering it, and he threatened to kill her next time.

Frightened and badly battered, she phoned a family friend in Seattle and confided in him. He called the Seattle police. That evening, Blue was arrested in his dorm while he showered.

Six weeks after the semester had started, Blue was back in a cell at the penitentiary, and Anne returned to Walla Walla. She called me late one Friday afternoon, and said she had forgiven Blue. She told me that, after he served six months to a year for a parole violation, she and Blue would try college again, but not at the University of Washington.

Washington State's prisoner education program ended that semester. And so did Washington State's sponsorship of higher education extension courses at the Washington State Penitentiary.

Prison: Look for Yourself

Decades of literature about prisons have given us the idea that prisons are draconian institutions where street criminals, killers, rapists, armed robbers, and child molesters, become "alienated" and "hardened," and where inmate subcultures indoctrinate relatively nonviolent criminals to be really violent.[21]

"No one who had experienced an American prison of the fifties or sixties from the inside," says Currie, "or who had worked closely with those who had, could fail to be impressed by the prisons' capacity to induce bitterness, to close off legitimate opportunities for inmates on release, and generally cripple their ability to cope with the demands of the larger world."[22]

My experience with prisons since 1970 has left me with a different impression: Every day, street criminals *arrive* at prison gates already bitter, alienated, and crippled; many of these men exit prison physically and mentally healthier, better educated, and better prepared for the rigors of the larger world than on the day they walked in.

Take a look at modern prison. Try to arrange a visit to a federal or state prison. In fact, spend several days talking to staff and inmates about the work, vocational, educational, and recreational activities. Eat with inmates in the dining hall. Attend education classes. Visit the law library. Watch vocational training, barbering or computer science, for instance. Hang around the gymnasium and big yard during recreation. Listen to the inmates playing basketball, lifting weights, shooting pool. Enjoy the manicured lawns and flower beds. Ask someone about the weekend movie.

Browse cellblocks. Walk around. Look at cells. Smell the air. Sit with inmates in a television room. Watch them while they watch Sunday afternoon football or the World Series on a color television.

Wander around the visiting room and inmate factories too. Check the medical and dental facilities. Talk with the psychologists and psychiatrists. Before you leave, visit the drug and alcohol counseling program. Listen for laughter.[23]

Prisons and jails have become a part of America's welfare system.[24] Nearly a million inmates are comfortably imprisoned, while 5 million to 10 million hustlers are still on the streets, knowing sooner or later they too will join companions inside federal or state prisons. In prison, street criminals say they "dry out," "clean up," "take it easy," and "program." The food is hot and plentiful, recreation time is virtually endless, mental health and drug counseling are encouraged, educational and vocational training programs are ample, civil rights are protected, and professional medical and dental care is free.[25]

Now the courts are adding to the list of inmates' benefits by protecting criminals from unsavory prisons. A federal judge recently refused to send a drug dealer to prison, because drugs are too freely available inside.[26] How many judges refuse to allow youngsters to live in public housing projects where drugs are plentiful and violence is an everyday occurrence? How many judges permanently remove children from violent family environments where alcoholic and drug-addicted parents create an unhealthy, unsavory, unsafe family culture?

Popcorn, T-Cool, Red Hog, Itch, School Yard, Miss Ann, Cuzz, and the others have a life on the street. It is the only life they have known, and for them, going to jail and prison is an inevitable fact of that life. But for them imprisonment doesn't matter, because prison often provides them with a quality of life better than the one they leave behind. Take a look on the street too.

Steeped in prison life, now spend a few days in an American ghetto, places like those where my informants grew up. In Los Angeles, visit Watts. Look at Harlem at 145th Street. Take a subway to East Harlem. Stroll around the housing projects on Seattle's Yesler Way.[27] In San Francisco, hang around Hunter's Point. If you dare, spend a few hours in the early evening at Fifty-ninth and California near Chicago's Cook County Jail, which holds over 10,000 inmates. Look at the public housing projects in New Orleans, Cleveland, Detroit, and Miami. Or spend an evening in Kansas City, Missouri, on the street corner at Prospect and Twenty-third Street. Walk around apartment buildings. Check for garbage in the halls, look for vermin. How warm are apartments in December? Is there running water?

Walk around outside. Look at children's playground equipment. Spend time in the local public hospital. Share a meal with residents, or eat at the community kitchen or a local mission or shelter. Talk to residents about the quality of their lives. Watch mothers send children off to school. Get off the street before dark. Listen for gunfire. Watch out for gangs. Look at gang graffiti on the walls. Listen for laughter.

Are Prisons Too Costly?

Since 1980 the state and federal prison population has increased from 329,821 to 883,593—a rise of 168 percent.[28] Since 1985 the federal correctional system, supported by frightened Americans and politicians fearing reelection loss, has increased its inmate population by 100 percent.[29]

Forty-two states have reported plans to build new prisons for 100,000 more inmates at a $5 billion cost.[30] Federal politicians want to build more and even larger prisons too.[31] But critics argue that we don't need more prisons because imprisonment has had little effect on street crime.[32]

Let's consider several issues while we assess prison's value to American society. We know for sure that, while violent street criminals are imprisoned, they won't murder and rape lawful citizens; that's the point of putting them there. But the trick is learning how to use prisons for the advantage of lawful citizens. This requires knowing which types of criminals to keep in prison and then putting these inmates to work at full-time activities that will benefit them as well as the taxpayers. Working every day doesn't hurt lawful citizens, and it surely won't harm imprisoned felons.

Nearly all states spend less money on corrections than on police protection.[33] A comparison of expenditures on corrections and police protection for all states and the District of Columbia shows that, with the exception of the District of Columbia, Georgia, Kansas, Nevada, and Tennessee, all states spend less money on corrections than on police. Despite these expenditures, no one argues to cut police budgets and reduce police staffing levels, even though street police don't stop street criminals from committing crimes.

Critics say prisons are expensive and ineffective.[34] But how expensive is prison? Let's consider correctional expenditures as a percentage of a state's total financial expenditures (for these purposes, I call this figure the correctional allocation rate). In the early 1990s California's correctional allocation rate was 2.4 percent; this included the cost of correctional institutions for men, women, and juveniles, as well as other types of institutions, allocations for probation, pardon, and parole, and other correction-related costs. California had a 1.4 percent correctional allocation rate for men's prisons.*

California's relatively low correctional allocation rate isn't unique. Florida spends 3.0 percent; Illinois, 1.9 percent; Massachusetts, 1.7 percent; Michigan, 3.0 percent; New York, 2.2 percent; New Jersey, 2.0 percent; and, Texas, 2.3 percent. Alaska, Maine, Minnesota, and Tennessee had the highest annual correctional operating expenditures per inmate,[35] yet their correctional allocation rates were 1.8 percent, 1.3 percent, 0.9 percent, and 2.3 percent, respectively. Annual imprisonment costs in the federal prison system ($14,456 per person) are less than the annual state average ($15,586).

Boot Camps: A Policy Mistake

Analyses of the causes and conditions of crime aren't valuable to policymakers, whose only concern is trying to find some way of reducing crime without remedying its causes; altering criminals' behavior is their primary concern.[36] Boot camps are an example of policymakers' failure to understand the complexity of deviant behavior.

The Violent Crime Control and Law Enforcement Act of 1993, introduced in the House of Representatives by Jack Brooks (Democrat, Texas) and in the Senate by Joseph R. Biden, Jr. (Democrat, Delaware), supported by the Clinton administration, and backed by Republican congressmen, has proposed spending $6 billion on new prison construction with $150 million earmarked for 10 military-style bootcamp prisons.[37] Attorney General Janet Reno said, "These are for kids who have got to understand that there is no excuse for putting a gun up beside somebody's head and hurting them—and that they are going to be punished but that there will be programs after the punishment to help them come back."[38]

Offenders' first six to eight years of family life failed to instill discipline, values, ethics, morality, a strong self-image, and self-control.[39] But policymakers believe that in a few months in boot-

---

*The rates cited here were calculated by dividing correction expenditures for fiscal year 1990 (U.S. Department of Justice 1993a:12) by the total state spending for fiscal year 1991 (U.S. Department of Commerce 1992–306).

camp the intangibles of personality, discipline, values, and self-esteem can be infused by exposing mostly first-time offenders to a militarylike culture. They awaken in early morning to meet a strict schedule and strict discipline.[40]

Inciardi, Horowitz, and Pottieger note that "it seems doubtful that marching and chanting can overcome the behavioral patterns and value orientations that result in [crime]."[41] Bentayou reports that "specialists at the U.S. Justice Department's National Institute of Justice [said] the new boot camps have sucked up tens of millions in state and Federal corrections dollars for construction and millions more for operations. Yet no one has shown clearly that this approach to punishment actually helps turn young lawbreakers away from crime."[42]

Young offenders' behavior in bootcamp will no doubt be better than it was on the street.[43] But that's to be expected, and it illustrates only that prisoners can comply well with the demands of captors. Versatility keeps criminals alive.

In the long run, however, bootcamps are likely to show that young offenders just temporarily replace one set of behaviors with another set without altering cognitive processes or repairing low mental health.[44]

Prisons in Social Context

While we're reinvigorating inner cities with industries and building prisons and offering food, recreation, health, and education to convicted felons, let's not forget about Ace. He and hundreds of thousands of children like him must be protected and removed from the influence and abuse of parents like Maniac. Unless we act in a significant way to protect children, the flow of boys and girls into America's juvenile institutions and adult prisons will never end. Let's spend less time and less money educating drug dealers and convicted felons, the killers and rapists, and more time and money safeguarding youngsters like Ace.

Today's rates of street crime are high. Inner cities need development. Should we stop building prisons? Of course not. Repairing urban environments is one priority; building prisons is another one. We should not consider prison expenditures and urban renewal to be mutually exclusive policy options.

There are few nonviolent cultures.[45] America is a complex urban society and will always have violent and nonviolent crime.[46] Purging the streets of all criminals, stopping all violent criminal behavior, closing all prisons, ending all child abuse are admirable but unrealistic objectives.

Policymakers should ask basic policy-related questions: How much nonviolent and violent street crime is America willing to tolerate? How many people should be imprisoned? What is an acceptable rate of incarceration? How many killers, rapists, bank robbers, child molesters, and so on, do we want imprisoned? What recidivism rate is acceptable? How many children will courts permit to be beaten and neglected? Perhaps addressing issues like these can direct policymakers toward significant policy decisions.

5

The Street

Street hustling is mundane.[1] Life on the street for an adult hustler is cold: there are few material or hedonistic rewards; sexual partners are often difficult to find; status and prestige rewards are absent; there is little sense of personal power, except when feeling particularly narcissistic from too much cheap wine; and there is a constant risk of being beaten or stabbed by drunk or angry hustlers.[2]

Popcorn, Wolf Man, Paris, and the other informants didn't choose to sell drugs and engage in other low-level street crimes because they didn't want a career[3] as a high school teacher, insurance salesman, attorney, or manager of a Starbuck's coffee shop.* Nor did these informants forsake the thrill of driving a Formula One racing car or playing football in front of 60,000 screaming fans at the University of Washington's Husky Stadium[4] for the excitement of standing on a street corner peddling rock cocaine in Seattle's cold wintery drizzle.

These hustlers' economic lives are a series of defaults, not career choices.[5] They stand on sidewalks as helpless children do, waiting for the criminal justice or social welfare system to care for them.[6] When that doesn't happen, they satisfy their needs in the easiest, most familiar ways. They steal from sleeping drunks and passersby, shoplift at local stores, sell small quantities of heroin and rock cocaine, panhandle, and even steal cash and drugs from each other. Their life trajectory was set in motion decades earlier in early childhood, and they can't stop it now.

---

*No informants worked at legitimate jobs, not even for a day, during the years of this research.

Social Networks and Hustling

The success of an adult hustler's adaptation depends on weak social ties distributed over a wide geographic area. After years of teenage hustling, doing time in jails and prisons, and staying in missions and shelters, a hustler has amassed an array of acquaintances.

Hustlers' street networks are diffusely distributed and extend between cities throughout the Northwest (Portland, Oregon; Seattle, Washington; Vancouver, British Columbia) and even into major cities in the greater West, such as Los Angeles, San Francisco, Fresno, and Phoenix, among others. Street social life in these networks is guided by a simple question: What can he or she do for me now? The result is subsets of instrumental networks. Two or three men, for instance, get together to shoplift and sell stolen property or panhandle enough money to buy a bottle of Wild Irish Rose, a high-alcohol-content wine. But once the wine has been drunk and the goods sold, hustlers go their own way.

Reciprocity between street hustlers fresh out of prison and those who've been outside a while is strong. These men have an understanding based on common need. If an established hustler refuses aid to a former inmate just "back on the set," he can be sure his lack of cooperation will be reciprocated.

To become established again in Seattle, a hustler must face the scene at First and Pike. On a typical day there, the street scene changes as the day grows old. By late morning, there is action on each of the four corners, and it spreads for two blocks north and south and three blocks east.

Street folks and tourists mix well in daylight hours. Tourists don't bother the drug runners and addicts, ex-convicts, street hustlers, and the others lurking around. And street folks usually don't bother tourists, except to hustle a quarter. Tourism is a valuable industry in Seattle, a protected industry, and, to be sure, "one-time" (the police) are close by.

Drug sellers don't bother each other unless a stranger gets pushy and tries to expand his territory by nudging into someone else's corner. Expansion is OK if the "businessmen" know each other.

"There's lots of corners, plenty of customers, and nobody wants trouble, that kind of trouble from one-time. When runners be out there, they be clocking. When you're slinging packets, you got to work against the clock. It's only a matter of time before one-time rolls by and you're out of business for a while," said Popcorn.

In downtown Seattle, or anywhere else, drug dealers don't kill each other over territory, said Popcorn. Anyway, drug dealers "messing with each other" cost time; time costs them money. Street drug dealers have only a brief time to "dish soup" (sell heroin) or sling cocaine, make some cash, and retreat into hiding in a cheap apartment or motel room with a bottle of "I," a few rocks, a couple of strawberries.

Rock sellers fill the street by midevening. Stand on a street corner near the Pike Place Market and wait a few minutes. Teenage runners holler like barkers in a dark sideshow. "Soup, soup, soup, soup, soup." They advertise most loudly when tourists are not around, on rainy and cool wintery Sundays, late in the day.

Nightly, drug sellers silently advertise their poison while they pack a pay-n-park lot across the street from the Market Cafe, as well as many other places in the area. A runner who tips his head slightly backward signals, "I'm cool!" (I'm selling drugs!) to a prospective customer who drives or walks by. When a customer makes eye contact, the rock seller pauses to read the area before he approaches the buyer. In this open-air market of misery, a drug-hungry citizen can buy "papers" of heroin, weed by the joint, speed, or pills (uppers, downers, and every other kind).

Prostitutes (hookers, rock whores) hanging on the corners, day or night, are for sale, too. Professionals usually do not work here. This place is for runaway teenage girls, strawberries, and raspberries, waiting to barter sex for money or a rock.

Street cops are always hanging around somewhere or gliding down alleys on mountain bikes. Sellers and customers don't pay them too much attention, though. But things do get crazy on the street, and when that happens, one-time rolls up with a bus and rounds up everybody in business.

"Shit," says Popcorn, "they can even book you on that fucking bus." One-time parks the bus on the street where Hawk and Benny run their scam, and walks away from it, leaving it empty. It's a message that street folks must share their territory with the West Precinct.

The late-night sideshow does not end until 3:00, 4:00 in the morning. Even then, dealers and drug laborers work late-night and early-morning traffic. Addicts geek here and there. The sideshow disappears with the darkness, giving way to a daytime street crew, walking out of missions and cheap hotels, crawling out from under cardboard blankets or from inside bedrolls pushed into doorways and laid on sidewalks and shoved under bushes in downtown parks. That is life renewal on the street.

Missions and Shelters

Just out of prison, a hustler who isn't met at the prison by a girlfriend, wife, or relative has no place to go. Years of free meals and sleeping in a bed in a warm prison cell have left him reluctant to sleep on a park bench or under a cardboard blanket on a concrete sidewalk. He wants a place to stay, food, and alcohol and drugs. To get those things, he needs today's street "currency," cocaine.

With cocaine he can buy anything, and with it he can barter for anything. But to get cocaine, he must find a homeboy, road dog, or partner who knows the street. Locating a road dog or partner after years in prison can be a problem. As a street hustler ages, he has fewer companions on the street. Prison has taken many away. Some have died from drug overdoses or alcohol-related diseases or AIDS. Others have been killed on the street. Still others have been overcome by addiction and no longer have the energy for crime.

Yesterday a hustler was protected in a sanctuary. Today he seeks a connection to cocaine and stays in a mission or shelter in Pioneer Square or along Seattle's beautiful waterfront. Popcorn's first stop after his release from the Seattle jail in early January 1989 was the Union Gospel Mission in Pioneer Square.

"You gotta be a lame motherfucker to starve," says 36-year-old Preacher, a former California and Washington state prison inmate, a 25-year veteran of the street. Fact is, street folks all over the western United States know that Seattle is generous.

This was illustrated for me one night when I walked down the main street of Palo Alto, California. A block ahead of me, a young fellow, about 30, was walking slowly in my direction. Pedestrians walked by him, and he stuck out his hand. "Spare change?" he asked quietly.

Soon, his filthy hand, with dirt caked under his long yellowish fingernails, came toward me. He wore a tattered cardigan sweater covered by an unzipped prison jacket; his beard was a few days old; his eyes were bloodshot. I pulled out my roll of ones.

"Yeah, bud, here ya go." I put a dollar bill on his palm. He was taken aback. He stared at it.

"I was watching ya come down the street," I said, "asking those straight folks for change. Lemme give ya a hint. Use a cup. Get an old coffee cup out of the garbage."

We talked. He had just been released for the third time, from Tracy, a California state prison. "Why are you hanging around California?" I asked.

"Waiting for a check," he said.

"A check?"

"Social security, man. For a disability. I gave the government the cops' address here. They said they'd get me the check when it comes in."

"Where you staying?"

"In the park. Down there," he motioned with his hand, pointing somewhere down the dark street.

"Cops are going to track you down when it comes in?" He nodded yes. "Then what? What are ya gonna do after you get your check?"

"Going to Seattle. Had some friends inside who stayed up there. They said it was a good place to go. No hassles."

The Seattle mission St. Martin de Porres caters to homeless men over age 50. I volunteered there, helping to feed and keep them company. A staff member there said most are former inmates and alcoholics. A mission bus picks them up at a gathering spot on the street and brings them to the mission by early evening. I helped serve them thick tuna fish sandwiches, pumpkin pie, and chocolate or vanilla ice cream. A dime buys a cup of coffee, a minibox of washing machine detergent, a disposable razor. Towels, bath soap, and local phone calls are free.

But as with other missions and shelters, patrons must leave by 6:30 in the morning. Men who are ill aren't forced back to the street. They can spend a day or two inside resting on a mattress. Once well, however, it's back outside. Seeing old men on the street bothered me. Where were their children or grandchildren?

Missions limit the number of nights that a patron can stay each month. On "Mother's Day," when welfare checks arrive, there are usually as many mattresses at any mission as there are patrons wanting one. But weeks later, when the checks have been spent on drugs and wine, sleeping places are often in short supply. In the late

Table 3. Number of days per week that different meals are served, by mission

	Breakfast	Lunch	Dinner
Bread of Life	5		7
Lutheran Compass Center	2	1	1
Millionaire Club	6		5
St. Martin de Porres	7		7
Service Center		7	2
Matt Talbot Center		5	
Orion Center[a]		6	6
Pike Market Senior Center[b]		4	
Salvation Army Harbor Light		6	
Morrison			5
Peniel Mission			6
Union Gospel Mission			7

[a] For youngsters 11–20 years old.
[b] For adults age 55 and over.

afternoon, usually around 5:00, men get in line. Early arrival ensures a spot on a floor mattress.

Daily meals are not served at each site. I've listed Seattle's missions in Table 3, above, indicating the number of days each week that breakfast, lunch, or dinner is served.

Popcorn says mission food is palatable, but he doesn't like to eat at religious missions. "Bread of Life. Breakfast, you know. You gotta listen to an hour of Jesus Christ before you eat. They serve dinner too, but you gotta listen to another hour of Jesus Christ. Fuck dat." Panhandling alcoholics have time to stand in line; they fill the chapel and then eat, before they beg for money and drink.

The Morrison is Seattle's worst shelter, according to street folks, worse than any prison anyone has ever been in. Men's mattresses are placed on the floor, separated from others with a rectangle of white painted lines around it, creating a private area enclosed by invisible walls. Women sleep on bunk beds, away from the men's area.

Near the end of a month, although mattresses and money are in short supply, it's a good time to buy stolen property or pick strawberries. That's the give and take of the street.

Popcorn hated staying in missions. "Stayin' in a shelter is just like jail. You gotta wait in lines for meals. It's boring, too. You just be walkin' around starin' at the floor. Some guys be talkin' shit to women. The people is the worst. Some of them's crazy. It's dangerous too, jail. Ya can be all righ'. It's just how you carry yourself and don't mess with people. And, you gotta be out by 6:30. Fuck dat, man. I'd rather be in jail, man, where they treatcha like a man."

Popcorn admitted, though, that missions have advantages. "It be good sometimes. You get clothes and soap, shampoo, razors. If ya know somebody up there in the property room of a mission, you can get some extra stuff—pants, suits, like that. You can sell that stuff out here on the street."

However, Itch had another opinion; he would risk going to jail, either on a drug-hustle or shoplifting, rather than stay in a mission. "You get tired of staying in missions and shelters. I ain't like them other dudes in them places, man. There's nothing but overgrown niggers up in them places, living a curfew. It's worse than the joint. That ain't for me. You gotta work the system."

Missions and shelters also are handy when a guy's girlfriend or wife throws him out. T-Cool had been staying with his girlfriend, somewhere in south Seattle. "I was drinkin', one thing led to another, bitch call da cops." Not much of an explanation, but he didn't need one.

"DVPA?" I asked. Washington State's Domestic Violence Protection Act is supposed to protect women against abuse.

T-Cool responded, "Ah. I didn't hit her or nothin'. She wadn' bleedin' or nothin'. The cops were cool and didn' arrest me. They told me to leave and let her chill for a couple of days. I came downtown."

Choosing a Product and Building a Business

Now that he was out of jail, Popcorn wanted to build a drug business. But first he needed a place to stay; his time was running out at the mission. I drove him to his sister's place in the CD, and as much as he claimed to hate it, he asked if he could stay awhile. He had no money, but she knew that he would soon have cocaine. So for now, he had a roof over his head. He needed cocaine and planned to sell flake and rock. This time he said he would avoid selling heroin. Cocaine can bring a seller high profits.[7]

Ernesto, a Los Angeles cop, explained to me dealers' primary motive in choosing to deal: "Look! We're doing what we know how to do; they're doing it the way they know how. Selling rocks is what they know how to do. Simple, huh?"

Cocaine or heroin ("product") is mixed ("cut" or "stepped on") by a drug supplier with a powder ("cutter"). The most common cutter is inositol, but cocaine sellers use corn sugar, vitamin B_1, aspirin, procaine, and acetaminophen. The product is then purchased by a local dealer, someone like Popcorn. The ratio of cocaine to cutter determines the relative purity of heroin and cocaine. A good cut, say dealers, is about 95 percent cocaine. A dealer in Seattle in 1989–90 paid $40 a gram, or about $1,200 an ounce (one ounce has 28 grams, about the quantity of medication in an acetaminophen capsule); in the Midwest, at the same time, an ounce of cocaine was approximately $1,800. Heroin was more expensive; depending on its purity, it ranged from $4,000 to $6,500 an ounce; for personal use, high-purity heroin could be cut 10–12 times.

Seattle cocaine dealers have many sources. Small street hustlers who rock up cocaine themselves often buy it from local Bloods and Crips. T-Bone was purportedly responsible for transporting cocaine to Seattle from Los Angeles in heavily armed automobile convoys, with the car carrying the drugs positioned between a lead and a trail car. Dealers with a large clientele might buy sizable quantities of cocaine from southern California connections, who bring it to Seattle or to the Tri-Cities (Yakima, Pasco, and Kennewick) in eastern Washington; law enforcement authorities in California told me that the Mexican Mafia brings cocaine and heroin into south-central Washington from southern California.[8] 'Dre told me he bought cocaine at $15 a gram, or about $400 an ounce, from Mexican Mafia cocaine suppliers in the Tri-Cities.

Drug entrepreneurs say big money can be made by transporting cocaine into Washington State. 'Dre said, "Give me a full month run and I could make about a few hundred thousand, say, a quarter of a million. I used to fly to California and go to an old car dealer dude. He'd pack a cylinder with it and I'd junk it when we got back [to Seattle]. Now, shit, after we got connected with them Cubans and Mexicans in Yakima, we don't need to do that shit. I'd drive over there, and they'd put cocaine in tires, heads, muffler system, cooler, radiator. You'd be surprised at where they stash that stuff. I saw a kilo of coke stashed in a radiator built around a radiator!"

In 1989–90 in Washington State, cocaine supplies were high. Addiction was affordable, and drug sellers didn't feel constrained to sell it. Fang, a rock dealer from southern California, told me: "I sell it, they use it, and that ain't my problem. I don't give a fuck. No way, man! It's on them, not me. I sell it. They buy it. I don' make 'em buy it. We all gotta live." Every cocaine dealer I know shares Fang's opinion.

Some dealers mix 23 grams of 95 percent pure cocaine with 5 grams of cutter: this mixture contains about $900 worth of 95 percent pure cocaine, and it sells for $1,800 an ounce at the point of sale. Some dealers use 95 percent pure cocaine to mix a "50-50 cut": 50 percent cutter, 50 percent cocaine.

The dealers I spoke with told me they had pride in their product and would not sell a 50-50 cut. Drug sellers said, if the cut is too high, customers will buy their drugs from someone whose cocaine is not so diluted. An 80-20 mix might be packaged as an "8-ball," or 3.5 grams (one-eighth ounce), and sold for $275–$300. Seven grams (one-quarter ounce) sell for $500; 14 grams (one-half ounce) bring $900.

Cocaine dealers get hooked on their product. An addicted dealer, like Juan, will support his habit by altering the ratio of cocaine to cutter. If he had mixed an 80-20 cut prior to his addiction, he might prepare a 70-30 or 60-40 mixture afterward, and smoke, snort, or inject what he does not mix. While his habit worsens, which, say addicted sellers, it always does, he dilutes his mixture more and more, and eventually the product is so weak that his customers buy from another dealer. Now he is out of business and has a cocaine habit too, which might cost hundreds of dollars a day. 'Dre fell victim to rock. "The best dope dealer has been a dope fiend. I used to smoke, Lord have mercy, $500 a night, all myself."

A dealer cooks his own rocks. He mixes in a glass container a thimbleful of cut cocaine and about the same quantity of baking soda and a few drops of water. The mixture is gently shaken and cooked in a microwave for eight seconds on high or until the ingredients rock up. The rock is cut into pieces, selling for $10 (the size of a pencil eraser or a bit smaller), $20, and $50. Some dealers make a "primo"; that is, they add marijuana to the rock mixture before it is cooked.

Fang says a $10 rock made of 95 percent pure cocaine cut to 80-20 or 70-30 by a dealer contains about half of a tenth of a gram of cocaine. Mixed this way, a rock yields a profit of approximately $200 a gram, or $5,600 an ounce, at the point of sale.

There are rock counterfeiters who sell rock "look-alikes." During the day, Seattle dealers sell phony rocks to unsuspecting customers, who are almost always white folks driving expensive cars. They told me, if a customer is willing to buy cocaine in broad daylight, "they dumb enough to buy shit."

In a quick transaction, dried chewing gum or squashed Certs pass as a cocaine rock. Customers are clever, too. Some regular drive-up customers try to switch a phony rock that they've made and stashed under their tongue for a cocaine rock sold by a runner. With this in mind, a runner will not permit a drive-up customer to taste a rock before it is purchased. Most dealers do not sell phony rocks. It damages customer relations.

Memories of Good Ol' Days

Popcorn had been in the drug business before, and his memories of it motivated him. He recalled his drug-selling experiences for me. Popcorn left his alternative high school and started to "run papers" of heroin.* He worked and stayed with his cousin DC in an apartment at Twentieth and Walker in the CD. Popcorn bragged that DC's elder brother, Lewis, was "the one who got heroin started in Seattle." DC and Popcorn did well selling heroin. Life was easy then.

"Man, we had money, clothes, a car, girls. We didn't work but a couple hours a day. Suppliers and dealers, man, they be livin' good. Look, man, dealin' heroin's easy, man. Here's whatcha gotta do. While you cut and balloon it, always have someone watch the windows. Wash everything. Bury it outside and use a place marker. Keep the balloons in your hand or mouth when you on the street.†

"I cut it with lactose and experiment with it 'til I get it right. Add three spoons o' cut [small ice-cream-tasting spoon], mix it, and give it to somebody who'll shoot it. If he like it [if it isn't too weak or too

---

*A "paper" of heroin is a street idiom. A paper is a dose, or a "fix," which is approximately equivalent to the leveled quantity of a Baskin-Robbins ice-cream-tasting spoon. The drug is wrapped in a piece of plastic taken from a bag and finally packaged in tin foil. It is also packaged in waterproof balloons or condoms.

†If a runner is shaken down by street cops, he can swallow heroin balloons. He must hope, however, that the balloons don't break. If the balloons remain intact, he can either vomit them up or wait to retrieve them from his stools. A runner can also keep balloons in his hand, throw them when he runs from police, and retrieve them later.

strong], it be OK. A knock-off tip [an amount in the tip of an ice-cream-tasting spoon] is $20."

Popcorn sold less heroin as cocaine's popularity grew. Cocaine eventually overtook heroin sales. "Flake, at first, that was the thing then. When rock came along [1984], I switched." Business blossomed. So did DC's addiction to heroin, cocaine, and speedballs.*

Popcorn took over the business and rented his own place, the upper half of an old green duplex, one block west of Ezzel's, on the southern edge of Blood territory. To hear him tell it, he stayed in a suburban palace. I saw it; it was shabby and dilapidated, but he was proud of it. It was his, for a while.

At first, he used his apartment as a rock house, buying cocaine in Seattle from California-based sources (some rock houses sell heroin too. A "shooting gallery" is different from a rock house).[9] He rocked up cocaine in his kitchen, cut it, and sold it at his front door.

His sales expanded, and he became increasingly fearful that a steady flow of customers up the side steps to this apartment would draw police attention. So he moved his business operation to an apartment rented by a welfare mother. Cocaine paid his rent, and he traded it for sex. When he became fearful that that operation was attracting the police, he moved into the apartment of another welfare mother. The payment plan stayed the same.†

Popcorn was an honest businessman. Customers received a substantial quantity of high-quality rock at a reasonable price. Popcorn even ran "specials": buy a $100 rock, get a $50 rock free. He also offered "bump-ups," or "double-ups": a $20 bill buys a $50 rock.

Popcorn's social life was good, too. "I had enough money to support a house and a couple of skeezers. They're like queens and run the house and watch over my other women. Skeezers, they [are] like strawberries but different. Skeezers are better than that. They got values.[10]

"Skeezers'll sleep with you for drugs, but they won't leave you if

---

*A mixture of heroin and cocaine that's heated, liquefied, and injected is a speed-ball. Inciardi (1986:81–82) notes that the term *speedball* was used by "the heroin-using community as early as the 1930s, and [was known] as *whizbang* as far back as 1918." In 1982, Inciardi notes, speedballing killed actor John Belushi.

†Hamid's (1992) research in Central Harlem, New York City, describes "freak houses," temporary residences in abandoned buildings shared by male and female rock smokers who have lost their apartments, or "berths," in relatives' homes. The freak house residence pattern has been developing since 1990.

times get bad. Strawberries'll say, 'Fuck you, man,' and go find someone else. They got to have that rock. I had a lot of strawberries. A lot. I fucked 'em all, too." Popcorn smiled brightly.

"All girls that smoke are not strawberries. You ask them to do something fo' da c'aine you give 'em, and they look at you like you crazy. There be some who will give up their right arm for a rock. If you got a strong sexual nature, it be even more intense.

"A bitch who'd tear your doorknob off to get into your car to get to the dope, that a strawberry. You could ride downtown and the bitch [would] suck you[r] dick or you[r] partner's—anything you want.

"Sex? Yeah, it good on c'aine. You be sucking on a pipe while they suck on you! I'd like to have girls sitting on my lap; I'd be in her. You get it easier with c'aine while they be tweekin' and geekin'.

"I had a private strawberry named Joy. 'Nisie [Denise; one of Popcorn's long-term skeezers] had her, too. Denise [would] get Joy. Joy be finger-fuckin' Denise, and I be gettin' Joy from behind. 'Nisie'd like to have her titties sucked while she was smokin'.

"Denise get crazy sometimes. She be tweekin' about me tellin' Joy, 'I love you.' 'Nisie be smokin' the pipe in the corner, and she'd run over and pound on me, when I be fuckin' Joy. Other girls came through [Popcorn's apartment], and I'd ask Denise if she wanted them, and I'd get some head from Joy. Sometimes, I get four, five girls in a motel. They be doin' each other and I be watchin', smokin' my pipe, and they be suckin' each other's titties.

"After you be smokin' for a long time, it's not hard to get it up, you know. It gets hard tryin' to get it off, though. I hear some dudes who been smokin' for years can't get it up, you know. They just sittin' around watchin' girls doin' girls. They like it, too.

"Denise get jealous? Ah. If it's in public, it's all right, like Joy givin' me head and Denise finger-fuckin' Joy. If it's out where everybody can see it, it be all right, you know."

Popcorn ran the drug business for about 10 years. On that rainy afternoon in the CD, the day we met, it ended. That day, he lost his apartment, skeezers, and strawberries. His landlord didn't care; there are no leases signed between street hustlers, like Popcorn, and landlords. A drug seller doesn't have a checking account; he pays with drugs, or week to week or month to month with cash. No rent receipts are necessary, and landlords do not offer one. Even in run-down neighborhoods in the CD, cocaine profits keep rent high.

One night, Popcorn and I were in line waiting to buy chicken at Ezzel's. A neighborhood rock dealer came in. He saw Popcorn and immediately complained about the local rents. A ramshackle apartment near Ezzel's, not too far from Popcorn's former rock house, was renting for $600–$700 a month.

When Popcorn went to jail, his girls joined other "drug families" and found new drug boyfriends. Social flexibility is the key to keeping a roof overhead. For instance, Popcorn's skeezer, Denise, moved in with her uncle Oscar (her father's brother) and began to date a Blood, whose territory was a block away. For expediency, Denise was willing to live with her uncle, even though, according to Popcorn, Oscar had forced Denise to sleep with him when she was 11 or 12 years old.

Once, during my fieldwork, Denise invited Popcorn on a friendship tip to join her for Sunday dinner at Oscar's. Popcorn liked Denise. He called her Butter, " 'cause she the real thang, and she got *some* butt." I drove him to Oscar's house.

Oscar owns his house and rents space to welfare mothers and their kids. Oscar, a loan shark, claims his money on paydays and on "Mother's Day." Oscar buys food stamps on the street at half-price and uses them at Costco, a discount store, to buy food, which he sells on the street at a bit less than face value. He also sells drugs for the Bloods and Crips.

Many people stay at Oscar's: Denise and her two preschool kids; one of Popcorn's sisters and her baby; two of Popcorn's teenage nieces (daughters of two of his other sisters, who stay elsewhere); Denise's two teenage sisters and their two kids; one of Denise's preschool nephews (whose mother lives elsewhere); and two of Denise's cousins and their two kids.

Each teenage mother smokes rock, and has a Crip or Blood boyfriend who supplies the rocks. These girls are usually given rocks worth $200, whenever they need it. They sell $100 worth for cash, which they hand over to their boyfriend, and then keep $100 worth of rocks, which they smoke or sell, or both.

Popcorn and I left Oscar's hungry. There was no food, but there was cocaine—and there were hungry children.

"Doin' Good": Crime Folklore of the Street

Riches, cars, women—these are the fantasies of street drug sellers. Bourgois writes that in East Harlem, New York, the "crack economy and street culture are experienced as the most realistic routes for wealth and long-term success. Entry-level jobs are not seen as viable channels for upward mobility by high school dropouts. . . . The underground economy is more than material sustenance; it is also the most meaningful arena for the pursuit of prestige and meaning."[11]

The street is the place of wonderful memories that breed tomorrow's fantasies. Drug folklore tells dramatic and exciting accounts of dealers "doing good." I haven't seen ostentatious displays of wealth among cocaine sellers. Rock sellers use their profits for rent, food, and gas for old cars. I don't know a rock seller who owns a car; after all, ownership requires literacy skills, proper identification, a permanent residence.

Stories about cocaine wealth are far more common than material evidence of it. These stories always come from drug sellers who claim to have lived a life of splendor last year or before they lost their wealth and went to prison.

Popcorn told me, "You know, man, I made thousands and smoked up thousands. It's all gone now." After a long pause, he smiled and shook his head slightly up and down, as if to acknowledge to himself and to me that once he had been successful in a risky business.

Despite threats of jail and prison, drug sellers stand out on corners selling drugs. Street drug sellers don't fear street cops, getting busted, going to prison or jail, violent street competition, or heroin or alcohol addiction. These things are the exciting hazards of a drug seller's life. However, they are fearful of cocaine addiction. That fear has become a theme in cocaine folklore, connecting cocaine addiction to the loss of property and social life, the inevitable consequences of the addiction, the stories say.

A Hispanic heroin dealer, Juan, did six months in the Seattle jail for drug distribution. About age 30, an ex-marine (he had a marine tattoo on his arm), and a high school graduate, Juan had a juvenile history of burglaries, car thefts, truancy, and other kid stuff. Juan said that his cousin got him into the heroin business.

"We was doing good, you know. I tried to get a straight job, but it didn't work out. Bussing tables, waiting on people, that wasn't for me, man, you know. So I got into it with my cousin. Little stuff at first. I delivered heroin for him all over this fucking town.

"Where? Seafirst [Bank] Building, lawyers' offices, businesses, everywhere, man. There's addicts all over, respectable folks, too.

"Business got better. More deliveries. My cousin, he hired me to help him cut it, weigh it, package it, and he hired some kids to drive it around town. Couple hundred a day, they'll keep quiet and do a good job.

"Doing good, man, we was doing good. My cousin started doing a little coke, nothing heavy, you know what I mean. Little, little more, little more, soon that's all he was fucking doing. He started shooting heroin, too, with the coke. He's all fucked up.

"I took over the business, 'cause he started losing customers, you know. Prices went up. He started cutting it too thin and shorting 'em on quantities. Shit, man, he fucked up a good thing, you know.

"I built it back up again. Got the customers back and more. I bought my family a big house, new furniture. Kids got everything, man, everything. New cars. And I kept business away from them. I rented an apartment up near Broadway [Capitol Hill]. I had to hire some new guys to help me cut and package the shit.

"Money? I was making so much money that I hired a dude just to count it.

"I was doing good for about a year, maybe more. Then I started using cocaine. Six fucking months later, man, six *fucking* months, I lost everything. My business was gone, my ol' lady left me and took the kids. Bank got my house. Repo'ed my car and furniture. That, my friend, is what cocaine'll do to you.

"Heroin's different. You can shoot in the morning and in the afternoon. Shit's mellow, man. Dudes do their business all day, no one knows they're up. Coke ain't like that."

There are tales about the effects of smoking rock cocaine. 'Dre told me: "Yeah! They two kinds o' rock smokers. 'Rock patients,' they tweek artists, geekers. They fire the dope and burn it up right away. And 'smokers'—they knowledgeable smokers who uses it carefully and stretches it."

"Geekin'," said Popcorn, "that's when you lose your senses when you're not aware of reality around you. When you want it so bad you do anything for it. Everybody be geekin' a little different. I know a dude who think bugs be crawlin' all over him. He take one hit, one hit, that's all, and he start scratchin', scratchin' all over, man. He rip the skin off his arms and make himself bleed, man.

"Some people can handle it, some can't. They take a hit, they start tweekin'. My brother take a hit and he get down on the floor, lookin'. Others look out the window or talk. Other dudes, they be gettin' crazy and paranoid. My cousin like that. Take a hit and he starts runnin' around, look out the windows, think the cops comin'. Everybody does it different. It depends on the man. Limousine Tony [a pimp] took a hit and pull his 'ho'e over to him, say, 'Come here, bitch.' He be lookin' all around fo' da police.

"Down in Portland I knew this girl named Butterfly who started tweekin', take off all her clothes and scratch herself." He roared, laughing.

"Bloods'd give dis guy Albert a rock, just to watch him geek. Albert stuttered. Da Bloods, they say, 'What's your name? Spell it." He go, 'A-A-A-Albert.' They be laughin'."

Albert was a 14-year-old drug laborer and wannabe Blood who stayed in the CD with his grandmother. I was with him when he was arrested for selling rocks.

Cocaine sellers and addicts also said that cocaine is not addictive and is not a cause of violent behavior.

Popcorn said: "It's not addictive to the sense that you got to have it. You just like the exhilarating feeling it gives you. After you broke, all you can say is, 'We had fun.' That's what me and my brother said after we hustled up $700, $800, and smoked it up. Coke's not like heroin or cigarettes, where you start to shake. You might crave it like ice cream, but you don't got to have it. Some people will do anything for the cocaine, others won't. They'll keep their morals."

Fang said: "Folks don't be gettin' violent on heroin and don't be on rock. Some dudes be geekin' and get crazy, start to fight, stick somebody, or somethin' like dat, you know. It ain't the rock, man. It's the man. Some dudes, they get violent. Comin' off rock don't make you kill nobody. Crazy motherfuckers kill people, it don't make no difference what they be smokin'."

Popcorn's assertion that cocaine is not addictive surely didn't match the reality of his actual experiences. Despite that, as far as he and many other sellers are concerned, cocaine is not addictive. So much for learning from experience.

Connections to Cocaine

Forced to stay with his sister and her kids and whoever else shared her welfare apartment, Popcorn was motivated to move out. He needed cocaine. There are several strategies for getting it. A hustler can borrow cash, but that is unlikely; when cash is concerned, reciprocity fades. Or he can get cocaine on credit, which is likely; there is so much cocaine on the street that it can be borrowed with "interest." Or he can barter for cocaine using "slum," phony jewelry stamped 14K; many hustlers high-side using slum bracelets, necklaces, rings, or expensive-looking watches. Slum is a portable bank account. Or he can shoplift a few radios, cameras, Walkmans, or similar items. A fence, a broker in stolen objects, will very likely buy these items.

Every hustler working Seattle's streets knows about "Chinaman's Corner," a Pioneer Square fencing operation, run by an Asian American out of a small corner grocery store. "The Chinaman is tight enough," said David, who sold him eight new Sony Walkmans at five dollars each. "Chinaman sold 'em for $20." I saw stolen merchandise for sale in a display case.

Popcorn traded a $10 slum bracelet, which he'd found in his sister's room, for three $50 rocks. He cut each one into pieces; the larger pieces sold for $20 each, and the smaller ones for $10. He rebagged them, putting the chunks into small sealable bags, and had a wannabe gang member in the CD sell them. He made $90, gave the laborer $20, and kept $70. To this, he added the profits from selling a half dozen five-dollar watches, which he'd shoplifted. Now, in a day or two, he was back in the drug business.

Drug Customers

Popcorn wanted to stay out of jail for a while, and he still wanted to move away from his sister. To do this, he needed "safe" customers. Rock-addicted welfare women are exploited by male and female drug sellers. They are easy, available sources of income. Popcorn's sister was one entry point into that network; he also knew them from years on the street, and from listening to other drug sellers talk about them. He sold them rocks, but he said he did it with dignity.

"I front off [sell cocaine] to welfare women, but I don't want to dog no person [he didn't want to take advantage of them]. My brother's girlfriend has five, six kids. She get a $900 welfare check and food stamps. I had this girlfriend who got $900 a month for three kids, and $70, $77 a month foodstamps for each one, and pay $64 rent. She smokin' it all up. I see some of 'em who couldn't pay that $64. They smokin' that up. That's what that c'aine doin' to 'em."

Within a month, Popcorn had moved out of his sister's apartment and was sharing residences with eight women. In exchange for rock cocaine, they provided him a place to sleep, food, sex, and paid him cash, which he used to buy flake cocaine that he rocked up and sold. He stayed with one woman for a week or two, and during that time, he used the other apartments for drug sales.

'Dre also sold cocaine to welfare women and used their welfare checks as collateral. "Them bitches don't buy their babies diapers, but they buy that dope." 'Dre explained how he did it. In his account, he played his role and a woman's by altering his voice.

'Dre said to the woman, "I'm wanna use you spot [her apartment] to sell some dope out of."

" 'Dre, man, I don't have no food in here."

'Dre reassured her. "I call my partner; he buy y'all some groceries."

'Dre said he and his road dog would "move on in there. We'd cook, cut, and sell rock right out their places. I'd give 'em a $20 [rock] for every $100 I made. Then, they'd buy a quarter ounce for $200 [nearly a 100 percent profit] from me, rock it and sell it, and make $600, so they can buy more from me!

"Pussy and dope'll sell on the street all the time. When nothing else was goin', I'd sell pussy. Dope'd sell behind it. Women be comin' into the apartment, lookin' to have sex with me for my dope."

Miss Ann hustled welfare mothers, too. Most of her money went to cop heroin.[12] "I was a prostitute [as a teenager]. Money was good. Can't do dat no mo', man. My husband [a common law marriage to a man 10 years her junior] don' want me to do dat. I sell drugs.

"Women on welfare with three, four, five kids, they get a big check. Fou' kids get 'em $500 and $250 in food stamps. Man, I knew dis bitch, she gettin' $700 welfare, $300 food stamps, and $100 child support, and by the fifth, sixth [of the month], she be broke. She had a five-year-old who say, 'Mommy, don't smoke up your check.'

"Feel bad? Me? Shit, motherfucker. It's on them.

"Yeah, gangs do it, too. Gangs up there [in the CD] give welfare mothers cocaine. They sit there and watch 'em smoke it. She'll buy money orders to pay her bills [she doesn't have a checking account], and she'll cash them and use the money for rock. Listen up, buddy row. Cocaine—that's the biggest pimp.

"Here ya go, buddy row, here's how I did it. All ya needs is five, six women with $1,000 each a month [in welfare money and food stamps]. I get a room, maybe two, in a motel. I use one for the kids. I sit in there and play with the kids, watchin' TV, while da mothers be in da other room smokin', smokin'. They be smokin' more than their checks and food stamps, and I'd dog 'em. I make 'em give back them diapers, milk, and meat to the grocery store, and get that cash.

"Ya need protection, man. Everybody out there know what you doin' and know they'd be cash up in there. I hired a dude, he stand at the door with a pistol.

"I be gettin' rock from a dude in the gang, and I owe him the money. If ya don' pay, it's his ass [the supplier], your ass [the smoker], or my ass [the seller], and *baby*, it *ain't* gonna be my ass!"

Miss Ann lost her children to rock. Child Protective Services took her 11-year-old and 9-year-old sons. "I was smokin', smokin' every day. I gave my kid [referring to her 11-year-old] to some folks to take care o' him while I smoked. I gave them money and coke to watch him. I'm gonna get him back. I don't know when, man. I gotta clean up first. That be tough."*

Apparently Popcorn also found it tough to stay away from rock. After living with welfare women for about six months, he fell prey to the rock pipe. He started smoking again, and before long he was on the street, back in the Union Gospel Mission. As we saw early in the book, one night in the CD, he was stopped by police and arrested for possession of drug paraphernalia, his rock pipe. Saved.

"The Program"

In 1988, Washington State began its largest drug and alcohol treatment program, the Alcoholism and Drug Addiction Treatment Support Act (ADATSA).[13] Its 1988–90 budget of $41 million targeted street alcoholics, but the program has progressively incorporated more drug patients, especially pregnant women and parents of young children. By April 1990, 1,600 patients were being treated in residential and out-patient programs.

*Fetal cocaine exposure has been associated with congenital abnormalities and permanent neurophysiological damage (see Heidemann and Goetting 1990; Phibbs et al. 1991). Inner-city elementary school teachers told me crack babies (youngsters whose mothers smoked rock cocaine during pregnancy) are entering classrooms with learning disabilities and serious behavior problems. A first-grade teacher in Akron, Ohio, said crack children often display very violent behavior, such as punching and kicking other children in the face, during minor playground scuffles.

Miss Ann would have been the ideal residential client: a home-less, illiterate, heroin-addicted, unmarried, chronically alcoholic mother of three children. After some prodding from me, Miss Ann scheduled an interview with an ADATSA in-take counselor. She was hopeful that a drug counseling program would improve her chances of getting her nine-year-old son, her youngest child, back from Child Protective Services. I hoped it wouldn't.

The goal of ADATSA is rehabilitation, but that goal is not shared by many patients. The Seattle jail supplies inmate-patients, who then stay in a pleasant minimum-security facility north of the city. Inmate-patients stay in their own rooms and can wear street clothes. Best of all, the ADATSA program is coed. This aspect enthused Popcorn.

Drug addicts and alcoholics on the street can get into the reha-bilitation program, too. But all the drug addicts and alcoholics I know say they can't do it. One Sunday afternoon in a Pioneer Square tavern, David talked about why he couldn't do the program.

Cold Rainier beer frosted the outside of the pitcher. It sat in front of David, who faced me in a wooden booth near the pool tables. David had been barred from this tavern, but since he was with me, the bartender let him stay. We sat in the back, near two pay 'n play pool tables.

Willie, a pudgy, middle-aged white man, joined us. He sat next to David. David had introduced me to Willie just minutes earlier. Willie had been sitting up front, alone, near the main window, sip-ping on a half-full pitcher of beer. Willie's thick, yellowish finger-nails were oddly long, at least an inch. Dirt was packed between the curve of each nail and the fleshy tip of the finger. Heavy beard, dirty clothes, no money (someone had given him the pitcher, Willie said) identified him as a refugee from a local mission.

A middle-aged blonde woman with dark bags slightly visible un-der her eyes played pool with a well-built black fellow, nicely dressed. She sipped a schooner of ice water, her smooth full lips touching the schooner, leaving a red lipstick mark behind on the rim. She smiled casually at David while she circled the table, sinking striped balls one by one. She played well.

David sat motionless, eyes open wide, as if he were in a trance. "She's got a beautiful smile," he observed. "She reminds me of Es-ter." The blonde's smiles were his thrills.

Cold beer was the last thing David needed. His hands were still shaking from too much Wild Irish Rose the night before. But he wanted beer, so I bought it. He refused to eat.

"Stay out of his life," I told myself. "He's a drunk, a street thug, nothing will help him. Buy him beer, get what you want, go home." But I liked him, wanted to help. Unfortunately, I was 35 years too late.

David shook, smoked, drank his beer. Watching him made me nauseous.

"Can you get me into a program?"

"Treatment program?" I asked.

"Yeah. I can't handle this no more. I gotta get off the street. I gotta stop this."

"Yeah, I can take care of it for you."

"Today?"

"Nah. It's Sunday. Tomorrow. Monday, offices open up."

"Gotta be today, man. Today. I need help *now,* not Monday."

"Tomorrow, David, tomorrow. First thing, I'll call. Got a quarter?" A joke.

"If I do this, I want you there when I go in. I want you to visit me. Give me cigarette money. And be there when I get out. I ain't doin' it alone, man." Demands.

"I'll help you get in, but you gotta go through it alone. I can't be there every day, man. I got work to do, you know that. I'll make sure you got money in your account for all the Camels you can smoke."

"How quick can I get in?"

Willie piped in, "Couple weeks, at least."

"Is that right, Mark? Couple weeks!"

"Probably, David. It's not a fucking hotel, man. Takes time. Lots of people need help."

"Ain't gonna do it. Fuck it."

David poured more beer into his nearly empty schooner. He looked away at the blonde.

"She's beautiful, man. Reminds me of Ester." Back to fantasy.

ADATSA protected and nurtured Popcorn. He completed the in-house treatment and moved into a downtown Seattle hotel at ADATSA expense. Ninety days rent-free in a place I call the Homeboy Arms, a temporary residence for sober alcoholics and drug addicts.

The Homeboy Arms is not a glitzy place. On any afternoon, the lobby is full of middle-aged to old men sitting peacefully, staring through hazy lobby windows, smoking cigarettes, saying nothing. On the third floor overlooking a Pay 'n Park was Popcorn's room, a spot not much larger than a two-man prison cell. Fact is, new prison cells are bigger, better ventilated, better heated, air conditioned, brighter, better furnished, and quieter.

ADATSA provides its clients with a monthly stipend, paid to a "protective payee," a drug and alcohol counselor. This allocation is intended to support ADATSA out-patients while they search for a job and a permanent residence. Popcorn received $320 each month; $185 paid the rent and the balance was his. Popcorn had to pass a weekly urine test and attend meetings of Alcoholics Anonymous and Narcotics Anonymous to remain in the program.

Popcorn didn't use his allotment the way ADATSA had intended. He bought pawn shop goodies. A stereo, an electronic drum pad, a radio, and a television took relatively large chunks of cash out of his small budget. That didn't matter. Popcorn didn't save money, he didn't plan for the day the checks would stop. He planned for today.

Street people understood how ADATSA was being used by addicts. Listen to this conversation.

On a cold, drizzling, Friday afternoon, I went looking for Popcorn at the Homeboy, but he was gone. I wandered around the market area, looking for him or any addict or drug seller who wanted to chat. I didn't find anyone. It was still too early in the day for serious drug sellers and runners to be on the street hustling. Then, too, cold rain always drives them into hiding.

Leaning against a parking meter, I watched a teenage girl eat a plain cake donut and sip black coffee from a plastic foam cup. Her face was pocked with acne. She sat alone, dressed in a studded leather jacket. Her hair was heavily sprayed and twisted and knotted into an oddly shaped headdress. Tattooed spider webs spun out from under her metal studded, black leather, fingerless gloves. Real tattoos? She was daydreaming—of a happier time, I guessed. I felt her loneliness.

I looked away from her. Strolling down the street, I saw Popcorn coming toward me.

"Wha's up, homeboy!"

"Not'in', man. Same ol', you know."

"Where ya going?"

"Da hotel. Listen to some music. Play my drummin' machine."

He didn't want my company.

"Wanna eat later? Do some cruisin'?"

"Yeah."

A skinny black man in his early 30s sauntered up to us. It was Bobo. He said, "Popcorn, man, whatcha doin'?"

"Doin' good, doin' good."

"Where ya been, man? Ain't seen ya for a while."

"Just got outta treatment, man. Yeah."

Bobo laughed. "The *program!* Whatcha *do* that fo'?"

Popcorn shrugged. "I don't know."

Bobo asked, "How was it?"

"Good, man. Treatcha good. Nice up in there too. Better'n at jail."

They laughed, nodded knowingly.

Bobo asked, "Where you stayin' at, Popcorn?"

"At da hotel."

"They pay fo' it?"

Popcorn nodded yes. "Give me food money too."

Bobo said, "Listen, man, you gotta to come up to the crib, man. We barbecue some meat and kick it for a while. The ol' lady be workin' at Safeway. We got money, man. Ye-ah!"

Popcorn asked, "You up in da CD stayin' wit' your sister?"

Bobo shook his head no. "We moved, man. Got our own place up on University Ave."

"Yeah, OK, man. I try."

They nodded to each other. Bobo walked away. Trailing behind him, smoking an unfiltered Pall Mall, was his scrawny white wife, drawn cheeks, dark bags shadowing her eyes. I thought she would be a good poster woman for a ROCK COCAINE—JUST SAY NO campaign.

Popcorn's ADATSA support was about to end. That evening at dinner, I asked him about his future plans. "I don' know where I'm goin' after da program, man. I can go back into business if things get too bad. Ain't nothin' be makin' me go back to them missions."

Popcorn considered his options. He said he might move into Denise's house "to be wid her." Butter would let him move into Oscar's house, he said. But she now had a Crip boyfriend. Crips, as well as Bloods, were always hanging around Oscar's house. Denise had told him, "They be fighting outside and da girls be fighting inside." About a block from Oscar's, a Crip shot at a Blood. He missed. Butter and other girls staying in Oscar's house said jealousy over a girl's attention led to the shooting.

Popcorn rethought the idea of staying in a Crip hangout. Luckily, his common sense prevailed. "I be stayin' at the Homeboy. A motha-'fucker be gittin' killed around dat house, man." (Popcorn could rent a room at the Homeboy, after the program ended, at the same rate paid by ADATSA.)

Popcorn also thought about moving back in with his sister. But staying with her was his final option. He got an idea. He met Beverly during treatment. A 25-year-old rock addict, Beverly had a two-year-old son. Child Protective Services placed him in custody when she began drug treatment. Beverly's husband, also the father of her son, was a drug-addicted outlaw who was arrested on a parole violation and was returned to prison just after Beverly and Popcorn had completed in-house treatment.

Beverly sent Popcorn weekly letters, envelopes scented and embellished with red lipstick imprints. Once Beverly sent him color photographs of herself dressed in a transparent negligee, sitting on a bed, leaning against a large pastel silk pillow, her legs separated slightly. An invitation, thought Popcorn.

Popcorn's dilemma was that Beverly lived in a small town several hundred miles east and north of Seattle. A bus ticket was too expensive. I offered him bus money; he refused it. I offered to drive him there; he refused that too. Popcorn's fantasy about Beverly seemed to meet his needs. Reality takes work, so he was content to dream.

ADATSA ended. Popcorn moved back to the Union Gospel Mission. Time to begin again.

Plans Always Change

Hours before the peak commuting rush, missions empty homeless folks onto the sidewalks. They fill park benches and line up on the streets to panhandle nickels, dimes, and quarters, spare change to buy a bottle of wine, the first one of the day.

Popcorn and I had breakfast one morning about 7:00, at the Corner Restaurant, where First meets Pike; he was staying at a mission. The bar stools in the restaurant's tavern were nearly all occupied by then; men and women were drinking schooners of cold beer or a whiskey and a beer "back," watching "Good Morning, America."

In the restaurant, old men sat alone in seven reddish vinyl booths with taped tears and cracks, or on the dozen stainless-steel mushroom-shaped stools situated in front of a scratched, U-shaped formica counter. The cash register was located in the middle of the U, too far from the counter to give an advantage to snatch-and-run artists like David.

Nearly all the men smoked. Most of them had roll-your-own cigarettes, but a few men smoked tailor-made (packaged cigarettes). They held cigarettes close to their lips, taking long, deep draws to fill their lungs, their wrinkled faces registering pleasure.

The waitress served them one by one; no one looked at another man's meal. Some of the men ate eggs, toast, and potatoes; others, pancakes. Their toast was used to scrape their plates clean of drying yoke; hungry old men waste nothing. Most didn't eat meat; it's too expensive. A few lucky ones, savoring every mouthful, ate breakfast porkchops, thin, crusty, grill fried with mashed potatoes and gravy.

Popcorn and I sat in a window booth, so I could see the street. "Look at these guys, Popcorn. Shabby, huh? Sad. It's sad. These guys should be home with their grandkids, huh? Not living like this." That was bait. I awaited a reply.

"Best they got. Shit, I don't wanna end up like this."

"Fuck no, man, you'll get it together, get a job, money, an ol' lady. You'll be doing good soon." I lied. I paused. "If you don't straighten out, you'll never get out of that mission. Ever think about going for help, getting an 8:00-to-5:00, getting off the street? Man, if you don't leave that rock alone, you'll end up in the joint." I waited for an answer. None came. I dropped it.

My informants never considered the option of getting a straight job, working an 8:00-to-5:00 as a janitor or on a loading dock, nor did they seriously consider asking someone to help them create a straight lifestyle.[14] The fact is, in natural conversations inside prison and on the street, hustlers don't talk about selling cocaine and using the profits for community college tuition, or volunteering for community-funded vocational training programs.

Frankly, I became weary watching Popcorn do nothing but go to jail and sell and smoke rock cocaine. Acting as a surrogate father, on many occasions I pushed him to think about his future in a way that I constructed it. My vision for him included a job, a place to live, paying taxes, and accepting adult responsibilities. His irresponsibility annoyed me; he was wasting my tax dollars.[15]

One sunny Sunday afternoon, I listened to Popcorn and his road dog, CJ, converse about going straight. We were sitting at a small table in Starbuck's on Broadway.

I said to CJ, "Well, you been through the program [ADATSA]. You're a bright guy. Are you going to get a job?"

"A regular job? A straight one?"

"Yeah. A straight one, CJ. People do have straight jobs, you know." We laughed.

"Nah, that would hinder me at this point. I'm used to a particular lifestyle. I need a lump sum. I need to buy some more toys." CJ and Popcorn smiled, nodded in agreement.

That angered me. "We all want toys, CJ, but how are you going to get the money if you don't go to work?"

"I'm going to take my time, get a guitar, and try to get my band together, again. You'll hear me over the airwaves."

Sure, I thought to myself. I'll probably hear CJ playing in an inmate band in a prison auditorium. I pushed on him. "Yeah, but where you going to get the cash, CJ?"

Popcorn responded, "We going ta 'Laska." It was an idea I had implanted many months earlier. Salmon fishing pays very well.

"What? You two city fellas going to Alaska?" I kidded.

CJ said, "Yeah, man, we interviewed with the Northwest Passage Fishing Company the other day." Popcorn nodded slowly.

"Fishing. You guys. CJ and Popcorn in Alaska. Sounds like a Three Stooges story. Shit!" I teased.

CJ responded, "Lotta money in salmon. And it be safer than burglary!" A roar of laughter mixed in the air with the aroma of rich coffee.

"Well, when's this big plan gettin' underway?"

Popcorn replied, "Next week. I' gonna interview."

I said to Popcorn, "I thought you'd already been accepted?"

CJ interrupted, "I interviewed, and they said I could go."

Popcorn said, "Yeah, dat right."

I asked CJ, "Are you really going up there?"

"Man, what choices does I have? I ain't workin' for no goddamn McShit burgers, flipping hamburgers 'n shit like that there. Fuck dat." CJ was annoyed. Popcorn nodded his agreement.

CJ went on, "Look, man, da program got me a apartment down the street, give me some cash too. Doin' good for now, ya know, man. I can hold on like this, but I'm plannin'. Tomorrow's comin', right, *motherrrfuuuckerrr?*" He was annoyed at me for pushing him, challenging his plan.

I knew Popcorn and CJ wouldn't work on a fishing boat; fishing is hard work. I tried to repair a rip in the rapport. "What do you city fellas know 'bout salmon, hooks, chum, shit like that? You know, I had a friend who went up to Alaska in the summer, busted his ass, and he made a lot of money. You ready to work hard?"

Popcorn looked at CJ, waiting for his road dog to proclaim that fishing boat workers really don't work hard.

CJ answered, "Man, I know that. But you only up there for a few months."

Popcorn nodded. "Yeah, it's only for a few months."

I knew Popcorn didn't have an appointment for an interview. After nearly two years with him, I knew better. But I pretended and went along with the game. Several days later, we talked near the Pike Place Market. I asked if he had had his interview.

"What happened, man? How come you didn't go up to see 'em? There's good money in fish."

Popcorn started hopping nervously from foot to foot, swaying his shoulder front to back, turning his head slightly side to side. He did not look directly at me.

"That's shit, bullshit, man. They say they pay good, but they don't. They a bunch a white motha'fuckers who run them boats. They hates us niggers. You know dat, motherfucker."

I asked Popcorn if CJ had gone to Alaska. Popcorn had not seen him in a few days. I asked a few folks about CJ. I remembered that not too long ago, CJ said he wanted to take a bus to Chicago to visit his family. He said his father was a minister, his mother a social worker, and his sister lived in the same apartment building as Oprah Winfrey.

I had asked CJ, "Why don't you ask them for help? A few hundred bucks, you can get your guitar outta hock, get your band together again, huh?"

"Nope, not me. I left home when I was a kid, about 14, 15, and never went back. I'm gonna make it on my own. Beat them drugs, stay off that rock, make it, man. *On my own.* I ain't asking them, not for a motherfuckin' thing. When I go home, it'll be in a limo, ssstrrretch." A fantasy smile creased his face. A few days later I found CJ in jail, busted for theft. He had missed the boat. Indeed.

At 9:00 on a Monday morning, about two years after we first met, Popcorn and I drank coffee one final time at Starbuck's on Broadway. I felt as if I were abandoning him, leaving behind a helpless child.

Several months had passed since he had finished ADATSA, and he had stayed with his sister on and off and moved into the Union Gospel Mission many times. He was selling rocks and stolen watches and was talking about building up his drug business. Again, one last time, I talked to him about a straight job.

"OK, motherfucker, what's next in your life? Where do you go from here?"

Popcorn replied, "Got a idea."

"What?"

"Folks out there who got money want to buy stuff, right?"

"Yeah."

"What they need is to buy a book about where they can buy stuff."

"Huh?"

"Clearinghouse, man. Look. I sell them whities with bucks a catalog that lists all the books they can use to buy stuff. Self-help stuff, you know. How to fix the house, car, shit like that. They got kids on drugs, they can buy a booklet about what to do wid 'em." This idea made little sense to me.

"Well, look here, Popcorn. If these booklets you want to sell are already available to them, why do they need you?"

He paused, thinking. "'Cause I make it easy fo' 'em to get that shit, you know." He paused, again. "If I had a $1,000, I could turn it into a $100,000 real quick."

I knew what was coming. "Why don't you get a job and save the money?"

"Nah. I ain't gonna work for minimum wage. I'd rather do nothin' than work for two bucks an hour turnin' them fuckin' hamburgers or sweepin' some fuckin' flo's. I done 'at befo'e and it didn't work out, you know. I didn't get it on with my boss. Worked a couple days, and said, *'Fuck you, motherfuckers.'*"

"Let's go," I said. "Time to take you downtown. I gotta go home."

We drove in silence from Broadway to First and Pike. I thought about the years together: I knew his routine, it was mine too. He would spend the day walking and talking, and poppin' co'n. He would walk down First Avenue late in the afternoon, passing the Service Center and Wandering Raven, and stand in line at the Union Gospel Mission, waiting for a place to sleep. I pulled up in front of the Market Cafe.

"Hey, you take care of yourself, hear me? Stay the fuck away from rocks."

"Mark, man, think you can spare 75 cents for a soda? I'm a bit short."

"Yeah. Here." I put three quarters in his hand and reached into my pocket for my roll of ones. I had a five on top and gave it to him.

"This is bus money, Popcorn. Get on the right bus, OK bud?" He missed the point. We nodded at each other. He slid out of my car, gently pushing the door closed, and walked off. He didn't look back. He didn't look ahead either. We didn't see each other again. This research had ended.

A few months later I began to miss hanging out with Popcorn, CJ, T-Cool, Miss Ann, and the others. I drove to Seattle, looking for Popcorn. I looked everywhere, missions, shelters, the market, all his familiar haunts. I cruised the Central District, went to Ezzel's, and stopped to ask his Blood companions if they had seen him. "Don' know where he at," said a youngster about 12, a boy I hadn't seen before.

I walked the streets too, looking in bars and alleys, asking panhandlers and junkies, some I knew and others I didn't, if they had seen Popcorn. Hanging around near the Union Gospel Mission was CJ. "Seen Popcorn?" I asked.

"Nah, man, he ain't been around in a while," he replied. "Heard he went to St. Louis. He got people there, you know."

"What's he gonna do there?" I asked.

"Pop co'n, Mark, pop co'n. Dat's what he does," laughed CJ.

Street Culture

Street culture is a set of skills acquired during years of socialization on the street that enable hustlers' material survival. There are numerous material issues that affect young hustlers, including, for instance, where to sleep safely, how to behave properly in a mission, where and how to buy drugs, how to talk to street cops, where the best stores are for shoplifting, how to fence stolen property.

Street culture also has a unique worldview, which is a shorthand way of saying that street criminals, once victims of child abuse and neglect, come to the street with styles for perceiving and interpreting events that are similar to the lifestyles they experienced in their home as young children. Street culture has a set of distinctive themes that reflect hustlers' defensive worldview and its core ele-

ments—fear of unpredictable social interactions, of social attachments, of criticism, and of rejection.

Let there be no mistake about street culture and its effect on hustlers: Street hustlers learn adaptational skills on the street, but they
don't learn a defensive worldview on the street. This worldview is
the consequence of neglectful and abusive parenting.[16] Ace will be
emotionally and cognitively predisposed to street life after years of
brutal treatment by Maniac.

Street culture has a component that enables hustlers to hide their
fears with elaborate, self-protective, expressive behaviors: the verbal
bravado (loud, challenging, and often aggressive); aggressive and
sometimes violent interactions; and typical attitudes and beliefs
about social discourse, work, and personal responsibility.[17]

I've identified seven dominant themes in street culture:

1. *Street culture doesn't use guilt and shame as foundations for informal social control.* Informal social control is predicated on "role relationships [that are] established for other purposes and are components of role reciprocities."[18] Hustlers' social interactions with
others aren't based on closeness or responsibility.[19] Hustlers don't
honestly accept personal responsibility for behavior or display
genuine feelings of guilt or shame, even for serious criminal acts.
Fact is, they customarily blame criminal behavior on imperfections
in lawful society or on a nearby vulnerable target.

2. *Street culture permits personal irresponsibility by providing rationalizations, justifications, and excuses for irresponsible behavior.* These culturally acceptable defenses range from ideology ("America hates
us") and conspiracy theory ("America discriminates against us and
gives us drugs to eliminate us"), to material inadequacy ("If schools
were better I wouldn't need to steal or sell drugs"; "If our community had more businesses . . ."), to employment inadequacy ("If I
could find a job that suited me . . ."), to disease theory ("My father
drank, I have to drink"). I've never heard a criminal say, except in a
parole hearing, "I accept responsibility for my actions."

3. *Street culture doesn't value personal introspection, self-motivation,
lawful personal initiative, and creative thinking and problem solving.*
Luck and stealth are emphasized over hard work. Most street hustlers have little or no experience at lawful employment until they go
to prison and work their first lawful job. Hustling, quick and easy
scams, and exhausting money on drinking and partying, without a
thought about the future, are hustlers' preoccupations. "Shit, 8:00 to

5:00, that's fo' chumps," says Itch. Popcorn said he had had a "normal" job once, but he didn't intend to do it again.

4. *Street culture isn't future oriented.* Scholars who have studied criminals' view of motivation and personal change have, for the most part, collected data from prison inmates.[20] Hustlers in prison let society care for all their needs. Talking about personal change is easy, but their comments inside prisons almost never carry over to their behavior outside.

5. *Street culture values the status quo, not personal change.* Change frightens hustlers. To maintain the sameness of life, to prevent feelings of helplessness that arise with change, hustlers block change with legal and ideological obstacles. Often these obstacles result in unlawful behavior and a return to prison, where every day is the same, where options are few and ambiguity has been removed, and where social life is stable.[21] Almost 60 percent of all prisoners on parole violate parole[22] and return to jail or prison.

6. *Street culture doesn't renounce crime and substance abuse as self-destructive behaviors.* Street hustlers are comfortable hustling. They enjoy the irresponsible pleasures of alcohol and drug use, the care-free quality of committing crime with impunity, and a dependence on society for their well-being.[23] Participation in street culture prepares boys to be hustlers and prisoners, that's all.

7. *Street culture stresses individual plasticity that allows hustlers to conform by molding behavior and speech to the demands of immediate circumstances.* Hustlers are chameleons. They survive with behavioral plasticity and verbal stealth. Popcorn, David, T-Cool, Slim, and others will say whatever is necessary to get what they want.[24] Masters of verbal camouflage, they practice these talents in police stations, jails, and prisons.

During years in the criminal justice system, their skills mature. Hustlers have years of contact with police, courts, social workers, counselors, caseworkers, educators, psychologists, and other professionals working in the criminal justice system. They soon realize that if they are to adapt well, to receive the benefits of being in the system, or to manipulate it, they must speak as their captors do. Their once-restricted linguistic repertoires expand, and they learn to answer outsiders' questions using the jargon of rehabilitation, a speech code that is acceptable to lawful citizens[25] and one that signals to lawful citizens that hustlers have changed. This is cleverest of all hustlers' games.

However, criminals don't require too much linguistic stealth to fool lawful citizens or practitioners in the criminal justice system. Offenders are commonly asked by the courts if they "accept responsibility" for offenses. Accepting responsibility will, in many cases, lessen the sentence and restrictions imposed on offenders in prison. As a correctional programs specialist for the federal correctional system, I read the pre-sentence investigation (a court-ordered investigation of the offense and the offender's criminal and personal history) of many offenders; every one had accepted responsibility. But the court doesn't ask if the offenders are lying. Only a truly foolish offender wouldn't lie.

In years of listening to natural conversations in jails, prison cellblocks, and on city streets, I never heard hustlers talk about a desire to become lawful citizens or to work a lawful job. They didn't discuss the foolishness of their juvenile or adult crimes, or how remorseful they felt about hurting someone. On the street, hustlers don't talk about how long they waited in line at the unemployment office or about spending the profits from criminal activity for higher education. They don't discuss a desire to have a wife, children, and a home and garden. They never say they'd be proud to pay taxes, vote, or join the local parent-teacher association.

Who's Responsible for Street Crime

Street criminals' behavior is antithetical to social life in lawful society. But street culture isn't the cause of deviant and criminal behavior; it's the effect of enculturation in hostile families with brutal parents.

Irwin and Austin note that "social science should have taught us that all human behavior is only partially a matter of free will and that persons are only partially responsible for their deeds. Everyone's actions are always somewhat influenced or dominated by factors not of one's own making and beyond personal control."[26] Wolf Man, Pimping Slim, Donut, Donnie, and the others as preschool children couldn't control the brutality of their parents; however, as these street criminals aged and moved into teenage and adult years, they were aware of their own deviance and criminal behavior. They decided to use drugs and alcohol; they chose to commit crimes.

Street culture is not an excuse for or a cause of crime, but street culture does offer hustlers excuses. "On whom or on what can I blame my behavior?" hustlers ask. Society, prison, social workers, teachers, heroin, cocaine, alcohol, cops, girlfriends are handy reasons hustlers cite. This is hustlers' folk psychology, which Irwin and Austin would likely agree with. I don't.

What's missing in these folk explanations for deviance and crime is personal responsibility. When offenders are children aged 9, 10, and 11, it's easy to understand how they can be both criminal offenders and victims of brutal parents. Indeed, it's unfortunate that society has chosen to perpetuate child abuse by not acting on these young offenders' behalf long before they are arrested and committed to juvenile detention centers.

I've spent years on the street with rational, conscious criminals, both young and adult. These hustlers were once victims of abuse, but they were never victims of an ephemeral system of values and beliefs that compelled them to drink, use cocaine, burglarize houses, and commit drive-by shootings. They understand what crime is, they talk about it, they laugh about it, and they choose to commit it. Criminals, regardless of age, must be held accountable for their behavior and the violence and pain they inflict on victims.

There were a million confirmed cases of child neglect and abuse in 1993.[27] Every time judges, prosecutors, and social service workers return abused children to vile parents, these professionals exploit children in the name of a wish-fulfilling fantasy about "family life." The fact is that social service agencies and the juvenile justice system enable brutal parents to transform healthy young children into helpless and irresponsible adolescents and adult criminals.

We insist that criminals pay for their mistakes. But who pays for the mistakes of social workers and judges? Now Ace pays every time Maniac beats him. Perhaps the federal government, acting on behalf of child-victims, should hold social workers, judges, and prosecutors responsible for malfeasance when they enable child victimization. Perhaps these professionals ought to be financially accountable for cases of neglected and abused children who eventually end up in the public domain (jail, juvenile detention, prison). Perhaps if these professionals were to face criminal charges, they would become more aware of their bad decisions.

To keep youngsters off the street, away from youth gangs, and out of prisons, we must first protect them from mothers and fathers who neglect, beat, and abandon them. If we shirk our responsibility to protect children, then we too are accountable for street crime.

6 _____

Aging

The ethnographic observations and interviews in this book support a well-documented fact about criminality: criminal involvement increases from childhood to late teenage years and then slowly diminishes.[1] I think this phenomenon is not singularly the result of aging.

In this chapter, I discuss two types of hustlers whose propensity to commit crime has diminished. The first type is the loner, as they call themselves. David, in his 40s, and 'Dre and Miss Ann, in their mid- to late 30s, are loners who avoid continuous day-to-day companionship with active hustlers. They said less contact with active hustlers gets them into less trouble. Fact is, David is the only hustler I interviewed over age 40 who was arrested, and his offense was minor, public drunkenness and fighting. Despite their outlook, however, these loners occasionally formed short-term partnerships or tips for a quick hustle to make some money. And, of course, they never refused to share a bottle of Wild Irish Rose with a streetcorner group.

The second type is middle-aged hustlers who band together. During my research, Shy was the core member of a 12–15-member group of former prisoners in their mid-30s to late 40s[2] who had declared freedom from a dependence on jails and prisons and now devoted themselves to satisfying alcohol addictions. These are the men and women I call the porch people. On occasion one would be arrested for public drunkenness, street fighting, or harassing tourists, but after a day or two in jail,[3] he was back on the street.

Loners and porch people represent the street lifecycle's post-system stage.[4] All these hustlers begin using alcohol and drugs as adolescents, and with age, their addiction to alcohol and drugs increases. When this happens the threat of going to prison becomes a serious deterrent to criminal behavior. These hustlers simply don't want to risk being deprived of access to alcohol and drugs. A lifestyle of crime gives way to a lifestyle of addiction and the economic and social activities to support it.

Daily life for older addicted hustlers brings just two things: hustling and using drugs and drinking. Sometimes hustling brings a quick thrill, but crime is thrilling mostly as a conversation topic. It isn't too thrilling to awaken each day in a mission, a shelter, or on a piece of cardboard on a cold sidewalk with a hangover or a desperate need for a syringe full of heroin, a hit on the rock pipe, or a bottle of Wild Irish Rose.

Others' research has found that middle-aged offenders acquire full-time jobs, marry, or experience other positive changes in natal and conjugal families.[5] My informants didn't do these things.* The loners and porch people I met didn't lament life passing them by; there were no dramatic personal revelations; and they were no less rebellious than more active hustlers, just rebellious in a different way.[6]

Street and prison informants talk about "meaningful" life changes, and I looked for objective evidence of it. Penitentiary informants said that older guys get "tired," "learn their lesson," "leave the street to kids," "get beat up on the street," and "get tired of the hassle." But these avid hustlers have never worked or lived in lawful society and have never made any realistic attempt to do so.[7] They merely talk about it a lot.

My street informants, from their early 20s to mid-60s, showed no objective signs of social aging and gave no indications that they are

---

*Interviewing criminals about aging and crime offers insufficient data to understand the relationship and its process. Researchers often ask older offenders leading questions: "Do you feel that you've lost the opportunity to do [something]?" "You feel like you're on the outside of life?" (Shover 1985:133). Subjects' responses meet researchers' etic expectations because researchers tacitly acknowledge these responses as truthful and accurate.

To interpret criminals' dialogue well enough to adduce changes in values and attitudes, we must first understand the semantics of street culture and then watch these criminals on the street. Unless we do the latter, we'll never know if an ex-convict's employment actually lasted one day, a month, or a year; or if and how a marriage actually stabilized his life or if it exacerbated the tumultuous nature of his life.

ready to assume adult responsibilities. Popcorn, 'Dre, and other hustlers in their 30s and 40s sound and act like boys. They enjoy selling rock cocaine, hanging out, flirting with young strawberries and skeezers, drinking beer and ale, smoking rocks, and "raising hell."

These hustlers weren't arrested very often, but that's not an indication of social responsibility. Their worldview is boyish, their behavior irresponsible. None of them wants to leave behind their adolescent behavior in favor of working eight hours a day and paying taxes.

The Porch People

All the porch people I met are chronic alcoholics.[8] Some said they used heroin, cocaine, or both earlier in their lives, but now they want just alcohol.[9] Satisfying this addiction is a way of life. All day every day, they drink. They often work together to gather money for beer, wine, and marijuana. They beg money from tourists and local citizens, but they commit low-risk offenses as well. They shoplift cheap watches and sell them to other street people or teenagers hanging out on the corners; steal cash or a Walkman from an anonymous sleeping drunk whose road dog, in need of a bottle of wine, has abandoned him in an alley.

On a busy day it takes an hour to collect four dollars, enough for a fifth of Wild Irish Rose. A few more dollars can buy a fifth of Mickey's ale. In half an hour the wine and beer are consumed, and the gathering begins again.

Porch people's social network is a wide-reaching set of social ties to beggars all over the city. These beggars are the customary "owners" of panhandling spots on sidewalks and street corners. To use an owned spot temporarily, the user must know the owner. Should a temporary user who is not a member of the local network intrude on a man's corner, especially a high-profit spot, he may be assaulted or stabbed when the sun sets. Network members enable safer and easier panhandling.

Porch people don't have social and physical boundaries. There are no formal rituals of membership, no group jargon, no special attire. A stranger acquainted with a member becomes a member, as long as he is willing to share his bottle of Wild Irish Rose, Mickey's, and a joint. When an evening of panhandling and drinking ends, porch people who have not passed out in an alley stumble back to the porch, where they gather for protection; a street predator is less likely to assault or steal from members within the group.

Younger alcoholics whose bodies and minds haven't yet deteriorated work part-time jobs on Capitol Hill. Restaurant jobs, washing dishes, cleaning the kitchen late at night involve little responsibility, are easy to get, easy to abandon. In a kitchen a man can eat, steal food, and earn enough money for the next day's supply of alcohol and marijuana. These kitchen workers feel comfortable at that job; it is a common job for unmotivated prison inmates, and a common place to find homemade alcohol brewing in the warmth cast by the ovens in a prison's kitchen.

Twenty or 30 years earlier, these men survived as burglars, car thieves, fences of stolen property, and armed robbers. Some had been members of youth gangs, still carrying their gang tattoos. Now they have little energy for their old vocations. They choose not to compete against the high-energy street hustlers for the cash offered by the buyers of drugs. It is too much effort; it would take too much time away from drinking wine.

Their reason for quitting crime is not that they can't compete against, or are afraid of, more energetic criminals. These men have honed survival skills during decades on the street. Capitol Hill police say that on occasion one of the porch people will brutally beat or slash ("cut") another street addict.

Porch people have a comfortable way of passing their days. Imprisonment is, from their point of view, anathema: If inside, they would suffer intense pain from alcohol withdrawal; many fear it would kill them. So it is better to avoid prison and to continue drinking. During the five months we spent together, their routine was stable, few things happened that were unpredictable. A composite scene of daily life illustrates group patterns and its members' temperaments.

A Day in the Life of Street Alcoholics

It was late in the day, about 5:30. It had been raining and snowing. The bitter cold was unusual for Seattle.

Albert and Smokey, both very drunk, made a wobbly approach while Shy, Mark (his road dog), and I talked. Albert is a Nootka from Vancouver Island, British Columbia, and Smokey is an interior Salish from north-central Washington. Rick joined us too. I hadn't seen these men before. Shy introduced me.

"Hey, Rick, this here guy, he's a *grave robber*," Shy announced, pointing at me with a calloused, filthy hand, with unclipped fingernails blackened by greasy dirt. Rick, a black man from Fond du Lac, Wisconsin, was still sober and eager to talk.

"I thumbed to the Northwest in the '70s. I got a wife and two kids in the Tri-Cities. My old lady's white, man. Wine has been bringing *me* down." Rick said he was going back to Wisconsin as soon as spring came. Riding the rails is tough in winter, he noted.

Standing next to Rick, Albert wobbled from side to side, holding a near-empty jug of Thunderbird. Albert gazed at me, his toothless mouth half open, saliva bubbling over his lower lip, and he grabbed the right sleeve of my down jacket. "I think I'll take it. You can have *mine*," he grumbled, shaking a fist in my face, wobbling, and spraying me with saliva, simultaneously.

I asked Albert a few questions, which he answered. He said he had done 13 years in the Colorado State Penitentiary for manslaughter, a common offense among American Indian inmates. Albert had been hanging around Seattle's streets since he'd left the reservation as a teenager. It seemed he left Seattle only to do prison time or to run back to the reservation after committing a crime, to seek a hiding place among family members.

Before long Rome, a Yakima, appeared. He was drunk too. He said he had done five years at the Washington State Penitentiary for armed robbery. We chatted and got along well once he found out I knew Indian George (the name by which inmates knew him), an inmate who had been in the state penitentiary for nearly 20 years. Indian George, a Salish man from north of Seattle, was my first informant in a prison.

Chicken Wing Charlie, a white guy, wandered up and joined the group after washing dishes at a local restaurant a few blocks south on Broadway. His clothes cast an odor of grease, smelling like a deep fryer. Charlie fed his companions with the restaurant's food; he earned his nickname by stealing buckets of chicken wings. He told me he had been a marine, and he rolled up his sleeve to show me a corps tattoo.

"I got out in '70 and been on the street since November 1988, this time. I go through periods of being a wino and go to the street. I got two kids. Then I go straight, get a job and a place to live, and an ol' lady. Then something goes click, and I go off and start drinking."

Iron Man, a Lakota Sioux, Burnside Brian, a white guy, and DD, a Lillooet from interior British Columbia, soon walked up and joined Shy and his husky, Wimpy, Mark, Chicken Wing, Rick, Albert, Smokey, Rome, and me. Burnside Brian hung out mostly in Portland, taking his street name, which was tattooed on his arm, from the downtown Burnside neighborhood. When he traveled he hitchhiked and rode the rails. He said he enjoyed it in the summer. Brian talked freely and had comments about almost everything, but he didn't say much about himself. "I was state-raised in reform schools and prisons. I did 10 months in Oregon for attempting to kill a cop." A short term, a minor offense. Brian had swung a punch at a cop who was arresting him; he said now that he should have killed him.

DD stood back, drunk, listening, teetering at bit. More than any man I had met on the street in more than two years of ethnography, at the instant I saw DD, he frightened me. That surprised me. I had known men whose acts of violence were horrifying. I had seen inmates who had been stabbed to death with homemade prison knives, strangled to death with belts, and beaten in the face with steel chairs and calloused knuckles until their facial bones had shattered and eyes hung drooping from the sockets of a bloody pulp, nearly beyond recognition as something human.

DD had wild eyes, a look I hadn't seen in years, a vacant stare of an emotionless, thoughtless person capable of beating or killing another human. Without my asking, he told me he was a killer. "I did 16 months at Atascadero [one of California's facilities for psychotic criminals] for a vicious and malicious assault on an officer with intent to kill. I wanted to kill the motherfucker. He was beating me with his gun. I took it from him. I had one knee on his throat. I beat him in the mouth. I took his gun and stuck it in his mouth."

DD finished his tale. He was agitated, mumbling to himself; he walked away. I sighed with relief. DD's demeanor hadn't affected anyone else.

While I chatted, Chicken Wing Charlie turned away and strolled off, not saying a word. Soon he returned with some Mickey's ale and Cool Breeze. Charlie unscrewed the Mickey's, held the cap upside down between his thumb and forefinger, and poured ale into it. He held in front of him the capful of ale, paused for a moment, muttered something to himself, then slowly turned the cap upside down, letting the ale drip to the ground. I asked myself, Why is this guy wasting ale? "Why did you do that, Charlie?" I asked aloud.

"That's for the brothers. The ones who have died, and the ones who haven't got here yet."

Out came a plastic bag filled with marijuana; Charlie rolled a joint, handing it man to man. I passed, as I did on the Mickey's and Cool Breeze. The joint and cold ale and wine occupied everyone's attention, numbing their bodies in the wet, icy cold weather, and elevating their spirits.

When the Mickey's and Cool Breeze were gone, a hat was passed. In everyone's view I made a show of donating a few dollars and volunteered to make a run in the cold rain to get more booze, adding more money and a few extra bottles of Mickey's to the booty. So I had my entree.

That day we sat under the wide church eaves, on the spot where I had first met Shy. On dry days they sat there, too, drinking wine and beer, smoking marijuana, talking, listening to a portable radio. They slept on the front porch of an abandoned house, catercorner to the church, to the south.

Mark was the only white man. Flo, his Tlingit girlfriend from a beach village in southeast Alaska, said she had hooked up with Mark after Spanky, her Yakima Indian boyfriend, and Dog's partner, was arrested and jailed for assaulting a cop.

"Ah," said Shy, in a deliberate voice, emphasizing each syllable, "he was drinking. Ain't nothin'."

"Motherfucker's crazy," exclaimed Mark. Flo nodded in agreement with both comments.

The porch people and I visited regularly during the winter months. Always I brought Mickey's and Cool Breeze, gifts for my hosts. After a few weeks of regular visits, Shy offered me a seat on the porch, just to his left. Before that moment I hadn't been invited to join them on the porch; it was their home, and they hadn't welcomed me. So I stood on the muddy lawn in front of the porch of the abandoned house they knew as home, at Republican and Tenth; my feet got very cold standing for hours in cold mud.

The porch people didn't want to answer questions; in prison,

American Indian inmates form a closed group, with a rigid outer boundary that keeps staff and other inmates away. From my experiences inside I knew that time, patience, and silence were my allies.

Drinking, talking, and smoking cigarettes and marijuana is what they did. No one wanted to be interrupted or interrogated; in prison I had been able to corner an American Indian informant in the big yard or in a cellblock, or I could just sit at a table with him in a crowded dining hall; there, he couldn't escape. But the street is the criminal's venue.

So I waited for tidbits of data to pop up in conversations, or for events to occur that taught me something about each person or how the group operated. And when these things did emerge, I tried to sneak in a question here and there, but I couldn't predict if anyone would respond. Some days I was ignored; on other days I got some answers. It depended on members' moods and the group mood, the amount of alcohol consumed, the number of joints smoked.

Once Burnside Brian asked, "What are you writing—a book?"

"Maybe," I answered.

"That's cool," he took another sip of Cool Breeze. I waited for him to ask about my book, but he didn't care.

One Sunday morning about 10:00, Shy and Flo and Mark had finished a bottle of wine, smoked two joints, then took up a collection of panhandled money for a second bottle of Mickey's. I walked around the corner, bought coffee for myself and three bottles of Mickey's for them. When I returned, Flo's radio blared rock music. Popping in between songs was an advertisement for a local alcohol and drug rehabilitation program.

"Listen to that bullshit," yelled Shy.

"*No you can't,*" shouted Flo, "*You can never get well, you can never get well!* That shit pisses me off." A Mickey's was passed around, another joint too. When Flo got angry and yelled, the small tattoo on her right cheek bone looked as if it fluttered. It was supposed to be a quasi-artsy Northwest Coast Indian design, an oval encircling an eye, but it looked as though it had been done in the dark. Flo calmed down while she drank. That's how she got well.

Every week Shy talked about leaving Seattle, but he never did. Shy and Mark and Burnside Brian and others, too, talked about leaving town, hopping a freight to South Dakota, Florida, or Texas, to see relatives they said they had. Shy said South Dakota was not a place to visit in dead winter, but as soon as the cold gave way to warmth, he was going back to the Sioux country. He said he hadn't been able to visit the "res," things had happened there many years ago that kept him away now, a common element in American Indians' life history accounts.

Months passed, and Shy's past remained elusive to grasp; I knew almost nothing about him. His silence frustrated me. Finally I talked to a local cop. Shy had been a suspect in many burglaries, had convictions for burglary, robbery, and grand theft auto. The cop noted that in recent years Shy had been tame. Week after week Shy drank, begged for money, smoked marijuana. Even his begging was passive.

The porch stood one block east of Broadway, a street of restaurants, book stores, clothing boutiques, furniture stores, and brass and oak taverns that attract locals and tourists alike. Limited parking on Broadway forces folks to search up and down side streets, looking for a parking spot to squeeze in.

Sitting on the front edge of the porch, his sleeping bag behind him, Shy withdrew enough energy from deep inside to become opportunistic and gregarious, especially toward ladies; young perky ones were his favorites. He'd wipe his filthy fingers through his greasy hair, yanking it in place.

"Ladies, how are you this fine day?" Passersby tried their best not to hear a word. But he insisted.

"Ladies, ladies, give me a smile, a smile. How 'bout a drink, a little wine in the sunshine?" That would slow down their hurried pace, some even looked at him.

"Have a quarter, a dollar? Wimpy's hungry, could use some food." No one ever walked across the front yard, so Shy sent Mark, his road dog, or me to collect the offering.

Shy worked the porch; perhaps on a good day he'd stroll to Broadway, panhandle, and retreat to the porch. Mark worked downtown, mostly in Pioneer Square, around Wandering Raven. That's where he had been stabbed, in an alley near the Union Gospel Mission. Burnside Brian was mobile, so he wandered all over Capitol Hill and downtown, looking for tourists; he stayed away from the Pike Place Market area on nights he heard that the gangs would be roaming there. Flo never got too far from Mark, or from her Yakima companion when he wasn't in jail.

They'd start their migration here and there in midafternoon, if they had to go downtown; they'd catch locals and tourists going out to dinner or home from work. Getting back to the porch was their problem. If they worked Broadway, the panhandling was good anytime, and the porch was close by.

On Sunday afternoon, homeless people from all over Seattle arrived at the church across the street, to enjoy a free meal, wash their clothes, take a shower. Shy never joined the porch people on their jaunts, or anyone else. Either he chose to sit and drink, tucked away in his sleeping bag, or he left the porch and wandered to Reservoir Park.

Near the end of the winter in early 1989, on a bitter Sunday morning with the sky cloudless and shimmering blue, I returned to the porch about 9:00. Shy sat on the front edge, his body buried deeply inside his sleeping bag pulled up to his shoulders, his legs hanging over the chipped porch edge, and his blue wool hat pulled down over the tops of his ears.

Mark, tucked in his bedroll, lying near the junction of the porch and the house's front wall, slept under one of its boarded-up windows. A plywood sheet nailed to the frame of the front door was an impediment in the entryway; like so many other things in their lives, I thought, this entrance, too, was closed.

"Hey, what's up, Shy?"

"Trying to get high. Got any money?" He laughed. I handed over a few bucks; he offered me a hit on a joint.

Mark stirred, sat up. His eyes were shiny and bloodshot, his skin was gray, his lips were chapped and pieces of skin were peeling off. I hadn't seen him in a few days and thought he had been waylaid by wine and women in Pioneer Square, and had camped somewhere else for several days, as porch people did on occasion.

"Got stabbed, here, in the stomach," he slurred out. He pulled down the bedroll, stood up and pulled up his blood-stained sweatshirt and off-white insulated undershirt to show me the slash, about two inches long, in the upper right area of his abdomen, just below the mound where the ribs push up the skin. It had been stitched. He said while he had been asleep, he had passed out, and a stranger had attacked him and tried to take his bedroll. He said he was very drunk, but defended himself bravely, a proud man. That ability, he said, to ward off a "punk motherfucker," even while "shitfaced," was worth his life. Police made sure he was treated at a local hospital.

Shy listened to Mark's tale. "Can't trust anybody out here. I got two road dogs," he laughed in Mark's direction and petted Wimpy.

About a year later the sun shone on the Emerald City while the temperature rose to high 50s, low 60s. I walked along Broadway on my way to Starbuck's, a half block north and one block west of where the porch had stood until late 1989, when it was razed to make way for a lovely corner house. The porch people had been evicted.

Street life in the CD and downtown Seattle had captured my exclusive attention for nearly a year, but I hadn't forgotten the porch people. No matter how hard I tried, I couldn't forget DD. Time and time again over many months, I asked street folks about Shy: "You seen Shy? A big guy, an Indian, about 6 feet 3 inches and 240, 250. Hangs out on Capitol Hill?" Of course, my question just drew a stare.

A half block south from Starbuck's, an American Indian woman and a paper-thin white man were sitting on the sidewalk, begging in front of the church that once fed and showered homeless folks. The homeless were no longer fashionable, church parishioners' donations had dwindled, free Sunday dinners had ended.

The Indian woman, in her early 40s, was dressed in new denim overalls and ankle-high boots with soles barely scratched—mission clothes. Her partner, in his mid-30s, wore a stained white shirt and a thin cloth jacket half zipped. In front of them, poised in the middle of the sidewalk, lay a woven basket, their collection plate. Pedestrians couldn't miss it. That was the point. We've seen Benny and Hawk do this, too.

"Where ya from?" I asked.

"Wisconsin," said the woman.

"How'd ya get out here?"

"With ease." She laughed warmly. She had a nice smile, fairly good teeth, incisors somewhat staggered, but no visible cavities.

Her partner's face was marred with a half-dollar-sized patch of crusty blood caked between his eyes on the bridge of his nose. The tip of his nose had been attacked and was torn and raw. On both sides of his nose slices of skin had peeled off, and blood-soaked bandages covered the full length of his left thumb. Street folks don't carry first-aid kits, so someone else must have repaired the damage.

"What happened?" I asked.

"Don't ask!" he grumbled angrily, tipping back his head, throwing it to the right as if to dismiss the seriousness of the incident. An invitation to pry.

"When'd it happen?"

"Last night." The street fighter acknowledged the time reluctantly but proudly.

"Over what?"

He ignored the question. "They start 'em, I finish 'em," he said with finality. I didn't want to hear his heroic tale; I had heard many just like his. Finding Shy was my only business today. I fed the meter, dropped a dollar into the basket, and bought time. I looked at the woman.

"You guys know an Indian named Shy?"

"Yeah!" said the woman, with excitement in her voice.

"Know where he's staying?"

Without hesitation she answered, "He's at Reservoir Park." That's a park surrounding a small reservoir just a few blocks south and east of Broadway and around the corner from the East Precinct station house. I should have known he might be there.

"Do me a favor, huh? Tell 'im Mark's looking for him." Her look posed a silent question. "I'm an anthropologist; he knows me. Just tell him the guy who's writing a book about street folks wants to see him."

"Yeah, OK, I'll do it." She paused a moment. "We're trying to get enough for a bottle." It was almost 11:00 in the morning. I fed the meter again.

"Drinking the 'T'?" I joked.

"Nah," the lady smiled, "Thunderbird. It's cheaper."

I took my time and arrived at Reservoir Park a few hours later. I guessed it would take an hour or two for the Broadway beggars to collect a couple more dollars, buy a bottle, maybe two, of Thunderbird, wander to Reservoir Park, give my message to Shy, and guzzle the wine. They don't drink on Broadway: cops bust them for drinking alcoholic beverages from open containers on any street, but on high-traffic business streets they will get thrown into the back of a police car, hauled to the precinct, and stuck away in a holding cell. An unpleasant thought, for a thirsty man. Also, if Shy didn't want to see me for some reason, he would have time to hide.

I drove around the park looking for homeless folks. There, adjacent to a public toilet building, next to a few tennis courts, near a jogging track surrounding the reservoir, was their small camp.

I pulled up next to the public toilets, left my car running in the alley. I wouldn't be there long. No questions this time. Frankly, I had grown weary of misery. I thought to myself, If I can't do something to slow the growing number of unhappy people on the street and in jails and prisons, maybe I should just mind my own business. But I had to see Shy one final time. I missed his glibness; he let the world circle around him; he was a "be-er," a Buddhist would say.

About a dozen rolled-up bedrolls and numerous framed and soft backpacks and blankets were stacked against an anchor fence that separated the public toilet from the tennis courts. A few folks were sitting there; some had drifted into the porch people's group for a day or so, then moved on. I remembered their faces; alcohol dulled their memories of me.

A black guy was buried in a bedroll, stocking hat pulled down over the tops of his ears, convict-style headgear. A white woman sitting on the dirt was wrapped in an institution blanket; a tag revealed its origin in a local homeless program. She stared at me.

The camp was furnished with a short park bench. I stood behind it and to its left. At one end sat a Mexican man, skinny, scarred, and pimple-faced, dressed in black leather motorcycle pants and heavy biker boots ventilated by a gaping hole on the outside of the left foot. No motorcycle, though. Expressionless, he stared too, out of the corner of his left eye.

Looming in the center of the bench was a large figure, tucked away to its neck in a bedroll that had been wrapped up in a piece of heavy orange vinyl. Walkman headphones protruded downward from the lower edge of the navy blue stocking cap worn convict-style. Stolen, no doubt, from someone asleep.

"Shy here?" I asked the woman whose eyes never left my face.

"He's right there," she said in curt tone. Keeping her arms inside the bedroll, the woman tilted her head back and motioned with her chin to the figure on the center of the bench. I stepped around to the front: Shy.

At first, I didn't recognize him. He had grown a scraggly beard, his head drooped, he didn't look up. A small tin of Starkist tuna rested in the dirt, next to his bedroll. An orange-and-white price tag was stuck to the can's top. Pay 'n Save.

"Shy, remember me?" His head raised a bit. He looked at me and pulled an arm out of the bedroll. I reached toward him; we shook hands.

"How ya doin', man?" Shy said, slowly, very slowly, his lips barely opening. The style of speech reminded me of the middle-aged Muhammad Ali.

"Good. How're you, Shy?"

"O-K. Heard you writin' a book, eh?" he slurred.

"Got you in it, too, bud. I'm making you a star," I asserted. He didn't care. I felt foolish.

"Shy, where's Mark?"

"He's down in Portland. Got in a program, got an apartment, and he's living with his girlfriend. He's doin' good."

"You gonna get into a program?" The wrong question.

"Nah. It's too late for me."

"Never too late, Shy, never. Has life been OK out here?"

"Yeah, things are the same. You know. It's all right."

"Winter's coming up, Shy. You could always go back inside if things get too bad out here. Huh?" Shy nodded slightly. Our eyes met for an instant.

"I've done my time. This is better time." His eyes closed, his head drooped again.

I took out my roll of money and gave him a five that was rolled in the center. His left hand was curled and rested on the bench. I stuck the bill in his palm. Still filthy, calloused fingers curled slowly around it.

Shy was expressionless, motionless. I looked at him, one final time. "I'll see ya, Shy." He nodded and didn't look up.

Final Days with Loners

David

Early in the afternoon, about 1:00, I finished a hamburger and David drank his fourth, fifth, sixth beer; I did not count the bottles. We left the tavern and went looking for Dale and Bobbie and a brown paper bag.

Dale and Bobbie were a few blocks away, lurking in a Pioneer Square alley near a dumpster, not far from where Mark had been assaulted and stabbed. At that spot, I had seen drunks fight, or vomit and stumble and pass out, or grope and slobber over a drunk street woman.

David and I strolled toward Dale and Bobbie. Bobbie had a grip on a brown bag. Standing in the alley, they swiveled slowly at the waist, looking like wind-up toys, heads moving left to right, right to left, in a surveillance pattern, reading the street. In the big yard at the Oregon State Penitentiary, they learned how to "read." The Salem penitentiary had spit them back onto the street a few weeks before Popcorn and I met David in front of Chinaman's Corner, a year and a half ago. That was the last day David looked healthy. David, Bobbie, and Dale hung together occasionally; they were partners, said David, occasional criminals. He met them recently in a bar and formed a quick shoplifting tip.

David and I approached them. They got nervous, thinking I was an undercover cop. They had not remembered our first meeting. Again, David told them who I was, but they didn't believe it. Liars think everyone is lying. David grabbed the paper sack from Bobbie. Dale and Bobbie backed up.

"What's in there?" I asked. "Those motherfuckers are nervous, Bud. What's the deal?" David's tag is Bud.

David replied, "Cameras, motherfucker, cameras. Lemme show ya. See these little guys here? They even got price tags on 'em." Pay 'n Save.

"Hey, let me see," I said. Two Kodaks, one about $35, the other nearly $80; one Minolta, only $40.

"Wan' 'em?" David asked me.

"They're stolen, motherfucker. I can't be buying stolen shit. I'd be in jail with you."

David responded, "It ain't so bad up in jail. Look, man, 35 bucks for this one [the $80 camera], 25 for both of these cheap ones here. Shit, man, you got money, give me 60 for all of them. Hey, man, your kids would like 'em."

I became moralistic. "What would you do with the money, Bud, drink it up?"

"Fuck women, man. Fuuuck womennn!"

"What are you talking about, Bud? You haven't had pussy in years. You couldn't get that motherfucker up, it's so full o' goddamn Wild Irish Rose." A joke.

"Fuck you. Hey, asshole, lemme tell you what happened last Saturday night. I was sitting down by the Kingdome, out front of those fucking restaurants, drinking the 'I.' This goddamn stretch limo pulls up and stops right in front of me. White, man, white, long as a fucking city block.

"Back door opens up and there's three women inside. Fucking

beautiful too. This bitch says, 'You busy or you wanna come with us?' Took my bottle and climbed in.

"They was staying in the Hilton uptown, in a suite. Got there and they told me to take a shower, gave me a drink. A good drink, man, expensive scotch. Nice warm shower. One of them gave me a robe to put on and then we had some fun.

"All night, the three of us in bed [he had apparently lost count], rolling around. I licked and sucked on things I ain't never seen or heard about before. I was fucking them; they was fucking each other.

"Next morning, they called room service, got me breakfast, had their limo take me back down. Bitch give me $100 too. Motherrrfuuuuckerrr."

"Hey, now listen up, Bud. It was you and three women? Next time give me a call. We'll even up the odds some, huh?"

"Fuck you, asshole. I can take care of it myself. How much you gonna give me for these cameras? Sixty?"

"Forty, asshole. Listen, Bud, if I buy 'em, I don't want those motherfuckers, Bobbie and Dale, to get my money, hear me?"

David answered, "Yeah, yeah. You buy 'em for $60, I'll tell 'em I got $40, give 'em $20. We did the thing together, man. I got give 'em something."

"Give ya 40 for all of 'em, Bud."

"Forty! Shit, man, 50."

"Forty, Bud. I can't afford any more."

"OK. I'll tell 'em I got 25."

We walked to a cash machine two blocks away, I took a quick withdrawal and handed David two 20s.

Now I read the street, looking for West Precinct cops on silent mountain bikes. I didn't want to get arrested for buying or possessing stolen property. I remembered where it got Popcorn.

"Hey, Bud, if you sold all these to the Chinaman, how much would he give ya for 'em?"

"Fifteen. Twenty, most."

"Twenty! You fucked me, Bud." He smiled. I stuck three cameras in the two front pockets of my parka, not knowing if any one of them worked. The 40 bucks were social work, an informant's fee.

Success as a thief went to David's head. That signaled trouble. "Got a car?" David asked, already knowing the answer.

"Yeah. Need to go somewhere?"

"Mercer Island. A big Pay 'n Save over there has shelves of men's and women's cologne, perfume."

"I don't want to hear this. No way am I shoplifting with you."

"It's easy, man. All you gotta do is sit in your car. I'll do the rest. I go in, put some stuff under my coat, walk out. In an hour or two, we've cleaned them out."

"Yeah, great. And if you get caught?"

"No way. I never get caught. We can sell the stuff for $400, $500. Give you half for the use of your car. How 'bout it?"

"Fuuuck youuu, Bud. No way. I'm respectable, motherfucker. I can't be doin' kid shit like that."

"Punk."

David took off with Bobbie and Dale. They planned to rent a cheap motel room north of Seattle along Aurora Avenue. There they would drink and drink and drink until they passed out.

A few weeks passed; I had not seen David. I wanted to find him one last time. Saturday night at 9:00, it was pouring rain in Pioneer Square while I walked the wet, glistening sidewalks looking for David. I used the "PO" strategy, the parole officer scam David had taught me the day Dog badgered me. I wore jeans better looking than my street pair, a clean blue parka, and a pair of glasses that added a college look.

Street folks were trying to stay dry, standing beneath the broad limbs of trees squarely rooted near Wandering Raven. I approached a group of six. "Seen Bud?" They looked at me questioningly.

"I'm his PO. I need to find him. Know where he is?" They shook their heads no. No one questioned my PO scam. I handed each guy a dollar and moved on. More social work.

I saw a black guy standing in the doorway of the joint where I bought David coffee and donuts the first time. I had seen him on the street many times.

"Know Bud? David Seals."

"Yeah."

"Seen him lately?" No answer. I continued, "I'm his PO."

The guy jumped to attention. A prisoner's response to authority. "Seen him jus' da otha' day."

Sure, I thought. "Where?"

"He be puttin' his stuff over near the bleachers, near the Kingdome, you know?" The plausible reply.

"Have you seen him today, yesterday?" He shook his head no. I took out my roll of ones and handed him two. Surprise hit his face. "Now listen to me," I went on. "Tell Bud I need to see him tomorrow at noon at Chinaman's Corner. OK?"

Sunday, I was up early and walked down to Wandering Raven to watch the sidewalk fill up at 7:00 with homeless men filing out of missions. David was standing near Wandering Raven. It wasn't because he had heard I wanted to see him and felt a responsibility to meet me. Fact is, he was there because he was almost always there at that time of day.

The whites of his eyes were a red web of capillaries pumping yesterday's "I." Yellowish gop lumped below each eye. He wore a red lumberman's jacket he had stolen off the back of a drunk who had fallen unconscious in a Pioneer Square alley the night before.

Others hovering near Wandering Raven looked just as awful.* They walked aimlessly or sat helplessly in the chilly air of early morning near Seattle's glorious waterfront. I thought, Here they are, a depressing sight, a scene out of a movie about the "living dead."

"Where ya been, Bud?"

"Runnin' with those two dudes ya met [Dale and Bobbie]."

"Staying outta trouble?" A joke.

"Fuck no!"

"Haven't seen ya on the streets for weeks, man, weeks. You been in town?"

"Nah. We went up to Canada. Bobbie said we could score up there, near the border."

"Doing what?" He hesitated, didn't answer. I continued, "Come on, what difference does it make if I know?"

"Rippin' off stores, taverns, places like that."

"How?"

"Like we did it last night, uptown here at a club, the Kon Tiki."

This tale was going to take awhile. I needed coffee as badly as I knew David needed beer. We found a spot in Pioneer Square that was serving food and alcohol. The bar was about half full. Half the restaurant tables were full too. I ordered coffee and pancakes. David ordered a Budweiser. He refused to eat.

"So? What happened at the Kon Tiki?"

---

*Among homeless folks, rates of chronic mental illness, such as schizophrenia and affective disorders, range from about 10 percent to nearly 50 percent (U.S. General Accounting Office 1988:37–39).

"Yeah. Bobbie and Dale were in there drinking at a table, and I was at the bar. Taking it easy, too. Can't get too fucked up when you're pulling a job."

"Thanks, Bud, I'll remember that next time I pull a job." He didn't laugh.

"Why didn't you all sit together?"

"Looks suspicious, man. Like we were going to do something. I sat up at the bar drinking, getting to know the bartender. Put a 20 on the bar, like I had money, you know."

"Where'd ya get the 20?"

"Fuck that, man. Listen and quit asking all those fucking questions. What difference does it make where I got that motherfucking 20? Asshole.

"Now it's about 2:00, closing time, and the bartender needs to count the till. Bobbie goes out to the street to jigger [a prison term meaning "to stand watch"]. Dale watches the inside, case anyone tries to grab us."

"Now why would anyone want to stop you from stealing? It's not their motherfucking money." David didn't pay any attention.

"Bartender opens the cash drawer and that dumb motherfucker brought all the cash over to the bar, right in front of me, still talking at me like he was doing all fucking night.

"He put the money down, turned his head for a second. I grabbed it and we fucking ran before he knew what hit him. Out we went running down the street, turned a fucking corner and a goddamn cop was coming right at us. Turned around and we ran."

"Who's got the money, Bud?"

"I stuck the cash—must have been hundreds, man, hundreds— in a paper bag. We was running; I threw the bag under a car parked right across the street from this Thai restaurant up there. Figure I could go back later and get the bag. We split up. Two cops can't go three ways.

"Cop lost me and I went back for the cash. Fucking bag was gone. *Motherfucker. Gone.*"

"Where's Dale and Bobbie?"

"Gone too. Fuck them. I don't need them motherfuckers. I can deal with this shit without them assholes. Anyway, man, them motherfuckers are ex-cons and they attract cops. I don't want to go back to prison."

David's mood quickly changed. He stopped drinking his beer,

lit a cigarette, and looked as if he had suddenly dropped into a pit of sticky filth. His movements slowed and were exaggerated. He drifted away, heading somewhere inside, somewhere dark and hidden.

"You don't want to go back to prison. Why? Beats the shit out of what you've been doin' for the last couple years, don't it?"

"Prison's easy, man. But I'm living out here now. Look, man, I'm 'bout to die soon anyway."

"What do you mean, Bud?"

"I am so depressed, Mark. You couldn't spend one day walking in my shoes. You'd kill yourself. I can't take it no more, man. One more job, man, one more. That's it. I'm going to hold court in the street, Mark. If I make it, I'll have cash. Can live good then. If the cops bust me, fuck 'em. They ain't takin' me this time. Hold court right there in the street."

"What kinda job you gonna pull?"

"Armored car."

"Armored car. The feds'll throw you in prison for-fucking-ever, Bud."

"Told you, man, I'm going to do it and get away with it, or die. Made a call couple of days ago to a woman in Portland who's holding my piece. Told her about it and she's coming up today, tonight. Meeting her at Chinaman's at 9:00. She'll have my gun. We'll use her van. And she's bringin' a couple o' guys along too, to help out.

"In south Seattle. I been watching this armored car company for a long time now. Haven't told you everything, have I?" He laughed.

"I know it's dangerous, but I don't give a fuck. I'm alone, man, been alone all my life, been fighting all my life. Fuck it, it's over.

"I wanna die anyway, man. You know, man, I never had nobody in this fucking world. 'Lone man, I'm alone. Ever been really alone?" I shook my head no. David continued, "Alone, but I don't miss nobody. Can't miss nobody you ain't never had."

That was the final time I saw David. I checked the newspapers that day for a report of a robbery at the Kon Tiki the night before. I talked to some cops, too; no robbery, no chase. Several weeks later I asked around to find out if an armored-car robbery had occurred. None had. The talk of robbery was, I thought, Bud's metaphor for death, his only way to escape his loneliness, depression, and life-long misery.

Miss Ann

The Doubleheader wasn't far from where David drank and we had talked for the last time. Miss Ann and I sat at a table in the rear of the tavern; after this, we saw each other one more time.

Craig, her common law husband and junior by more than 10 years, was propped up against the jukebox, leaning on his left arm, head drooping, spellbound by Kenny G's "Song Bird." Craig was skeptical about my identity and never understood my relationship to Miss Ann. He never trusted me.

Miss Ann said, "I'm tryin' to get my boy back. I called ADATSA. They sent me some papers and I got an appointment tomorrow. Check this shit out wid me, huh? Make sure I got it right. If I get through it OK, I maybe can get him back.

"Where would we live? I don't know. I have to work that out."

We read the documents together. At age 37, she was functionally illiterate. I asked her about it. Reluctantly, painfully, she linked her poor school performance in childhood to her family life. Life fell apart at age 11, when her mother died.

"My mom died, I was too young for that to happen. It still bothers me. It hurted me. We was so close. I had a nervous breakdown. I was suicidal and went to a mental institution for a year and a half.

"By 15, I was on weed, reds, Valium, skipping school, forging checks. I practiced how to write [her father's] name. He didn't know it then. He woulda cooked my ass.

"I never had any childhood. Nine, I was doing the washing and cooking. My father put up a box in front of the stove. I went to the junior prom and got pregnant. I didn't know what I was doing. It was the 'If you love me' tip. Shit!

"What next? I went to Goodwill Literacy School for a little while. I quit that.

"Work? I ain't gonna get no job. My husband will take care of me. I ain't never had no job. I never had to work. My father didn't believe in that. I tried to work once, but I started getting sick. Craig has worked before. When I met him, he was working."

I saw Miss Ann the final time at about 9:00 in the evening on a Sunday, a few weeks later. She stood with Itch, 'Dre, Craig, School Yard, and a few other regulars who hung out near the convenience store across the street from the Morrison.

I drove up, parked my car at a yellow curb, leaving the motor running. They were drinking to my right. I depressed the button and the right-front side window slowly slid down. Before I could call to Miss Ann, a black dude I had not seen before trotted over and put his head in the window opening.

"Watcha wan', motherfucker?" he asked, as if I were an invader.

"Looking for Miss Ann."

"Who the fuck is you?"

The dude's loud voice caught Miss Ann's attention. I saw her take the last toke on a fifth of Wild Irish Rose. Cuzz was there too, nodding, sleepwalking in small circles. Miss Ann ran to my aid.

"Get your motherfucking black ass out da way, Stretch. This here's my man."

"Who?" he asked.

"None of yo'w motha'fucking business. Get your drunk black ass out da way. Get your head out da man's car, stink it all up 'n shit. You ain't bathed in 20 fuckin' years. Out da way."

Miss Ann grabbed Stretch's left shoulder with her right hand and moved him aside. She poked in her head.

"Hi, baby. Wha'cha doin'?"

"Looking for you, Miss Ann."

She purred. "Where you going, buddy row?"

"Where you gonna go?"

"I could use some food."

"Jump in. Get Cuzz. Let's feed her too."

"Hey, Cuzz, get on over here. Goin' for a ride with buddy row. Come on, bitch."

Cuzz looked up, a faint sigh of recognition rolled across her face, through the dark of the night and the heroin haze engulfing her. A spot of blood dried on the right side of her neck matched the stain on her collar.

We drove uptown to McDonald's across the street from the International Hotel. I left the car running and ran inside to get Cuzz a hamburger and Miss Ann a fish sandwich. I got french fries too, though they didn't ask for them. They told me not to buy anything to drink; they brought their own. An hour or two later, we got down to talking.

Miss Ann missed her appointment with an ADATSA in-take worker. She said she couldn't do the program now. She was afraid of the pain of heroin withdrawal, and she insisted a methadone habit is just as bad as a heroin addiction. A methadone program requires going somewhere every day at the same time. She was not prepared to do that.

Her approach to kicking was to reduce her heroin intake from $100 to $40 daily. After a few months, if she were successful, she would try ADATSA.

I dropped off Miss Ann. Craig was waiting for her, while 'Dre and Stretch and a few others were still drinking.

"Where you and Craig going to sleep tonight?" I asked her.

"I don' know. Too late now to get a good spot. Sleep in a doorway, I guess."

Cuzz said little all evening. When I dropped her off, she said, "Buddy row, sorry I couldn't help you more tonight, but I'm not feeling so good now. Know what I mean? I'll see you later. Here, take this, call me."

She wrote her mother's name and phone number on the inside of a matchbook and handed it to me. "My mother'll always know where I am. She can tell me you called."

I guessed the last time Cuzz's mother knew where she was she was doing a six-and-a-half year sentence in a Washington State women's prison. Cuzz said her mother hadn't visited her.

A few days later, I heard 'Dre had been arrested. I visited him in the Seattle jail; he didn't make bail. Busted, he thought he would have to go back to the Washington State Penitentiary, to serve time for assault. Three white men had attacked him in the parking lot of the Spaghetti Factory, a nice family restaurant on the north end of the Seattle waterfront. An unprovoked attack, he claims. He defended himself with a baseball bat he had in his car. Then too, he faced a few recent burglary charges.

"How many times you been across state now?" I asked

He paused a moment. "Been there two, three times. Who's countin'?"

Aging Street Hustlers

The street lifecycle suggests that some street criminals must proceed through a social maturation process before they seem to be willing to end or at least slow deviant and criminal behavior. But this depends, of course, on the nature of the criminals being studied and on complex variables whose interplay is inadequately understood.[10] My informants did not show evidence of true change in individual core values, identity, and empathy with victims.[11]

Talking about personal change is one thing; actually changing is another. Perhaps for these informants, whose lives have for decades been defined by roles in street culture, change is as tough as it would be for a lawful citizen who is told to relinquish his history, companions, thoughts, and feelings and fears, and replace them with someone else's.

While nearly all these middle-aged street hustlers rejected life inside prison and didn't commit crimes serious enough to return to prison, this shouldn't be understood as criminals going straight, because cessation of crime during middle age may be just temporary.

My experience as a correctional programs specialist in the federal correctional system revealed a fact: Many middle-aged criminals leave prison at ages 35–50 and don't commit a crime for 5, 10, 15, or 20 years. I recall an offender who was released from custody at age 43, after approximately 30 years of criminal activity that began in his early teens. His record had about five dozen arrests and numerous commitments to state and federal institutions. For 20 years after release at age 43, he was straight and his rap sheet showed no criminal activity. Then he was convicted of conspiracy to distribute marijuana and possession of an unregistered weapon. At age 63 he began a long prison term.

Many middle-aged prisoners swore the next time they were on the street they would give up crime. Stan promised. Wolf Man wanted to open a Mexican restaurant. Pinto was going into the car repair business. Blue had seemed eager to go along with the plans that Anne worked out for him. Prisoners' plans are programing talk.[12]

On the street, hustlers' lives tell a sad story. Middle age is associated with a reduced crime rate, but that doesn't bring hustlers peace and happiness, and it surely doesn't end the problems these aging hustlers cause American society.

7

Ethnography and Anti-Crime Policy

The findings of this research can provide policymakers with the significant facts about delinquents' and adult criminals' life trajectories, enable policymakers to conceptualize crime-related issues in a way that leads to effective anti-crime policies, and offer an ethnographic assessment of the effects of anti-crime policies on street criminals' behavior.

This street-level assessment of the policy process (that is, policy formation, implementation, and accountability) is an important contribution: it offers a firsthand opportunity to see how effective the education model of social change has been as the theoretical premise for social change among common street criminals like T-Cool, CJ, 'Dre, Twin, Body Count, and Popcorn.

Policies are based on theories; programs put theories into action.[1] When policymakers formulate anti-crime policies and implement programs, they engage in America's highest-stakes gamble: currently they are betting billions of tax dollars that the education model of social change will lower rates of street crime, reduce recidivism, and make America's streets safer. The view from the street shows they've lost this bet, yet policymakers keep gambling anyway.

True, formulating policy is difficult. Policymakers encounter complex social phenomena, must determine problems, and then do something about them.[2] Policymakers see what we see: youth gangs plaguing all midsized to large cities; prison inmates reoffending within weeks or months of release; alcohol and drug abuse associated with criminal activity. Policymakers initiate the policy process by asking questions about what they've seen: What are the determinants of street crime? Why do youth gangs form? Why are prisons ineffective at inmate rehabilitation? How does child brutalization contribute to street crime?

These are complex questions. Qualitative research, especially close-up ethnographic views of street culture and street criminals, can help policymakers conceptualize strategic anti-crime issues. Often however, social research doesn't reach policymakers, or if it does it's in a form that's difficult to use.[3] The findings of this research are straightforward.

Here are the significant facts about chronic criminals' life trajectories; for each stage of the street lifecycle, I have identified one fact that can become a major policy issue. (1) Childhood stage: Parental brutality causes young children to suffer permanent, irreversible cognitive and emotional damage. (2) Teenage stage: Cognitive and emotional damage suffered in early life expresses itself in adolescence when once-brutalized and -neglected youngsters age, are expelled from natal families and are untreated by school teachers and administrators, join youth gangs and delinquent youth groups, commit street crimes, and engage in alcohol and drug abuse. (3) System stage: Delinquent teenagers and adult street criminals seek sanctuaries, safe havens where the quality of life is more stable and positive than social life in natal households or on the street. These sanctuaries are jails and prisons, which become stable focal points in the lives of chronic street criminals. (4) Postsystem stage: Many chronic street criminals who are middle-aged and older have become so addicted to alcohol and drugs that going to prison is a deterrent, because imprisonment threatens easy access to drugs and alcohol. These hustlers choose to commit fewer serious crimes while addiction dominates their lives. But completing substance-abuse treatment doesn't ensure a crime-free life, because sobriety often throws these street criminals back into the system stage.

This chapter will focus on the findings of two research topics: brutalization of children and the effective use of prisons. I will use these findings as key policy issues for anti-crime initiatives which can be implemented on a national or state level.

National policy decisions, the high-stakes game of anti-crime initiatives, for instance, affect a broad political arena and are well-publicized political events. It may be difficult, if not impossible, for these findings or policy initiatives to reach the national agenda. This doesn't make these findings or initiatives less important, but it does suggest that social researchers must make themselves better known to national and state policymakers.

States and, particularly, cities have a more direct stake in formulating and implementing effective anti-crime policies than the federal government. In the social milieu of city neighborhoods, criminals exploit their neighbors, and once-abused and -neglected youngsters make a slow and inevitable trek to the street, where they begin the teenage stage of the street lifecycle.

A neighborhood is the operational unit, or the focal point, for the implementation of anti-crime policies. National- and state-level policymakers and interest groups are stakeholders who control policy formation but are often the people who know the least about neighborhoods. As a result of this, the policy process in cities and communities should unite government officials, community leaders, and neighborhood residents. To be sure, qualitative researchers who know the details of daily life in neighborhoods and their households should contribute to these discussions. Eventually all these stakeholders should be active in state-level policy planning.

Policies are instructions that policymakers give to policy implementers.[4] Policy initiatives offered here are global in scope and affect national, state, and local government. These initiatives don't account for state- and local-level sociopolitical and socioeconomic conditions. After all, it would be highly impractical to formulate policies while trying to account for all existing and future social and economic conditions that may affect all possible implementation sites.

Policy implementation should be a careful process. Policy implementers, whether they're city officials or state correctional agency directors, should ensure that policies are molded to fit local-level conditions (neighborhoods, prisons). Qualitative research can be helpful at this point, too, to determine if initiatives are appropriate for local conditions and, if so, how best to implement them. Once implementation begins there should be a continuous feedback process allowing policymakers and policy implementers to alter programs when the prevalence and severity of original conditions change.

Policymakers should remain open to fresh ideas and to feedback suggesting that programs aren't meeting a policy's original intent. Policymakers should be free to choose a theory that's more appropriate for a particular policy issue if policies and programs fail. If the operation of 50 state prisons hasn't stopped urban street crime, then building 25 more prisons most likely won't stop street crime either. If imprisoning tens of thousands of local-level drug sellers in federal prisons hasn't stopped streetcorner drug selling, then imprisoning 30,000 more local-level drug sellers won't stop it either. If mandatory sentencing has caused an increase in the ratio of imprisoned nonviolent offenders to violent street criminals,[5] then let's stop doing it. Policymakers who fail to learn from their mistakes are as destructive as the criminals they imprison.

Anti-Crime Initiatives:
An Ethnographic Assessment

Years of ethnography show that the criminal justice system and social service agencies have been doing many things badly. Courts and social service agencies have permitted parents and other adults responsible for child care to damage the bodies, the social lives, and the emotional well-being of young children. Adult socializers beat youngsters with their hands, fists, and feet, assail them verbally, and leave them for days and weeks without care and supervision. These parents ignore children's medical and dental needs, permit truancy, allow youngsters to be illiterate, encourage and support criminal activity by spending youngsters' illegally gained income, foster gang memberships through their own criminal deviance, and permit youngsters to be surrounded by repugnant adult behavior. These things Porkie's and Paris' mothers did to them, and Maniac does to Ace, and, worse yet, they have done it in front of our eyes.

Years of ethnography have found that the criminal justice system as well as our social service agencies aren't providing human services to high-risk noncriminals, the pre-adolescents, adolescents, and adults who survive on the margins of society and on the fringes of serious criminality. These people need drug and alcohol treatment, remedial education, medical and dental care, psychological counseling, vocational training, and a place to reside as much as convicted felons do. But to obtain the same level of care we offer killers, rapists, drug dealers, and thieves, socially marginal noncriminals must become felons. By the time they receive these services and social support from the lawful community, it's usually too late to alter their life trajectories dramatically.[6]

Years of street ethnography exploring the life trajectory of street criminals show that these men and women aren't members of criminal organizations such as the Aryan Brotherhood, Mafia, Medellín Cartel, Mexican Mafia, or other major drug cartels. These folks are "rabble,"[7] the ordinary street criminals who cycle between jails and prisons. They pack holding cells at city jails, clog our courts, burden our probation and parole officers with stacks of case files, fill prison cellblocks, and return to the streets time after time in a ritualized, predictable street-to-prison cycle.

My years of conducting prison ethnography, both as a participating observer and an observing participant, show that prisons don't hold a miraculous cure for criminality and its causes. Prisons warehouse criminals, that's all. Many scholars,[8] citizens, and policymakers wish this weren't true. Prisons, they believe, ought to diagnose and treat criminals and, somehow, prison teachers, psychologists, and correctional officers ought to transform rapists, murderers, armed robbers, thieves, serial killers, and cannibals into lawful citizens. But in my experience as a prison researcher and a federal correctional administrator, prisons just warehouse criminals. Prisons aren't "correctional" institutions, therapeutic environments, college preparatory schools, and vocational training institutes. Irresponsible street criminals go in, and most often, irresponsible inmates come out. Prison offers no guarantee of personal transformation.

Street hustlers cycle into and out of federal and state prisons as if these prisons have an open admission policy. Most prison inmates are repeat offenders or violent criminals.[9] Street-to-prison cycling imposes a financial burden on taxpayers, and the human cost to victims' families is enormous.

Rehabilitation requires awareness of one's own cognitive and social interactional difficulties, and achieving this awareness and altering thought and social processes are arduous, lifelong tasks.[10] More than a *program* is required to shift direction in a life trajectory; however, the simplicity of education, vocational training, and drug treatment programs as a remedy for the complex crime control issue is an attractive political solution to policymakers who care less about crime's causes than about government remedies for it.[11]

The current attitude toward program cures reminds me of Irwin's analysis of the "bogeyman," a simplistic construction for the career criminal. "It is not difficult," Irwin writes, "for us social scientists to understand the appeal of these simplistic [ideas], why they emerge at particular troublesome periods, and the diversionary functions they serve for the society's powers that be, who are trying to avoid making the hard decisions (which would be particularly hard on them) that would be required to bring the society out of uncertain times."[12]

Illiteracy, lack of job skills, and drug addiction have been earmarked as primary causes of crime. Learning to read and write, acquiring a vocational skill, and deciding to stop shooting heroin or some other drug are its simplest solutions. But these ethnographic data show that being a criminal is a lifestyle whose causes are far more complex than what can be accounted for by addiction and a lack of education. Initiating a desire to change this lifestyle and proposing rewards for doing it are based on cultural values, such as guilt and shame.[13] These ethnographic data show that T-Bone, T-Cool, Popcorn, David, Miss Ann, Itch, Twin, Body Count, and the others neither have nor want to acquire lawful values. My informants never took personal change seriously.

Life on the street for these ordinary street criminals isn't easier, better, or more morally acceptable than doing time in prison. Street survival is a daily struggle, and they know it. Each time they're released from jail or prison they must rebuild and renew social and economic life. These ethnographic data show that many criminals, faced with the displeasures of street life, welcome a return to prison. Some informants even vowed to return to prison well before their release, but that secret wasn't shared with citizens in prison tour groups, prison researchers, or parole examiners.

While some inmates can't wait to return, others vow "to go straight this time." Soon the chill of winter air and gnawing hunger wears on their resolve to stay out this time, and they steal or hurt someone, which gives them a "ticket home" to a warm cellblock, color television, hot food three times a day, and a right to complain about conditions of confinement.[14]

Hollywood depictions of prisons as miserable dungeons with demonic wardens are wrong. In fact, life in well-managed prisons usually doesn't hurt inmates. Most prisons are humane places that offer inmates a quality of life better than street hustling does. Prison provides a stable residence, plenty of food, a clean bed, recreation, education and vocational training, and access to medical, dental, and mental health care.[15] Social life is good too, and inmates almost always find street companions inside. The truth is, inmates have few lawful options, and most aren't socially and emotionally well suited for lawful jobs.

In years of research on the streets and in prisons and years of employment in the federal prison system, I didn't see miraculous changes.[16] Street criminals like my informants, despite the protestations otherwise made by some of them, don't want to live the way we do. We must realize the actual limitations on altering human emotions and cognition as well as the things prisons can realistically do before we can develop effective crime-control policies.

Our desire to transform criminals into law-abiding citizens and a belief that it can be done with a few treatment and education programs have prevented the formulation of crime-control policies that protect the safety of lawful citizens, that cut prison operating costs, and that offer inmates a responsible way to do time. Most criminals, despite prison staffers' best efforts, don't walk away from prison as productive American citizens. If we can enable them to become less destructive, we've succeeded.

This ethnography has led to these recommendations: (1) Children who are brutalized and neglected by their parents must be permanently placed in community residential homes. (2) Violent criminals must be housed in secure juvenile and adult institutions, those with fences, razor wire, high walls, and gun towers, to serve long sentences and to work full time.[17] (3) Nonviolent offenders should be placed in juvenile and adult residential homes,[18] to serve short sentences and to work full time.

Protecting Children

There are multiple pathways to criminality,[19] but these paths always begin at home. Irresponsible, drug-addicted parents are young boys' and girls' primary agents of enculturation. It isn't surprising that before long youngsters sound, act, and behave like street criminals.[20] After years of abuse and neglect, after years of being drawn into a criminal lifestyle, after years of becoming inextricably embedded in the street's social networks, it's too late to help most of them, who now cycle from cellblocks to street corners to cellblocks.

Public policy can help stop this if it's the right policy. "Most prisoners come from single-parent families, over one-quarter have parents who abused drugs or alcohol, and nearly one-third have a brother with a jail or prison record. Many produce the same sad experience for their children."[21] I advocate the removal of children from abusive and neglectful households and their permanent placement in small, long-term residential homes regulated by the federal government and funded with resources reallocated from federal and state correctional budgets. For every dollar spent on state correctional institutions about $0.85 goes to adult (male and female) corrections, and only $0.15 goes to juvenile corrections.[22] These spending allocations should be reversed, and the appropriation of resources reconsidered.

Children's homes should be funded with allocations from adult correctional programs. We now spend billions to educate and treat convicted killers, rapists, and thieves, and little to protect children before they become tomorrow's street hustlers. Protecting and educating children should be our first priority; rehabilitating violent adult recidivists, our last.

How many Americans would prefer spending tax dollars on care centers for preschool and elementary school children than on providing educational and vocational recreation facilities and modern dormitories for adult inmates? How many Americans would argue that Ace is better off with Maniac than in our care?

Hagan writes, ". . . little is known about how and when trajectories of criminal embeddedness can best be diverted, and it is important to note some of the difficulties of learning more about this."[23] I agree; it is difficult to obtain firsthand data on the sociopsychological processes that move children from natal homes to street corners, but this research has given us a glimpse into the effects that enculturation in harsh families has on youngsters.

This ethnographic research has revealed and reinforced significant findings about the role of child rearing and adolescent behavior. My informants' natal families were a social fabric of fragile and undependable social ties that weakly bound children to their parents and other socializers (stepparents, aunts, uncles, cousins, grandparents). Nearly all parents were alcoholics; many used other drugs too, such as marijuana, heroin, and cocaine. Many fathers were criminals; often they were drug dealers. Mothers, and sometimes grandmothers too, engaged in criminal activities with their husbands, brothers, sons, and nephews. Sometimes these women, the mothers in particular, were passive bystanders, but they always were active consumers of money and goods brought by crime.

My informants' parents usually didn't get along well with each other, especially when they were drunk.[24] Husbands beat their wives with fists or slashed them with knives; knife-wielding wives cut their husbands. Fathers and mothers beat their sons and daughters—whipped them with belts, punched them with fists, slapped them, and kicked them. In numerous documented cases, fathers forced their sons and daughters, or stepsons and stepdaughters, to engage in oral sex (father to child, child to father), anal intercourse (father to child), and vaginal intercourse (father to stepdaughter or daughter). Mothers of these children were knowing but passive bystanders, pretending not to know, fearful, they said, that they might be beaten or might have their supply of drugs cut off. The well-being and criminal pleasures of parents came first; children always suffered.

In this morass of anger and drunkenness and squalid human emotions, my informants were enculturated. Quite naturally, the outcome of this developmental process was consistent with adults' parenting style, which was a constant feature of the social environment. Neglected at home, my informants gradually pulled away from home life for street life. At first they stayed away for a few days or a week, but when they adjusted to street life, adolescents became embedded in social networks, and stints away from abusive caretakers grew longer.

Inner-city boys raised in isolated and often impoverished neighborhoods banded together in loosely knit social groups that afforded some protection and opportunities to make money. But these youthful street companions didn't guarantee one other personal safety or reduce one another's fear, nor could they assist one another in escaping street life.

These youngsters became like their parents. They too were academic and social failures. Irresponsible, uncooperative, and marginally literate, many became addicted to drugs and alcohol in junior high school, and delinquent behavior soon erupted. Early in the teenage years their social maturation ended when drug addiction and stints in juvenile detention stifled "normal" social interactions.[25]

These children, like their parents before them, took the path of least resistance to profitable, albeit unlawful, low-skill jobs. They became the burglars, the car thieves, the drug sellers, the pimps, the armed robbers. Eventually these street skills led to "training schools" (prisons for adolescents), and when these youngsters entered adulthood they were led away to prison.

This family drama is tragic, and worse yet, scholars have known for decades that family strife, lack of affection, exposure to violence, and parental abuse and neglect lead many children to adolescent delinquency and adult criminality.[26]

These ethnographic data, as well as other scholarly research, show that children are well embedded in street social networks by their middle teenage years.[27] Many of my informants were "hard" criminals by age 14.

"Children who grow up in *families* without love, support, and acceptance," Wright and Wright argue, "are more likely to become delinquents. Parents who fail to teach their children right from wrong, who fail to monitor the whereabouts, friends, and activities of their children, and who discipline their children erratically or harshly increase the chances that their children will become delinquent" (emphasis added).[28] Should we, the social scientists and concerned citizens of America, wait until statistical research tells us that *all* abused children become delinquents and adult criminals before we act to save children?

Wright and Wright's summary of research on family effect and delinquency tells us three things: (1) A healthy home as indicated by parent-child affection, cohesion, and involvement lowers the risk of delinquency. (2) Parent-to-child as well as child-to-parent attachments affect delinquency (this mutual interaction depends, in large part, on individual traits of parents and children). (3) Parental rejection is "one of the most significant predictors of delinquency."[29]

You won't have to look far to see parental rejection and its corollary, a lack of supervision. Look at city streets early in the morning, as I have done, and decide for yourselves what we should do about the 12-, 13-, and 14-year-old girls trading sex for drugs, and the boys and girls carrying loaded handguns. Go to juvenile institutions and talk with boys aged 12–16 who are murderers, armed robbers, and sexual molesters of still younger children, and ask about their early family life.

"'The child-welfare system stands over the bodies, shows you pictures of the caskets and still does things to keep kids at risk,'" notes Gelles.[30] Children abused and neglected by parents have been kept in dangerous home environments by a national policy insisting that families stay together, and this ill-conceived policy continues today, with Congress allocating over $1 billion for the family-preservation programs.[31]

Someone decided that keeping children together with their parents is more important than youngsters' long-term welfare. We have saved families that are so brutal and unconscionable that they have no right to their children, and by doing this we have lost the children forever. Perhaps Ace will enroll in a violence management program at his juvenile institution when he's 14.

There are millions of preschool boys in homes like Ace's who are now engulfed by deviant adults.[32] These ethnographic data show that the only sure way to end adolescent and young-adult criminality is to remove at-risk children from families where they have been neglected, abused, and rejected. Allowing Ace to remain at home with Maniac is absolute stupidity.

States, under federal policy leadership and funding, should put experts to work designing, building, and operating children's residential homes. These homes will differ from our current foster homes in several ways: they'll be staffed by professionally trained personnel; they'll be subject to strict standards of accountability; and they'll be regularly overseen by federal administrative officials. Full-time placement of at-risk, nondelinquent children in small community homes might, over the decades, save them from street culture and save us from their anger. In these surrogate families, they may have a more "normal" family life. Most important, they'll be removed from family discord, rejection, conflict, and violence, and receive supervision and positive parenting.[33] The federal government now spends billions on adult prisons and does an outstanding job of operating these institutions and developing and managing inmate programs. Surely the executives and managers who now provide psychological services, elementary school education, and recreational services to armed bank robbers, international drug dealers, white slavers, kidnapers, and child-molesters can provide these services to children in need.

These children's residential homes won't be institutions. I see bedrooms and bunk beds, toys in the backyard, and a kitchen and dining room. Each home will care for five or six children, about the same number as in a large family. These boys and girls will attend community schools, and staffers will seek community physicians and dentists as well as other services. Community businesses will realize support from federal and state funds. Children will experience a measure of love and protection beyond what they ever could have hoped for in their natal homes. I'm sure there are well-trained and educated counseling psychologists, teachers, social workers, and recreation specialists graduating from college and universities all over America who could fill these new federal staff positions. This is a win-win solution to child abuse and neglect.

Critics will find reasons not to remove children permanently from awful parents and place them permanently in these long-term community residential homes.[34] Wright and Wright and other scholars advocate empowering families as a primary policy remedy for delinquency.[35] As a public policy, family empowerment seen from the street level envisions therapists and social workers, all of whom will be well paid, visiting millions of households around America with the purpose of teaching parents who have proven histories of irresponsibility and neglect how to be better mothers and fathers.

I am not optimistic about family empowerment as a public policy.[36] The family "treatment" model is analogous to education and vocational training programs for inmates, a model that we know has serious flaws. Remember too, these programs pay the salaries of lawful citizens, the psychologists, the administrators, the social workers, the treatment "specialists," the consultants, and dozens of others who share the windfall of tax dollars initiated by taxpayers' fears of street crime. The federal oversight of community-based residential homes would ensure a strict accountability and containment of expenditures within that program.

Some experimental parent-training programs have produced positive results[37] and show that parents can be taught to be less destructive. But the critical issue is not what parents can learn to do while social workers supervise them; it is what they have already done and are likely to do again when social workers are absent. I doubt if we can reach all the lousy parents in America. At this point, we need more than small-scale, family-training experiments.

The ethnographic data reported in this book show delinquents' parents to be drug-addicted, violent criminals. After seeing the damage they inflict on youngsters, I don't trust the outcome of family advocacy programs. I don't trust the behavior of drug-addicted, highly irresponsible, often-violent fathers and mothers. I wouldn't allow these adults near my children. Would you allow your children to be reared by a heroin-addicted street criminal or a convicted killer who now claims to be "ready" for parenthood?

Even if these inmate and family programs don't work, many scholars will ask for more research money to evaluate program strengths and weaknesses, presenting findings in government reports, and government program administrators whose jobs depend on these funds will want more money for more "alternative" or "intensive" programs. Hundreds of millions of tax dollars will be wasted on reports and programs that don't save children or lower rates of street crime.

This ethnography shows that being a criminal, even a young criminal, is more than a series of criminals acts. It is more than a way of behaving; it is a way of life, a way of thought. But this way of living and thinking can be diverted if we identify at-risk boys and girls early enough.

Two community-based programs should be established: (1) school-based programs to identify, diagnose, and treat children who suffer from abuse and neglect and its emotional effects; and (2) therapeutic communities for delinquents suffering drug and alcohol addictions.[38]

School-based prevention and diversion[39] rely on public administration and professionals already employed in every community in America: schools and teachers, law enforcement officials, juvenile justice administrators and counselors,[40] community mental health professionals, and community college and university faculty members.

Boys from families like Ace's have already gone to school. Several years ago I interviewed Jane, a first-grade teacher. Jane was very concerned about the violent behavior she saw daily on the playground. Six- and seven-year-old boys, she said, picked fights and punched and kicked playmates. When young victims fell to the ground, aggressors "stomped them," Jane noted with horror in her voice. Little boys, seven, eight, nine years old, were intentionally kicking other boys in the face and wouldn't stop until they were pulled away. It reminded me of cellblock fights.

"Crack children," those whose mothers smoked rock cocaine while pregnant, were slowly entering Jane's and other teachers' classrooms. These boys and girls were often disruptive, inattentive, and difficult to teach, she said, and curricula were being developed especially for them.

Jane's school had social problems too, as well as intervention programs. Jane was highly disturbed by the increasing number of poorly fed and clothed children who attend her school. Teachers fed children breakfast and distributed winter coats and boots to boys and girls who came to school in frigid weather without them. It reminded me of a Seattle mission. Children regularly fell asleep in her classroom, not from boredom, but from exhaustion and hunger. This is an inner-city school in Akron, Ohio.

The "hard-core" poor constitute about 10 percent of people living in poverty, but their plight has had a disproportionate effect on violence and class and racial tensions.[41] I can only guess that children in Jane's school were the hard-core poor and that many will end up in Ohio's juvenile justice and adult correctional systems.

Despite Jane's and her colleagues' best efforts, their school had limited financial and staff resources, and at some point they had to give up on caring for their students.[42] As a society we let our children go hungry and freeze in the snow, yet prisoners, the men who rape, kill, and abuse children, are warm and well fed and attend fully equipped schools. I have seen prison inmates using better computer and recreational equipment than most children use in public schools. A computer is the last thing a killer or a rapist needs. Our priorities have gone awry.

Primary and secondary schools house children whose ages range from about 6 to 14, the period when help is critical. The responsibility for diagnosing maladapted children falls on the shoulders of school teachers and administrators. If they pass the buck by looking away or saying they already have too much to do, the buck won't stop until it gets to a penitentiary gate. That's where the buck always stops, at least for a while.

One of the most important administrative objectives for primary and secondary school principals should be coalition building with "community partners." Primary and secondary schools should be a community's hub for all services delivered to children.[43]

Schools are government agencies, and school policies, programs, procedures, guidelines, and budgets should be opened to public view. School administrators would benefit by pro-actively developing a community relations board (CRB), similar to those implemented in all federal prisons by the former director of the Federal Bureau of Prisons, J. Michael Quinlan. CRBs opened institutions to public view and enabled communities to discuss ideas and opinions with a prison's chief executive officer. CRB members came away from meetings with an understanding of policies and procedures for complex public institutions. In school board rooms, community professionals can design strategies to assist young children once they have been diagnosed with behavioral and emotional problems.

In a September 1993 training session for two dozen juvenile justice administrators at the National Institute of Corrections Academy, those attending had an opportunity to discuss juvenile justice issues. Uniformly, these administrators said they have a difficult time initiating or sustaining community involvement for obtaining treatment resources from outside their facilities for young offenders, for sharing information with other community agencies, and for building coalitions with law enforcement and other professional social service agencies.

Law enforcement officials, juvenile probation and parole agents, university faculty members, and community mental health professionals are busy people, but they shouldn't be too preoccupied to help community children. As government employees, that's what they are paid to do.[44]

Let's be realistic: Many people can teach classes filled with well-behaved, well-fed, highly motivated, middle-class students. But can you imagine teaching a classroom filled with kids like Popcorn, Wolf Man, Pinto, Paris, David, 'Dre, Miss Ann, Itch, School Yard, Oni, Red Hog, Slim, Leo, Donnie, Porkie, CJ, Shy, Mark, Black Hammer, Stan, Primetime, T-Dog, Twin, Vamp, and Body Count? Jane faces them every day, and she needs special training to do it properly.

Colleges of education should assist colleagues in community schools. Education professors collaborating with university colleagues in clinical psychology, social work, criminal justice, and other fields can design curricula to prepare education students for the reality of elementary school life in Akron or any city in America, where young teachers will face desperately poor or maladapted children. University faculty who have research and applied experience in education, psychology, social work, criminal justice, and so on, can surely assist teachers and administrators facing special challenges in primary and secondary schools.

Teacher training in colleges and universities must be highly interdisciplinary and should include lecture courses and seminars in clinical psychology, sociology, criminal justice, anthropology, political science, and public administration courses. College faculty members in these departments should assume the responsibility for developing courses exclusively for education students. It is the ultimate exercise in community service.

Police and social workers can help too. Community policing can strengthen communities by establishing and sustaining social networks linking school children to families and neighborhoods.[45] Intensive pro-active community policing, such as what I witnessed in Seattle neighborhoods, had a potential to link preteenagers, teenagers, and young adults to lawful segments of the community. Recall that many boys, girls, and young men and women on the street don't have access to literate and educated people, except police officers.

The Seattle neighborhood patrolmen I spoke with understood family histories, family problems, and community social networks. If strong coalitions were built among educational and social service agencies, a teacher, patrolman, or social worker might be able to save boys like Ace, wherever they live.

Youth crime has frightened citizens. Because of public perceptions that the juvenile justice system is too lenient[46] and public fears of street crime and gangs,[47] juvenile detention facilities and adult jails and prisons have been filled well beyond capacity.

A 1991 survey of 984 public and private juvenile detention centers, reception centers, training schools, and juvenile ranches shows that admissions increased to a record high of nearly 690,000 in 1990, with the largest increase in detention centers, from just over 400,000 in 1984 to 570,000 in 1990.[48]

Nonviolent delinquents need help too, before they commit serious violent acts and get deeply involved in drug use. In a comprehensive study conducted in Miami, Inciardi, Horowitz, and Pottieger note that "'serious delinquents' are not in need of rehabilitation. What they need is 'habilitation' or 'capacitation.' 'Rehabilitation' involves a process of renovation and repair and a returning to a useful and constructive place in society; it implies the restoration of something or someone damaged to a prior good condition." But the serious delinquents in the Miami study "were never in good condition in the first place. Most, disenfranchised socially, educationally, economically, and psychologically since birth, never developed the self-esteem, maturity, and value system necessary for effectively coping with contemporary society."[49]

Most adolescent gang members, for instance, don't want to be in gangs, and many aren't violent, but these boys as well as other adolescents lost on the street have nowhere to go, no one to turn to.[50] These older youngsters on the street, many of whom are drug addicted, must be treated in therapeutic environments.[51]

Therapeutic communities are essential for adolescent drug addicts and alcoholics. The purpose of therapeutic communities is consistent with the treatment needed by youngsters who have numerous cognitive, emotional, and psychological difficulties: "The treatment perspective . . . is that drug abuse is a disorder of the whole person; that is, the problem is the *person* and not the drug, and addiction is a symptom and not the essence of the disorder."[52]

Juvenile institutions shouldn't be places where adolescents are further damaged. "Harsh reformatory and prison sentences would likely do no more than turn 'serious delinquents' into 'serious adult criminals,'" note Inciardi, Horowitz, and Pottieger. "If the American system of criminal justice initiates . . . jail and penitentiary confinement at age 14, it will be paying for institutional space for these offenders for the rest of their lives. . . ."[53] They're right, and to prevent this from happening, community-based residential care for young children must begin long before youngsters become teenage delinquents and have suffered abuse and neglect at the hands of alcoholic, drug-addicted, angry fathers and mothers.[54]

Intervention programs must reach at-risk children under age 10, before they become drug-addicted or gang-affiliated delinquents, or both. There are numerous well-meaning juvenile delinquency programs[55] which retrain some delinquents, calming them down so they're less destructive in the community as well as less self-destructive. But delinquency intervention and parent-training programs are evidence that we have failed to reach children soon enough. "Successful intervention programs for juvenile delinquents" is America's most sadly misconceived goal.

Correctional Cost-Containment: Streamlining Programs

We must redefine and restructure our use of prison facilities. We build jails and prisons and create thousands of bed spaces, but we don't seem to know how to use prisons or what prisons actually do.*

Prisons are government agencies and, as administrative entities,

---

*Steffensmeier and Harner (1993) report that $20 billion was spent in 1991 on incarceration in state, federal, and local jails, and in the 1980s, prison construction alone cost $30 billion. Jails are 99 percent over capacity (U.S. Department of Justice 1993b), and 1,143 new prison bed spaces are needed weekly, nationwide (U.S. Department of Justice 1993a). Irwin and Austin (1994:3–4) note that, between 1980 and 1990, 4.1 million adults were in some form of custody; in 1990, the average daily

prison staffers process paperwork, feed, recreate, and warehouse felons, ensuring that they remain behind walls and razorwire fences. Prison inmate programs such as work assignments, remedial and high school education, and drug counseling are primarily a management tool designed to keep inmates busy, that's all.[56]

Inmates enter prison as enculturated street criminals. They are, for the most part, school dropouts. They have poor study skills at best and find little pleasure in reading and writing; they have little or no job experience; they have little ambition to work on the street full time;[57] and they aren't willing to make an independent effort to initiate and maintain the labor of "inner" change. Of course while they're in prison and community treatment centers, they talk about personal transformation and going straight, but we teach them this talk in our institutions as part of their resocialization. The fact is, the majority of them don't go straight and aren't transformed into lawful citizens. What they do well is talk sincerely about personal change.*

Street talk is an expressive component of street culture.[58] When inmates' and street hustlers' rehabilitation talk is understood in its natural context, it becomes clear that street hustlers use it as verbal play, to explore a social world they know little about. Hustlers derive pleasure from creating tales and telling these in a public forum for all to hear and enjoy. Street culture abounds with all sorts of tales, adventures, fantasies, lies, and distortions. These tales are streetcorner verbal art. I have given many examples: David's tale about the limousine and beautiful women; 'Dre's adventure hiding under campers and calling his grandmother by cellular phone; Popcorn's fishing job in Alaska; Miss Ann's nostalgic talk about regain-

---

population of adults on probation was 2.3 million; and in 1988, jails had nearly 10 million admissions.

America leads the world in the rate of imprisonment. As of December 31, 1991, the state and federal imprisonment rate was 310 per 100,000 of the resident population (U.S. Department of Justice 1993a:608, Table 6.58). Approximately 46 percent of state prisoners and 33 percent of federal prisoners are black (U.S. Department of Justice 1993a:622, Table 6.69, and 635, Table 6.83). State prisons house approximately 92 percent of all prisoners (U.S. Department of Justice 1993a:612, Table 6.61) (see also Raspberry 1991; for an analysis of the costs of imprisonment, see Malcolm 1991; Zedlewski 1987; and Zimring and Hawkins 1988).

*Prison therapy and education programs, as well as years of contact with social service agencies, have given street criminals and inmates a new vocabulary and way of talking about themselves, which has, in a sense, enabled them to create a folk psychology (see Bruner 1990).

ing custody of her children; CJ's talk about becoming a musician; David's plan to rob an armored car; and Wolf Man's plan to open a Mexican restaurant.

Going-straight talk is folklore and joins other tales like "The Great Drug Deal That Went Wrong." Hustlers' talk about personal change is analogous to children's talk about "what I'm going to do when I grow up." Youngsters aspire to become doctors, lawyers, firemen, and policemen, and these aspirations are expressed without a clue about the reality of achievement in modern American society, grade-point averages, the writing of research papers, the reading of thousands of pages in hushed libraries, college and graduate school entrance exams, tuition payments, and college debts. Our young storytellers and my criminal informants don't care about the realities; the pleasure comes in saying the words; the verbal ritual itself brings pleasure.[59]

When an eight-year-old child says he wants to be a neurosurgeon, we don't ask him for his opinion about Alzheimer's disease. I wouldn't trust his opinion, would you? Nor do I trust the opinions of 20-, 30-, and 40-year-old street criminals who've been in juvenile detention, jails, and prisons for most of their lives, telling me, "I'll make it this time."

Full-time productive work in the labor force is an indicator of social adulthood and a key marker in its definition.[60] If ordinary criminals standing on street corners around America are similar to my informants, they don't understand and share in the culture of a workaday world and a straight lifestyle, nor can they easily assume its responsibilities. My informants said they don't want to live a straight life anyway, and they haven't done it.

Here's one fact policymakers must understand: What criminals do doesn't depend on what they say they'll do or on how many programs we provide; it depends for the most part on what they've done.[61] No matter how hard we wish this weren't true, it is true most of the time, at least it was with my informants. High recidivism rates aren't an indicator of an administrative failure in the implementation of rehabilitation programs. Rather, recidivism is an indicator of how difficult it is to alter human cognition[62] and a life trajectory.

Even for those former criminals who do "make it," the truth is, when push comes to shove, lawful Americans really don't want them integrated into lawful society. Former inmates are the least likely prospective employees to be hired.[63] Be realistic: Will an office or restaurant manager hire, even at minimum wage, a 35-year-old, "rehabilitated," former inmate who has a GED (General Education Department certificate), a 15-year employment history in prison food service, LOVE and HATE tattoos on the backsides of his fingers, and a gang name tattooed on his neck, just above his shirt collar?

The cognition, attitudes, values, beliefs, speech, and style of social interaction typical among my informants are normal only in street culture and a street lifecycle. These people were beaten and neglected in childhood and thereby sentenced by their parents to a life on the margins of society. Popcorn, T-Cool, Twin, Body Count, Vamp, Itch, Miss Ann, and the others in this book had many opportunities to alter their lifestyles, but chose not to do it. Their life trajectory and life choices will not be the same as ours. Our best efforts to alter their life trajectories with remedies such as high school education, vocational training, and drug treatment usually waste our money.

The Comprehensive Crime Control Act of 1984 became law in November 1987, and mandated enhanced drug treatment for federal inmates.[64] States such as Illinois now provide comprehensive, residential (in-prison) drug treatment in therapeutic communities and postresidential (postrelease) drug treatment.

Comprehensive drug treatment is expensive. The Federal Medical Center (FMC) at Rochester, Minnesota, for instance, received accreditation for its drug abuse program from the Commission on Accreditation of Rehabilitation Facilities.[65] FMC Rochester is now the first accredited program among 31 similar programs at federal prisons. The program treats between 125 and 150 inmates in nine months of intensive therapy. The cost of housing an inmate at FMC Rochester is $68.02 daily, or $24,827 annually; the average annual cost of confinement is $20,072.[66] Over the nine-month course of drug treatment for 150 convicted felons who are drug addicts, taxpayers spend at least $2.7 million. Ask your U.S. congressmen what you got for your investment?

These ethnographic data show that putting my informants and others like them in prison classrooms, therapy sessions, and vocational training did not accomplish the desired result: lower rates of street crime. Popcorn stopped using heroin and cocaine, which was a sobering act; but sobriety, by itself, didn't repair his cognitive orientation, emotional damage, and decision-making style. In this case, drug therapy transformed a cocaine-addicted thief and drug seller into a sober thief and drug seller.

Recall that Miss Ann thought about drug treatment too, but decided to inject herself with heroin. David talked about alcohol treatment, but drank another pitcher of beer instead. Popcorn succeeded at drug treatment in a therapeutic community, but failed to straighten out, despite abundant financial and social support. Popcorn had no intention of getting off the street, no desire to find a job, no desire to stop selling cocaine. He just wanted a temporary residence and found comfort in Seattle's drug program.

Angelo told me about Robot, a 32-year-old Hell's Angel who went to court one day, a place he's been dozens of times:

"Robot was standing there in front of the judge. Robot was a real asshole. He had his head shaved and an engine of a Harley tattooed on the top of it, and bullet holes tattooed along the side of his head on his temples. A long knot of beard hung down to here [chest level]. A real fucking scuz.

"The judge told Robot he was going to recommend a drug rehab program. That shithead looked at the judge and said: 'Judge, look here. I'm going to do three things. Ride my Harley, take drugs, and chase pussy. Did you hear that, Judge? Ride my Harley, take drugs, and fuck. Save that drug program for someone who needs it.'"

A desire to change an addictive behavior and a commitment to do it are the minimum criteria for self-change.[67] But my informants, and I suspect other chronic street criminals as well, are as firmly committed to their familiar lifestyles and habits as we are to ours.[68]

Inmate education is well-meaning too. Since 1965 nearly 95,000 federal inmates have been involved in General Educational Development programs and have taken GED tests.[69] Even federal inmates who are not native English speakers are required to attend and pass courses in English as a second language. Yet recidivism rates, on average, for federal offenders are high: 22 percent were rearrested in one year; 34 percent within two years; and 42 percent were rearrested within three years, using statistics based on 1978, 1980, and 1982 data.* State prisoner recidivism rates are even higher: 39 percent were rearrested in one year; 55 percent were rearrested within two years; and 63 percent were rearrested within three years.[70]

---

*Federal inmate recidivism rates are based on aggregate data from a stratified, proportional, random sample of minimum-security (nonviolent, low-risk), medium-security (sometimes violent, moderate-risk), and high-security (violent, high-risk) inmates. The Federal Prison System doesn't report recidivism rates by offense categories for instant offenses (drug crime; property crime; violent crime) or by individual security levels (minimum; low; medium; high).

These recidivism rates were high 12 years ago, and now Irwin and Austin say they've skyrocketed.[71]

Should we support programs that don't work? If you or your children were to pay tuition for college or a vocational training program that provides little outcome as indicated by an objective measure, such as a national standardized test, would you continue to pay for it? Taxpayers support hundreds of thousands of inmates who receive GEDs, training in barbering and janitorial skills, and drug treatment. Every time a former inmate gets busted again, these resources are wasted. The fact is, no matter how much money we spend on education and treatment programs for chronic criminals like my informants, we will receive virtually no positive return on the investment.

Prior to funding and implementing yet another rehabilitation program or even approving allocations for implemented programs, I advocate testing rehabilitation programs (prison and community-based education, vocational training, and drug treatment) for economic viability. Here is the question to ask: Did an inmate who participated in a specific rehabilitation program stay employed long enough, after in-prison and community supervision terminated, to repay through state and federal income tax deductions and major consumer purchases (automobile or home purchases) his share of all program costs?

Let's test each major federal and state program. If taxpayers don't at least break even on these expenditures, I advocate streamlining all rehabilitation programs to meet minimum education and health standards that enable prison inmates to work full time in prison industries or in work programs that support prison industries.

Employing Inmates

"Criminality is much more than just a 'bad habit,'" write Walters and White, "crime and criminality tear at the very fabric of society."[72] An abundance of scholarly research shows that anti-social and delinquent tendencies emerge early in the lives of neglected, abused, and unloved youngsters, often by age nine.[73] My ethnographic data support these findings and show that, once these youngsters leave home and go to the street, they are at best difficult to extricate from street culture and its social networks.

Most violent crimes in America, the homicides, rapes, robbery, and aggravated assaults, are committed by young violent boys and

men between the ages of 13 and 29.[74] In 1991, 50 percent of an estimated 6.4 million nonfatal acts of violent crime were committed by
these adolescent and young-adult street criminals.[75] That's 3.2 million acts of violence against innocent citizens, mainly the poor,
young men, women, and children. Health care costs from 1987
to 1990 associated with this violent rampage are estimated at
$179 billion.[76]

Violent criminals must be held accountable for this behavior.
Let's stop apologizing for imprisoning them, stop finding excuses
in social science for their horrible behavior. Innocent citizens are
killed, maimed, and raped by young criminals who commit these
heinous acts because they are angry and violent. To suggest that unemployment, semiliteracy, or alcoholism or drug-addiction as isolated variables cause people to kill and rape is to overlook the
causes of the semiliteracy, addiction, and truancy among young
adolescents.

America should build as many prisons as it needs to house violent adolescents and adults in separate facilities. Prisons are good
business; they employ thousands of lawful citizens and keep violent
criminals off the street. Prison payrolls are pumped into local economies to keep stores open, to buy houses and cars, and to pay college
tuition. How many citizens would become unemployed if three or
four dozen prisons were to close?[77]

'Dre, Pinto, Pimping Slim, Wolf Man, T-Cool, Donnie, Leo, David,
and Donut, as well as other informants, were once teenagers in custody, and we should have kept them there. Citizens suffer each time
a probation officer and juvenile court judge make the bad decision
to release a violent adolescent to the community on the basis of a
belief that he is "a good boy who will change."

A rational decision 20 years ago would have stopped Pimping
Slim's assault on the world. But instead the court gave him second,
third, and fourth chances, until he ended up at Soledad state prison
in Soledad, California, for murder. Fact is, none of my informants
straightened out as they aged; they've just altered their style of deviance. All my informants who were violent teenagers have been
even more violent as adults.[78] When will we learn?

If juvenile court judges, social workers, probation officers,
and program managers believe a few years in an institution, an "anger management" program, and "intensive" probation will transform teenage killers into lawful, healthy citizens, then you should
become foster parents and welcome these boys into your home. For

our safety, violent adolescents and young adults should stay in prison.

Don't apologize for being angry at violent adolescents and adults. We can offer once-violent criminals serving long sentences in secure prisons an opportunity to accept full-time employment. This will manage their time and pay them a reasonable wage, which they can use to learn how to become financially responsible: they can reimburse state correctional agencies for prison housing, medical care and drug treatment, food and recreation; they can also pay court costs, restitution to victims, and court-ordered alimony and child support.*

All American prisons should be "factories with fences."[79] Prison programs have little effect on recidivism,[80] but prison industries and their rewards can improve the quality of prison life for staff and inmates.[81] Remedial education, vocational training, and substance-abuse treatment should be geared toward transforming illiterate or semiliterate, addicted, often out-of-control inmates into productive full-time employees. Many prison jobs (food service, indoor maintenance, outdoor grounds-keeping) can employ even semi-literate English speakers as well as non-English-speaking inmates full time.

Community college and four-year college programs for violent inmates serving multidecade sentences shouldn't be supported with tax dollars; these inmates, like anyone else, can borrow tuition and fees and enroll in college after serving a prison sentence, or they can attend classes in the evening, after working eight hours to earn tuition costs. If inmates were to have to work for tuition money, many fewer would "cherish" higher education.[82]

Community standards are benchmarks for prison operations and programs. In the federal prison system the effectiveness of inmate programs, such as mail delivery and dental care, are measured against community standards. If it takes three days for a letter mailed in New York City to be delivered to an address in Los Angeles, then inmates' mail shouldn't take much longer.

Daily work is the minimum community standard for free Americans, and there's no reason imprisoned Americans, our felons, shouldn't be held to the same standard. Why should criminals in

---

*The Federal Bureau of Prisons enacted the Financial Responsibility Program, which enables inmates to meet financial responsibilities. Should inmates refuse to participate, privileges such as furloughs (obtainable only by nonviolent, minimum-security inmates) and transfers to other institutions are denied.

prison be permitted to survive on the public dole? We are all obligated to work and pay taxes. In a humane environment work isn't cruel or unusual in any way.[83]

Work is rehabilitation. Of course there will be inmates who refuse job assignments. The consequences for them should be similar to those for any American who chooses to be unemployed: an immediate loss of all earned privileges and perquisites.[84] Popcorn didn't work and didn't have 75 cents for a soft drink. I bought it; should you? While you commute to work to earn a salary out of which taxes are paid, convicted felons participate in "leisure-time programs." It's time we give them an opportunity to support themselves. Their acceptance of this responsibility is their first step toward adulthood and rehabilitation.

Keeping violent offenders in institutions where industries run smoothly is the trick, but it's being done in California and Oregon. Oregon prison industries manufacture work clothes, "prison blues," and export them to Italy, Japan, and other countries; California prison industries export prisoner-made clothing too, to Japan and Malaysia. Inmate workers earn $6–$8 an hour and are learning to be financially responsible, with their wages garnisheed for room, board, and restitution.[85]

Over the next decade correctional agencies must plan carefully to introduce light industries into prisons. This will be particularly important if the incarceration rate continues at or exceeds its current rate of 329 per 100,000 residents. The number of inmates nearly tripled between 1980 and 1992,[86] and with new federal and state crime control legislation mandating life in prison for offenders who commit a third serious felony, state and federal inmate populations will steadily increase.

Imagine, if you would, the possibility of doubling or even tripling the current number of inmates, about 1 million, to 2 million or even 3 million, each one serving a sentence in excess of 5 or 10 years. What will these inmates do every day?

Full-time inmates should have full-time jobs, working either to produce goods of value or at services supporting the production of these goods. American labor leaders complain that inmate laborers compete against union workers.* What are the alternatives? We can

---

*In 1990 while I was employed by the Federal Bureau of Prisons as special assistant to the regional director, North Central Regional Office, Kansas City, Missouri, several members of Congress tried unsuccessfully to terminate federal prison indus-

spend billions on education, drug treatment, and leisure-time programs for inmates, with little hope for rehabilitation on a massive
scale and for the dramatic lowering of recidivism rates among a high
percentage of inmates like my informants, who are quite likely to
recidivate. Or we can reduce the costs of imprisonment by putting
inmates to work full time, manufacturing goods with economic
value in American as well as foreign markets.

Inmate workers who are paid minimum wage or slightly above
will not compete against union workers and others who earn much
higher wages.[87] What's more, inmate workers locked behind secure
walls and fences cannot perform, for reasons of prison security,
many jobs that free citizens do. In fact, American inmate-workers
may be the labor force that competes against Third World workers
for lower-paid jobs. Careful long-term planning and collaboration
between state and federal correctional administrators and private-
sector leaders and union representatives can ensure that inmate-
workers and ordinary citizens are engaged in complementary
endeavors.

With the influx of new inmates into state and federal prisons, correctional agencies could create, say, 500,000 full-time inmate jobs.
Although this represents a trivial increase in the number of new jobs
created in the American economy,[88] these jobs may have a dramatic
effect on correctional institutions.

Research at USP Lompoc has shown that a full-scale prison industries program was the foundation for a reward-based correctional culture that kept maximum-security inmates peaceful, 98 percent of whom had proven histories of violence. Penitentiary rates of
violence (armed and unarmed assaults against staff and inmates)
were low, inmate and staff morale was high, and prison industries
generated revenues that exceeded the institution's annual operating
budget.[89]

Fifty state legislatures should issue a clear mandate to directors
of departments of corrections to develop and implement full-time
industrial work programs (state prisons house about 80 percent of

---

tries, under pressure from American labor leaders, who asserted that federal inmates were displacing union workers. My research (Fleisher 1989; Fleisher and Mc-
Carthy 1988) shows the positive social and financial effects obtained for staffers and
inmates by prison industries at USP Lompoc, and I participated in discussions with
central office administrators, who developed briefing material for the Federal Bureau of Prisons' director and executive staff.

all sentenced inmates).[90] America's growing population of older inmates, and even inmates in wheelchairs, can be offered employment in prison industries' offices and quality-control areas.[91]

Prison industries complemented by nonindustrial inmate service jobs will pay financial and social dividends to taxpayers, and may be our most effective policy tool in cutting street crime. Cost savings from prison operations can be reallocated to fund school and community-diversion programs and the activation and operation costs for thousands of small community-based homes for children. Anything less than enabling inmates to work full time squanders tax dollars, promotes inmates' social irresponsibility, and is public policy at its worst.

Regardless of prison industries' success at saving correctional costs and promoting safe, humane environments for inmates and staffers, let's not lose sight of America's most urgent social objective: to protect children from bad parents and save them *before* they commit the crimes that bring them to juvenile and adult prisons.

Nonviolent Offenders: Residential Work Centers

Most offenders entering federal prisons today are first-time adult drug offenders with no violent history.[92] The Comprehensive Crime Control Act of 1984 mandated that federal prisons be used as high-cost dumping grounds for nonviolent adult drug hustlers.[93]

I talked to Drake, a 23-year-old black inmate in a large midwestern prison. He had attended school through 11th grade and then dropped out. His record showed no juvenile or adult convictions, no prior commitments, and no arrests until agents from the federal Drug Enforcement Administration arrested him for selling a few cocaine rocks.*

Drake was sentenced to 10 years and served nearly 9 years before release. Estimating the annual cost of imprisonment and postrelease supervision, Drake's custody cost taxpayers nearly $250,000.

Consider Joe, a "typical" nonviolent offender in federal custody.

---

*The Anti–Drug Abuse Act of 1986, Public Law 99-570, Section 21-844(a), mandates a minimum sentence of 5 years and a maximum sentence of 20 years for a first conviction for "possession of a mixture of substance that contains a cocaine base" if the quantity of cocaine exceeds five grams (approximately a quarter of an ounce). A second cocaine-possession conviction requires the same mandatory penalty for three grams.

Joe grew up in a city with a population between 50,000 and 100,000 in a mountainous, largely rural, western state. Joe's father was a blue-collar minimum-wage worker employed at both day and evening jobs. Joe remembers his father coming home after the evening job, drinking a fifth of liquor, and passing out in the living room.

Joe said his mother worked as the director of a Head Start program. She was out of town so much on business that she had little time to watch over her seven children. Joe's sister was the oldest child and performed maternal duties for all her siblings, including Joe (he was second in the birth order).

Joe said his parents had little or no interaction with him or his siblings, except for doling out punishment, which he refused to discuss. When I asked him about it, his eyes opened widely, his back straightened, his hands clenched, his voice turned hard.

Joe was arrested for the first time for truancy at age 13. About leaving his parents' house permanently at age 15, he said, "They didn't miss me."

"Why?" I inquired.

"They had a lot of other kids around," said Joe coldly.

Truancy and fighting in school continued until Joe quit school in the seventh grade and began selling marijuana full time on the street. Joe didn't join a street gang because there weren't gangs in his city then.

At age 15, he began living with a 15-year-old girl who became his common law wife, and he fathered a daughter. Selling marijuana met their financial obligations. Joe had many arrests for drug selling and was sent repeatedly to reform school. Joe said, "My wife stuck with me." At age 18, Joe was arrested for conspiracy to distribute cocaine and was sentenced to several years in state prison. Shortly after his release, Joe was arrested and returned to state prison, where he stayed to his mid-20s. During his second prison term, his wife left him. After that release, they "remarried" and had a second child. Joe resumed selling marijuana and branched out into flake cocaine sales. His drug business flourished, but he had a $500–$600-a-day cocaine habit, which gobbled up the profits.

After years of dealing drugs, Joe was arrested in 1989 for several offenses, including cocaine distribution and a firearms violation. At age 30, Joe is serving a federal and a concurrent state sentence and will serve time on a second state sentence after he completes his present term.

Joe says he is older now and tired of "living this way." After release from custody this time, he plans to work as a drug counselor, helping kids. It is a way of giving something back to the community, he says. His postrelease residence will be somewhere in Seattle's Central District, where his father has brothers and sisters.

When we finished talking, Joe stood up and walked slowly toward the door. Then he stopped, turned around, paused a moment, and said quietly: "A fortune passed through my hands over the years, and I gave other people a fortune by using cocaine. If I can stay straight next time, I got it made." I wouldn't bet on it.

We've spent billions to imprison men like Joe and Drake, and this hasn't solved the problem of street crime and drug use. But when I think about Joe, Popcorn, Drake, and other addicts I've known on the streets and in prisons, I recall Sweetwater's words, a life-long heroin addict. "Ya know," Sweetwater said with certainty in his voice, "drugs ain't no problem. *Usin'* drugs, now *dat* is da motha'-fuckin' problem. How ya gonna keep dem motha'fuckers from wantin' dat shit? Know what I' sayin'? Dat's whatcha gotta worry 'bout. How ya gonna stop dem crazy motha'fucka's from wantin' to shoot dat her'on or smoke da dick? Wantin' 'at shit [drugs] come from inside a man."

By protecting children from the misery inflicted by terrible caretakers, we may be able to alleviate the pain inside many youngsters and adults that leads them to do drugs. But in the meantime, I don't advocate imprisoning thousands of minor drug sellers like Joe and Drake. I recommend that we stop arresting and clogging courtrooms, jails, and prisons with minor drug offenders.[94] Each time we send a drug seller like Popcorn, Drake, or Joe to prison, someone takes his place. They have nothing to lose by doing time, enrolling for in-prison drug treatment, and enjoying a leisure-time program. We gain nothing at a high cost.

Today we can gain thousands of prison beds by releasing from secure facilities nonviolent drug offenders and placing them in minimum-security community work camps.[95] The drug dealers I hung with for years didn't hurt anyone. If we're going to imprison them despite this, let's put them to work. The last thing a semiliterate drug dealer needs to know is the proper use of commas and semicolons.[96] These men need to know how to use a paint brush, a broom and rake, and a pick and shovel, and then we need to put them to work under careful supervision, repairing highways, cleaning vacant lots in communities, doing laborers' work on community renewal projects, painting government buildings, mowing lawns and raking leaves, among other things.

If we are going to continue to use imprisonment as a primary crime-control technique, then inmates must be given an opportunity to work in our, and their, communities and earn an income. It isn't sufficient for inmates to talk about going to work. Rehabilitation is hard work; hard work is rehabilitating.

A Final Message

About 6 million crimes of violence, over 12 million crimes of theft, and nearly 15 million household crimes occurred in 1992.[97] Building more prisons will have little effect on these statistics or the sociogenic factors of delinquency.[98] Community streets can be safer though, if we reduce the number of delinquent boys on street corners. But safeguarding the streets from dangerous teenagers must begin when boys are five, six, seven years old.

When I think about children being hurt by their parents, I hear Angelo's words: "I knew [Ace would] get the shit knocked out of 'im. There was nothing we could do. Nothing!" Perhaps when policymakers recognize that child abuse relates directly to crime, they'll pay more attention to the causes and conditions that move some boys to the streets.

Delinquent boys aren't the problem; brutal parents are. Courts have confounded this problem by permitting abusive and neglectful parents to have second chances. Outcries to save the family must be ignored; addicted mothers' claims that they'll "do it better next time" are empty promises.

The juvenile justice system and social service agencies must save children even if it means losing already depraved families. Had we protected Popcorn, Miss Ann, School Yard, Itch, T-Cool, Twin, Body Count, David, 'Dre, Shy, CJ, Pimping Slim, Paris, Wolf Man, Porkie, T-Bone, and the others before age 8 or 10, they might not have become beggars and thieves.

Notes
Glossary
References
Index

Notes

Introduction

1. Elder 1985:31–32.
2. See Howell 1989; Robarchek 1980.
3. See Elliot et al. 1985; Hawkins and Weis 1985; Johnson 1979; Thornberry 1987.
4. See Lévi-Strauss 1966:17.
5. See Brown 1992; Bernstein 1983; Diesing 1991; Kuhn 1986.
6. See Frake 1964:112.
7. Malinowski 1922; see also Agar 1980, 1986; and Atkinson and Hammersley 1994.
8. See Palmer 1968; Katz 1988; Lyons 1968; Fillmore 1973.
9. Bruner 1986:92.
10. See Inciardi, Lockwood, and Pottieger 1993:59.
11. See Bauman and Sherzer 1974; Hymes 1974; Gumperz and Hymes 1964.
12. Adler 1993.
13. Gottfredson and Hirschi 1993; Hindelang et al. 1981; Osgood et al. 1988; Rojek and Erickson 1982; Rowe et al. 1990; Wolfgang et al. 1972.
14. Cf. Liebow 1967; Letkemann 1973; Klockars 1974.
15. Goodenough 1957:167; see also Spradley 1972.
16. See Inciardi, Horowitz, and Pottieger 1993:44.
17. Sapir 1927, as quoted in Pike 1954:11; see also Vigil and Long 1990:57.
18. Conley 1985; Elder 1975; George 1993.
19. Conley 1985:110, see also pp. 97–112; see also Neugarten and Datan 1973.
20. See Elder 1985:17 for a discussion of life course.
21. Boyer and James 1982; Edelbrock 1980; Kufeldt and Nimmo 1987; Nye 1980; Weisberg 1985.
22. Elder 1985:31–32; see also Sampson and Laub 1992.

23. Blumstein and Cohen 1987:985.

24. Nagin and Land 1993:329; see also Blumstein 1983; Blumstein, Farrington, and Moitra 1985; Blumstein et al. 1986; Farrington 1986; Gottfredson and Hirschi 1988, 1990; Greenberg 1977; Hirschi 1983; Irwin 1985a; and Weiner 1989.

25. Weiner 1989:41.

26. Gottfredson and Hirschi 1990:266–267; see also Gottfredson and Gottfredson 1992; and Irwin and Austin 1994:20–23.

27. Nagin and Land 1993:329.

28. Blumstein and Cohen 1987:986.

29. Hill and Mannheim 1992:381.

30. Chomsky 1959.

31. See Damasio 1992; Damasio and Damasio 1989; Damasio et al. 1990; Kandel and Hawkins 1992; and Shatz 1992.

32. Chomsky 1965; see also Bernstein 1975, 1964.

33. See Cazden 1973.

34. See Tyler 1969.

35. See Atkinson and Hammersley 1994:251.

36. Irwin and Austin 1994:22–23.

37. See Currie 1985.

38. Rist 1994:549.

39. Rist 1994:551–552.

40. Bernard 1988:32.

Chapter 1. Street Ethnography

1. See Anderson 1978, 1990; Faupel 1991; Hannerz 1969; Hanson et al. 1985; Inciardi, Horowitz, and Pottieger 1993; Klockars 1974; Liebow 1967; Letkemann 1973; Valentine 1978; and Whyte 1943.

2. Adler 1993:11.

3. Spradley 1970.

4. Adler 1993; Fagan 1989; Short and Strodtbeck 1965.

5. See also Irwin and Austin 1994; and Shover 1985.

6. See also Bernard 1994:209.

7. Bernard 1988:151.

8. See Adler 1993:11, 20–21.

9. See Bernard 1988:170; see also Phillips 1987.

10. See Bernard and Killworth 1993.

11. See Altman 1974.

12. See Bernard 1988; and Biernacki and Waldorf 1981.

13. Fagan 1989:641.

14. See Fleisher 1989 for a discussion of penitentiary fieldwork.

15. Adler 1993:18.

16. Fleisher 1989.

17. See Huff 1989:530.

18. See also Huff 1989:531.

19. See Price 1992.

20. See Liebow 1967.

21. See Fleisher 1989 for a discussion of prison fieldwork and interviewee selection.

22. See Laub and Sampson 1993.

23. See Chomsky 1965.

24. See Hill and Mannheim 1992; and Wierzbicka 1993; see also Geertz 1984.

25. See Maultsby 1975; he recognized irrational thought in speech.

26. See Bruner 1986; and Bernstein 1975.

27. See Dingwall and Whitaker 1974.

28. Adler 1993:20–21.

29. Becker 1963; Carey 1972; Johnson 1975; Whyte 1943.

30. Adler 1993:13, 15.

31. Adler 1993:200 fn. 6.

32. Adler 1993:15; see also Douglas 1976.

33. Fleisher 1989.

34. See also Adler 1993; and Whyte 1943.

Chapter 2. Distorted Families

1. Leach 1968.

2. See Erikson 1975.

3. Bruner 1986:66–67.

4. Snyder and Huntley 1990:199; see also Akers 1977; Akers et al. 1979; Farrington 1978; Gottfredson and Hirschi 1990; Hirschi 1969, 1983; Kandel and Mednick 1991; Parker and Asher 1987; and Sutherland and Cressey 1970.

5. Widom 1992; Loeber and Stouthamer-Loeber 1987.

6. Patterson 1980.

7. See Adler 1993:22.

8. See also Sampson and Laub 1993.

9. See Crouch and Milner 1993; Bronfenbrenner 1974; and Newson et al. 1993.

10. See McCord 1977; and Robins 1979.

11. See Gross 1992.

12. See Walters and White 1989; and Howell 1989.

13. See Wolfgang and Ferracuti 1967.

14. Gottfredson and Hirschi 1990:90–91, 95–98; see also Akers 1984; Gough 1948; Hall and Lindzey 1978:8; and Robins 1978.

15. Sanchez Jankowski 1991; Hagedorn 1988; Vigil 1990; see also Nagin and Farrington 1992:520; Sampson 1985; and Wilson 1987.

16. Garbarino 1989; Kufeldt and Nimmo 1987; Marsh et al. 1978; and Dygdon et al. 1987.

17. Keniston 1970; Elder 1978, 1980; Smelser and Erikson 1980; Kerckhoff 1990; see also Chudacoff 1989.

18. Dwivedi 1993:52–53.

19. Kelly 1993b.

20. See Bruner 1986; Walters and White 1989; Yochelson and Samenow 1976; and Wilson and Herrnstein 1985; see chapter 3, "Adolescent Survival," for additional examples.

21. Fox Butterfield, *New York Times,* personal communication, 1992.

22. Hammett et al. 1992.

23. Hirschi 1969; Gottfredson and Hirschi 1990.

Chapter 3. Adolescent Survival

1. See Bing 1991.

2. See Padilla 1992.

3. See Inciardi, Horowitz, and Pottieger 1993:185–189.

4. Weis and Hawkins 1981.

5. Wilson and Herrnstein 1985:242, 243, and 244.

6. Emler et al. 1987; see also Miller 1958, 1975.

7. See Akers et al. 1979; Erickson 1971; Erickson and Empey 1965; Esbensen and Huizinga 1993; Hepburn 1977; Jensen 1972; Reiss and Rhodes 1964; Short 1957; Thrasher 1927; Tittle et al. 1986; Voss 1964; Warr 1993; Warr and Stafford 1991; and West and Farrington 1977.

8. Hirschi 1969; Reiss 1988.

9. Burgess and Akers 1966; Cloward and Ohlin 1960; Cohen 1955; Miller 1958; and Sutherland and Cressey 1970.

10. Decker 1993:1.

11. Elliott et al. 1985; Zimring 1981.

12. Esbensen and Huizinga 1993:569.

13. See Reiss 1988.

14. Esbensen and Huizinga 1993:583.

15. Fagan 1990:207.

16. Hirschi 1969.

17. Liska and Reed 1985.

18. Backman et al. 1978; Thornberry et al. 1985; Fagan and Pabon 1990; Kandel 1975.

19. Frude 1991.

20. Olweus 1978, 1979, 1980, 1984.

21. Coie et al. 1982.

22. Milich et al. 1982.

23. Peretti and McNair 1987.

24. Sherif et al. 1961; see also Meyenn 1980.

25. Tajfel 1982.

26. Frude 1993:76.

27. Hazen et al. 1984; Rubin et al. 1982; Milich et al. 1982; Cairns et al. 1988.

28. Coie and Dodge 1983.

29. See Monti 1993.

30. Frude 1993:81–82.

31. Cohen 1955; Short and Strodtbeck 1965.

32. Esbensen and Huizinga 1993:575.

33. Hirschi 1969.

34. Clark 1965:3.

35. Short and Strodtbeck 1965; see also Cohen 1955.

36. See Katz 1988:52–79.

37. Barnes 1979; Braucht 1980; Cotton 1979; Donovan and Jessor 1985; Elliot et al. 1985; Frances et al. 1980; Goodwin 1976; Goodwin et al. 1974; Jessor and Jessor 1977; Johnston et al. 1978; Kelly 1993a, 1993b; Roe 1944; Wechsler and Thum 1973.

38. Hirschi 1969:159; cf. Giordano et al. 1986.

39. Miller 1958 discusses male speech.

40. Gottfredson and Hirschi 1990:177–178; see also Cloward and Ohlin 1960; Cohen 1955; Elliott and Voss 1974; Farrington 1987; Thornberry et al. 1985.

41. Inciardi, Horowitz, and Pottieger 1993; Inciardi, Lockwood, and Pottieger 1993.

42. Hirschi 1969.

43. Wilson and Herrnstein 1985:231.

44. Kelly 1993a; see also Whyte 1943 for a discussion of "corner boys."

45. See Campbell 1984.

46. See Jackson and McBride 1992.

47. Kardiner 1939, 1945; see also Levine 1973; and Whiting and Child 1953.

48. Klein 1971.

49. See, for example, Bourgois 1990, 1991, 1995; Fagan 1989; MacLeod 1987; Sanchez Jankowski 1991; Taylor 1990; and Williams 1989.

50. McPherson et al. 1992:158–159.

51. Klein 1971.

52. Cf. Sanchez Jankowski 1991.

53. See Hagedorn 1988; Huff 1989; Klein 1971; Short and Strodtbeck 1965; Vigil 1988; and Yablonsky 1959, 1962.

54. Decker 1993.

55. Reiss 1988.

56. See Padilla 1992.

57. See MacLeod 1987; Sullivan 1989; and Swartz 1987.
58. See Emshwiller 1992.
59. See Price 1992; and Williams 1989.
60. See Carley 1991; and McPherson et al. 1992.
61. See Padilla 1992.
62. Fagan 1990.
63. See Sullivan 1989.
64. See Fagan and Chin 1989; and Inciardi and Pottieger 1990.
65. See Inciardi, Horowitz, and Pottieger 1993:117; *Chicago Tribune* 1988; and Emshwiller 1992.
66. See Fleisher 1989.
67. Decker 1993; Fagan 1989; Hagedorn 1988; Horowitz 1983; Klein and Maxson 1985; Miller 1975; Taylor 1990; Vigil 1988.
68. Horowitz 1987; Moore 1978.
69. Short 1990.
70. See Sanchez Jankowski 1991.
71. Decker 1993; Fagan 1989; Fagan et al. 1986; Klein 1971; Spergel 1989; Short 1974; Short and Strodtbeck 1965.
72. See Fagan et al. 1986.
73. Short 1990:3; Fagan 1990:207.
74. See Klein et al. 1991.
75. See Sanchez Jankowski 1991.
76. Klein 1971; Padilla 1992; see also Marwell et al. 1988.
77. See Decker 1993; Klein 1971; and Suttles 1972.
78. See Moore 1978; and Vigil 1988.
79. Vigil 1990.
80. Wilson and Herrnstein 1985:235.
81. See Rodriguez 1993; Diaz 1991; Diaz and Peterson 1991; and Moore 1978.
82. See Rodriguez 1993.
83. Wilson and Herrnstein 1985:235.
84. Sanchez Jankowski 1991.
85. Vigil 1988.
86. Cf. Sanchez Jankowski 1991.
87. Esbensen and Huizinga 1993; Padilla 1992.
88. Decker 1993:19.
89. Moore 1978; Vigil 1988.
90. See Lyman and Potter 1991; Peele 1985; and Preble and Casey 1969.
91. See Jackson and McBride 1992.
92. U.S. General Accounting Office 1988:111; see also Shlay and Rossi 1992.
93. U.S. General Accounting Office 1988:111.
94. See Hagan 1991; and Sullivan 1989.
95. See Adler 1993: chapter 4.

96. See Feld 1981.

97. See Blau 1977.

98. Adler 1993:74; Decker 1993; Vigil 1993.

99. Granovetter 1973:1361; cf. Hawkins and Fraser 1985:5; see also Blau 1977; Giordano et al. 1986; Hansell and Wiatrowski 1981; and Killworth et al. 1984.

100. McPherson et al. 1992:158.

101. Laub and Sampson 1993:304.

102. See also Hirschi 1969:159.

103. See Inciardi 1992:277; Irwin 1970; and Fleisher 1989.

104. Cf. Laub and Sampson 1993:304.

105. Coleman 1988, 1990.

106. Gottfredson and Hirschi 1990:89–90.

107. Granovetter 1974.

108. See Cook 1986; Granovetter 1974, 1985, 1992; Tittle 1980; and Williams and Hawkins 1986.

109. Cf. Cloward and Ohlin 1960.

110. Sampson and Laub 1993.

111. Caspi 1987; Caspi et al. 1993.

112. Thrasher 1927; see also Short 1987:16.

113. Klein 1971:13.

114. Cohen 1990:10.

115. Esbensen and Huizinga 1993:569; Miller 1980:121 (see also Horowitz 1990); and Klein and Maxson 1989.

116. Short 1990:3.

117. Short 1990.

118. Decker 1993:8; Fagan 1989:649; Cloward and Ohlin 1960; Huff 1989:528–529.

119. Jeffrey Fagan, September 1993, class lecture, "Definitions of Gangs," at the National Institute of Corrections Academy, Longmont, Colorado.

120. See Fortes 1945.

121. Hippler 1974:140, 170; Whyte 1943:272–276.

122. Thrasher 1927; Shaw and McKay 1942; see also Bursik 1988; Byrne and Sampson 1986; Greenberg et al. 1985; Kornhauser 1978; Laub 1983; Sampson 1987; Shannon 1984; and Weis and Sederstrom 1981.

123. Boykin 1983; Heath 1989; Katz 1985; Williams 1987.

124. Wilson and Herrnstein 1985:311.

125. Sampson 1985.

126. Klein and Maxson 1989; Spergel 1989.

127. See Wilson 1987; MacLeod 1987; and Vigil 1990.

128. See Fagan 1989:661–662.

129. Huff 1989.

130. *New York Times* 1993a: A11.

131. See Bursik and Grasmick 1993.
132. See Liebow 1967.
133. Fagan 1989:662; see also Bohannan 1957.
134. See Gottfredson and Hirschi 1990; and Schwartz 1987.
135. Emshwiller 1992; see also Padilla 1993.
136. See Weber 1946.
137. See Goffman 1959, 1967; and Lang and Lang 1961.
138. Papajohn 1994:2.
139. Taylor 1990.
140. See Cloward and Ohlin 1960; Curry and Spergel 1988; Hagedorn 1988; and Spergel 1984.
141. Fleisher 1990.
142. Petersilia et al. 1990.
143. Fagan 1989:649–650; Moore 1978:106–109; and Keiser 1969.
144. See Moran 1989.
145. See Fagan 1989.
146. Detective Robert F. Windrim, Street Gangs Unit, Los Angeles County Sheriff's Department, September 1993, class lecture, "Street Gangs, Managing Gangs, and Deviant Groups," at the National Institute of Corrections Academy, Longmont, Colorado.
147. Gabe Kovnator, CYA, gang intelligence coordinator, personal communication.
148. Fagan 1989:661.
149. See Dillon 1993; and Sheldon et al. 1992.
150. See Horowitz 1983, 1990.
151. See Eckland-Olson 1982; and Katz 1988.

Chapter 4. Sanctuaries

1. Carroll 1993:E1.
2. Fleisher 1989.
3. Martin 1993.
4. Carroll 1993:E2.
5. Bernard 1994:138–139.
6. Cf. Irwin 1985a:48–51.
7. Cf. Irwin 1985a:50.
8. Petersilia et al. 1990; see also Irwin 1970, 1985a.
9. Irwin 1985a:50–51.
10. Irwin 1985a:98.
11. Cf. Feely 1979.
12. Warren Lebeau, Bureau of Indian Affairs, detention specialist, personal communication, 1992.
13. U.S. Department of Justice 1990a.
14. Irwin 1985a:45.
15. See Fleisher 1989.

16. McPherson et al. 1992.

17. See Fleisher 1989.

18. See Bernstein 1975.

19. See Burstein 1977; Freidman and Esselstyn 1965; Frontline 1985; Fishman 1986, 1990; Glaser 1964; Holt and Miller 1972; Howser et al. 1983; Jessiman 1984; Lowenstein 1984; Morris 1967; Sack 1977; Sack et al. 1976; Schneller 1975; and Schwartz and Weintraub 1974.

20. See Irwin 1970:107–148 for a discussion of adjustment issues for prison inmates released in the mid-1960s; my informants shared many of those issues.

21. See Clemmer 1958; Davidson 1974; Irwin 1980, 1985a; and Sykes 1958.

22. Currie 1985:76.

23. Cf. Rideau and Wikberg 1992.

24. Butterfield 1992.

25. See Flynn 1992.

26. *New York Times* 1993b.

27. See Raban 1991:273.

28. Irwin and Austin 1994:1.

29. Simon et al. 1993.

30. Irwin and Austin 1994:1.

31. National Criminal Justice Association 1993.

32. Irwin and Austin 1994:172–173; see also Hammett et al. 1992; and Steffensmeier and Harner 1993.

33. U.S. Department of Justice 1993a:4.

34. Irwin and Austin 1994; see also Currie 1985:89–90.

35. U.S. Department of Justice 1993a:13.

36. Wilson 1983:50–51.

37. National Criminal Justice Association 1993:4.

38. Knight Ridder / *Chicago Tribune* 1993.

39. Gottfredson and Hirschi 1990:272.

40. See Klein-Saffran 1991; MacKenzie and Souryal 1991; and Morash and Rucker 1990.

41. Inciardi, Horowitz, and Pottieger 1993:194.

42. Bentayou 1992:28.

43. See Austin et al. 1993.

44. See Kelly 1993a:451; and MacKenzie and Shaw 1993.

45. See O'Nell 1979, 1989; Paddock 1982; and Robarchek 1980.

46. See Currie 1985:100.

Chapter 5. The Street

1. See Inciardi 1975; Letkemann 1973; and Sutherland 1937; cf. Katz 1988.

2. See Irwin and Austin 1994:143.

3. See Adler 1993; Langer 1977; Letkemann 1973; and Sutherland 1937.

4. See Adler 1993; Jackson 1972; Katz 1988; Maurer 1974; and Miller 1978.

5. See Johnson et al. 1985; Mieczkowski 1986; and Tunnell 1993.

6. Irwin and Austin 1994:136.

7. See Jacobs 1990:28–30; see also Inciardi and McBride 1990, for a discussion of drug legalization.

8. See Fleisher 1989; and Buentello 1992.

9. See Bourgois, n.d., 1991, 1995.

10. See Inciardi, Lockwood, and Pottieger 1993:59.

11. Bourgois, n.d.:35; see also Holden 1989.

12. See Preble and Casey 1969.

13. See Simon 1990; see also Baumann et al. 1985; Brown et al. 1983; Farr et al. 1986; King County 1986a, 1986b; Lunday and Kalob 1985; Rossi et al. 1986; Snow and Anderson 1987; and Struening and Susser 1986.

14. Cf. Wilson and Herrnstein 1985:147.

15. See Berk et al. 1980; Orsagh and Witte 1981; Zeisel 1982; and Freeman 1983, for a discussion of unemployment and its relationship to crime.

16. Dwivedi 1993; Frude 1991, 1993.

17. Hippler 1974; Kelly 1993a.

18. Kornhauser 1978:24.

19. Walters and White 1989.

20. See Cusson and Pinsonneault 1986; Irwin 1970; Levinson et al. 1978; Meisenhelder 1977; and Shover 1983, 1985.

21. See Walters 1990:163–164.

22. Irwin and Austin 1994:121.

23. Ellis 1962.

24. Katz 1988.

25. Bernstein 1975, 1977.

26. Irwin and Austin 1994:169.

27. Ingrassia and McCormick 1994:53.

Chapter 6. Aging

1. See Blumstein 1983; Blumstein et al. 1985; Blumstein et al. 1986; Cohen 1955; Farrington 1986; Glueck and Glueck 1968; Gottfredson and Hirschi 1988, 1990; Greenberg 1977; Hirschi and Gottfredson 1983; Irwin 1970: 174–204; Levinson et al. 1978; Rowe and Tittle 1977; Matza 1964; Shover 1985; Weiner 1989; and Zimring 1981.

2. See Irwin and Austin 1994:138.

3. Irwin 1970:176.

4. See Irwin and Austin 1994:138–139.

5. Shover 1985:153–154; see also Laub and Sampson 1993.

6. See also Shover 1985:132; Levinson et al. 1978; and Gove 1985.

7. See Adler 1993; Braithwaite 1989; Brown 1991; Shover 1983, 1985; Meisenhelder 1977; and Petersilia 1980.

8. See also American Psychiatric Association 1987:165–175.

9. See also Chein 1964.

10. See Wilson and Herrnstein 1985; and Hogan and Jones 1985.

11. Cf. Levinson et al. 1978.

12. Cf. Gove 1985; and Jolin and Gibbons 1987.

Chapter 7. Ethnography and Anti-Crime Policy

1. Pressman and Wildavsky 1984:xxii.

2. See Lindblom 1968:13.

3. See Rist 1994:550.

4. Nakamura and Smallwood 1980:31.

5. Campaign for an Effective Crime Policy 1993.

6. See Anderson 1990; Farrington et al. 1986; Granovetter 1985, 1992; McCord 1979, 1991; Nagin 1991; Padilla 1992; and Wolfgang 1980.

7. Irwin 1985a.

8. See Feeley and Simon 1992.

9. See Logan 1991:57; see also Gottfredson and Gottfredson 1988; Gottfredson and Hirschi 1990; Greenberg 1983; and Wolfgang et al. 1972.

10. See Andrews et al. 1990; and Walters and White 1989.

11. See Wilson 1983:50–51.

12. Irwin 1985b:3.

13. Gross and Rayner 1985; cf. Brim and Kagan 1980; and Braithwaite 1989.

14. See Hofer 1988.

15. See Bonta and Gendreau 1990; Toch 1977; and Wormith 1984.

16. Cf. McCarthy 1994.

17. See also Duxbury 1993.

18. See also Leukefeld and Tims 1988.

19. Huizinga et al. 1991:104.

20. See Hawkins 1993; and Loeber and Dishion 1983.

21. DiIulio 1994:25.

22. U.S. Department of Justice 1993a:12.

23. Hagan 1993:487.

24. See Currie 1985:206.

25. Darling and Steinberg 1993.

26. See Loeber and Dishion 1984; Glueck and Glueck 1950; Mercy et al. 1993:20; and Wright and Wright 1994:193–194.

27. See also Esbensen and Huizinga 1993; Inciardi, Horowitz, and Pottieger 1993; and Inciardi, Lockwood, and Pottieger 1993.

28. Wright and Wright 1993a:1; see also Wright and Wright 1994.

29. Wright and Wright 1993b:17.

30. Gelles as quoted in Ingrassia and McCormick 1994:54.

31. See Ingrassia and McCormick 1994:53; see also McCord 1978.

32. See Duster 1987; Garbarino 1989; Gibbs 1987; Hotaling et al. 1989; and Wilson 1987.

33. See Loeber et al. 1984; Tremblay et al. 1991; and Zigler et al. 1992.

34. See Ingrassia and McCormick 1994; and McCord 1978.

35. Wright and Wright 1993a; see also Melaville and Blank 1991.

36. See also Wilson 1983.

37. See Karoly and Rosenthal 1977; Martin 1977; Patterson et al. 1982; and Walters and Gilmore 1973.

38. See Mercy et al. 1993; and Inciardi, Horowitz, and Pottieger 1993: 196–197.

39. See Crime Concern 1992; Gottfredson 1986; Greenwood 1985; Inciardi, Horowitz, and Pottieger 1993; Kingsley 1989; Kodluboy and Evenrud 1993; Stephens 1993; and Sautter 1995.

40. See Sullivan 1993.

41. Milton S. Eisenhower Foundation 1993.

42. See also Inciardi, Horowitz, and Pottieger 1993:199.

43. See New York City, Department of Juvenile Justice, Family Ties Program 1992; Williamson et al. 1993; see also Chesney-Lind and Shelden 1992; Inciardi, Horowitz, and Pottieger 1993; Inciardi, Lockwood, and Pottieger 1993, for a review of juvenile justice programs and their success.

44. See Howitt and Moore 1993.

45. See Bottoms 1990; and Sherman 1983.

46. See Bernard 1992; Inciardi, Horowitz, and Pottieger 1993; see also Hirschi and Gottfredson 1993.

47. See Irwin and Austin 1994:5.

48. Parent 1993.

49. Inciardi, Horowitz, and Pottieger 1993:196.

50. See Esbensen and Huizinga 1993; Chesney-Lind and Shelden 1992; Cummings and Monti 1993; Inciardi, Horowitz, and Pottieger 1993; and Inciardi, Lockwood, and Pottieger 1993.

51. See De Leon 1990; De Leon and Ziegenfuss 1986; and Lipton and Wexler 1988.

52. Inciardi, Horowitz, and Pottieger 1993:197.

53. Inciardi, Horowitz, and Pottieger 1993:193; see also Schwartz 1989.

54. See Straus 1991.

55. See Hawkins and Catalano 1992; Krisberg et al. 1989; Krisberg 1991; and Lerner 1990.

56. See DiIulio 1991:114.

57. See Fagan 1992.

58. See Campbell 1986.

59. See Geertz 1984; and Wierzbicka 1993.

60. See Clausen 1986; and Smelser and Erikson 1980; see also Elder 1978, 1980.

61. See Dembo et al. 1993.

62. See Hollin 1993.

63. Irwin and Austin 1994:126.

64. See Edwards 1994.

65. Burcum 1993.

66. Federal Bureau of Prisons 1992.

67. See Orford 1985; and Tuchfeld 1981; see also Prochaska et al. 1992.

68. See Agar 1973; Chein et al. 1964; Feldman 1968; Gould et al. 1974; Hanson et al. 1985; Preble and Casey 1969; Rosenbaum 1981; Spradley 1970; Sutter 1966; and Waldorf 1973.

69. Federal Bureau of Prisons 1992:1.

70. Federal Bureau of Prisons 1990; see also U.S. Department of Justice 1992a.

71. Irwin and Austin 1994:129–131.

72. Walters and White 1989:9.

73. See Geismar and Wood 1986; Loeber and Dishion 1983; Loeber and Stouthamer-Loeber 1986; and Snyder and Patterson 1987.

74. U.S. Department of Justice 1993a; see also U.S. Department of Justice 1990b.

75. U.S. Department of Justice 1992b.

76. Miller et al. 1993.

77. See Carlson 1992.

78. See also Fagan 1993.

79. Burger 1986.

80. See Irwin and Austin 1994; and Saylor and Gaes 1992.

81. See Fleisher 1989; and Fleisher and McCarthy 1988.

82. See Hutchison 1994; cf. Pell 1994.

83. See Fleisher 1989.

84. See Erlich 1994.

85. Erlich 1994.

86. U.S. Department of Justice 1993c:2.

87. These observations about inmate jobs and their effect on union workers were stimulated as the result of personal commmunication in 1994 with Professor Thomas Ulen, professor of law and economics, College of Law, Institute of Government and Public Affairs, and Department of Economics, University of Illinois, Champaign-Urbana. Professor Ulen is not responsible for these remarks.

88. Professor Thomas Ulen, personal communication, 1994.

89. Fleisher 1989.

90. U.S. Department of Justice 1993c.

91. See Flynn 1992.

92. See Simon et al. 1993; see also Blumstein 1993.
93. Edwards 1994.
94. See Hagedorn 1994:216.
95. See DiIulio 1991.
96. See Bell 1990.
97. U.S. Department of Justice 1994:73.
98. See Belenko and Fagan 1987; Irwin and Austin 1994; Inciardi 1988; Klein and Maxson 1985; and Klein et al. 1991.

Glossary

baby gangster A young gang member; abbreviated as "BG."

balloon A prison term that refers to a balloon or condom used to conceal drugs when attempting to smuggle them into a prison or jail.

beaten out To have relinquished gang membership and endured a beating similar to that of being *courted in,* except that being beaten out is far more severe. Rules that prohibit punching to the face in courting in may be suspended, and weapons (e.g., bats) may be used. Members who wish to exit a gang that requires this ritual beating but who refuse to submit to the ritual become the target for extremely severe or even fatal injuries, and there is no limit to the number of beatings they might receive. Each time they are spotted by gang members, they will be beaten or shot at. Gangs express this directive as "stomp on sight" or "shoot on sight." The only way to escape these repeated beatings is to move, according to a former member of a Hispanic gang that has practiced the stomp-on-sight.

bunk Heroin that is too weak to stop the pain of withdrawal.

clique A group with a long-range plan for a specific purpose. A clique is larger than a tip, has a socioeconomic and political hierarchy, and forms to sell drugs. Some informants use the terms *tip* and *clique* synonymously, but that seems to be idiosyncratic. The term *klika* is used by Hispanic gang members to designate their group.

clocking Selling drugs on the street within an allocated time. When the term is used by street-corner drug sellers, or *runners,* it has several connotations. It means "to work or put in time on the street; to have a limited amount of time to sell drugs" (runners anticipate that the police will spot them, and they'll be forced to flee); "to anticipate arrest" (runners say it's just a matter of time before they'll be arrested). I didn't hear the term used by people selling drugs out of drug houses. Nor is this term used by inmates who sell drugs in jail or prison.

cluck, clucker To behave as a chicken during a *rock* high: the smoker bends over, stares at the floor or ground, searching for specks of rock. This behavior, or type of *tweek,* is called a cluck; someone who is clucking is a clucker.

courted in To have withstood a ritual gang-initiation beating. The beating has few rules: the assaulters usually don't use weapons (bats, knives), and don't intend to injure the initiate severely; the initiate may punch back. Gang members say this ritual is a "heart check," a test of a person's willingness to endure pain for the gang. Initiation into a girl's gang also often requires a beating by members. In gangs composed of both males and females, a female initiate may have the choice of either being courted in or having sex with all the male gang members. Female gang members who have been courted into a mixed-gender gang say that the beating gives them a status equal to the males' status.

Some gangs require that an initiate "walk the line," that is, walk slowly between two rows of gang members who punch the initiate. Although the rules for walking the line differ among gangs, it's common to find that initiates aren't permitted to punch back; assaulters may not be permitted to punch an initiate in the mouth, eyes, or nose, although punches to the sides of the head are permitted. Some gangs require an initiate to walk the line twice.

Street gang members in prison use this type of gang assault to punish a gang member who has violated gang rules or who has refused to give himself sexually to his peer gang members. In this case, the beating is intentionally inflicted on the victim's face, with the purpose of causing severe swelling. After the beating, the victim is displayed in public by marching him around prison grounds. A gang may try to conceal the victim from prison authorities by wrapping a towel around his head. After the beating and while the victim's face is severely swollen, his fellow gang members call him a pumpkin head. Pumpkin heads tell authorities that the injuries are the result of an accident.

crack The smokable form of cocaine; also known as *rock.* A law enforcement source said that the term *crack* derives from the splits (cracks) that appear in the surface of the cocaine mixture when it's prepared in large quantities (see Inciardi, Lockwood, and Pottieger 1993:4). That same source attributes the origin of the term to the Jamaican Posse, because they were among the first drug dealers to cook and distribute large quantities of crack cocaine. Seattle informants preferred the term *rock.*

cut; cutter To mix drugs with a substance that expands the drug's volume and reduces its potency; synonymous with *step on.* The expression "to get a good cut" refers to obtaining drugs that aren't diluted too much, resulting in low potency. A substance that is mixed with drugs is a cutter.

dealer A person who is responsible for the distribution and sale of drugs; a manager who supervises lower-level people.

dish soup To sell cocaine.

dog To persist in wanting something from someone; to hound someone. Street criminals say the "one-time is dogging 'em."

dog food Heroin.

drug house A place (house, private apartment, public housing apartment) where illegal drugs are bought and sold.

freak house A temporary residence in an abandoned building, for drug addicts that have lost their own apartments or have been ejected from relatives' homes.

friend A generic term for a relationship. As used by street criminals this term doesn't have the same connotations as it has in middle-class vocabularies. In everyday speech on the street and in jails and prisons, the term *friend* is rarely spoken. Terms such as *partner, road dog,* or *homey,* among others, are preferred.

front off To give drugs on credit; a near synonym for selling drugs. The term is often used to suggest that a drug seller has done someone a favor by "fronting off" drugs. The connotation is that the drug seller is a trusting person who's willing to do a favor for someone in need.

full-fledged A term used to describe a gang member who is committed to gang activity; synonymous with *real-deal.*

gang A generic law enforcement and criminological term that refers to a street or prison gang. The term isn't used by members of street and prison gangs in natural conversation.

gang banger An initiated member of a street gang.

geeking Exhibiting anxiety caused by coming down from a cocaine high. A person is geeking when he or she runs around in a panic, looking for more drugs or trying to get the money to buy more drugs.

glass dick An instrument used to smoke *crack,* or *rock,* cocaine. This term's complex connotations combine rock addiction with the acts of oral sex that are often associated with the addiction. Males use the term to emphasize the insatiable nature of another man's rock addiction: "He cayn't stop suckin' da glass dick."

half-stepping Behaving as a gang member in a way that indicates you are not fully committed to gang activity.

high siding Wearing stylish clothes; walking with a strut.

'hood An abbreviated form of *neighborhood.* This term connotes the nature of social life in a neighborhood.

homeboy (also homey, homes) A term used to denote a social affiliation. This affiliation may be based on a criterion such as neighborhood residence or on an affiliation with a street or prison gang. *Homey* and *homes* are diminutive forms of *homeboy,* and are often used as terms of address between people who wish to denote symbolically a close social tie. In prison it's common for the terms *home, homes,* and *homey* to be used in a manipulative strategy by someone who is trying to entice another inmate into a relaxed relationship so that he will become vulnerable to physical or sexual attack or some type of hustle. *Homeboy* is used most often as a term of reference: "Slim is a homeboy." The terms *home, homes,* and *homey* are used nearly interchangeably as terms of address: "Hey, home"; "What's up, homes?"; "How ya programin', homey?"

jack, jacker   To steal something (drugs, money) from a criminal; someone who jacks is a jacker.

jigger   To watch out for law enforcement authorities during the commission of a crime; a person who is positioned as a lookout (a jigger) is said to be jiggering.

kick, kick out   Something (drugs, money, alcohol) shared with someone else: "Gimme a kick out on dat [alcohol, rock pipe]"; "Can ya gimme a kick [some cash]?"

mover   A person who imports (moves) drugs into the United States.

nodding drugs   Drugs that make users sleepy (e.g., prescription cough syrup, heroin).

one-time   Police.

original gangster   An honorific gang term that refers to a gang member or former gang member who has been accorded a high degree of respect. The term is abbreviated in speech: "T-Cool's an OG." OG has two meanings, depending on the age of the speaker. Former gang members who are now in their 30s and 40s say OGs are men in the founding generation (late 1960s, early 1970s) of contemporary gangs, such as Crips and Bloods; these middle-aged former gang members never give a female the status of OG. Nor have I ever heard young male gang members call a female gang member of any age an OG. Today's young gang members say an OG is a male who is so attached to his gang and committed to gang activities that he remains a member even after receiving serious gang-related injuries and serving time in juvenile detention, jail, or prison. Many young gang members say that they eagerly anticipate the day when they will become OGs.

paper   A dose of heroin; a quantity sufficient for a fix.

partner   Someone with whom specific activities are shared: a crime partner, drinking partner, drug partner.

pick-up man   Someone who delivers drugs to drug sellers on the street and collects the revenue of drug sales.

poppin' co'n   "Popping corn," or running scams or hustles.

primo   A mixture of marijuana and *rock* cocaine.

product   A term for drugs (heroin, cocaine).

raspberry   A male who trades sex for drugs; the male counterpart of a *strawberry.*

real-deal   A term used to describe a gang member who is committed to gang activity. This term connotes a person's willingness to commit violent acts as part of gang activity. Synonymous with *full-fledged.*

road dog   A partner or street companion. A social affiliation based on reciprocity and trust. Road dogs run simple hustles together or may be crime partners. The term connotes of a degree of relationship closer than *homeboy;* homeboys may or may not be road dogs. This term is used more commonly among adult criminals than among adolescents.

rock   The smokable form of cocaine; also known as *crack.*

row dog   A prison term used by an inmate to refer to another inmate whose cell is located on the same tier, or row, of cells as his own. A row dog is the prison counterpart of a *road dog* on the street.

run, runner   To sell drugs; someone who sells drugs on the street is a runner, also known as a *worker.*

sagging   Wearing pants slung low on the hips.

set   A localized subset of a gang. Crips and Bloods, for instance, have hundreds of sets, each one named and associated with a specific territory, such as Green Street Crips, Santana Block Crips, 117th Street Watts Crips, and Harvard Park (Los Angeles) Brims (Bloods).

shake down   To search.

shooting gallery   A place where drugs are injected.

shotcaller   A gang's consensual leader who calls the shots.

skeezer   A woman who trades sex and companionship for drugs. Informants differentiate skeezers from *strawberries* by saying that relationships with skeezers are longer lasting than relationships with strawberries; a man may share a residence with a skeezer for weeks or months. A skeezer, like a strawberry, is a man's companion only while he can keep her supplied with drugs.

slum   Phony gold jewelry.

soup   Cocaine.

speedball   A mixture of heroin and cocaine that is injected.

step on   To mix drugs with a substance that expands the drug's volume and reduces its potency; synonymous with *cut.*

straight shooter   A glass or metal instrument ("shooter") used to smoke crack.

strawberry   A woman who trades short sexual encounters for drugs.

supervisor   Someone who supervises the sale of drugs and pays *runners.*

supplier   A person who is the connection between *movers* and a drug distribution *clique.*

syrup   Prescription cough syrup that causes severe drowsiness.

tag   A nickname used as a term of address or reference by people on the street and by inmates in jail and prison. A person's tag often denotes a physical trait ("Shorty"), a characteristic ("Chubby"), or a propensity for committing a particular type of crime ("Killer"). People are either given a tag by their peers or derive one on their own. A tag is an element in maintaining a street persona.

tip   A small group, often composed of two or three people, that has a specific economic function; members of a tip may be *partners*. A drug-selling tip has a consensual leader and little in the way of a social hierarchy. Prison inmates use the term *tip* in reference to small groups that have a specific function (e.g., inmates who enjoy lifting weights together are a tip). Prison inmates also use the term *tip* to denote a person's affiliation with street and prison gangs. An inmate in a gang (tip) is said to be tipped.

tweeking   Behaving in a particular way while high on *rock.* There are varieties of tweeks; some have names (e.g., *clucking*), some don't.

veterano   A term used by Hispanic gang members to refer to someone who has remained active in his *klika* (*clique*) and who is experienced in criminal activities and gangs; a veteran, a leader, usually in his 20s or 30s.

warrior   A gang member whose violent behavior is well known. Gang members often claim to be warriors, and thus express the notion that they are fully committed to gang activity or to the gang's ideology.

worker   A person who sells drugs on the street for a dealer; also known as a *runner.*

References

Adler, Patricia. 1993. *Wheeling and Dealing: An Ethnography of an Upper-level Drug Dealing and Smuggling Community.* 2nd edition. New York: Columbia University Press.

Agar, Michael H. 1973. *Ripping and Running: A Formal Ethnography of Urban Heroin Addicts.* New York: Seminar Press.

———. 1980. *The Professional Stranger.* New York: Academic Press.

———. 1986. *Speaking of Ethnography.* Beverly Hills, Calif. Sage.

Altman, J. 1974. Observational Study of Behavior: Sampling Methods. *Behaviour* 49:227–267.

Akers, Ronald L. 1977. *Deviant Behavior: A Social Learning Approach.* 2nd edition. Belmont, Calif.: Wadsworth.

———. 1984. Delinquent Behavior, Drugs, and Alcohol: What Is the Relationship? *Today's Delinquent* 3:19–47.

Akers, Ronald L., M. D. Kron, L. Lanza-Kaduce, and M. J. Radosevich. 1979. Social Learning and Deviant Behavior: A Specific Test of a General Theory. *American Sociological Review* 44:636–655.

American Psychiatric Association. 1987. *Diagnostic and Statistical Manual of Mental Disorders.* 3rd edition. Washington, D.C.

Anderson, Elijah. 1978. *A Place on the Corner.* Chicago: University of Chicago Press.

———. 1990. *Streetwise: Race, Class, and Change in an Urban Community.* Chicago: University of Chicago Press.

Andrews, D. A., Ivan Zinger, Robert D. Hoge, James Bonta, Paul Gendreau, and Francis T. Cullen. 1990. Does Correctional Treatment Work? A Clinically Relevant and Psychologically Informed Meta-analysis. *Criminology* 28(3):369–404.

Atkinson, Paul, and Martyn Hammersley. 1994. Ethnography and Participant Observation. In *Handbook of Qualitative Research,* ed. Norman K. Denzin and Yvonna S. Lincoln, pp. 248–261. Thousand Oaks, Calif.: Sage.

Austin, James, Michael Jones, and Melissa Bolyard. 1993. *The Growing Use of Jail Boot Camps: The Current State of the Art.* Washington, D.C.: U.S. Department of Justice, National Institute of Justice.

Backman, Jeral G., Patrick M. O'Malley, and Jerome Johnston. 1978. *Adolescence to Adulthood: Change and Stability in the Lives of Young Men.* Vol. 6, *Youth in Transition.* Ann Arbor, Mich.: University of Michigan Press.

Banks, J., and J. Grambs. 1972. *Black Self-concept.* New York: McGraw-Hill.

Barnes, G. E. 1979. The Alcoholic Personality: A Reanalysis of the Literature. *Journal of Studies on Alcohol* 40:571–623.

Baumann, D. J., C. G. Beauvais, and D. F. Schultz. 1985. *The Austin Homeless: Final Report Provided to the Hogg Foundation for Mental Health.* Austin, Tex.: Hogg Foundation for Mental Health.

Bauman, R., and Joel Sherzer. 1974. *Explorations in the Ethnography of Speaking.* Cambridge: Cambridge University Press.

Becker, Howard. 1963. *Outsiders.* New York: Free Press.

Belenko, Steven, and Jeffrey Fagan. 1987. *Crack and the Criminal Justice System.* New York: New York City Criminal Justice Agency.

Bell, Raymond. 1990. Prison Schools Need a New Curriculum. *Philadelphia Inquirer,* October 19, p. 19A.

Bentayou, Frank. 1992. The New Chain Gangs. *The Progressive* (August):28–30. The Progressive, Inc., Madison, Wis.

Berk, Richard A., Kenneth J. Lenihan, and Peter H. Rossi. 1980. Crime and Poverty: Some Experimental Evidence from Ex-Offenders. *American Sociological Review* 45:766–786.

Bernard, H. Russell. 1988. *Research Methods in Cultural Anthropology.* Newbury Park, Calif.: Sage.

——. 1994. *Research Methods in Cultural Anthropology: Qualitative and Quantitative Methods.* 2nd edition. Thousand Oaks, Calif.: Sage.

Bernard, H. Russell, and Peter D. Killworth. 1993. Sampling in Time Allocation Research. *Ethnology* 32(2):207–125.

Bernard, Thomas J. 1990. Angry Aggression among the "Truly Disadvantaged." *Criminology* 28(1):73–96.

——. 1992. *The Cycle of Juvenile Justice.* New York: Oxford University Press.

Bernstein, Basil. 1964. Elaborated and Restricted Codes. In *Ethnography of Communication,* ed. John J. Gomperz and Dell H. Hymes, pp. 55–69. Special issue of *American Anthropologist* 66(6), part 2.

——. 1975. *Class, Codes and Control: Theoretical Studies towards a Sociology of Language.* New York: Schocken.

Bernstein, R. J. 1983. *Beyond Objectivism and Relativism: Science, Hermeneutics, and Praxis.* Philadelphia: University of Pennsylvania Press.

Biernacki, Patrick, and Dan Waldorf. 1981. Snowball Sampling: Problems and Techniques of Chain Referral Sampling. *Sociological Methods and Research* 10(2):141–163.

Bing, Leon. 1991. *Do or Die.* New York: HarperCollins.

Blau, Peter M. 1977. *Inequality and Heterogeneity.* New York: Free Press.

Block, J. H., N. Haan, and M. B. Smith. 1969. Socialization Correlates of Student Activism. *Journal of Social Issues* 25:143–177.

Blumstein, Alfred. 1983. Selective Incapacitation as a Means of Crime Control. *American Behavioral Scientist* 27:87–108.

———. 1993. Making Rationality Relevant. *Criminology* 31:1–16.

Blumstein, Alfred, and Jacqueline Cohen. 1987. Characterizing Criminal Careers. *Science* (August 28):985–991.

Blumstein, A., D. P. Farrington, and S. D. Moitra. 1985. Delinquency Careers: Innocents, Desisters, and Persisters. In *Crime and Justice: An Annual Review of Research*, Vol. 6, ed. Michael Tonry and Norval Morris, pp. 187–219. Chicago: University of Chicago Press.

Blumstein, A., J. Cohen, J. A. Roth, and C. A. Visher, eds. 1986. *Criminal Careers and "Career Criminals."* Washington, D.C.: National Academy Press.

Bohannan, Paul. 1957. *Justice and Judgment among the Tiv.* London: Oxford University Press.

Bonta, James, and Paul Gendreau. 1990. Reexamining the Cruel and Unusual Punishment of Prison Life. *Law and Human Behavior* 14(4):347–372.

Bottoms, Anthony E. 1990. Crime Prevention Facing the 1990s. *Policing and Society* 1(1):3–22.

Bourgois, Philippe. n. d. Living with Crack: Survival and Self-destruction in *el Barrio*. Manuscript. San Francisco: San Francisco Urban Institute (1600 Halloway Ave., ADM 556, 94132).

———. 1990. *Hypotheses and Ethnographic Analysis of Concealment in the Underground Economy: The Economic and Ideological Dynamics of the Census Undercount.* Ethnographic Exploratory Research No. 6. March. Washington, D.C.: U.S. Bureau of Census, Center for Survey Methods Research.

———. 1991. Shooting Gallery Notes. Russell Sage Foundation, Working Paper No. 22. New York: Russell Sage.

———. 1995. *In Search of Respect: Selling Crack in El Barrio.* Series in Structural Analysis in the Social Sciences. New York: Cambridge University Press.

Boyer, Debra, and Jennifer James. 1982. Easy Money: Adolescent Involvement in Prostitution. In *Justice for Young Women: Close-up on Critical Issues*, ed. S. Davidson, pp. 73–79. Tucson, Ariz.: New Directions for Young Women.

Boykin, A. W. 1983. The Academic Performance of Afro-American Children. In *Achievement and Achievement Motives*, ed. H. P. McAdoo and J. L. McAdoo, pp. 322–371. San Francisco: Freeman.

Braithwaite, John. 1989. *Crime, Shame and Reintegration*. Cambridge: Cambridge University Press.

Braucht, G. Nicholas. 1980. Psychosocial Research on Teenage Drinking: Past and Future. In *Drugs and the Youth Culture*, ed. F. R. Scarpitti and S. K. Datesman, pp. 109–143. Beverly Hills: Sage.

Brim, Orville G., Jr., and Jerome Kagan. 1980. Constancy and Change: A View of the Issues. In *Constancy and Change in Human Development*, ed. Orville G. Brim, Jr., and Jerome Kagan. Cambridge, Mass.: Harvard University Press.

Bronfenbrenner, Urie. 1974. Is Early Intervention Effective? *Teacher's College Record* 76(2):279–303.

Brown, C., et al. 1983. *The Homeless of Phoenix: Who Are They and What Should Be Done?* Report for the Consortium for the Homeless, Phoenix, Ariz.

Brown, J. David. 1991. The Professional Ex-: An Alternative for Exiting the Deviant Career. *Sociological Quarterly* 32:219–230.

Brown, Karen McCarthy. 1992. Writing about "the Other." *Chronicle of Higher Education* (April 15):A56.

Bruner, James. 1986. *Actual Minds, Possible Worlds*. Cambridge, Mass.: Harvard University Press.

———. 1990. *Acts of Meaning*. Cambridge, Mass.: Harvard University Press.

Buentello, Salvador. 1992. Texas Turnaround: New Strategies Combat State's Prison Gangs. *Corrections Today* 54(5):58–60.

Burcum, Jill. 1993. Drug Program on "Cutting Edge." *Rochester Post-Bulletin* (Minnesota), February 20.

Burger, Warren E. 1986. Factories with Fences. In *The Dilemmas of Punishment*, ed. Kenneth C. Haas and Geoffrey P. Alpert, pp. 349–356. Prospect Heights, Ill.: Waveland.

Burgess, Robert L., and Ronald L. Akers. 1966. A Differential Association-Reinforcement Theory of Criminal Behavior. *Social Problems* 14:128–147.

Bursik, Robert J. 1988. Social Disorganization and Theories of Crime and Delinquency: Problems and Prospects. *Criminology* 26:519–551.

Bursik, Robert J., Jr., and Harold G. Grasmick. 1993. *Neighborhoods and Crime: The Dimensions of Effective Community Control*. New York: Lexington Books.

Bursik, Robert J., Jr., Harold G. Grasmick, and Mitchell B. Chamlin. 1990. The Effect of Longitudinal Arrest Patterns on the Development of Robbery Trends at the Neighborhood Level. *Criminology* 28:431–450.

Burstein, J. Q. 1977. *Conjugal Visits in Prison*. Lexington, Mass.: Lexington Books.

Butterfield, Fox. 1992. Are American Jails Becoming Shelters from the Storm? *New York Times*, July 19, "The Nation" section, p. 4.

Byrne, James M., and Robert J. Sampson. 1986. Key Issues in the Social Ecology of Crime. In *The Social Ecology of Crime*, ed. James M. Byrne and Robert J. Sampson, pp. 1–22. New York: Springer-Verlag.

Cairns, R. B., B. D. Cairns, J. J. Neckerman, and S. D. Gest. 1988. Social Networks and Aggressive Behavior: Peer Support or Peer Rejection. *Developmental Psychology* 24:815–823.

Campaign for an Effective Crime Policy. 1993. Evaluating Mandatory Minimum Sentences. Washington, D.C.: Campaign for an Effective Crime Policy (918 F St., 20004).

Campbell, Ann. 1984. *The Girls in the Gang*. New York: Basil Blackwell.

———. 1986. The Street and Violence. In *Violent Transactions: The Limits of Personality*, ed. Anne Campbell and John J. Gibbs, pp. 115–132. New York: Basil Blackwell.

Cantor, D., and K. C. Land. 1985. Unemployment and Crime Rates in the Post–World War II United States: A Theoretical and Empirical Analysis. *American Sociological Review* 50:317–332.

Carey, James T. 1972. Problems of Access and Risk in Observing Drug Scenes. In *Research on Deviance*, ed. Jack D. Douglas, pp. 71–92. New York: Random House.

Carley, Kathleen. 1991. A Theory of Group Stability. *American Sociological Review* 56:331–354.

Carlson, Katherine A. 1992. Doing Good and Looking Bad: A Case Study of Prison/Community Relations. *Crime and Delinquency* 38(1):56–69.

Carroll, Jerry. 1993. Prison Is Author's Muse: Inmate Pushes Book from Behind Bars. *San Francisco Chronicle*, November 3, pp. E1–E2.

Caspi, Avshalom. 1987. Personality in the Life Course. Special Issue: Integrating Personality and Social Psychology. *Journal of Personality and Social Psychology* 53(6):1203–1213.

Caspi, Avshalom, Donald Lynam, Terrie E. Moffitt, and Phil A. Silva. 1993. Unraveling Girls' Delinquency: Biological, Dispositional, and Contextual Contributions to Adolescent Misbehavior. *Developmental Psychology* 29(1):19–30.

Cazden, C. B. 1973. Problems for Education: Language as Curriculum Content and Learning Environment. *Daedalus* 102:135–148.

Chein, I., Donald L. Gerard, Robert S. Lee, and Eva Rosenfeld. 1964. *The Road to H: Narcotics, Delinquency, and Social Policy*. New York: Basic Books.

Chesney-Lind, Meda, and Randall G. Shelden. 1992. *Girls, Delinquency, and Juvenile Justice*. Pacific Grove, Calif.: Brooks/Cole.

Chicago Tribune. 1988. Drug Gangs in Los Angeles Spell It Out for Their Recruits. May 27, p. 6.

Chomsky, Noam. 1959. A Review of B. F. Skinner's "Verbal Behavior." *Language* 35:26–58.

———. 1965. *Aspects of the Theory of Syntax*. Cambridge, Mass.: MIT Press.

Chudacoff, H. P. 1989. *How Old Are You? Age Consciousness in American Culture*. Princeton, N.J.: Princeton University Press.

Clark, K. 1965. *Dark Ghetto*. New York: Harper and Row.

Clausen, J. A. 1986. *The Life Course: A Sociological Perspective*. Englewood Cliffs, N.J.: Prentice Hall.

Clemmer, Donald. 1958. *The Prison Community*. New York: Holt, Rinehart and Winston (originally published in 1940).

Cloward, Richard, and Lloyd Ohlin. 1960. *Delinquency and Opportunity*. New York: Free Press.

Cohen, Albert K. 1955. *Delinquent Boys: The Culture of the Gang*. New York: Free Press.

———. 1990. Foreword and Overview. In *Gangs in America*, ed. C. Ronald Huff, pp. 7–21. Newbury Park, Calif.: Sage.

Cohen, L. E., M. Felson, and K. C. Land. 1980. Property Crime Rates in the United States: A Macrodynamic Analysis, 1947–1977; with Ex Ante Forecasts for the Mid-1980s. *American Journal of Sociology* 86:90–118.

Coie, J. D., and K. A. Dodge. 1983. Continuities and Changes in Children's Social Status: A Five-Year Longitudinal Study. *Merrill-Palmer Quarterly* 29:261–282.

Coie, J. D., K. A. Dodge, H. Coppotelli. 1982. Dimensions and Types of Social Status: A Cross-Age Perspective. *Developmental Psychology* 18:557–570.

Coleman, James S. 1988. Social Capital in the Creation of Human Capital. *American Journal of Sociology* 94:S95–120.

———. 1990. *Foundations of Social Theory*. Cambridge, Mass.: Harvard University Press.

Coleman, James S., and Thomas Hoffer. 1987. *Public and Private High Schools: The Impact of Communities*. New York: Basic Books.

Conley, James T. 1985. A Personality Theory of Adulthood. In *Perspectives in Personality: A Research Annual*, Vol. 1, ed. Robert Hogan and Warren H. Jones, pp. 81–115. Greenwich, Conn.: JAI Press.

Cook, Philip J. 1986. The Demand and Supply of Criminal Opportunities. In *Crime and Justice: An Annual Review of Research*, Vol. 7, ed. Michael Tonry and Norval Morris, pp. 1–27. Chicago: University of Chicago Press.

Cotton, N. S. 1979. The Familial Incidence of Alcoholism: A Review. *Journal of Studies on Alcohol* 40:89–12.

Crime Concern. 1992. Family, School, and Community: Towards a Social Crime Prevention Agenda. Working Paper. London: Crime Concern.

Crouch, Julie L., and Joel S. Milner. 1993. Effects of Child Neglect on Children. *Criminal Justice and Behavior* 20(1):49–65.

Cummings, Scott, and Daniel J. Monti. 1993. *Gangs: The Origins and Impact of Contemporary Youth Gangs in the United States.* Series in Urban Public Policy. Albany: State University of New York Press.

Currie, Elliot. 1985. *Confronting Crime.* New York: Pantheon.

————. 1989. Confronting Crime: Looking toward the Twenty-first Century. *Justice Quarterly* 6(1):5–25.

Curry, G. D., and I. A. Spergel. 1988. Gang Homicide, Delinquency and Community. *Criminology* 26(3):381–405.

Cusson, M., and P. Pinsonneault. 1986. The Decision to Give Up Crime. In *The Reasoning Criminal: Rational Choice Perspectives on Offending,* ed. D. Cornish and R. Clarke, pp. 72–82. New York: Springer-Verlag.

Damasio, Antonio R. 1992. Aphasia. *New England Journal of Medicine* 326(8): 531–539.

Damasio, A. R., H. Damasio, D. Tranel, and J. P. Brandt. 1990. Neural Regionalization of Knowledge Access: Preliminary Evidence. In *Cold Spring Harbor Symposia on Quantitative Biology.* Vol. 55, *The Brains,* pp. 1039–1047. Cold Spring Harbor: Cold Spring Harbor Laboratory Press.

Damasio, Hanna, and Antonio R. Damasio. 1989. *Lesion Analysis in Neuropsychology.* London: Oxford University Press.

Daniels, Steve. 1987. Prison Gangs: Confronting the Threat. *Corrections Today* (April):66, 126, 162.

Darling, Nancy, and Laurence Steinberg. 1993. Parenting Style as Context: An Integrative Model. *Psychological Bulletin* 113(3):487–496.

Davidson, Theodore. 1974. *Chicano Prisoners: The Key to San Quentin.* New York: Holt, Rinehart and Winston.

Decker, Scott H. 1993. Gangs and Violence: Collective and Individual Involvement. Paper presented at the 1993 American Society of Criminology Conference, Phoenix, Ariz.

De Leon, George. 1990. Treatment Strategies. In *Handbook of Drug Control in the United States,* ed. James A. Inciardi, pp. 115–138. Westport, Conn.: Greenwood Press.

De Leon, George, and James T. Ziegenfuss. 1986. *Therapeutic Communities for Addictions.* Springfield, Ill: Charles C. Thomas.

Dembo, Richard, Linda Williams, Jeffrey Fagan, et al. 1993. The Relationships of Substance Abuse and Other Delinquency over Time in a Sample of Juvenile Detainees. *Criminal Behaviour and Mental Health* 3(3):158–179.

Diaz, Kevin. 1991. Among the Disciples. *Star Tribune* (Minneapolis), August 4, pp. 1, 20A–22A.

Diaz, Kevin, and David Peterson. 1991. Gangs: How Large a Threat? *Star Tribune* (Minneapolis), August 4, pp. 1, 22A.

Diesing, P. 1991. *How Does Social Science Work? Reflections on Practice.* Pittsburgh: University of Pittsburgh Press.

DiIulio, John J. 1991. *No Escape: The Future of American Corrections.* New York: Basic Books.

———. 1994. The Question of Block Crime. *Public Interest* 17(Fall):3–32.

Dillon, Sam. 1993. Board Played Down New York City School Crime, Chancellor Says. *New York Times,* November 24, p. B14.

Dingwall, William Orr, and Harry A. Whitaker. 1974. Neurolinguistics. In *Annual Review of Anthropology,* Vol. 3, ed. Bernard J. Siegel, pp. 323–356. Palo Alto, Calif.: Annual Reviews.

Donovan, John E., and Richard Jessor. 1985. Structures of Problem Behavior in Adolescence and Young Adulthood. *Journal of Consulting and Clinical Psychology* 53:890–904.

Douglas, Jack D. 1976. *Investigative Social Research.* Beverly Hills: Sage.

Douglas, Jack D., and John M. Johnson, eds. 1977. *Existential Sociology.* New York: Cambridge University Press.

Duster, Troy. 1987. Crime, Youth Unemployment, and the Black Urban Underclass. *Crime and Delinquency* 33(2):300–316.

Duxbury, Elaine B. 1993. Correctional Interventions. In *The Gang Intervention Handbook,* ed. Arnold P. Goldstein and C. Ronald Huff, pp. 427–437. Champaign, Ill.: Research Press.

Dwivedi, Kedar Nath. 1993. Child Abuse and Hatred. In *How and Why Children Hate: Study of Conscious and Unconscious Sources,* ed. Ved Varma, pp. 46–71. London: Jessica Kingsley.

Dygdon, J. A., A. J. Conger, and S. P. Keane. 1987. Children's Perceptions of the Behavioral Correlates of Social Acceptance, Rejection, and Neglect in Their Peers. *Journal of Clinical Child Psychology* 16:2–8.

Eckland-Olson, S. 1982. Deviance, Social Control, and Social Networks. *Research in Law, Deviance, and Social Control* 4:271–299.

Edelbrock, Craig. 1980. Running Away from Home: Incidence and Correlates among Children and Youth Referred for Mental Health Services. *Journal of Family Issues* 1:210–228.

Edwards, Calvin R. 1994. The Federal Sentencing Reform Act: The Implementation in the Federal Bureau of Prisons. Ph.D. dissertation in public administration, University of Southern California (Washington, D.C., branch).

Elder, Glen H., Jr. 1975. Age Differentiation and the Life Course. *Annual Review of Sociology* 1:165–190.

———. 1978. Family History and the Life Course. In *Transitions: The Family and the Life Course in Historical Perspective,* ed. T. K. Hareven, pp. 17–64. New York: Academic Press.

———. 1980. Adolescence in Historical Perspective. In *Handbook of Adolescent Psychology,* ed. J. Adelson, pp. 3–46. New York: John Wiley and Sons.

———. 1985. Perspectives on the Life Course. In *Life Course Dynamics,* ed. Glen H. Elder, Jr., pp. 23–49. Ithaca, N.Y.: Cornell University Press.

Elliot, Delbert, and Harwin Voss. 1974. *Delinquency and Dropout.* Lexington, Mass.: Lexington Books.

Elliot, Delbert, David Huizinga, and Suzanne S. Ageton. 1985. *Explaining Delinquency and Drug Use.* Beverly Hills: Sage.

Ellis, Albert. 1962. *Reason and Emotion in Psychotherapy.* Secaucus, N.J.: Lyle Stuart.

———. 1987. A Sadly Neglected Cognitive Element in Depression. *Cognitive Therapy and Research* 11(1):121–146.

Emler, N., S. Reicher, and A. Ross. 1987. The Social Context of Delinquent Conduct. *Journal of Child Psychology and Psychiatry and Allied Disciplines* 28:99–109.

Emshwiller, John R. 1992. Rival Street Gangs Discover Capitalism, the Legitimate Kind. *Wall Street Journal,* June 22, pp. A1, A6.

Erickson, Maynard L. 1971. The Group Context of Delinquent Behavior. *Social Problems* 19:114–129.

Erickson, Maynard L., and Lamar T. Empey. 1965. Class Position, Peers, and Delinquency. *Sociology and Social Research* 49:268–282.

Erikson, Erik H. 1968. *Identity: Youth and Crisis.* New York: Norton.

———. 1975. *Life History and the Historical Moment.* New York: Norton.

Erlich, Reese. 1994. US, as well as China, Exports Prison Goods. *The Christian Science Monitor,* February 9, p. 8.

Esbensen, Finn-Aage, and David Huizinga. 1993. Gangs, Drugs, and Delinquency in a Survey of Urban Youth. *Criminology* 31(4):565–589.

Fagan, Jeffrey. 1989. The Social Organization of Drug Use and Drug Dealing among Urban Gangs. *Criminology* 27(4):633–669.

———. 1990. Social Processes of Delinquency and Drug Use among Urban Gangs. In *Gangs in America,* ed. C. Ronald Huff, pp. 183–219. Newbury Park, Calif.: Sage.

———. 1992. Drug Selling and Licit Income in Distressed Neighborhoods: The Economic Lives of Street-level Drug Users and Dealers. In *Drugs, Crime, and Social Isolation: Barriers to Urban Opportunity,* ed. Adele V. Harrell and George E. Peterson, pp. 99–146. Washington, D.C.: Urban Institute Press.

———. 1993. Interactions among Drugs, Alcohol, and Violence. *Health Affairs* (Winter):65–79.

Fagan, Jeffrey A., and K. Chin. 1989. Initiation into Crack and Cocaine: A Tale of Two Epidemics. *Contemporary Drug Problems* 16:579–618.

Fagan, Jeffrey A., and Edward Pabon. 1990. Contributions of Delinquency and Substance Use to School Dropout among Inner City Youths. *Youth and Society* 21:306–354.

Fagan, Jeffrey, Karen V. Hansen, and Michael Jang. 1983. Profiles of Chronically Violent Delinquents: Empirical Test of an Integrate Theory. In *Evaluating Juvenile Justice*, ed. James Kleugel, Beverly Hills: Sage.

Fagan, Jeffrey, Elizabeth Piper, and Melinda Moore. 1986. Violent Delinquents and Urban Youths. *Criminoloby* 24(3):439–466.

Farr, R., P. Koegel, and A. Burnham. 1986. *A Study of Homelessness and Mental Illness in the Skid Row Area of Los Angeles*. Los Angeles: Los Angeles County Department of Mental Health.

Farrington, David P. 1978. The Family Backgrounds of Aggressive Youths. In *Aggression and Anti-Social Behavior in Childhood and Adolescence*, ed. L. A. Hersov, M. Berger, and D. Schaffer, pp. 73–93. Oxford: Pergamon.

———. 1986. Age and Crime. In *Crime and Justice: An Annual Review of Research*, Vol. 7, ed. Michael H. Tonry and Norval Morris, pp. 189–250. Chicago: University of Chicago Press.

———. 1987. Prediction and Classification: Criminal Justice Decision Making. In *Crime and Justice: An Annual Review of Research*, Vol. 9, ed. Donald M. Gottfredson and Michael Tonry, pp. 53–101. Chicago: University of Chicago Press.

Farrington, David P., Lloyd E. Ohlin, and James Q. Wilson. 1986. *Understanding and Controlling Crime: Toward a New Research Strategy*. New York: Springer-Verlag.

Faupel, Charles. 1991. *Shooting Dope*. Gainesville: University of Florida Press.

Federal Bureau of Prisons. 1990. Recidivism among Federal and State Offenders. Research Bulletin, November. Office of Research and Evaluation, Bureau of Prisons, Washington, D.C.

———. 1992. GED Program Celebrates 50th Anniversary. *Monday Morning Highlights* (August 3). Information, Policy, and Public Affairs Division, Washington, D.C.

Feeley, Malcolm. 1979. *The Process Is the Punishment*. New York: Russell Sage.

Feeley, Malcolm, and Jonathan Simon. 1992. The New Penology: Notes on the Emerging Strategy of Corrections and Its Implications. *Criminology* 30(4):449–474.

Feld, Scott L. 1981. The Focused Organization of Social Ties. *American Journal of Sociology* 86:1015–1035.

Feldman, Harvey W. 1968. Ideological Supports to Becoming and Remaining a Heroin Addict. *Journal of Health and Social Behavior* 9:131–139.

Fillmore, Charles. 1973. A Grammarian Looks to Sociolinguistics. In *Report of the 23rd Annual Round Table Meeting on Linguistics and Language Studies—Sociolinguistics: Current Trends and Prospects*, ed. Roger W. Shuy, pp. 273–287. Washington, D.C.: Georgetown University Press.

Fishman, Laura T. 1986. Repeating the Cycle of Hard Living and Crime: Wives' Accommodations to Husbands' Parole Performance. *Federal Probation* 50(4):44–54.

——. 1990. *Women at the Wall: A Study of Prisoners' Wives Doing Time on the Outside.* Albany: State University of New York Press.

Fleisher, Mark S. 1989. *Warehousing Violence.* Newbury Park, Calif.: Sage.

——. 1990. *An Ethnographic Evaluation of Street-to-System Cycling of Black, Hispanic, and American Indian Males.* Joint Statistical Agreement 88-19. Washington, D.C.: U.S. Bureau of Census, Center for the Survey Methods Research.

Fleisher, Mark S., and Daniel McCarthy. 1988. Wage Earning and Social Control at the United States Penitentiary at Lompoc, California. Paper read at the American Society of Criminology, Chicago.

Flynn, Edith E. 1992. The Graying of America's Prison Population. *The Prison Journal* 72 (1 and 2):77–98.

Fortes, Myer. 1945. *The Dynamics of Clanship among the Tallensi: Being the First Part of an Analysis of the Social Structure of the Trans-Volta Tribe.* London: Oxford University Press.

Frake, Charles. 1964. A Structural Description of Subanum "Religious Behavior." In *Exploration in Cultural Anthropology,* ed. Ward Goodenough, pp. 111–129. New York: McGraw-Hill.

Frances, R. J., S. Timm, and S. Bucky. 1980. Studies of Familial and Nonfamilial Alcoholism. *Archives of General Psychiatry* 37:564–566.

Freeman, Richard B. 1983. Crime and Unemployment. In *Crime and Public Policy,* ed. by J. Q. Wilson, pp. 89–106. San Francisco: Institute for Contemporary Studies.

Friedman, S., and T. C. Esselstyn. 1965. The Adjustment of Children of Jail Inmates. *Federal Probation* 29:55–59.

Frontline. 1985. The Lifer and the Lady. Transcript #304. Boston: WGBH Educational Foundation (125 Western Ave., 02134).

Frude, Neil. 1991. *Understanding Family Problems: A Psychological Analysis.* Chichester, England: John Wiley and Sons.

——. 1993. Hatred between Children. In *How and Why Children Hate: Study of Conscious and Unconscious Sources,* ed. Ved Varma, pp. 72–93. London: Jessica Kingsley.

Garbarino, James. 1989. The Incidence and Prevalence of Child Maltreatment. In *Family Violence,* ed. L. Ohlin and M. Tonry, pp. 219–261. Chicago: University of Chicago Press.

Geertz, Clifford. 1984. "From the Native's Point of View": On the Nature of Anthropological Understanding. In *Culture Theory: Essays on Mind, Self, and Emotion,* ed. R. A. Shweder and R. A. Levine, pp. 123–136. New York: Cambridge University Press.

Geismar, Ludwig L., and Katherine M. Wood. 1986. *Family and Delinquency: Resocializing the Young Offender.* New York: Human Sciences Press.

George, Linda K. 1993. Sociological Perspectives on Life Transitions. *Annual Review of Sociology* 19:353–373.

Gibbs, J. P. 1987. Social Processes in Delinquency: The Need to Facilitate Empathy as well as Sociomoral Reasoning. In *Moral Development through Social Interaction,* ed. W. Kurtines and J. Gewirtz, pp. 301–321. New York: John Wiley and Sons.

Giordano, P. C., S. A. Cernkovich, and M. D. Pugh. 1986. Friendships and Delinquency. *American Journal of Sociology* 91:1170–1202.

Glaser, D. 1964. *The Effectiveness of Prison and Parole System.* Indianapolis: Bobbs-Merrill.

Glueck, Sheldon, and Eleanor Glueck. 1950. *Unraveling Juvenile Delinquency.* Cambridge: Harvard University Press.

———. 1968. *Delinquents and Nondelinquents in Perspective.* Cambridge, Mass.: Harvard University Press.

Goffman, Erving. 1959. *The Presentation of Self in Everyday Life.* Garden City: Doubleday Anchor.

———. 1967. *Interaction Ritual: Essays on Face-to-Face Behavior.* Garden City: Doubleday Anchor.

Goodenough, Ward H. 1956. Componential Analysis and the Study of Meaning. *Langauge* 32:195–216.

———. 1957. Cultural Anthropology and Linguistics. In *Report on the Seventh Annual Round Table Meeting on Linguistics and Language Study,* ed. Paul Garvin, pp. 167–173. Monograph Series, Language and Linguistics 9. Washington, D.C.: Georgetown University Press.

Goodwin, D. W. 1976. *Is Alcoholism Hereditary?* New York: Oxford University Press.

Goodwin, D. W., F. Schlusinger, N. Moller, L. Hermansen, G. Winokur, and S. B. Guze. 1974. Drinking Problems in Adopted and Nonadopted Sons of Alcoholics. *Archives of General Psychiatry* 31:164–169.

Gottfredson, Denise C. 1986. An Empirical Test of School-based Environmental and Individual Interventions to Reduce the Risk of Delinquent Behavior. *Criminology* 24:705–731.

Gottfredson, Michael R., and Don M. Gottfredson. 1988. *Decisionmaking in Criminal Justice.* 2nd edition. New York: Plenum.

Gottfredson, Michael R., and Travis Hirschi. 1988. Science, Public Policy, and the Career Paradigm. *Criminology* 26:37–56.

———. 1990. *A General Theory of Crime.* Stanford, Calif.: Stanford University Press.

———. 1993. A Control Theory Interpretation of Psychological Response on Aggression. In *Aggression and Violence: Social Interactionist Perspec-*

tives, ed. Richard B. Felson and James T. Tedeschi, pp. 47–67. Washington, D.C.: American Psychological Association.

Gottfredson, Stephen D., and Don M. Gottfredson. 1992. *Incapacitation Strategies and the Criminal Career.* Sacramento: Law Enforcement Information Center.

Gough, Harrison. 1948. A Sociological Theory of Psychopathy. *American Journal of Sociology* 53:359–366.

Gould, Leroy C., Andrew L. Walker, Lansing E. Crane, and Charles W. Lidz. 1974. *Connections: Notes from the Heroin World.* New Haven, Conn.: Yale University Press.

Gove, W. 1985. The Effect of Age and Gender on Deviant Behavior: A Biopsychological Approach. In *Gender and the Life Course,* ed. A. Rossi, pp. 115–144. Washington, D.C.: American Sociological Association.

Granovetter, Mark S. 1973. The Strength of Weak Ties. *American Journal of Sociology* 78:1360–1380.

———. 1974. *Getting a Job: A Study of Contacts and Careers.* Cambridge, Mass.: Harvard University Press.

———. 1985. Economic Action and Social Structure: The Problem of Embeddedness. *American Journal of Sociology* 91:481–510.

———. 1992. The Sociological and Economic Approaches to Labor Market Analysis: A Social Structural View. In *The Sociology of Economic Life,* ed. Mark Granovetter and Richard Swedberg, pp. 233–263. Boulder, Colo.: Westview Press.

Greenberg, David F. 1977. Delinquency and the Age Structure of Society. *Contemporary Crises* 1:189–224.

———. 1983. Age and Crime. In *Encyclopedia of Crime and Justice,* ed. Sanford H. Kadish, pp. 30–35. New York: Free Press.

Greenberg, Stephanie W., William M. Rohe, and Jay R. Williams. 1985. *Informal Citizen Action and Crime Prevention at the Neighborhood Level.* Washington, D.C.: National Institute of Justice.

Greenwood, Peter. 1985. *The Juvenile Rehabilitation Reader.* Santa Monica, Calif.: Rand Corporation.

Gross, Jane. 1992. Collapse of Inner-City Families Creates America's New Orphans. *New York Times,* March 29, "The Nation" section, pp. 1, 15.

Gross, J. L., and S. Rayner. 1985. *Measuring Culture: A Paradigm for the Analysis of Social Organization.* New York: Columbia University Press.

Gumperz, J. J., and Dell Hymes. 1964. The Ethnography of Communication. *American Anthropologist* 66(6), special publication.

Hagan, John. 1991. Destiny and Drift: Subcultural Preferences, Status Attainments, and the Risks and Rewards of Youth. *American Sociological Review* 56:567–582.

———. 1993. The Social Embeddedness of Crime and Unemployment. *Criminology* 31(4):465–491.

Hagedorn, John M. (with Perry Macon). 1988. *People and Folks: Gangs, Crime and the Underclass in a Rustbelt City.* Chicago: Lake View Press.

———. 1994. Homeboys, Dope Fiends, Legits, and New Jacks. *Criminology* 32(2):197–219.

Hall, Calvin S., and Gardner Lindzey. 1978. *Theories of Personality.* 3rd edition. New York: John Wiley and Sons.

Hamid, Ansley. 1992. *Ethnographic Follow-up of a Predominantly African American Population in a Sample Area in Central Harlem, New York City: Behavioral Causes of the Undercount of the 1990 Census.* Final Report for Joint Statistical Agreement 89-28. Washington, D.C.: Center for Survey Methods Research, Bureau of the Census.

Hammett, Marcella, Kenneth E. Powell, Patrick W. O'Carroll, and Sharon T. Clanton. 1992. Homicide Surveillance—United States, 1979–1988. *Morbidity and Mortality Weekly Report* (May 29):1–33. Atlanta: U.S. Department of Health and Human Services, Centers for Disease Control.

Hannerz, U. 1969. *Soulside.* New York: Columbia University Press.

Hansell, Stephan, and Michael D. Wiatrowski. 1981. Competing Conceptions of Delinquent Peer Relations. In *Sociology of Delinquency,* ed. Gary F. Jensen, pp. 93–108. Beverly Hills: Sage.

Hanson, William, George Beschner, James M. Walters, and Elliot Bovelle, eds. 1985. *Life with Heroin: Voices from the Inner City.* Lexington, Mass.: Lexington Books.

Hawkins, D. F. 1993. Inequality, Culture, and Interpersonal Violence. *Human Affairs* (Winter):80–95.

Hawkins, J. David, and Richard Catalano. 1992. *Communities That Care.* San Francisco: Jossey-Bass.

Hawkins, J. David, and M. W. Fraser. 1985. The Social Networks of Street Drug Users: A Comparison of Competing Propositions of Control and Cultural Deviance Theories. *Social Work Research and Abstracts* 21:3–12.

Hawkins, J. David, and Joseph Weis. 1985. The Social Development Model: An Integrated Approach to Delinquency Prevention. *Journal of Primary Prevention* 6:73–97.

Hazen, N. L., B. Black, and F. Fleming-Johnson. 1984. Social Acceptance: Strategies Children Use and How Teachers Can Help Children Learn Them. *Young Children* 39:26–36.

Heath, S. B. 1989. Oral and Literate Traditions among Black Americans Living in Poverty. *American Psychologist* 44:367–373.

Heidemann, Sabrina M., and Mark G. Goetting. 1990. Passive Inhalation of Cocaine by Infants. *Henry Ford Hospital Medical Journal* 38(4):252–254.

Helms, Janet E. 1992. Why Is There No Study of Cultural Equivalence in Standardized Cognitive Ability Testing? *American Psychologist* 47(9):1083–1101.

Hepburn, John R. 1977. Testing Alternatives Models of Delinquency Causation. *Journal of Criminal Law and Criminology* 67:450–460.

Hill, Jane, and Bruce Mannheim. 1992. Language and World View. *Annual Review of Anthropology* 21:381–406.

Hindeland, M., T. Hirschi, and J. Weis. 1981. *Measuring Delinquency*. Newbury Park, Calif.: Sage.

Hippler, Arthur E. 1974. *Hunter's Point: A Black Ghetto*. New York: Basic Books.

Hirschi, Travis. 1969. *Causes of Delinquency*. Berkeley: University of California Press.

———. 1983. Crime and the Family. In *Crime and Public Policy*, ed. James Q. Wilson, pp. 53–68. San Francisco: Institute for Contemporary Studies.

Hirschi, Travis, and Michael Gottfredson. 1983. Age and the Explanation of Crime. *American Journal of Sociology* 89:552–584.

———. 1993. Rethinking the Juvenile Justice System. *Crime and Delinquency* 39(2):262–271.

Hofer, Paul. 1988. Prisonization and Recidivism: A Psychological Perspective. *International Journal of Offender Therapy and Comparative Criminology* 32:95–106.

Hogan, Robert, and Warren H. Jones, eds. 1985. *Perspectives in Personality: A Research Annual*, Vol. 1. Greenwich, Conn.: JAI Press.

Holden, Constance. 1989. Street-Wise Crack Research. *Science* (246, December 15):1376.

Hollin, Clive R. 1993. Advances in the Psychological Treatment of Delinquent Behaviour. *Criminal Behaviour and Mental Health* 3(3):142–157.

Holt, Norman, and Donald Miller. 1972. *Explorations in Inmate-Family Relationships*. California Department of Corrections, No. 46 (January). Sacramento: California Department of Corrections.

Horowitz, Ruth. 1983. *Honor and the American Dream: Culture and Identity in a Chicano Community*. New Brunswick, N.J.: Rutgers University Press.

———. 1987. Community Tolerance of Gang Violence. *Social Problems* 34(5):437–450.

———. 1990. Sociological Perspectives on Gangs: Conflicting Definitions and Concepts. In *Gangs in America*, ed. C. Ronald Huff, pp. 37–54. Newbury Park, Calif.: Sage.

Hotaling, Gerald T., and Murray A. Straus, with Alan J. Lincoln. 1989. Intrafamily Violence, and Crime and Violence Outside the Family. In *Family Violence*, ed. L. Ohlin and M. Tonry, pp. 315–375. Chicago: University of Chicago Press.

Howell, Signe. 1989. "To Be Angry Is Not to Be Human, But to Be Fearful Is": Chewong Concepts of Human Nature. In *Societies at Peace: Anthropological Perspectives*, ed. Signe Howell and Roy Willis, pp. 45–59. London: Routledge and Kegan Paul.

Howitt, Pamela S., and Eugene Arthur Moore. 1993. Pay Now So You Won't

Pay Later: The Effectiveness of Prevention Programming in the Fight to Reduce Delinquency. *Juvenile and Family Court Journal* 44(2):57–67.

Howser, J., J. Grossman, and D. MacDonald. 1983. Impact of Family Reunion Program on Institution Discipline. *Journal of Offender Counseling, Services and Rehabilitation* 8:27–36.

Huff, Ronald C. 1989. Youth Gangs and Public Policy. *Crime and Delinquency* 35:524–537.

Huizinga, David, Finn-Aage Esbensen, and Anne Wylie Weiher. 1991. Are There Multiple Paths to Delinquency. *Journal of Criminal Law and Criminology* 82(1):83–118.

Hutchison, Kay Bailey. 1994. Should Inmates Get Student Aid? *USA Today,* March 17, p. 13A.

Hymes, Dell. 1974. *Foundations in Sociolinguistics: An Ethnographic Approach.* Philadelphia: University of Pennsylvania Press.

Inciardi, James A. 1975. *Careers in Crime.* Chicago: Rand McNally.

———. 1986. *The War on Drugs: Heroin, Cocaine, Crime and Public Policy.* Mountain View, Calif.: Mayfield.

———. 1988. *Crack Cocaine in Miami.* Newark: University of Delaware.

———. 1992. *The War on Drugs II: The Continuing Epic of Heroin, Cocaine, Crack, Crime, AIDS, and Public Policy.* Mountain View, Calif.: Mayfield.

Inciardi, James A., and Duane C. McBride. 1990. Legalizing Drugs: A Harmless, Naive Idea. *The Criminologist* 15(5):1, 3–4.

Inciardi, James A., and A. E. Pottieger. 1990. Kids, Crack and Cocaine. *Journal of Drug Issues* 20:181–194.

Inciardi, James A., Ruth Horowitz, and Ann E. Pottieger. 1993. *Street Kids, Street Drugs, Street Crime: An Examination of Drug Use and Serious Delinquency in Miami.* Belmont, Calif.: Wadsworth.

Inciardi, James A., D. Lockwood, and Ann E. Pottieger. 1993. *Women and Crack-Cocaine.* New York: Macmillan.

Ingrassia, Michele, and John McCormick. 1994. Why Leave Children with Bad Parents? *Newsweek,* April 25, pp. 52–54, 55–56, 58.

Irwin, John. 1970. *The Felon.* Englewood Cliffs, N.J.: Prentice Hall.

———. 1980. *Prisons in Turmoil.* Boston: Little, Brown.

———. 1985a. *The Jail.* Berkeley: University of California Press.

———. 1985b. The Return of the Bogeyman. Speech delivered to the American Society of Criminology Annual Meeting, San Diego, California.

Irwin, John, and James Austin. 1994. *It's about Time: America's Imprisonment Binge.* San Francisco: Wadsworth.

Jackson, Bruce. 1972. *Outside the Law.* New Brunswick, N.J.: Transaction.

Jackson, Robert K., and Wesley D. McBride. 1992. *Understanding Street Gangs.* Placerville, Calif.: Copperhouse.

Jacobs, James B. 1977. *Stateville: The Penitentiary in Mass Society.* Chicago: University of Chicago Press.

———. 1990. Imagining Drug Legalization. *The Public Interest* (101, Fall): 28–42.

Jensen, Gary F. 1972. Parents, Peers, and Delinquent Action: A Test of the Differential Association Perspective. *American Journal of Sociology* 78: 562–575.

Jessiman, Edwin Martin. 1984. A Study of the Factors Relating to Perceptions of Family Support of Inmates Serving Sentences in the Maine State Prison. Ph.D. dissertation, University of Connecticut.

Jessor, Richard, and Shirley L. Jessor. 1977. *Problem Behavior and Psychosocial Development: A Longitudinal Study of Youth.* New York: Academic Press.

Johnson, Bruce D., Paul J. Goldstein, Edward Preble, James Schmeidler, Douglas S. Lipton, Barry Spunt, and Thomas Miller. 1985. *Taking Care of Business: The Economics of Crime by Heroin Abusers.* Lexington, Mass.: Lexington Books.

Johnson, John M. 1975. *Doing Field Research.* New York: Free Press.

Johnson, Richard E. 1979. *Juvenile Delinquency and Its Origins.* Cambridge: Cambridge University Press.

Johnson, Steve. 1993. Some Truants Learn Deadliest of Lessons. *Chicago Tribune,* November 19, pp. 1, 8.

Johnston, Lloyd D., Patrick M. O'Malley, and Leslie K. Eveland. 1978. Drugs and Delinquency: A Search for Causal Connections. In *Longitudinal Research on Drug Use,* ed. D. B. Kandel, pp. 137–156. Washington, D.C.: Hemisphere.

Jolin, A., and D. C. Gibbons. 1987. Age Patterns in Criminal Involvement. *International Journal of Offender Therapy and Comparative Criminology* 31: 237–260.

Kandel, Denise B. 1975. Reaching the Hard-to-Reach: Illicit Drug Use among High School Absentees. *Addictive Diseases* 1:465–480.

Kandel, Denise, and Mark Davies. 1991. Friendship Networks, Intimacy, and Illicit Drug Use in Young Adulthood: A Comparison of Two Competing Theories. *Criminology* 29(3):441–467.

Kandel, Elizabeth, and Sarnoff A. Mednick. 1991. Perinatal Complications Predict Violent Offending. *Criminology* 29(3):519–529.

Kandel, Eric R., and Robert D. Hawkins. 1992. The Biological Basis of Learning and Individuality. *Scientific American* 267(3):70–86.

Kardiner, Abram. 1939. *The Individual and Society.* New York: Columbia University Press.

———. 1945. *The Psychological Frontiers of Society.* New York: Columbia University Press.

Karoly, P., and M. Rosenthal. 1977. Training Parents in Behavior Modification: Effects on Perceptions of Family Interaction and Deviant Child Behavior. *Behavior Therapy* 8:406–410.

Katz, Jack. 1988. *Seductions of Crime.* New York: Basic Books.

Katz, J. H. 1985. The Sociopolitical Nature of Counseling. *The Counseling Psychologist* 13:615–624.

Keiser, R. Lincoln. 1969. *The Vice Lords: Warriors of the Street.* New York: Holt, Rinehart and Winston.

Kelly, DeLos. 1982. *Creating School Failure, Youth Crime, and Deviance.* Los Angeles: Trident Shop.

Kelly, Thomas M. 1993a. Neo-cognitive Learning Theory: Implications for Prevention and Early Intervention Strategies with At-Risk Youth. *Adolescence* 28(10):439–460.

———. 1993b. An Advanced Criminology Based on Psychology-of-Mind. *Journal of Offender Rehabilitation* 19(3/4):173–190.

Keniston, K. 1970. Youth as a Stage of Life. *American Scholar* 39:631–654.

Kerckhoff, A. C. 1990. *Getting Started: Transition to Adulthood in Great Britain.* Boulder, Colo.: Westview.

Killworth, Peter D., H. Russell Bernard, and Christopher McCarty. 1984. Measuring Patterns of Acquaintanceship. *Current Anthropology* 25(4): 381–397.

King County. 1986a. *Homelessness Revisited.* Seattle: Housing and Community Development Division, Department of Planning and Community Development.

———. 1986b. *Emergency Shelter Study Update.* September. Seattle: Housing and Community Development Division, Department of Planning and Community Development.

Kingsley, Ronald. 1989. A Peer Connection Program: An In-school Resource for High-Risk, Delinquency-Prone Students. *Juvenile and Family Court Journal* 40:20–29.

Klein, Malcom W. 1971. *Street Gangs and Street Workers.* Englewood Cliffs, N.J.: Prentice Hall.

Klein, Malcom W., and Cheryl L. Maxson. 1985. "Rock Sales" in South Los Angeles. *Sociology and Society Research* 69:561–565.

———. 1989. Street Gang Violence. In *Violent Crime, Violent Criminals,* ed. Neil A. Weiner and Marvin E. Wolfgang, pp. 198–234. Newbury Park, Calif.: Sage.

Klein, Malcom W., Cheryl L. Maxson, and Lea Cunningham. 1991. "Crack," Street Gangs, and Violence. *Criminology* 29:623–650.

Klein-Saffron, Jody. 1991. Shock Incarceration, Bureau of Prisons Style. *Research Forum* 1(3, July). Federal Bureau of Prisons, Office of Research and Evaluation, Washington, D.C.

Klockars, Carl. 1974. *The Professional Fence.* New York: Free Press.

Knight-Ridder/*Chicago Tribune.* 1993. Senate Endorse Ban on Assault Weapons. November 18, Section 1.

Kodluboy, Donald W., and Loren A. Evenrud. 1993. School-based Interventions: Best Practices and Critical Issues. In *The Gang Intervention Hand-*

book, ed. Arnold P. Goldstein and C. Ronald Huff, pp. 257–299. Champaign, Ill.: Research Press.

Kornhauser, R. R. 1978. *Social Sources of Delinquency: An Appraisal of Analytic Models*. Chicago: University of Chicago Press.

Krisberg, Barry. 1991. Are You Now or Have You Ever Been a Sociologist? *Journal of Criminal Law and Criminology* 82(1):141–155.

Krisberg, Barry, James Austin, and Patricia Steele. 1989. *Unlocking Juvenile Corrections: Evaluating the Massachusetts Department of Youth Services*. San Francisco: National Council on Crime and Delinquency.

Kufeldt, Kathleen, and Margaret Nimmo. 1987. Youth on the Street: Abuse and Neglect in the Eighties. *Child Abuse and Neglect* 11:531–543.

Kuhn, T. S. 1986. *The Essential Tension: Selected Studies in Scientific Tradition and Change*. Chicago: University of Chicago Press.

Lang, K., and G. Lang. 1961. *Collective Dynamics*. New York: Thomas Y. Crowell.

Langer, John. 1977. Drug Entrepreneurs and Dealing Culture. *Social Problems* 24:377–385.

Laub, John H. 1983. Urbanism, Race, and Crime. *Journal of Research in Crime and Delinquency* 20:183–198.

Laub, John H., and Robert J. Sampson. 1993. Turning Points in the Life Course: Why Change Matters to the Study of Crime. *Criminology* 31(3):301–325.

Leach, Edmund. 1968. *A Runaway World: 1967 Reith Lectures*. BBC London. Oxford: Oxford University Press.

Lerner, Steve. 1990. *The Good News about Juvenile Justice*. Bolinas, Calif.: Common Knowledge Press.

Letkemann, Peter. 1973. *Crime as Work*. Englewood Cliff, N.J.: Prentice Hall.

Leukefeld, Carl G., and Frank M. Timms, eds. 1988. *Compulsory Treatment of Drug Abuse: Research and Clinical Practice*. Rockville, Md.: National Institute on Drug Abuse.

Levine, R. 1973. *Culture, Behavior, and Personality*. Chicago: Aldine.

Levinson, D., C. Darrow, E. Klein, M. Levinson, and B. McKee. 1978. *The Seasons of a Man's Life*. New York: Knopf.

Lévi-Strauss, Claude. 1966. *The Savage Mind*. 2nd edition. Chicago: University of Chicago Press.

Liebow, Elliot. 1967. *Tally's Corner*. Boston: Little, Brown.

Lindblom, C. E. 1968. *The Policy Making Process*. Englewood Cliffs, N.J.: Prentice Hall.

Lipton, Douglas S., and Harry K. Wexler. 1988. Breaking the Drug-Crime Connection. *Corrections Today* (August):144, 146, 155.

Liska, Allen E., and Mark D. Reed. 1985. Ties to Conventional Institutions and Delinquency: Estimating Reciprocal Effects. *American Sociological Review* 50:547–560.

Loeber, Rolf, and Thomas J. Dishion. 1983. Early Predictors of Male Delinquency: A Review. *Psychological Bulletin* 94(1):68–99.

———. 1984. Boys Who Fight at Home and School: Conditions Influencing Cross-Setting Consistency. *Journal of Consulting and Clinical Psychology* 52(5):759–768.

Loeber, Rolf, and Magda Stouthamer-Loeber. 1986. Family Factors as Correlates and Predictors of Juvenile Conduct Problems and Delinquency. In *Crime and Justice: An Annual Review of Research*, Vol. 7, ed. Michael Tonry and Norval Morris, pp. 29–149. Chicago: University of Chicago Press.

———. 1987. Prediction. In *Handbook of Juvenile Delinquency*, ed. Herbert C. Quay, pp. 325–382. New York: John Wiley and Sons.

Loeber, Rolf, Thomas J. Dishion, and Gerald Patterson. 1984. Multiple Mating: A Multistage Assessment Procedure for Identifying Youths At Risk for Delinquency. *Journal of Research in Crime and Delinquency* 21:7–31.

Logan, Charles H. 1991. Who Really Goes to Prison? *Federal Prison Journal* 2(3):57–59.

Lowenstein, A. 1984. Coping with Stress: The Case of Prisoners' Wives. *Journal of Marriage and the Family* 46:699–708.

Lundy, G. F., and D. L. Kalob. 1985. Struggling to Make It: A Study of Homelessness in New Orleans. A paper prepared for Associated Catholic Charities, Loyola University, New Orleans, Louisiana.

Lyman, M., and G. W. Potter. 1991. Drugs in Society. Cincinnati, Ohio: Anderson.

Lyons, J. 1968. *Introduction to Theoretical Linguistics.* Cambridge: Cambridge University Press.

McCarthy, Colman. 1994. Committed to a Hard-Found Peace. *Washington Post*, February 1.

McCord, Joan. 1977. A Comparative Study of Two Generations of Native Americans. In *Theory in Criminology*, ed. Robert F. Meier, pp. 83–92. Beverly Hills: Sage.

———. 1978. A Thirty-Year Follow-up of Treatment Effects. *American Psychologist* 33:284–289.

———. 1979. Some Child-rearing Antecedents of Criminal Behavior in Adult Men. *Journal of Personality and Social Psychology* 37:1477–1486.

———. Family Relationships, Juvenile Delinquency, and Adult Criminality. *Criminology* 29(3):397–417.

MacKenzie, Doris Layton, and Clare C. Souryal. 1991. Boot Camp Survey. *Corrections Today* (October):90–96.

MacKenzie, Doris Layton, and James W. Shaw. 1993. The Impact of Shock Incarceration on Technical Violations and New Criminal Activities. *Justice Quarterly* 10(3):463–487.

MacLeod, Jay. 1987. *Ain't No Makin' It: Leveled Aspirations in a Low-Income Neighborhood*. Boulder, Colo: Westview Press.

McPherson, J. Miller, Pamela A. Poplielarz, and Sonja Drobnic. 1992. Social Networks and Organizational Dynamics. *American Sociological Review* 57(2):153–170.

Malcolm, Andrew H. 1991. More Cells for More Prisoners, But to What End? *New York Times,* January 18, pp. 9–10.

Malinowski, Bronislaw. 1922. *Argonauts of the Western Pacific*. London: Routledge and Kegan Paul.

Marsh, P., E. Rosser, and R. Harre. 1978. *The Rules of Disorder*. London: Routledge and Kegan Paul.

Martin, B. 1977. Brief Family Therapy Intervention: Effectiveness and the Importance of Including the Father. *Journal of Consulting and Clinical Psychology* 45:1001–1010.

Martin, Dannie. 1993. *Committing Journalism: The Prison Writings of Red Hog*. New York: North.

Marwell, Gerald, Pamela E. Oliver, and Ralph Prahl. 1988. Social Networks and Collective Action: A Theory of the Critical Mass III. *American Journal of Sociology* 94:502–534.

Matza, David. 1964. *Delinquency and Drift*. New York: John Wiley and Sons.

Maultsby, M. C. 1975. *Help Yourself to Happiness through Rational Self-counseling*. New York: Institute for Rational Living.

Maurer, David W. 1974. *The American Confidence Man*. Springfield, Ill.: Charles Thomas.

Meisenhelder, T. 1977. An Exploratory Study of Exiting from Criminal Careers. *Criminology* 15:319–334.

Melaville, Atelia I., and Martin J. Blank. 1991. *What It Takes: Structuring Interagency Partnerships to Connect Children and Families with Comprehensive Services*. Washington, D.C.: Education and Human Services Consortium.

Mercy, James A., Mark L. Rosenberg, Kenneth E. Powell, Claire V. Broome, and William L. Roper. 1993. Public Health Policy for Preventing Violence. *Health Affairs* (Winter):7–29.

Merton, R. K. 1949. *Social Theory and Social Structure*. New York: Free Press.

Meyenn, Robert J. 1980. School Girls' Peer Groups. In *Pupil Strategies: Explorations in the Sociology of the School,* ed. Peter Woods, pp. 108–142. London: Croom Helm.

Mieczkowski, T. 1986. Geeking Up and Throwing Down: Heroin Street Life in Detroit. *Criminology* 25:645–666.

Milich, R., S. Landau, G. Kilby, and P. Whitten. 1982. Preschool Peer Perceptions of the Behavior of Hyperactive and Aggressive Children. *Journal of Abnormal Psychology* 10:497–510.

Miller, Gale. 1978. *Odd Jobs*. Englewood Cliffs, N.J.: Prentice Hall.

Miller, T. R., M. A. Cohen, and S. B. Rossman. 1993. Victim Costs of Violent Crime and Resulting Injuries. *Health Affairs* (Winter):187–198.

Miller, Walter B. 1958. Lower Culture as a Generating Milieu of Gang Delinquency. *Journal of Social Issues* 14(3):5–19.

———. 1975. *Violence by Youth Gangs and Youth Groups as a Crime Problem in Major American Cities.* Washington, D.C.: U.S. Department of Justice, National Institute for Juvenile Justice and Delinquency Prevention.

———. 1980. Gangs, Groups and Serious Youth Crime. In *Critical Issues in Juvenile Delinquency,* ed. David Shichor and Delos H. Kelly, pp. 115–138. Lexington, Mass.: Lexington Books.

Milton S. Eisenhower Foundation. 1993. *Investing in Children and Youth, Reconstructing Our Cities: Doing What Works to Reverse the Betrayal of American Democracy.* Washington, D.C.

Monti, Daniel J. 1993. The Culture of Gangs in the Culture of the School. *Qualitative Sociology* 16(4):383–404.

Moore, Joan (with Robert Garcia, Carlos Garcia, Luis Cerda, and Frank Valencia). 1978. *Homeboys.* Philadelphia: Temple University Press.

Moran, Richard. 1989. Bring Back the Mafia. *Newsweek,* August 7, p. 8.

Morash, Merry, and Lila Rucker. 1990. A Critical Look at the Idea of Boot Camp as a Correctional Reform. *Crime and Delinquency* 36(2):204–222.

Morris, P. 1967. Fathers in Prison. *British Journal of Criminology* 7:424–430.

Nagin, Daniel S. 1991. On the Relationship of Past and Future Participation in Delinquency. *Criminology* 29:163–190.

Nagin, Daniel S., and David P. Farrington. 1992. The Onset and Persistence of Offending. *Criminology* 30(4):501–523.

Nagin, Daniel S., and Kenneth C. Land. 1993. Age, Criminal Careers, and Population Heterogeneity: Specification and Estimation of a Nonparametric, Mixed Poisson Model. *Criminology* 31(3):327–362.

Nakamura, R. T., and F. Smallwood. 1980. *The Politics of Policy Implementation.* New York: St. Martin's Press.

National Coalition for the Homeless. 1989. *American Nightmare: A Decade of Homelessness in the United States.* Washington, D.C.: National Coalition for the Homeless.

National Criminal Justice Association. 1993. Clinton, Republicans Unveil Respective Anti-Crime Packages. *Justice Bulletin* 13(8):1–5.

———. 1994a. House Approves $28 Billion Comprehensive Crime Bill; Congress Expected to Vote on Final Bill by Memorial Day. *Justice Bulletin* 14(4):1–2.

———. 1994b. Congress Vows to Restore Byrne Formula Grant Program, Begins Appropriations Process; House Drafts Crime Bill. *Justice Bulletin* 14(3):1–2, 9–11.

Neugarten, B., and N. Datan. 1973. Sociological Perspectives on the Life

Cycle. In *Life Span Development Psychology: Adult Socialization,* ed. P. Baltes and W. Schaie, pp. 53–69. New York: Academic Press.

Newson, John, Elizabeth Newson, and Mary Adams. 1993. The Social Origins of Delinquency. *Criminal Behavior and Mental Health* 3(1):19–29.

New York City, Department of Juvenile Justice, Family Ties Program. 1992. *The First Eighteen Months: A Resource Guide for Establishing Family Preservation Programs in the Juvenile Justice System.* New York: New York City.

New York Times. 1993a. Los Angeles Gets Plan to Ease Gang Problem. October 14, p. A11.

———. 1993b. Judge Won't Send Prisoner Back to a Drug-Mart Prison. November 17, p. A13.

Nye, F. Ivan. 1980. A Theoretical Perspective on Running Away. *Journal of Family Issues* 1:274–299.

Olweus, Dan. 1978. *Aggression in the Schools: Bullies and Whipping Boys.* Washington, D.C.: Hemisphere.

———. 1979. Stability of Aggressive Reaction Patterns in Males: A Review. *Psychological Bulletin* 86:852–875.

———. 1980. Familial and Temperamental Determinants of Aggressive Behavior in Adolescent Boys: A Causal Analysis. *Developmental Psychology* 16:644–660.

———. 1984. Aggressors and Their Victims: Bullying at School. In *Disruptive Behaviour in Schools,* ed. N. Frude and H. Gault, pp. 57–76. Chichester, England: John Wiley and Sons.

O'Nell, Carl W. 1979. Nonviolence and Personality Dispositions among the Zapotec. *Journal of Psychological Anthropology* 2:301–322.

———. 1989. The Non-violent Zapotec. In *Societies at Peace: Anthropological Perspectives,* ed. Signe Howell and Roy Willis, pp. 117–132. New York: Routledge.

Orford, J. 1985. *Excessive Appetites: A Psychological View of Addictions.* New York: John Wiley and Sons.

Orsagh, Thomas, and Ann D. Witte. 1981. Economic Status and Crime: Implications for Offender Rehabilitation. *Journal of Criminal Law and Criminology* 72:1055–1071.

Osgood, D. Wayne, L. Johnston, Patrick M. O'Malley, and Jerald D. Bachman. 1988. The Generality of Deviance in Late Adolescence and Early Adulthood. *American Sociological Review* 53:81–93.

Paddock, John. 1982. Antiviolence in Oaxaca, Mexico: Archive Research. Paper presented at the meeting of the American Society of Ethnohistory, Nashville, Tennessee.

Padilla, F. 1992. *The Gang as an American Enterprise.* New Brunswick, N.J.: Rutgers University Press.

———. 1993. Working Gangs. In *Gangs: The Origins and Impact of Contem-*

porary Young Gangs in the United States, ed. Scott Cummings and Daniel J. Monti, pp. 173–192. Albany, N.Y.: State University of New York Press.

Papajohn, George. 1994. Traveling Gang Summits Losing Steam. *Chicago Tribune,* May 29, "Chicagoland" section, pp. 1–2.

Parent, Dale G. 1993. Conditions of Confinement. *Juvenile Justice* 1(1):2–23. U.S. Office of Juvenile Justice and Delinquency Prevention, Washington, D.C.

Parker, J., and S. Asher. 1987. Peer Relations and Later Personal Adjustment: Are Low-accepted Children at Risk? *Psychological Bulletin* 102:357.

Patterson, Gerald R. 1980. Children Who Steal. In *Understanding Crime,* ed. T. Hirschi and M. Gottfredson, pp. 73–90. Beverly Hills: Sage.

Patterson, G. R., P. Chamberlain, and J. B. Reid. 1982. A Comparative Evaluation of a Parenting Training Program. *Behavior Therapy* 13:638–650.

Peele, S. 1985. *The Meaning of Addiction.* Lexington, Mass.: Lexington Books.

Pell, Clairborne. 1994. Should Inmates Get Student Aid? *USA Today,* March 17, p. 13A.

Peretti, P. O., and A. McNair. 1987. Self-perceived Psychological and Social Characteristics of the Sociometric Isolate. *Education* 107(4):310–311.

Petersilia, Joan. 1980. Criminal Career Research: A Review of Recent Evidence. In *Crime and Justice: An Annual Review of Research,* Vol. 2, ed. Norval Morris and Michael Tonry, pp. 321–379. Chicago: University of Chicago Press.

Petersilia, Joan, Allan Abrahamse, and James Q. Wilson. 1990. The Relationship between Police Practice, Community Characteristics, and Case Attrition. *Policing and Society* 1(1):23–38.

Phibbs, Ciaran S., David A. Bateman, and Rachel M. Schwartz. 1991. The Neonatal Costs of Maternal Cocaine Use. *Journal of the American Medical Association* 266(11):1521–1526.

Phillips, Denis C. 1987. Validity in Qualitative Research. *Education and Urban Society* 20(1):9–24.

Pike, Kenneth. 1954. *Language in Relation to a Unified Theory of the Structure of Human Behavior,* Vol. 1. Glendale: Summer Institute of Linguistics.

Povich, Elaine S. 1993. It's a Federal Offense. *Chicago Tribune,* November 14, section 4, pp. 1, 7.

Preble, Edward, and John Casey. 1969. Taking Care of Business: The Heroin User's Life on the Street. *International Journal of Addictions* 4:1–24.

Pressman, J. L., and A. Wildavsky. 1984. *Implementation.* 3rd edition. Berkeley: University of California Press.

Price, Richard. 1992. *Clockers.* Boston: Houghton Mifflin.

Prochaska, James O., Carlo C. DiClemente, and John C. Norcross. 1992. In Search of How People Change. *American Psychologist* 47(9):1102–1114.

Raban, Jonathan. 1991. *Hunting Mister Heartbreak: A Discovery of America.* New York: HarperCollins.

Raspberry, William. 1991. Why Are So Many People in Prison? *Washington Post,* January 4, p. A17.

Reiss, Albert J., Jr. 1988. Co-offending and Criminal Careers. In *Crime and Justice: An Annual Review of Research,* Vol. 10, ed. Michael Tonry and Norval Morris, pp. 117–170. Chicago: University of Chicago Press.

Reiss, Albert J., Jr., and A. Lewis Rhodes. 1964. An Empirical Test of Differential Association Theory. *Journal of Research in Crime and Delinquency* 1: 5–18.

Rideau, Wilbert, and Ron Wikberg. 1992. *Life Sentences.* New York: Time Books/Random House.

Rist, Ray C. 1994. Influencing the Policy Process with Qualitative Research. In *Handbook of Qualitative Research,* ed. Norman K. Denzin and Yvonna S. Lincoln, pp. 545–557. Thousand Oaks, Calif.: Sage.

Robarchek, Clayton A. 1980. The Image of Nonviolence: World View of the Semai Senoi. *Federated Museums Journal* (Malaysia) 25:103–117.

Robins, Lee N. 1978. Aetiological Implications in Studies of Childhood Histories Relating to Antisocial Personality. In *Psychopathic Behavior,* ed. R. Hare and D. Schalling, pp. 255–271. New York: John Wiley and Sons.

———. 1979. Sturdy Childhood Predictions of Adult Outcomes: Replications from Longitudinal Studies. In *Stress and Mental Disorders,* ed. James E. Barrett, Robert M. Rose, and Gerald L. Klerman, pp. 219–235. New York: Raven Press.

Rodriguez, Luis J. 1993. *Always Running: A Memoir of La Vida Loca, Gangs Days in Los Angeles.* Willimantic, Conn.: Curbstone.

Roe, A. 1944. The Adult Adjustment of Children of Alcoholic Parents Raised in Foster-homes. *Quarterly Journal of Studies of Alcohol* 5:378–394.

Rojek, D., and M. Erickson. 1982. Delinquent Careers: A Test of the Career Escalation Model. *Criminology* 20:5–28.

Rosenbaum, Marsha. 1981. *Women on Heroin.* New Brunswick, N.J.: Rutgers University Press.

Rosenthal, Robert, and L. Jacobson. 1968. *Pygmalion in the Classroom.* New York: Holt, Rinehart and Winston.

Rossi, Peter H. 1989. *Down and Out in America.* University of Chicago Press.

Rossi, Peter H., G. A. Fisher, and G. Willis. 1986. *The Condition of the Homeless of Chicago.* Amherst: Social and Demographic Research Institute, University of Massachusetts; and Chicago: National Opinion Research Center.

Rowe, Alan R., and Charles R. Tittle. 1977. Life-cycle Changes and Criminal Propensity. *Sociological Quarterly* 18:223–236.

Rowe, D., D. W. Osgood, and W. A. Nicewander. 1990. A Latent Trait Approach to Unifying Criminal Careers. *Criminology* 28:237–270.

Rubin, K. H., T. Daniels-Beirness, and M. Hayvren. 1982. Social and Social-Cognitive Correlates of Sociometric Status in Preschool and Kindergarten Children. *Canadian Journal of Behavioural Science* 14:338–349.

Sack, W. H. 1977. Children of Imprisoned Fathers. *Psychiatry* 40:163–174.

Sack, W. H., J. Seidler, and S. Thomas. 1976. The Children of Imprisoned Fathers: A Psychosocial Exploration. *American Journal of Orthopsychiatry* 46:618–628.

Sampson, Robert. 1985. Neighborhood and Crime: The Structural Determinants of Personal Victimization. *Journal of Research in Crime and Delinquency* 22:7–40.

———. 1987. Urban Black Violence: The Effect of Male Joblessness and Family Disruption. *American Journal of Sociology* 93(2):348–382.

Sampson, Robert, and John Laub. 1992. Crime and Deviance in the Life Course. *Annual Review of Sociology* 18:63–84.

———. 1993. *Crime in the Making: Pathways and Turning Points through Life.* Cambridge, Mass.: Harvard University Press.

Sanchez Jankowski, Martin. 1991. *Islands in the Street: Gangs and American Urban Society.* Berkeley: University of California Press.

Sapir, Edward. 1927. Anthropology and Sociology. In *The Social Sciences and Their Interrelationship,* ed. W. F. Ogburn and A. Goldenweiser, pp. 97–113. Boston: Houghton Mifflin.

Sautter, R. Craig. 1995. Standing Up to Violence. Kappan Special Report. *Phi Delta Kappa* (January). Phi Delta Kappa, Inc., Bloomington, Ind.

Saylor, William G., and Gerald G. Gaes. 1992. The Post-Release Employment Project. *Federal Prisons Journal* 2(4):32–36.

Schneller, D. P. 1975. A Study of Some Social and Psychological Effects of Incarceration on the Families of Negro Prisoners. *Criminology* 14:402–412.

Schwartz, Gary. 1987. *Beyond Conformity or Rebellion: Youth and Authority in America.* Chicago: University of Chicago Press.

Schwartz, Ira M. 1989. *(In)Justice for Juveniles—Rethinking the Best Interests of the Child.* Lexington, Mass.: D. C. Heath.

Schwartz, M. C., and J. F. Weintraub. 1974. The Prisoner's Wife: A Study in Crisis. *Federal Probation* 38:20–27.

Shannon, Lyle W. 1984. *The Development of Serious Criminal Careers and the Delinquent Neighborhood.* Washington, D.C.: U.S. Department of Justice, Office of Juvenile Justice and Delinquency Prevention.

Shatz, Carla J. 1992. The Developing Brain. *Scientific American* 267(3):61–67.

Shaw, Clifford R., and Henry D. McKay. 1942. *Juvenile Delinquency and Urban Areas.* Chicago: University of Chicago Press.

Sheldon, Randall G., Ted Snodgrass, and Pam Snodgrass. 1992. Comparing Gang and Non-gang Offenders: Some Tentative Findings. *Gang Journal* 1(1):73–86.

Sherif, M., O. J. Harvey, B. J. White, W. R. Hood, and C. W. Sherif. 1961. *Intergroup Conflict and Cooperation: The Robbers' Cave Experiment*. Norman: University of Oklahoma Press.

Sherman, Lawrence W. 1983. Patrol Strategies for Police. In *Crime and Public Policy*, ed. J. Q. Wilson, pp. 145–163. San Francisco: Institute for Contemporary Studies.

Shlay, Anne B., and Peter H. Rossi. 1992. Social Science Research and Contemporary Studies of Homelessness. *Annual Review of Sociology* 18:129–160.

Short, James F. 1957. Differential Association and Delinquency. *Social Problems* 4:233–239.

––––––. 1974. Collective Behavior, Crime, and Delinquency. In *Handbook of Criminology*, ed. D. Gibbons, pp. 403–449. New York: Rand McNally.

––––––. 1987. Exploring Integration of the Theoretical Levels of Explanation: Notes on Juvenile Delinquency. Albany Conference on Theoretical Integration in the Study of Deviance and Crime, State University of New York at Albany, Department of Sociology. Manuscript.

––––––. 1990. *Delinquency and Society*. Englewood, Cliffs, N.J.: Prentice Hall.

Short, James F., and Fred L. Strodtbeck. 1965. *Group Process and Gang Delinquency*. Chicago: University of Chicago Press.

Shover, Neil. 1983. The Latest Stages of Ordinary Property Offender Careers. *Social Problems* 31:208–218.

––––––. 1985. *Aging Criminals*. Beverly Hills: Sage.

Simon, Eric, Gerald Gaes, and William H. Rhodes. 1993. Hindsight: Effectiveness of Simulating the Impact of Federal Sentencing Legislation on the Future Prison Population. Paper presented at the 45th Annual Meeting of the American Society of Criminology, Phoenix, Ariz.

Simon, Jim. 1990. Drug-treatment Records "Shoddy." *Seattle Times*, April 28, pp. A1, A14.

Smelser, N. J., and E. H. Erikson, eds. 1980. *Themes of Work and Love in Adulthood*. London: McIntrye.

Snow, David A., and Leon Anderson. 1987. Identity Work among the Homeless: The Verbal Construction and Avowal of Personal Identities. *American Journal of Sociology* 92(6):1336–1371.

Snyder, James, and Debra Huntley. 1990. Troubled Families and Troubled Youth. In *Understanding Troubled and Troubling Youth*, ed. Peter E. Leone, pp. 194–225. Newbury Park, Calif.: Sage.

Snyder, James, and Gerald Patterson. 1987. Family Intervention and Delinquent Behavior. In *Handbook of Juvenile Delinquency*, ed. Herbert C. Quay, pp. 216–243. New York: John Wiley and Sons.

Spellacy, F. 1977. Neuropsychological Differences between Violent and Nonviolent Adolescents. *Journal of Clinical Psychology* 33(4):966–969.

———. 1978. Neuropsychological Discrimination between Violent and Nonviolent Men. *Journal of Clinical Psychology* 34(1):49–52.

Spergel, Irving A. 1984. Violent Gangs in Chicago: In Search of Social Policy. *Social Service Review* 58(2):199–226.

———. 1989. Youth Gangs: Continuity and Change. In *Crime and Justice: An Annual Review of Research,* Vol. 12, ed. Norval Morris and Michael Tonry, pp. 171–275. Chicago: University of Chicago Press.

Spradley, James. 1970. *You Owe Yourself a Drunk: An Ethnography of Urban Nomads.* Boston: Little, Brown.

———. 1972. Foundations of Cultural Knowledge. In *Culture and Cognition: Rules, Maps, and Plans,* ed. J. P. Spradley, pp. 3–40. San Francisco: Chandler Press.

Steffensmeier, Darrell, and Miles D. Harner. 1993. Bulging Prisons, and Aging U.S. Population, and the Nation's Violent Crime Rate. *Federal Probation* 57(2):3–10.

Stephens, Ronald D. 1993. School-based Interventions: Safety and Security. In *The Gang Intervention Handbook,* ed. Arnold P. Goldstein and C. Ronald Huff, pp. 219–256. Champaign, Ill.: Research Press.

Straus, Murray A. 1991. Discipline and Deviance: Physical Punishment of Children and Violence and Other Crime in Adulthood. *Social Problems* 38(2):133–152.

Struening, E. L., and E. Susser. 1986. *First Time Users of the New York City Shelter System.* New York: New York State Psychiatric Institute.

Sullivan, Barbara. 1993. Working the Trenches. *Chicago Tribune,* December 1, section 2, p. 1.

Sullivan, Mercer L. 1989. *"Getting Paid": Youth Crime and Work in the Inner City.* Ithaca, N.Y.: Cornell University Press.

Sutherland, Edwin. 1937. *The Professional Thief.* Chicago: University of Chicago Press.

———. 1947. *Criminology.* 4th edition. Philadelphia: J. B. Lippincott.

Sutherland, E., and D. R. Cressey. 1970. *Criminology.* 9th edition. New York: J. B. Lippincott.

Sutter, Alan G. 1966. The World of the Righteous Dope Fiend. *Issues in Criminology* 2:177–222.

Suttles, G. 1972. *Social Construction of Communities.* Chicago: University of Chicago Press.

Sykes, Gresham. 1958. *The Society of Captives.* Princeton, N.J.: Princeton University Press.

Tajfel, Henrie. 1982. Social Psychology of Intergroup Relations. In *Annual Review of Psychology,* ed. Mark R. Rozenzweig and Lyman W. Porter, pp. 1–39. Palo Alto: Annual Reviews.

Tannenbaum, Frank. 1938. *Crime and the Community.* Boston: Ginn.

Taylor, Carl S. 1990. *Dangerous Society*. East Lansing: Michigan State University Press.

Taylor, I., P. Walton, and J. Young. 1973. *The New Criminology: For a Social Theory of Deviance*. London: Routledge and Kegan Paul.

Thornberry, Terence P. 1987. Toward an Interactional Theory of Delinquency. *Criminology* 25:863–891.

Thornberry, Terence P., Melanie Moore, and R. L. Christenson. 1985. The Effect of Dropping Out of High School on Subsequent Criminal Behavior. *Criminology* 23:3–18.

Thrasher, Frederic M. 1927. *The Gang: A Study of 1,313 Gangs in Chicago*. Chicago: University of Chicago Press.

Tittle, Charles R. 1980. *Sanctions and Social Deviance: The Question of Deterrence*. New York: Praeger.

Tittle, Charles R., Mary Jean Bruke, and Elton F. Jackson. 1986. Modeling Sutherland's Theory of Differential Association: Toward an Empirical Classification. *Social Forces* 65:405–432.

Toch, Hans. 1977. *Living in Prison: The Ecology of Survival*. New York: Free Press.

Tremblay, Richard E., Joan McCord, Helene Boileau, Pierre Charlebois, Claude Gagnon, Marc LeBlanc, and Serge Larivee. 1991. Can Disruptive Boys Be Helped to Become Competent? *Psychiatry* 54:148–161.

Tuchfeld, B. 1981. Spontaneous Remission in Alcoholics: Empirical Observations and Theoretical Implications. *Journal of Studies on Alcohol* 42: 626–641.

Tunnell, Kenneth D. 1993. Inside the Drug Trade: Trafficking from the Dealers' Perspective. *Qualitative Sociology* 16(4):361–381.

Turner, R. H., and S. J. Surace. 1956. Zoot-Suiters and Mexicans: Symbols of Crowd Behavior. *American Journal of Sociology* 62:214–220.

Tyler, S. A., ed. 1969. *Cognitive Anthropology*. New York: Holt, Rinehart and Winston.

U.S. Department of Commerce. 1992. *State Government Finances: 1991*. Washington, D.C.: Government Printing Office.

U.S. Department of Justice. 1990a. *Drugs and Crime: 1989. Research in Action: 1989 Drug Use Forecasting Annual Report*. Washington, D.C.

———. 1990b. *Age-specific Arrest Rates and Race-specific Arrest Rates for Selected Offenses, 1965–1988*. Washington, D.C.: Federal Bureau of Investigation.

———. 1992a. *Recidivism of Felons on Probation, 1986–1989*. Washington, D.C.: Bureau of Justice Statistics.

———. 1992b. *Criminal Victimization in the United States, 1991*. Washington, D.C.: Bureau of Justice Statistics.

———. 1993a. *Sourcebook of Criminal Justice Statistics—1992*. Washington, D.C.: Bureau of Justice Statistics, Office of Justice Programs.

———. 1993b. Jail Inmates 1992. *Bureau of Justice Statistics Bulletin* (August). Washington, D.C.

———. 1993c. Prisoners in 1992. *Bureau of Justice Statistics Bulletin* (May). Washington, D.C.

———. 1994. *Criminal Victimization in the United States, 1992.* Washington, D.C.: Bureau of Justice Statistics, Office of Justice Programs.

U.S. General Accounting Office. 1988. *Homeless Mentally Ill: Problems and Options in Estimating Numbers and Trends.* Report to the Chairman, Committee on Labor and Human Resources, U.S. Senate, Washington, D.C.

Valentine, Bettylou. 1978. *Hustling and Other Hard Work: Life Styles in the Ghetto.* New York: Free Press.

Vigil, James D. 1988. *Barrio Gangs.* Austin: University of Texas Press.

———. 1990. *Cholos and Gangs: Culture Change and Street Youth in Los Angeles.* In *Gangs in America,* ed. H. Ronald Huff, pp. 116–128. Newbury Park, Calif.: Sage.

———. 1993. Gang Conflict in an Urban Housing Project. Paper presented at the 1993 American Society of Criminology conference, Phoenix, Ariz.

Vigil, James D., and John M. Long. 1990. Emic and Etic Perspectives on Gang Culture: The Chicano case. In *Gangs in America,* ed. H. Ronald Huff, pp. 55–68. Newbury Park, Calif.: Sage.

Voss, Harwin L. 1964. Differential Association and Reported Delinquency Behavior: A Replication. *Social Problems* 12:78–85.

Waldorf, Dan. 1973. *Careers in Dope.* Englewood Cliffs, N.J.: Prentice Hall.

Walters, Glenn D. 1990. *The Criminal Lifestyle.* Newbury Park, Calif.: Sage.

Walters, Glenn D., and Thomas White. 1989. The Thinking Criminal: A Cognitive Model of Lifestyle Criminality. *Criminal Justice Research Bulletin* 4(4). Huntsville, Tex.: Sam Houston State University, Criminal Justice Center.

Walters, H. I., and S. K. Gilmore. 1973. Placebo versus Social Learning Effects on Parental Training Procedures Designed to Alter the Behavior of Aggressive Boys. *Behavior Therapy* 4:311–377.

Warr, Mark. 1993. Age, Peers, and Delinquency. *Criminology* 31(1):17–40.

Warr, Mark, and Mark Stafford. 1991. The Influence of Delinquent Peers: What They Think or What They Do? *Criminology* 29(4):851–866.

Weber, Max. 1946. *From Max Weber: Essays in Sociology,* ed. H. Gerth and C. W. Mills. New York: Oxford University Press.

Wechsler, H., and D. Thum. 1973. Teenage Drinking, Drug Use, and Social Correlates. *Quarterly Journal of Studies on Alcohol* 34:1220–1227.

Weiner, Neil Alan. 1989. Violent Criminal Careers and "Violent Career Criminals." In *Violent Crime, Violent Criminals,* ed. Neil Alan Weiner and Marvin E. Wolfgang, pp. 35–138. Newbury Park, Calif.: Sage.

Weis, Joseph G., and David J. Hawkins. 1981. *Preventing Delinquency.* Washington, D.C.: U.S. Office of Juvenile Justice and Delinquency Prevention.

Weis, Joseph G., and John Sederstrom. 1981. *The Prevention of Serious Delinquency: What to Do?* Washington, D.C.: Government Printing Office.

Weisberg, D. Kelly. 1985. *Children of the Night: A Study of Adolescent Prostitution.* Lexington, Mass.: Lexington Books.

West, D. J., and D. P. Farrington. 1977. *The Delinquent Way of Life: Third Report of the Cambridge Study in Delinquent Development.* London: Heinemann Educational Books.

Whiting, J. W. M., and T. L. Child. 1953. *Child Training and Personality: A Cross-Cultural Study.* New Haven: Yale University Press.

Whyte, William F. 1943. *Street Corner Society: The Social Structure of an Italian Slum.* Chicago: University of Chicago Press.

Widom, Cathy Spatz. 1992. *The Cycle of Violence.* National Institute of Justice, Research in Brief series. Washington, D.C.: U.S. Department of Justice.

Wierzbicka, Anna. 1993. A Conceptual Basis for Cultural Psychology. *Ethos* 21(2):205–231.

Williams, C. 1987. *The Destruction of Black Civilization.* Chicago: Third World Press.

Williams, Kirk, and Richard Hawkins. 1986. Perceptual Research on General Deterrence: A Critical Overview. *Law and Society Review* 20:545–572.

Williams, Terry. 1989. *The Cocaine Kids: The Inside Story of a Teenage Drug Ring.* Menlo Park, Calif.: Addison-Wesley.

Williamson, Deborah, Michelle Clark, and Paul Knepper. 1993. Teen Court: Juvenile Justice for the 21st Century? *Federal Probation* 57(2):54–58.

Wilson, James Q. 1983. *Thinking about Crime.* New York: Basic Books.

Wilson, James Q., and Richard Herrnstein. 1985. *Crime and Human Nature.* New York: Simon and Schuster.

Wilson, William J. 1987. *The Truly Disadvantaged.* Chicago: University of Chicago Press.

Winfree, L. Thomas, Jr., G. Larry Mays, and Teresa Vigil-Backstrom. 1994. Youth Gangs and Incarcerated Delinquents: Exploring the Ties between Gang Membership, Delinquency, and Social Learning Theory. *Justice Quarterly* 11(2):229–255.

Wolfgang, M. E. 1980. Some New Findings from the Longitudinal Study of Crime. *Australian Journal of Forensic Sciences* 13:12–29.

Wolfgang, Marvin E., and F. Ferracuti. 1967. *The Subculture of Violence.* London: Tavistock.

Wolfgang, Marvin E., Robert M. Figlio, and Thorsten Sellin. 1972. *Delinquency in a Birth Cohort.* Chicago: University of Chicago Press.

Wormith, J. S. 1984. The Controversy over the Effects of Long-term Imprisonment. *Canadian Journal of Criminology* 26:423–437.

Wright, Kevin N., and Karen E. Wright. 1993a. A Policy-Makers Guide to Controlling Delinquency and Crime through Family Interventions. Paper prepared for the Office of Juvenile Justice and Delinquency Prevention, U.S. Department of Justice, OJP-91-006. Washington, D.C.: U.S. Department of Justice.

———. 1993b. *Family Life and Delinquency and Crime: A Policymakers' Guide to the Literature.* Office of Juvenile Justice and Delinquency Prevention. Washington, D.C.: U.S. Department of Justice.

———. 1994. A Policy Maker's Guide to Controlling Delinquency and Crime through Family Interventions. *Justice Quarterly* 11(2):189–206.

Yablonsky, L. 1959. The Gang as a Near-Group. *Social Problems* 7:108–117.

———. 1962. *The Violent Gang.* New York: Macmillan.

Yeudall, L. T., and D. Fromm-Auch. 1979. Neuropsychological Impairments in Various Psychopathological Populations. In *Hemisphere Asymmetries of Function and Psychopathology,* ed. J. Gruzelier and P. Flor-Henry. New York: Elsevier–North Holland Biomedical Press.

Yeudall, L. T., D. Fromm-Auch, and P. Davies. 1982. Neuropsychological Impairment of Persistent Delinquency. *Journal of Nervous and Mental Disease* 170(5):257–265.

Yochelson, S., and S. E. Samenow. 1976. *The Criminal Personality.* Vol. 1, *A Profile for Change.* New York: Aronson.

Zedlewski, Edwin W. 1987. Making Confinement Decisions. *Research in Brief* (July). Washington, D.C.: National Institute of Justice.

Zeisel, Hans. 1982. Disagreement over the Evaluation of a Controlled Experiment. *American Journal of Sociology* 88:378–396.

Zigler, Edward, Cara Taussig, and Kathryn Black. 1992. Early Childhood Intervention: A Promising Preventative for Juvenile Delinquency. *American Psychologist* 47:997–1006.

Zimring, Franklin. 1981. Kids, Groups and Crime: Some Implications of a Well-Known Secret. *Journal of Criminal Law and Criminology* 72:867–885.

Zimring, Franklin, and Gordon Hawkins. 1988. The New Mathematics of Imprisonment. *Crime and Delinquency* (October):425–436.

Index

325